T0322978

Norges Bank 1816–2016

Norges Bank 1816–2016

EINAR LIE

In cooperation with

JAN THOMAS KOBBERRØD,
GJERMUND FORFANG RONGVED,
AND
EIVIND THOMASSEN

OXFORD
UNIVERSITY PRESS

UNIVERSITY PRESS

Great Clarendon Street, Oxford, OX2 6DP,
United Kingdom

Oxford University Press is a department of the University of Oxford.
It furthers the University's objective of excellence in research, scholarship,
and education by publishing worldwide. Oxford is a registered trade mark of
Oxford University Press in the UK and in certain other countries

© Norges Bank 2020

The moral rights of the author have been asserted

First Edition published in 2020

Impression: 1

All rights reserved. No part of this publication may be reproduced, stored in
a retrieval system, or transmitted, in any form or by any means, without the
prior permission in writing of Oxford University Press, or as expressly permitted
by law, by licence or under terms agreed with the appropriate reprographics
rights organization. Enquiries concerning reproduction outside the scope of the
above should be sent to the Rights Department, Oxford University Press, at the
address above

You must not circulate this work in any other form
and you must impose this same condition on any acquirer

Published in the United States of America by Oxford University Press
198 Madison Avenue, New York, NY 10016, United States of America

British Library Cataloguing in Publication Data
Data available

Library of Congress Control Number: 2019953080

ISBN 978-0-19-886001-3

Printed and bound by
CPI Group (UK) Ltd, Croydon, CR0 4YY

Links to third party websites are provided by Oxford in good faith and
for information only. Oxford disclaims any responsibility for the materials
contained in any third party website referenced in this work.

Preface and Acknowledgements

The present book is largely based on a book published in Norwegian, *Norges Bank 1816–2016*, authored by Jan Thomas Kobberrød, Eivind Thomassen, Gjermund Forfang Rongved, and myself. The project, financed by Norges Bank, engaged two PhD candidates and a number of masters students who provided invaluable material and insights from a number of more detailed topics in the institution's long history. Drafts by the authors was presented to a committee set up to aid the work of this history and a parallel, related project on the monetary development and history of Norway (Eitrheim, Klovland, and Øksendal, *A Monetary History of Norway 1816–2016*). The members of the committee were Harald Bøhn and Jan Fredrik Qvigstad from Norges Bank, Tore Eriksen, Professor Knut Sogner, and Senior Lecturer Tobias Straumann. The gratitude expressed in the Norwegian version, to the committee and the authors of *A Monetary History of Norway*, Øyvind Eitrheim, Jan Tore Klovland, and Lars Fredrik Øksendal, and to the candidates and students involved, must also be extended with regard to the present book.

The book in Norwegian was planned and structured by me as a project manager. The chapters was drafted by my co-authors and myself, then read and commented on in the author group, and in the final phase slightly edited by myself before being sent to the publisher.[1] The present version is considerably shortened, passages of greatest interest to a Norwegian audience have been omitted or rewritten, and some topics of presumably larger general interest have been deepened and extended. The difference in structure, length, and to some extent interpretations, are most evident in the first part of the book and the chapters covering the interwar years. Chapter 4-6 have been shortened, given some textual supplements, and edited on the basis of the corresponding chapters in the Norwegian book from 2016. The postwar chapters, originally authored by Eivind Thomassen, are mostly shortened, 'de-Norwegianized', and sandpapered in terms of arguments and interpretations. Consequently, even though the text and interpretations, as well as any shortcomings and errors, in the final version are solely my responsibility, the present book is deeply rooted in and indebted to our *Norges Bank 1816–2016*.

The cover image shows a motif from the reverse side of the Norwegian 1000-krone banknote issued by Norges Bank 1949–75. The motif engraved in copper plate is

---

[1] In *Norges Bank 1816–2016*, Kobberrød wrote the chapters covered by ch. 1–4 and 6 in this book. Rongved wrote about the universal coin and SMU, and Norges Bank during WWI (ch 5 and 7). Kobberrød wrote two and Thomassen one chapter on the 1920s, which is rewritten and transformed to ch. 8 in the present book. Ch 9 and 10 is based on my own drafts in Norges Bank 1816–2016. The postwar era was covered by Thomassen alone, though the chapter on the oil fund was written by him and me together. The introduction and conclusion was written by me in Norges Bank 1816–2016, and rewritten for this book.

based on the Norwegian painter Edvard Munch's painting 'History', which is among the monumental paintings decorating the assembly hall at the University of Oslo. The copper plate motif was engraved by Henry Welde, a graphic designer at Norges Bank's Printing Works.

Finally, I would like to thank Øyvind Eitrheim, Jan Fredrik Qvigstad, and Juha Tarkka for comments to this book, as well as Jan Thomas Kobberrød, Gjermund Forfang Rongved, and Eivind Thomassen for reading and commenting upon selected chapters.

Einar Lie

Contents

List of Figures

Introduction

Norges Bank 1816–2016

This is a book on the 200-year history of Norges Bank, a central bank in a relatively small and remote country. It is—to some extent, but only to some extent—a contribution to the relatively broad literature on the history of national central banks. The present Norges Bank is a modern, well-functioning central bank, with strong likenesses to similar institutions in other countries.

The first central banks evolved gradually from commercial banks and partly public banks, which got involved in creating markets for payments and credits, raising loan for the state, and liquidating public debt. Newer central banks, established in the nineteenth and twentieth centuries, have to a larger extent been established with a specific purpose, related to note issuing, securing the value of the currency over time, and providing financial stability.

Most central banks in what we used to call the first and second world were established during these centuries. We find a variety of differences, due to national economic and political conditions, and not least the situation in which they have been established. Still, they may and have been studied in light of the same key elements: the function of note issuing, guardian of the value of the currency, stabilizer of the financial system, and partly as an agent for making public debt liquid, an old function of several central banks, which has been revitalized after the recent financial crisis.

The history of central banking has become a relatively coherent field because it can and has been approached by general economic and monetary theory. The historiography of central banks is to a large extent produced by economists, who recognize key elements in the arts of central banking—growth of money, stability and inflation, international cooperation, autonomy versus political dependency, etc.—over the last centuries. Important contributions to the literature, such as Charles Goodhart's influential *The Evolution of Central Banks* and Curcio Giannini's *The Age of Central Banks*, identify key aspects of central banking, as they have developed over time. They differ in the ways in which the core of central bank activities are identified. Goodhart emphasizes financial stability, expressed in the function as lender of last resort; Giannini, the construction of means of payments and their relation to the state. The difference has, however, elements of a friendly family feud. Both Goodhart and Giannini were economists and central bankers. The basic elements of their narrative and analysis are relatively similar and well known to central bankers and scholars trained in macroeconomic theory and monetary analysis. The two books also share a

Norges Bank 1816–2016. Einar Lie, Oxford University Press (2020). © Norges Bank.
DOI: 10.1093/oso/9780198860013.001.0001

teleological touch, as they both explicitly aim at explaining how central banks have developed into the relatively coherent and easily identifiable organizations across nations we know in the present time. In a recent contribution by Stefano Ugolini, these teleological elements are evaded by applying a functional approach, focusing on the development of the core functions of modern central banking (money issuing, managing the payment system, lending of last resort, monetary policy, financial supervision).[1] By structuring the analysis on the development of what economic theory describes as core central banks functions, an organizational presentism in avoided (how certain organizations developed into becoming contemporary central banks)— to be replaced with a presentism based on contemporary central banking functions.

This book can be read as a history of a small central bank, or rather, how Norges Bank developed into being a modern central bank. Still, it is not primarily a contribution to monetary history or to the historiography of central bank functions, such as principles for note issuing, price stability, and the handling of financial stress (though the topics often appear in the following chapters). To some extent, we share Forrest Capie's modest and immodest ambition in his preface to *The Bank of England: 1950s to 1979*, to follow the institution's development and write a book based on 'what the bank did, how it did it, and if possible, an explanation [of] why it did it the way it did'.[2]

Of course, more needs to be said about the principles guiding the selection of topics and research interests guiding a book. Capie's history of the Bank of England in the postwar period is, for example, closely tied to Britain's growth and economic development, and Bank of England's changing role in contributing to this development. This book on Norges Bank is to a larger extent centred around the relations between the bank and the political institutions; how the bank's role has been shaped and reshaped by perceptions of what kind of financial services Norway needed, how economic policy was coordinated, and how discretionary power was distributed between the elected bodies, the executive branch, and underlying institutions with a defined mandate.

In central bank literature, 'independence' is a recurrent topic.[3] If a central bank should be able to pursue a policy for redeeming the notes in silver, keep inflation down, or serve as a lender of last resort in a crisis, it will need to be in control of specific policy instruments. 'Independence' is from political institutions, which, in theory and practice, are more vulnerable to popular discontent with specific policy measures. In a historical study of Norges Bank (and most other central banks), the central bank's fundamental *dependence* is more striking than its independence. Many state institutions have some sort of independence from political institutions. Some, like courts,

---

[1]   Stefano Ugolini, *The Evolution of Central Banking: Theory and History* (Palgrave Macmillan, 2017).

[2]   Forrest Capie, *The Bank of England: 1950s to 1979* (Cambridge University Press, 2010), xx.

[3]   See e.g. Gianni Toniolo, Fondazione Adriano Olivetti, and Fondazione Adriano Olivetti, *Central Banks' Independence in Historical Perspective* (W. de Gruyter, 1988); Forrest Capie, Geoffrey Wood, and Juan Castañeda, 'Central Bank Independence in Small Open Economies', in *Central Banks at a Crossroad: What Can We Learn from History?* ed. Michael D. Bordo, et al. (Cambridge University Press, 2016). Simone Polillo and Mauro F. Guillén, 'Globalization Pressures and the State: The Worldwide Spread of Central Bank Independence', *American Journal of Sociology* 110, no. 6 (2005); Michael Bordo, 'Long Term Perspectives on Central Banking', *What is a useful central bank* (2011).

universities, and government statistical agencies, have normally had a stronger and deeper-rooted independency in performing their activities than Norges Bank. Norges Bank has always enjoyed some sort of independence, most consistently in internal, administrative matters. Nevertheless, the institution itself was constructed by its political superiors, and its tasks and structure have been defined and redefined by political institutions throughout the past centuries. 'Independency' is fundamentally something given to the bank, dependent as it is on trust and authority from the elected powers that defines its roles and tasks. The Norwegian historian Jens Arup Seip once described the Supreme Court—which is formally independent from government, as a part of the constitution's division of power—as 'a rocking wimpy in the wake of the State ship', as the court rarely challenged legislation that might be at odds with generally formulated paragraphs in the constitution. This might be an overly pointed formulation with regard to the judicial system. As a description of Norges Bank's role in society the metaphor is relatively free from frictions: Norges Bank has been shaped and reshaped by the wake of the state ship, even though the bank at times has influenced its course and speed, as everything of some weight being tied to a large ship might do.

Norges Bank has been an integrated part of Norwegian economic development from the complicated birth of the new nation-state after the Napoleonic Wars, until the days of the present nouveau-richness. In his influential *Political Order and Political Decay*, Francis Fukuyama examines the long-term history of the institutional structure of society to find the elements of why and how some countries develop mature democratic institutions, a rule of law, and incorrupt governance with a large problem-solving capacity. His one-liner, 'getting to Denmark', has become famous (at least in Denmark), as a metaphor for the gradual and complex formation of a prosperous and well-governed society. With regard to the development of modern political and economic institutions, understanding the getting to Norway is no less challenging than the getting to Denmark. If we should construct a prism, an optic for understanding the getting to Norway, Norges Bank is a useful starting point.

Norges Bank was established in 1816 with a dual purpose: to bring order and stability to the chaotic monetary system following the Napoleonic Wars and provide Norway with a bank—no banks existed in the Norwegian part of the Danish-Norwegian Kingdom, from which Norway was separated in the Kiel Treaty in 1814. Norway should, according to the treaty, be a part of a new union with the Swedish kingdom. A constituent assembly was thrown up and created an independent constitution when the Swedish crown prince and his army was still occupied on the continent. After a short war in the fall, Norway entered a loose union with Sweden, with its own parliament (the Storting), armed forces, ministries, state budget, and separate currency. The new state was financially weak, without traditions for independent government, least not democratic institutions. Complaints about mismanagement and bribery among public officials had also been numerous through the 1700s.

On this fragile stage, the complicated and costly effort to establish a note-issuing bank with assuring reserves in silver and a large lending capacity took place.

International and homemade ideas intersected with conflicting popular and elected interests, and geographical and cultural specificities.

After long, heated debates and popular protests, the bank was established and came into operation as a note issuer and lender to businesses and public life. The bank's formal and de facto role changed with better communications, growth in the economy and financial system, and with modern parliamentarism and new political constellations, such as the labour movement in the twentieth century. In the last phase of its long history, the oil age has made a fundamental impact on Norges Bank's functions. First in handling currency and exchange rates in an economy increasingly dominated by one single product traded in US dollars, and later as a manager for the Norwegian oil fund, for the time being the world's largest sovereign wealth fund.

The Parliament's Bank

The two central purposes behind the construction of the bank conflicted for a long time: the bank was born in the inflationary climate during and after the Napoleonic Wars, which strongly affected the Danish-Norwegian monetary system. The problems it inherited were multiplied by the new Norwegian state, which needed money to establish the elements of a government framework and affirm its independence against Sweden in 1814. However, no financial means were available, and there was no apparatus or authority to rapidly raise revenues by taxing the population. The national assembly's solution in 1814 was to produce more banknotes and guarantee their value, which the assembly's most earnest men realized was not a viable strategy. In 1816, a new guarantee of the value of banknotes, now at a considerably lower level, followed the decision to create Norges Bank, but the guarantee still promised a much higher future monetary value than the present one.

Norges Bank was to be the instrument to raise the value of the krone towards the new target value. This was the bank's monetary purpose. The second purpose was to be a bank, simply a provider of loans to businesses and the public. A separate Norwegian bank had been wanted by the business elites from the 1700s, and the non-existence of a bank in Norway was seen as a main reason for the relatively slow economic development in this northern part of the Dano-Norwegian kingdom centred in Copenhagen.

The first savings bank was formed in 1822 and the first commercial banks only around the middle of the century. Yet until that time, Norges Bank was the only bank for Norwegian savers and merchants. Credit sources existed, such as private lenders and merchants who would sell against payment at a later time. But, far in to the 1800s, engaging in lending to ordinary customers was Norges Bank's central function. Contrary to the intentions in its regulatory framework—and in authoritative theoretical literature on note-issuing banks—Norges Bank mainly came to provide long-term mortgages to the public. The lending business only shifted to the new banks slowly, and the bank of issue progressively went from being a bank for loan customers to a bankers' bank.

This dual purpose, with highly conflicting aims, characterized Norges Bank's activities in its first decades: it was supposed to create order in the monetary system, in practice to bring the value of the newly created speciedaler up to the level promised in 1816. Furthermore, it was supposed to provide loans and credit to the public. The first purpose implied a restrictive, contractionary policy; the second implied the opposite.

The two defined purposes did not mean that the bank was given independence in its work to reach the goal set in 1816. Formally and in reality, Norges Bank was under the instruction of the Storting; the Storting laid down the framework for the bank's operations. This included the timing for moving the rate towards the daler value set in 1816. The central bank's exercise of judgement in the period to 1842, when the guaranteed value was achieved, primarily rested with the Storting, while Norges Bank conducted its lending activities within the scope defined by the same institution.

Initially, Norges Bank was a privately owned bank under state control. In 1816, the private ownership dissolved naturally, yet it was also a necessity. The bank's basic capital, a silver reserve, could hardly be derived from other sources than the country's inhabitants. A substantial silver tax was imposed and collected, which was met with resistance and strong protests in many places. The tax payments varied, and ownership in the new bank was given against payment, calculated according to the amount of the individual contribution. The tax and ownership entailed expectations that bank branches would be established in all regions of the country—but especially in those areas where the silver tax payments were largest. The political response was first to set up formal branches with their own management, followed by offices supplementing these branches.

Mountains and fjords markedly divide the geography of Norway. In 1814, the political and administrative Norway had lost its former centre, Copenhagen. Nothing else existed then and there. Norway eventually obtained a centre, in the capital Kristiania, later named Oslo. However, tension between the centre and periphery is the most persistent cause of conflict in Norwegian political history, and Norges Bank's development represents a small part of that history.

The head office was not located in the country's biggest city at the time, Bergen, nor the political and administrative capital Kristiania, but in the more peripheral Trondheim, reducing the head office's scope for instructing and controlling the increasingly decentralized network. The managers of the branches and offices, mostly the nations' best citizens, were appointed by the Storting. The branches set their own lending rates, and hence there was no shared, national discount rate. Admittedly, Trondheim defined the quotas for the distribution of loans among the branches. But if the conditions failed to be met, the only means of sanction was a reprimand in the form of a letter. In this respect, it is more accurate to regard Norges Bank up until the 1890s more as a loose network of regional and local banks under the control of the Storting rather than a unified institution with a uniform leadership. This framework implied not only the strong formal and de facto dependence of political organs, but it also precluded the possibility for the Trondheim leadership to manage Norges Bank as an independent institution.

Effective realities, which are important to assimilate in seeking to comprehend the bank's evolution, underlay the institution's establishment: Norges Bank was part of the state financial infrastructure, at the same time as it had many private owners. As a private enterprise, the capital had to be managed responsibly with an acceptable annual return. Not least, it became a highly branched bank that provided loans to ordinary customers. Contrary to central bank wisdom in western Europe, the bank's balance was increasingly filled with long-term mortgages. A high demand for loans with good collateral was met by the bank, at the expense of the ability to respond quickly to cyclical changes in the economy and pressure on the silver reserves.

Throughout the 1800s, the customer-lending activity was gradually reduced with the emergence of savings and commercial banks. However, a large branch network remained in place until the end of the 1900s, although this made more sense during the bank's first eighty years than in the following one hundred.

Master in Its Own House—and That of Others

The new Norges Bank Act of 1892 changed the character of the institution. The Storting's micromanagement was scaled back to the benefit of the bank's own organs. The head office, which was soon moved to Kristiania, took on a stronger formal management role of the branches. Norges Bank operated using a key policy rate and with clearer rules for banknote issue and metal cover. By law and in practice, Norges Bank developed a stronger character as a bankers' bank. The role was unexpectedly put to the test in 1899 during the so-called Kristiania crash, when a number of banks encountered difficulties. Norges Bank stepped in as lender of last resort. By virtue of this function Norges Bank's management became the decisive and executive actor in handling the crisis.

The formal independence the law conferred upon Norges Bank was managed in a way that contributed to strengthening the institution's position. Conversely, the First World War weakened the institution's credibility and authority. Norway stayed neutral but the government increasingly took part in commercial activities, to secure the country's production and deliveries of food, fuel, and other necessities. As in many other countries, the central bank stretched itself to support the needs of the government. However, the overall government policy lacked coordination and discipline, with the result being strong growth in the money supply and government debt. In Norway, the international postwar crisis was followed and amplified by an extensive banking crisis caused by the credit boom during and just after the war. Subsequently, the economy was exposed to further stress as a result of a monetary policy that re-established the Norwegian krone at its pre-war value through a persistent resumption policy that came to a conclusion in 1928.

The interwar years was the most dramatic period of Norges Bank's history, marked by crises and major external headwinds—and by Nicolai Rygg's firm and long-lasting leadership. The banking crisis had to be resolved by Norges Bank. The government and the Ministry of Finance played a more peripheral role. The central bank also conducted monetary policy and exchange rate policy with a considerable degree of independence in the 1920s, through the collapse of the gold standard in 1931, and up to the outbreak of the Second World War.

Norges Bank has never before, nor since, been given such an independent and controversial role as during the interwar years. In the 1920s, central bank policy was in step with the Conservative majority's political line. It was, in broad terms, in accord with the general 'rules of the game' of the established metal standards, where convertibility at times had to be secured or re-established through austerity monetary measures. The new thorny road to resumption differed, however, from the one in Norges Bank's early decades of the 1800s in two respects: it was swifter and harder; and it happened in a new political and social context, with mass unemployment, universal voting rights, and a growing, radical labour movement.[4]

Norges Bank was brought into a bitter conflict with the Labour Party, as the foremost defender of the alienated capitalist order. However, even in its seemingly most independent decade, Norges Bank depended on support from political institutions. When government backing in resumption policies seemed to have been lost with the Labour Party's victory at the 1927 parliamentary election, the bank's governor contributed to bringing the new Labour government down. This was a pyrrhic victory at a peak of its influence, illustrating both its independence from and deep dependence on elected powers and institutions.

From the end of the 1920s, the Labour Party and economists with a new theoretical orientation came to portray Governor Rygg as the prime example of traditional conservative doctrinarism. When the two old parties, the Conservative Party and Liberal Party (both founded in 1884) lost their long-lasting grip on executive power in the 1930s, Norges Bank's superiority in monetary and exchange rate policies became an area of open conflict.

The Government's Bank

The Second World War dealt a blow to central bank independence. In the decades that followed, Norges Bank did not regain its former role. The trend in other countries also entailed stronger political coordination of monetary policy in a broad sense, but not to the same extent as in Norway. The new Labour Party regime marked its distance from the policy advocated by Norges Bank during the interwar years, at the same time as it scrapped many of the traditional monetary policy instruments. Credit controls and a stable, low interest rate were key elements of the policy. Interest rate changes were unequivocally made on the basis of the government's assessments, not those of the central bank. However, the changing relationship between the government and

---

[4] This point is in line with Barry Eichengreen's more general analyses, see e.g. Barry Eichengreen, *The European Economy since 1945: Coordinated Capitalism and Beyond* (Princeton University Press, 2008), 30–1.

Norges Bank was in line also with new principles for organizing government, and for how semi-autonomous state institutions should be managed. The general strategy in the postwar years was to strengthen the government and ministerial capacity and authority in formulating and coordinating politics. This strategy underlined the dependency of a number of state institutions, and was intended to increase the weight of political institutions and the efficiency of government planning and policies.

The central bank's postwar governors complied—Gunnar Jahn (1946–54) out of loyalty and necessity, Erik Brofoss (1954–70) and Knut Getz Wold (1970–85) out of free will and conviction. While monetary policy was hardly pursued in a traditional sense, a rising number of tasks linked to foreign exchange control and regulation were assigned to the bank. Norges Bank also assumed other tasks. In the postwar period, the institution's leaders retained a high degree of administrative autonomy within in the state apparatus. This autonomy was partly used to take on new tasks, e.g. in the government's planning and implementing of regional development policies, which underlined Norges Bank's position as an integral part of the political and administrative system.

In the 1970s and 1980s, central banks were given an increasingly independent role in Western countries. In Norway, the picture is less clear. Regulation of lending and interest rates remained rigorous until the mid-1980s. The era of credit regulation ended with a bang on the back of an economic boom, followed by tightening and a financial crisis. The tightening entailed the return of interest rate setting to Norges Bank, after forty years of exile. Nevertheless, these decades were not among the institution's best moments. Norges Bank's leadership was ridden with internal conflicts in the 1970s and early 1980s, at times displayed openly. After a long planning period, Norges Bank acquired a new head office in the mid-1980s. The building was remarkably expensive at a time of fiscal tightening and calls for wage moderation.

Ironically enough, a new Norges Bank Act was adopted in the mid-1980s, after a legislative review stretching back to the 1960s. The entire process clearly indicated that this was not one of the nation's most pressing issues. Throughout the constrained postwar period, the act of 1892, which marked the former formal independence, was retained. Now that the pendulum was about to shift, a new act would finally come into force that would mark postwar dependence.

A Central Bank in an Open Parvenu State

Over the past twenty-five years, the central bank has gradually progressed towards greater independence regardind monetary policy. 'Nominal anchoring' became a mantra from of the mid-1980s, as a reaction to inflation and the numerous devaluations of previous years. In the 1990s, the international trend was to switch to inflation targeting and Norges Bank's management argued in favour of adopting the new 'best practice'. The new trend was met with scepticism within senior management at the Ministry of Finance and the government, primarily because the tripartite cooperation in wage determination was based on the notion that the krone exchange rate should remain fixed, i.e. the interest rate was to be used to stabilize the exchange rate, not inflation. Cooperation in income settlement had been on a return in many European countries since the 1980s. In Norway, it was revitalized in the late 1980s, and the policy framework constructed around income settlements also came to provide a framework for Norges Bank's exchange rate setting and monetary policy measures in the following decade.

However, from the turn of the century inflation targeting was established, at the same time as the oil fund (now named the Government Pension Fund Global) grew at a surprisingly fast pace. In parallel with the expansion of this new activity, the former branch offices and activities not related to the work on monetary policy and financial stability were substantially reduced, resulting in a sharp decline in the bank's operating costs. The oil fund was managed by Norges Bank, and it grew into an integral part of the bank's overall activity and institutional self-understanding. From the very start in the early nineteenth century, parliament and Norges Bank wanted to avoid taking part in financing the state or in any kind of debt management on behalf of government. The mirrored activity, the somewhat more attractive activity of managing government wealth, has, however, fallen smoothly into the central bank's activities. Fund management has on the whole been successful, without any particularly serious controversies or episodes, even though the large losses associated with active management put the governance system of the fund to the test in 2009. Inflation targeting would in normal times easily have led to decisions that would be a burden or unpopular among politicians or the population at large. However, Norway has not experienced normal times in the past fifteen to twenty years. After the turn of the century, external inflationary impulses have been subdued, and since the financial crisis erupted there has been low growth without inflationary pressures in trading partner countries. At the same time, domestic activity has been robust thanks to relatively high oil prices and strong government finances.

Today, defending of the value of money is beginning to take on a form and expression connected to the more traditional defence of the value of money, as interest rates have been raised to keep inflation within prescribed boundaries. Yet, this has been the guiding principle for Norges Bank's activity throughout its history. During the first decades of the bank's history, the Storting assumed important elements of this mission. The defence of monetary stability was more or less suspended during the two world wars. In the postwar period the government removed it from Norges Bank—without entirely leaving the mission to anyone else. At times other tasks have been dominant, such as ordinary banking activities, foreign exchange control, and investment management on a large scale in international markets.

The following chapters examines Norges Bank's shifting role and importance over 200 years. Norges Bank has at times been a moving force behind important changes and decisions. More often, its tasks and roles have been shaped by external forces; partly international models and agreements, but mainly by the institutions of parliament and government. The central aim of this book is to trace and explain these changes over the past two centuries.

1

A Bank of Issue Forged in
Silver and Tears

World events led to Norway becoming an independent state in 1814. In 1807, the Kingdom of Denmark-Norway could no longer maintain its neutrality and sided with the French in the Napoleonic Wars. In the Treaty of Kiel at the beginning of 1814, Norway was ceded to Sweden, which had been part of the winning coalition. During the spring, however, a national assembly was convened in the name of national independence, a constitution was adopted, and a number of new government institutions were created. A predictable but very short war against superior Swedish forces followed in the autumn. The terms reflected a desire for peace and a civilized relationship with their neighbour: Norway was permitted to retain its constitution, administration, defence, and right to its own monetary system, and became part of a personal union with the Swedish king as head of both states.

To begin with, the new Norwegian institutions did not include a bank of issue. The constituent assembly was unable to agree on what form such a bank should take. A number of concerns featured in the discussions of 1814. First, it was clear that a bank of issue would need to be given the role of bringing order to a chaotic and hugely inflated monetary system. This role was combined with the need for an ordinary bank that could issue credit; no such bank existed in 1814, and the absence of a bank in Norway was considered one of the reasons for the country's weak economic performance and lasting economic dependence on Denmark. A third concern was the relationship with government finances. In a proposal made for the constituent assembly, the bank would become a key instrument for government borrowing. However, the assembly did not want a permanently established bank of issue to play a role in financing government—which is why the proposal was rejected.

Norges Bank was formed two years later by resolution of the Storting, the country's new parliament. The bank was not given any explicit role in government financing. But the other two tasks—providing credit for the public and stability in the monetary system—were fundamental to the bank's creation and almost every discussion of its operations for the next quarter of a century. When chartering Norges Bank in 1816, the Storting resolved that the Norwegian monetary unit—the speciedaler—should be convertible into silver at an exchange rate that was well above the notes' purchasing power and market value at the time.

One fundamental premise in all of the proposals that proliferated in 1816, influenced by the monetary chaos during the Napoleonic Wars, was that the value of the

Norges Bank 1816–2016. Einar Lie, Oxford University Press (2020). © Norges Bank.
DOI: 10.1093/oso/9780198860013.001.0001

nation's new paper money must be backed by silver. With the fledgling state short on both money and credibility, value needed to be protected through sufficient holdings of silver. These were raised through forced subscription levied on estimated wealth, during the crisis years following the war. 'The bank question' thus became an acid test for the authority and legitimacy of the political and administrative bodies of the new state.

The Chaotic Monetary System

The strongly expressed desire to tie the value of money to silver was founded in long and costly historical experience. In times of war, of which there were plenty in the Europe of the seventeenth and eighteenth centuries, it was less the exception than the rule that the money supply would expand rapidly as a result of the governments' need to finance warfare and supplies. Sweden and Denmark-Norway were not immune to this, especially during the Napoleonic Wars, which hit the stability of all European monetary systems.

Norway's own experience, as part of the integrated union of Denmark-Norway, thus followed a fairly common pattern. A systematically bullion-based monetary system was introduced in 1736, with the creation of a privately owned bank authorized by the Crown to issue banknotes. These notes could be converted into silver at a fixed rate. At the same time, the Crown was able to borrow money—notes—from the bank, and this option was exercised in tight situations. By 1757, the stock of paper money was so large that silver convertibility had to be suspended. In 1773, the Crown assumed the bank's liabilities. In 1791, an attempt was made to reconstruct the inflated system. A new privately owned bank of issue was formed with authority from the Crown, this time with an explicit cap on how many notes could be issued in relation to the value of its silver reserve, and the original bank of issue was closed.

This system collapsed when the so-called Hamburg Crisis hit Denmark-Norway in 1799, which was ultimately a result of changes to trading patterns caused by the war in Europe.[1] Many trading houses had problems meeting their international commitments. The regulations protecting the silver reserve put clear limits on how much credit could be issued to troubled trading houses—as the metallic system prescribes. To help both the state and the business sector, however, the original bank of issue from 1736 was reopened, and the old banknotes were once again made legal tender. Such was the situation in 1807 when the British navy bombarded Copenhagen, seized the Dano-Norwegian fleet, and so forced the country out of neutrality and into an alliance with France. From this point, its financing needs soared. By 1812, after five years of war, the silver value of notes in circulation had fallen to just 7 per cent of what it had been before the crisis in 1799.[2]

---

[1] Nicolai Rygg, *Norges Banks historie*, vol. 1 (Norges Bank, 1918), 24–31.
[2] Einar Lie et al., *Norges Bank 1816–2016* (Fagbokforlaget, 2016), 27ff.

The year 1813 brought a new reform that would have major implications for the new Norwegian state. A new national bank—the Riksbank—was created, and old banknotes were exchanged for new notes from this bank. The silver content was set at 10 per cent of the previous level. This was more than the market value of the notes would justify. The 10 per cent was thus a promise for the future, and the notes were not made convertible. The bank did not have a silver reserve, but the notes would be secured against all available property in the realm. This move had some similarities to the assignats issued during the French Revolution, which were backed by the value of properties confiscated from the church.[3]

The Riksbank had two branch offices: one in Copenhagen and one in Kristiania (today's Oslo). The Kristiania branch was covered by a special and, in theory, beneficial clause permitting it to retain any silver exchanged for notes to build up its own reserve. This was only beneficial on paper, however, as nobody would want to exchange silver for paper money at the rate offered, nor would anybody want to relinquish any silver in normal trading. Gresham's law, which applies regardless of whether people have heard of it, once again came into play: bad money drives out good. People hoarded silver and silver coins rather than putting them into circulation along with paper money that was constantly falling in value to well below the promised level.

The value of paper money fell further during the winter of 1813/14. The Treaty of Kiel—the agreement between the United Kingdom and Sweden on the one side, and Denmark-Norway on the other, which transferred Norway from Denmark to Sweden—was signed in January 1814. Encouraged by the Danish crown prince, a constituent national assembly convened at Eidsvoll, a small estate 70 miles north of Kristiania, to form a new state with its own constitution. By this time the financial situation was precarious. A decision to create a new permanent bank of issue could be put back until the first ordinary session of the Storting, the new legislative assembly, which we will return to shortly. The question of financing the new state now under formation, however, could not be postponed. For the state to function, it would need to be able to finance a small administration, some supplies, and, not least, a small army in order to be able to assert its sovereignty vis-à-vis the Swedish king.

The debate about the financing of the state overlapped with the issue of how the monetary system should be stabilized. A majority of the assembly wanted both stabilization and further financing of the state through expansion of the money supply. The talks on increasing the money supply and the implications of this took place on 13 May 1814, a few days before the unanimous resolution that gave Norway its constitution. Constitution Day—17 May—is still celebrated annually with speeches, flags, and processions, while 13 May is now all but forgotten, except for specialist historians. A boisterous debate arose between those for and against printing more money, with loud applause and cheering accompanying the most notable contributions. One

---

[3] Rebecca L Spang, *Stuff and Money in the Time of the French Revolution* (Harvard University Press, 2015); Michael D. Bordo and Eugene N. White, 'A Tale of Two Currencies: British and French Finance During the Napoleonic Wars', *The Journal of Economic History* 51, no. 2 (1991).

procedural consequence of this debate was that the members of the assembly decided against a British model for Norway's national assembly. At subsequent meetings of the Storting right through to the present day, no applause or expression of displeasure is permitted either during or after speeches.

The proponents of expansion in order to assert national independence won the day. The national assembly decided to convert the Kristiania branch of the Riksbank into a temporary Norwegian national bank with the right to issue paper money. Specifically, the bank was to issue a sum of 14 million riksbankdaler—equivalent to more than a 50 per cent increase in the money supply—to shore up the state's precarious finances. At the same time, a commitment subsequently known as the Eidsvoll Guarantee was made, namely that old and new notes would at a future date be convertible into silver at a rate of 53.33 per cent of their silver value following the devaluation when the Riksbank was formed in 1813. However, the assembly had already resolved that existing debts to citizens, dating from the union with Denmark, would be honoured. The Eidsvoll Guarantee was thus simultaneously a promise made and a promise broken, just like the decision on devaluation in Copenhagen the previous year.[4]

This decision has been much discussed and criticized since, both because it continued the inflationary spiral, and because, for that very reason, it was a promise that could not be kept. One vocal critic was the topcivil servant at the Ministry of Finance, Jørgen Vogt, who would go on to be one of the most influential civil servants and politicians of the era, serving almost uninterrupted as a minister in various departments from 1825 to 1857.[5] He was against the printing of new notes supplied with a guarantee of future value in the first place and was subsequently one of its sternest critics. All international experience indicated that the notes' market price would be determined not by a new political promise but by their purchasing power, he argued. 'Suffice to mention Sweden, Denmark, Austria, France, England, the United States of America. How could one believe that the word of our national assembly would prove the magic wand that the most powerful nations have been unable to find?'[6]

Neither contemporary nor modern monetary policy principles lend credibility to the guarantee. But this is not the only relevant perspective on the matter. Both then and since, the Eidsvoll assembly has been viewed as falling roughly into two camps. One was the 'union party', who were either friendly towards Sweden or took a more pragmatic view of the high politics of Kiel, and believed that the constitution should reflect a future union with Sweden. The other was the 'independence party', which was in the majority and wanted in principle to establish Norway as an independent nation. Within the latter camp, most wanted the Danish crown prince Christian Frederik as king, and some even envisaged a future reunion with Denmark, albeit in a very different form to before.

---

[4] Francis Sejersted, *Den vanskelige frihet 1814–1851* (Cappelens forlag, 1978), 32.
[5] Paul Thyness, 'Jørgen Herman Vogt', Norsk Biografisk Leksikon, https://nbl.snl.no/Jørgen_Herman_Vogt.
[6] Den Norske Rigstidende 64 (12 August 1815), p. 4, quoted in Martin Austnes, *Kampen om banken: et historisk perspektiv på utformingen av det nye norges bank- og pengevesen Ca. 1814–1816* (Norges Bank, 2016), 92.

The assembly's view of further monetary expansion supported by a guarantee was also split largely along these party lines.[7] The 'independence party' naturally wanted and needed more resources to build a Norwegian state and establish defences against the Swedes. In a stronger state, a modern state, this new expenditure might have been funded through taxation, or by borrowing at home or abroad. But there was no Norwegian state beyond the four walls of Eidsvoll. It was very doubtful whether the state would have the possibility and authority to collect taxes. Only the most daring investor would have lent to the new state. If Norway was to declare independence, printing money was the only real option.

It has been pointed out that the decision to print money has as much in common with the financing of revolutions as with the financing of young nations. The great revolutions of the late eighteenth century were largely financed by printing money. In the American case, this was without any formal funding. As Benjamin Franklin reflected,

> And indeed the whole is a mystery even to the politicians, how we have been able to continue a war four years without money, and how we could pay with paper that had no previously fixed fund appropriated specifically to redeem it. This currency, as we manage it, is a wonderful machine. It performs its office when we issue it; it pays and clothes troops, and provides victuals and ammunition; and when we are obliged to issue a quantity excessive, it pays itself off by depreciation.[8]

The stock of paper money in the US grew from 10–15 million dollars to 250 million dollars during the revolutionary period—in subsequent years these notes were as good as worthless.

Revolutionaries can also confiscate property, from their opponents and from individuals and institutions unaligned with the revolutionary ideal and the revolutionary fraternity. This was done in America, and the same principle was also applied in France, where confiscated land was the formal collateral for the issue of assignats, the revolutionary currency. In practice, there were no limits on the issue of these instruments, and here too they rapidly lost their value. Financially, these arrangements were hazardous. One way or another, though, they did bankroll revolutions that changed the history of both nations and the world.

In the new Norway, where the idea was to pull together as a nation, the confiscation route was out of the question, and the possibilities for raising heavy taxes in the near term were non-existent. The independent party therefore opted for the only feasible way of giving the government purchasing power. With the Danish Crown's excesses and the devastating inflation of the Napoleonic Wars on the political agenda, however, money could not be printed simply in the hope that it would be accepted by future

[7] Ibid., 100ff.

[8] Benjamin Franklin quoted in James Buchan, *Frozen Desire: The Meaning of Money* (Farrar Straus Giroux, 1997), 154; see also Austnes, *Kampen om bankenEt historisk perspektiv på utformingen av det nye Norges bank- og pengevesen ca. 1814–1816*, 94–5.

holders of the notes. A new guarantee, albeit on the optimistic side, needed to be issued. All in all, this was the only possible way forward.

Models and Inspirations

The years from 1814 to 1818, when vital elements in the compromises surrounding the note-issuing bank was finalized, were one of the greatest periods of upheaval in Norwegian history. But here too, the changes were rooted in the recent past. And the solutions chosen came to cement an institutional framework that would set its stamp on the bank's activities for almost the whole of the nineteenth century. Three parallel discussions (at least) evolved around the establishment of the bank. One had to do with the core monetary policy issue—the balance between the need to issue paper money and the need to stabilize the value of money. The second concerned how the new bank of issue should be financed. A third issue was the role the new bank should play in the longer term—who and what it was to finance. In all of these areas, hybrid solutions were found, shaped by lessons learned in other countries, the political balance of power, and preconceptions about the relationship between money, power, and credit. The main elements in the line compromises came with the decision to establish the bank in 1816. The founding decisions came to decide how Norges Bank should be financed and how it should be governed and controlled. The foundation of the bank also comprised a plan for monetary restoration and guidelines for the bank's future function and policies. However, new parliament decisions in 1818 came to alter and soften the principles for monetary restoration, which came to drag out into the following decades.

Between the constituent assembly of 1814 and the Storting of 1816 that finally resolved to establish Norges Bank, there was extensive analysis and debate on what form a new bank should take. An institution with a large silver reserve was to be created in a relatively impoverished country, with only a very thin crust of people with any real available means. At the same time, the state—through the Norwegian branch of the Riksbank—owed large amounts of silver to the holders of inflated notes circulating from the Danish period and exacerbated by the expansion the previous year. All plans included exchanging these notes for notes from the new bank of issue. There was a broad consensus that the bank should be privately owned, with a silver reserve to back the value of its notes. Next, there needed to be a mechanism to bring order to the monetary system and prevent future relapses. Finally, there needed to be rules for how the bank's lending activities should be organized once it got under way.

When it came to international models, the previous Dano-Norwegian period dominated. The system introduced in 1736 of issuing notes backed by silver was considered exemplary, whereas the Crown-induced inflationary period that culminated in the years of the Napoleonic Wars represented the fall from grace. This position, based on recent, first-hand experience, was shared across the battle lines. More remote ideals, from both theory and practice in other countries, would also play a role, but with only scattered support and varying authority. There was no real academic environment for the discussion of these issues. A university had been founded in Kristiania in 1811 and was home to a chair in the rather singular combination of 'botany and economic science'. But its holder, academic pioneer Christen Smith, would never become embroiled in the national debate. In 1816, when the talks on the formation of Norges Bank were at their most intense, he and eighteen other members of an expedition to the Congo lost their lives to hostile natives and contagious diseases—a trip said to have inspired Joseph Conrad's *Heart of Darkness* more than seventy years later.[9]

Despite an underdeveloped academic environment, parts of the relatively outward-looking Norwegian bourgeoisie—the officials and the merchants—were familiar with relevant foreign writings. For example, Adam Smith's *The Wealth of Nations* was translated into Danish (also the written language in Norway) as early as 1779, only three years after the publication of the original. Most orders for the book came from Norwegian readers, primarily leading figures in the merchant class.[10] In the absence of domestic banks, Norwegian lenders, merchants, and shipowners dealt directly with the big financial centres, primarily Hamburg and its Danish twin city of Altona, and in some cases London. There was frequent reference in the Norwegian debate to the role of the Bank of England—both the bank's traditional relationship with the state and the changes in the bank's policies during the war years from 1797 onwards.

In all of the proposals seriously debated by the national assembly, convertibility to silver was a fundamental principle. Another was that the bank should not belong to the executive, either on paper or in practice. The original assembly at Eidsvoll was supposed to have chartered a bank, but this did not happen. There was a proposal for this, prepared either by or for the Danish crown prince Christian Frederik. The original has been lost, but we know its key features from detailed comments made by Carsten Tank, a shipowner and timber merchant who was a member of the provisional Norwegian government set up in March 1814 and responsible for the Ministry of Finance. In this proposal, the bank was to have very considerable capacity to issue notes, backed by government bonds in the bank's reserve. The circulation of means of payment backed by government debt is a recurring theme in many early European banks of issue,[11] but here the proposal was directly linked to the Crown's use and misuse of the printing press in the last phase of the Dano-Norwegian union.[12] Tank's experience-based scepticism about such an arrangement was shared by much of the assembly.

These two functions—a bank independent of the executive and with a duty to convert notes into silver—defined the universe of possibilities for the institution that

---

[9] Preben Munthe, *Christen Smith: botaniker og økonom* (Aschehough, 2004).
[10] Hans Degen, 'Om Den Danske Oversættelse Af Adam Smith Og Samtidens Bedømmelse Af Den', *Nationaløkonomisk Tidsskrift* 3, no. 44 (1936); Niels Banke, 'Om Adam Smiths forbindelse med Norge og Danmark', *Nationaløkonomisk Tidsskrift*, no. 93 (1955).
[11] Michael D. Bordo et al., 'Introduction', in *Central Banks at a Crossroads: What Can We Learn from History*, ed. Michael D. Bordo, et al. (Cambridge University Press, 2016).
[12] Austnes, *Kampen om banken*, 111ff.

could be created. When concrete proposals were drawn up on this basis, a number of principles and interests emerged as irresolvable.

The historian Martin Austnes has noted a central, liberal line from the Norwegians' demands for their own bank under the Dano-Norwegian union in the late eighteenth century through to the discussions of 1814–18, and from this sprang a related debate around the possible relaxation of the issuing monopoly that was created with the establishment of Norges Bank in 1816. The calls for a Norwegian bank came from various quarters, but most prominently from the affluent and internationally oriented merchant bourgeoisie around Kristiania. Their wealth came mainly from trading in timber, for which Britain was by far the most important market.[13] In their arguments, the British model took centre stage. The Bank of England's role as an international model is well known. In the Norwegian debate, however, the Old Lady of Threadneedle Street was not held up as an example to be copied. Criticism of the existing banking system centred on the issuing monopoly which was based in Copenhagen and had overly close links with an economically expansionary Crown. The merchants wanted the monopoly to be relaxed, with the Norwegians allowed to open their own banks with an independent right to issue money. These banks would be wholly private and kept completely separated from government finances. Opinions varied on how the value of the new banks' notes would be secured, but there was a consensus that the threat to a fixed value lay in the state directly or indirectly being able to finance itself through the banks' operations. There were clear and considerable differences between the banks of issue in Copenhagen and London, but discussion of the Bank of England—with its strong legal rights and long and prominent history—was dominated by the similarities with regard to the banks's role in financing of the state.[14]

On the other hand, the British banking system outside London, most notably in Scotland, was portrayed in a positive light. Several Norwegian observers argued that competition between the banks led to plentiful credit and predictable values (very much like Adam Smith in *The Wealth of Nations*). In Scotland, there was no issuing monopoly, no central bank, and, for a long time, no specific regulation, not even for metallic cover. The calls for Norwegian banks did not therefore always include a requirement for bullion to back the notes they issued; after 1814, as mentioned earlier, this requirement was universal. Fears of the central power assuming control of the monetary system, and scepticism about privileges and monopolies, would survive the turning point that the Napoleonic Wars provided.

Jacob Aall (1773–1844), a leading merchant bourgeois and member of the Eidsvoll assembly who also authored a number of papers on economic theory, portrayed the modern credit system as a double-edged sword. It had a unique capacity to generate growth in trade and production; but it could also be used to fund harmful and illegitimate political projects. Aall was a consistent advocate of a fixed metal standard. But

---

[13] John Peter Collett and Bård Frydenlund, *Christianias Handelspatrisiat: En elite i 1700-tallets Norge* (Andresen & Butenschøn, 2008); Austnes, *Kampen om banken*, 57ff.
[14] Austnes, *Kampen om banken*, 53–4.

he also found positives in the Scottish system, with its strong credit-generating capacity, where the existence of multiple private, competing issuers made it difficult for the executive to abuse the monetary system. Affinity for the Scottish model also prevailed in Norwegian intellectual circles. When the university in Kristiania announced a chair in economics in the mid-1870s, it was advertised as a competition under the title 'On banks of issue'. The winner, Ebbe Hertzberg, spent a lot of time criticizing the Bank of England's strong position, relationship to the state, and strict rules on metallic cover. He too singled out the Scottish system as a better model for a bank of issue, or rather a network of banks of issue, in a country like Norway.[15]

Opposed to this liberal position were a number of speakers from the farmer and official classes, who in various ways were sceptical not only about how the credit system might be misused by political authorities, but also about how trading and finance houses might enrich themselves once the money-based economy became more established. We will illustrate this with a concrete discussion of how the new bank was to be raised and financed, an operation inseparable from the reconstruction of the existing Riksbank and its inflated notes.

After the constituent assembly at Eidsvoll rejected the original proposal for a bank linked to the executive's finances, a committee was appointed to draw up a fresh proposal. This proposal was considered at the first meeting of the new parliament—the Storting—in autumn 1815, and a revised proposal was presented the following year. While these specific proposals were rejected as a basis for a combined process of reconstruction and creation of a bank of issue, key features were retained in the final decision. In brief, the idea was that the old riksbankdaler should quickly be phased out in favour of new notes called speciedaler. This was to be done by allowing the old notes to be used to subscribe for shares in the new bank alongside silver in a set ratio. The new bank would also be strengthened, and subscription for shares made more tempting, if the bank took over the Riksbank's charges on all taxable property in the country. These would provide future revenue. The nominal value of the shares was set in such a way that, in principle, the Eidsvoll Guarantee was honoured. But the old notes had to come into the hands of people with silver, who were then forced to invest metal and notes in shares in the new bank.

Fear of Speculation and 'Jew-houses'

For the more affluent classes who had or could get hold of silver, there were undoubtedly opportunities here for arbitrage, to use a modern term. Those who only had banknotes with a low and diminishing value needed to offload them before they became worthless, and there was no obligation for anyone to buy the notes at a particular price. In addition, the bank's ownership would belong to those same classes, which were very small in Norway. It was not a landed aristocracy (which for all

---

[15] Ebbe Hertzberg, *Om Kredittens Begreb og Væsen* (Malling, 1877).

practical purposes did not exist in Norway, where farmers formally or effectively owned their own land) but a commercially oriented bourgeoisie who were seen as the silvered potential shareholders in the bank of issue.

Both factors were forcefully pointed out in the ensuing debate. The farmers called for a broad wealth tax to provide the basis for the combined operation of monetary reconstruction and creation of a bullion fund for the new bank. They also demanded that the Eidsvoll Guarantee be honoured in full, with old notes exchanged for new notes in such a way that the silver value remained the same. Farmers also wanted the new bank to be a 'national bank'. This was a term that covered many different solutions in terms of both organization and ownership. What they had in common was a move away from a solution where a limited financial elite ended up with control of the bank.[16]

Strong normative criticism arose during the course of the debate. This was generally fuelled by equality ideals expressed at Eidsvoll, but also targeted the merchant bourgeoisie and the practices and mentality ascribed to them. These were people addicted to luxury and excess—there are echoes here of the eighteenth-century debate about trade and modernity in Denmark-Norway.[17] Internationally oriented trading houses, especially where big money was involved, were considered particularly suspect. They were seen by many as a potential corrupting influence on national solidarity. It is also striking how fear of the Jews and 'Jew-houses' (a term sometimes used as a general metaphor for finance houses) abounded in the debate, not only among farmers but also among the more heterogeneous group of central and local officials. The original plan, with notes having to be converted via owners of silver, could favour 'Jew-houses'. Subsequent solutions, where riksbankdaler could be exchanged directly for new notes at some point, could also favour 'Jew-houses' through speculation until such time as the old notes were out of circulation.

Allow me a brief digression here. Article 2 of the Eidsvoll Constitution actually banned Jews and Jesuits from Norway. The clause was formulated succinctly and directly, making no allowance for exceptions. There was no real Jewish community in Norway, but there were various individuals and families, and a number of deportations took place in autumn 1814 and 1815. The clause and its implementation are particularly incongruous when one considers that the Norwegian Constitution was regarded as strikingly liberal in terms of the right to vote, legal rights, freedom of speech, and freedom of the press. Early research noted the economic motives behind the so-called 'Jew clause'.[18] More recent research has increasingly highlighted political and ideological factors. The founding fathers wanted to build a strong sense of national community, whereas the prevailing view was that Jews generally formed their own communities wherever they settled. However, the belief that internationally oriented economic

---

[16] Austnes, *Kampen om banken*, ch. 4.

[17] Håkon Evju, 'Velstandens forbannelser. Kriseforståelsen og synet på forholdet mellom rikdom og moral i Norge, 1807–1813', I: *Veivalg for Norden 1809-1813*. Akademika forlag 2013, ch. 6.

[18] Frode Ulvund, *Fridomens grenser 1814-1851* (Scandinavian Academic Press, 2014); Håkon Harket, *Paragrafen: Eidsvoll 1814* (Dreyers forlag, 2014).

activity could serve to undermine the national, combined with the associations made between Jews, international trade, and finance, makes the two difficult to separate.

The Jew clause would nevertheless come to play a part in the Norwegian state's financial history. In 1818, finance minister Herman Wedel (who had opposed the clause at Eidsvoll) travelled to London to raise a badly needed government loan. Norway had had to assume a share of Denmark-Norway's government debt under the Treaty of Kiel, and the general crisis after the Napoleonic Wars had led to states of emergency and a sharp decline in government revenue. In London, however, Rothschild refused to receive Wedel, referring to the Jew clause, and is also said to have urged other finance houses not to lend to Norway.[19] A very expensive short-term loan was subsequently raised in Stockholm. The public finance crisis was resolved in 1822 through a large loan brokered by the finance house of Hambro. Joseph Hambro travelled to Norway twice that year to negotiate the loan. He too was Jewish and should have been denied entry under a strict interpretation of the constitution. But then there would probably not have been any loan. The literature on the Jew clause has indicated that this episode led to a more pragmatic application of the clause, which came up for renewed debate in the 1840s and was eventually abolished in 1851.[20]

The Decision to Create Norges Bank is Taken

The question of a guaranteed exchange rate for the riksbankdaler had split the constituent assembly and would also come to divide the ordinary and extraordinary meetings of the Storting that considered it. From 1816 onwards, the split was along different lines. While the divide in the constituent assembly was between the 'union party' and 'independence party', it now ran along more established social strata. The merchant bourgeoisie wanted to ditch the guarantee. Based on the liberal views held by parts of this group, one would expect a guarantee, especially one given by the country's constituent assembly, to be cherished as an immovable legal framework for future actions. As exporters, however, they undoubtedly stood to lose from a major upward revaluation of money. The discussions also took place during a crisis that greatly reduced this group's financial capacity and political strength. A standard theme in Norwegian historiography has been the absence of a highly affluent *grande bourgeoisie*, ever since the dramatic decimation of this group during the crisis following the Napoleonic Wars.[21]

The farmers in the assembly, on the other hand, argued strongly in favour of upholding the guarantee. It is not given, neither in theory nor in the light of comparable episodes, that the relatively non-wealthy layer of the population would take this

---

[19] Ingerid Hagen, *Blåfargen fra Modum: en verdenshistorie: Blaafarveværket 1776–1821* (Scandinavian Academic Press, 2014), 150.
[20] Ulvund, *Fridomens Grenser 1814–1851*, 210–16.
[21] See e.g. Francis Sejersted, 'Den Norske Sonderweg', in *Demokratisk kapitalisme* (Pax, 2002).

position. If we look at the US, the middle classes—especially away from the economic centres on the east coast—were opposed to the plan of Alexander Hamilton, the US secretary of finance, to reform the monetary system on the basis of previous guarantees given for the value of American revolutionary currency, and create a new federal bank. There are obvious differences of scale and structure between the IOUs circulating in the US and the government-backed riksbankdaler in peripheral Norway, not least concerning the American debate on federal versus state authority. But there are also clear similarities in the proposed reforms and in the debate that ensued. The revolutionary notes in the US fell sharply in value after their introduction. The criticism was that those who had received them early got back their face value, whereas those receiving them at lower real values would make a substantial profit. Here too, there were obvious speculative incentives, which will always abound with future price promises on which demonstrable realities can cast doubt. The strongest American criticism from the non-wealthy, however, leaned towards not redeeming at the guaranteed rate, because this would favour money people and speculators who were sitting on large sums.

This position is easier to understand than the opposition from the Norwegian farmers. Their understanding was that the rural population's personal property was almost exclusively in the form of paper money, whereas the more affluent part of the population also had assets in the form of uncoined silver, and to some extent hard currency. Upholding the guarantee would therefore be relatively more important for farmers' wealth—their wealthier countrymen would also be able to use their access to silver and currency to make speculative gains in the event of continued uncertainty about the guarantee or its postponement. This reasoning is easy to understand, although nobody actually knew who held the notes. The presumption was that there would be more with the merchant bourgeoisie. It is tempting to assume that the strong opposition to 'speculation' in this monetary situation also dominated the positions taken on this issue, in the sense that the farmers wanted to remove opportunities for arbitrage, both real and suspected.

The solution for the establishment of Norges Bank entailed a series of compromises between the different groups involved. The reconstruction of the existing monetary system was largely achieved through a traditional tax solution. Parts of the old notes were withdrawn through a one-off tax on wealth and income. Norges Bank then extended a large loan to the temporal Riksbank, which was used to redeem the old notes. This loan was to be repaid over ten years, and in practice this would place clear restrictions on the bank's financial activities. The state itself obtained the money through new taxes. When the decision to charter the bank was taken, early in 1816, a further fall in banknote values since spring 1814 had further undermined the Eidsvoll Guarantee. A small majority of the Storting therefore resolved to abandon this promise, carry out a fresh devaluation, this time by 62.5 per cent, and declare that the new notes would be fully convertible from 1 January 1819. Combine the three devaluations of 1813, 1814, and 1816, and simple arithmetic gives a remaining silver value of just 2 per cent of what was originally guaranteed by the Dano-Norwegian Crown.

Subscription for the bank's shares was the key issue. A two-track solution was adopted which, at least in principle, made concessions to both the bourgeois-liberal wing and those who had criticized previous drafts for favouring an elite and wanted a bank under 'national' control. Plan A was to try to establish a privately owned bank. Such companies are normally created by issuing shares to those with the funds and inclination. This would be the first track: if it succeeded, an ordinary limited company would be formed, where the general meeting appointed a Supervisory Council to handle appointments and oversee the bank's activities. But the benefits of subscribing for shares were moderated from the early proposals. The loan to fund the redemption of old notes would also burden the bank and its future shareholders.

A majority of the Storting clearly suspected that this voluntary solution might fall short, and a Plan B was included from the outset. If voluntary subscription failed, the state would need to ensure sufficient compulsory subscription for shares to build the bank's silver reserve. With this solution, it would be decisions of the Storting that established the bank by raising funds from a large number of people. The Storting itself would then ensure that this diverse shareholder base had influence. It was generally assumed that those who would be forced into ownership would be those with good incomes and property. And such people were, for the most part, also those who were entitled to vote in elections to the Storting. If there were to be compulsory subscription, the Storting would thus install itself as the bank's general meeting, with direct influence in particular over the appointment of the bank's senior officers.[22]

The Silver Fund, the Crisis, and Union Politics

While debate raged openly between different tiers of society over what form the bank should take, a tug-of-war was playing behind the scenes over the future of the monetary system between Norwegian politicians and the Swedish crown prince, which ultimately boiled down to what form the Swedish-Norwegian personal union should take. The Swedish king at the time was ageing, enfeebled, and childless. In 1810, the French general Jean-Baptiste Jules Bernadotte was elected crown prince and heir to the Swedish throne. Alongside a brilliant military career, Bernadotte had been governor of the commercial and financial centre of Hamburg in 1807–9, demonstrating excellent administrative skills and building a considerable private fortune. He returned to Sweden in 1814 and effectively took over the Crown, which had a firm grip on the country's executive. Adopting the Swedish name Karl Johan (sometimes anglicized as Charles XIV John), he was strongly committed—first as crown prince and from 1818 as king—to strengthening both his own position and that of Sweden in Norway. This was due partly to his own personal ambitions, and partly to criticism from the Swedish nobility that he had given Norway too much independence in the wake of the brief war that followed the adoption of the constitution on 17 May 1814.

---

[22] Lie et al., *Norges Bank 1816–2016*, 39.

The constituent assembly and the first meetings of the Storting strove to ensure national control of the monetary system and, in one form or another, a new bank of issue. From Karl Johan's papers and extensive correspondence on the establishment of a Norwegian monetary system, it is clear that he envisaged a different solution, primarily an amalgamation of Norwegian and Swedish institutions. He sanctioned the Storting's resolution to create Norges Bank in 1816, but, like many others, clearly assumed that voluntary subscription would fail. Only 40 per cent of the minimum reserve of 2 million speciedaler was raised under Plan A. The crown prince's papers suggest that he was inclined to use his own considerable wealth to supply the silver reserve.[23] He thought that the Storting should convene again, which would have opened the door to new solutions. The government disagreed; in December 1816 it decided to move on with Plan B's forced subscription according to the parliament's resolution.

Karl Johan was, however, not alone in the attempts to slow down the process. By late 1816, the depression following the Napoleonic Wars had reached Norway. Voluntary subscription for the bank's shares fell a long way short. In no part of the country did it raise the sums stipulated in the plan, although the shortfall was greatest in the south-east, home to the wealthiest bourgeoisie and the centre for timber exports. Timber is a long-term and capital-intensive business, and the combination of economic crisis and scarce credit hit the region particularly hard. Along the south-western coast and in the middle of the country, the economy was more diverse, and the impact less dramatic. Bergen, then the country's largest city, was the centre for the healthier and more liquid fishing industry. The situation here was better, and no less than 90 per cent of compulsory contributions were made before the deadline.[24]

The economic slump decimated incomes and wealth across the country, but was particularly devastating for the so-called 'timber patricians' in the south-east in 1815–18. Anecdotes from the pre-war days tell of one having Madeira wine in his fountains, while another would send his best clothes to London to be properly washed and starched. This kind of conspicuous consumption disappeared with the crisis and ensuing bankruptcies, and the economic and social elite was more or less wiped out by the crises and taxes of the years before 1820. One of the big timber merchants, Haagen Mathiesen, made it through the crisis and then spent many years abroad. On his return in 1829, he commented: 'The middle class is no more.' It was not the middle class as we know it today that he had in mind, but the old affluent bourgeoisie that he knew from the years before the crisis struck in 1815–16.[25]

This meant that many of those expected to be the best taxpayers disappeared, while others saw their taxable capacity reduced. Since the bank proposals of autumn 1815, which were criticized for creating a bank financed and controlled by a wealthy elite, the tax base had become broader and more general. The payments required to finance

---

[23] Sverre Steen, *På fallittens rand*, vol. 2, Det frie Norge (Cappelen, 1953), 173.
[24] Lie et al., *Norges Bank 1816–2016*, 50.
[25] Francis Sejersted, *Den vanskelige frihet: Norge 1814–1850* (Pax, 2001), 171.

Norges Bank, coming on top of taxes to reconstruct the old monetary system, would affect a larger part of the population than simply the moneyed class. Public protests ensued. Karl Johan's agents were said to have fanned the flames, and the crown prince himself believed that the Norwegian attempt to finance a monetary system and bank of issue would fail. The financial situation was 'for thinking men [...] a sign of how impossible it was for the Norwegians to build an independent state'.[26]

Large farmers' marches were organized in autumn 1818 to demonstrate against the silver tax. There had been various protests by farmers during the Dano-Norwegian era, normally against local officials, asking the Crown to show lenience and make allowances. We find the same elements in the protests of 1818. One of the leaders of the marches put it as follows, in a public letter of complaint over the collection and seizure of assets to build the bank's silver reserve: 'Who is guaranteeing the bank for us? Is it His Majesty the King or the crown prince? If neither, one might be tempted to conclude that we have no real security for our deposits.'[27] In other words, the new institutions' legitimacy and credibility were not universally established. The most critical situation arose in September 1818, when large groups of farmers marched on the capital. Troops were called out, and Kristiania's civil corps was mobilized and armed. Groups of farmers were arrested in a number of operations, but with a few exceptions they were released once the demonstrations had broken up.

Other problems were also piling up at this time. It was thought that the rapid withdrawal of old riksbankdaler notes at the same time that Norges Bank was putting its own notes into circulation might cause liquidity problems. It was therefore decided to set up special loan and discounting centres with an independent right to issue their own speciedaler notes during a transition phase.

Even so, there were shortages of means of payment for ongoing business and taxes during the reconstruction process. Protests were rife, and even though people needed the money, old riksbankdaler notes were ceremoniously burned in public places. But not everything went on the fire. It turned out that one of the four directors of the Riksbank, David Thrane, was behind a substantial amount of cash going missing. The money had been embezzled for private speculation in France. The scandal came at the worst possible time, just before the Storting convened in 1818.[28] The case was considered by both the government and the Storting. After Thrane himself was stripped of his assets and declared bankrupt, his father and the three remaining directors guaranteed the remaining debt and interest. In the end, not everything was paid—two of the guarantors, although wealthy men by the standards of the day, went bankrupt a year or two later—and the outstanding interest was covered by the Storting.

This case—referred to by historians as the greatest scandal of the 'civil servant state' era (1814–84)—warrants a brief digression. Thrane was ruined, but avoided lengthy

---

[26] Ibid., 30.

[27] Halvor Hoel in *Christiania Intelligentsedler*, 27 October 1817, quoted in Sonja Serina Finstad Johansson, 'Til Christiania for at Søge Forlindring de store Tyngsler: Bondetogene på østlandet og bøndenes motstand mot skattepolitikken i 1818', masters thesis, University of Oslo (2009), 41.

[28] Harald Espeli and Yngve Nilsen, *Riksrevisjonens historie 1816–2016* (Fagbokforlaget, 2016), 24–7 and 40.

imprisonment. This was partly because Norwegian civil and criminal legislation was in its infancy, and the case was considered under the old Dano-Norwegian rules. In the years and decades that followed, however, a huge effort went into new legislation, expanding auditing and control systems, and extensive spot-testing. The penalties for embezzlement were also stepped up to levels approaching the draconian. In 1831, a bailiff was charged with a missing sum of 21,000 speciedaler, far less than Thrane had taken. Some had been embezzled, but the figure also included tax arrears for which his subordinates were responsible. The bailiff was nevertheless sentenced by the Supreme Court to a lifetime of hard labour. The combination of control measures, strict penalties, and, perhaps in particular, the development of a strong sense of integrity among civil servants meant, however, that cases of embezzlement and the like were only sporadic from the 1840s onwards.

The issue of integrity also had a broader dimension, which was more relevant for the distribution of the burden when it came to the formation of the new bank and the reconstruction of the old monetary system. The possibility of certain groups enriching themselves at the expense of others featured frequently in the debate—the speculation incentive has already been mentioned. When it came to collecting taxes, especially in the cities, there were strong protests against what was considered to be favouritism. Discretion was applied here from top to bottom. The Storting first divided taxes into regions, based partly on previous tax assessments, customs revenue, a census performed in 1815, and the judgement of elected officials. Within each region, the tax burden was divided between the different municipalities by separate elected commissions, and at a local level between individual taxpayers by newly formed committees. Also at these lower levels, previously reported information was used, supplemented with considerable discretionary powers.

There is a wealth of old anecdotal material about how officials exercised these powers in ways that benefited them at the expense of others, which is to some extent reflected in the interpretations of historians. Now that all of the material on the silver tax has been digitalized, there has recently been extensive analysis of whether members of the political elite really did use their discretionary powers to ease the burden on their own regions, their own local communities, and their own pockets. The benchmark here was the sum of all available objective material, and the analysis looked at whether the use of discretionary powers deviated systematically from this in favour of those wielding them. The conclusion of this work, which has the revealing title of 'Honest elites', is that there is generally a slightly negative correlation between personal interests and the impact of the discretionary element in these tax assessments. Some decisions will inevitably have been questionable, with fierce taxes being levied in a turbulent economic situation, but the material as a whole indicates that the ideals of impartiality and objectivity dominated in this complex assessment process.[29]

---

[29] Second essay in Edda Torsdatter Solbakken, 'The Wealth of a Young Nation: On Voting Rights, Financing Plights, and Long-Run Wealth Inequality in Norway' (University of Oslo, 2018).

Timetable Abandoned

The political situation, the economic crisis, and the extensive protests against heavy taxes meant that the tempo and approach of the entire web of reforms was raised at the Storting of 1818. Norges Bank's most senior governing body—the Storting-appointed Supervisory Council—proposed postponing conversion of the new speciedaler notes into silver by one year. The background to this was that collections for the silver reserve were going slowly, and the bank needed more time to gain an overview of overall holdings and prepare for conversion to metal. An alternative proposal was put forward by two representatives of Norges Bank itself: one a member of the Supervisory Council and one a member of the Executive Board. Both were businessmen and major taxpayers who needed liquidity and credit to meet their commitments.

This proposal won the support of the Storting in the demanding economic, financial, and political situation that prevailed. The literature on the central bank has held this up as the great failing in the implementation of the act of 1816 that would make the subsequent road to parity so long and rocky. The two representatives argued that rapid conversion to silver would restrict Norges Bank's ability to supply credit to alleviate the economic situation. This was undoubtedly correct. The Storting's preparatory committee, in which one of the two played a key role, also noted that Norges Bank's management needed a free hand to constrict or expand the money supply in order to guide it towards parity. As they wrote: 'This is the safest way for the bank to keep them at par, and the only way in which the bank can be put in a position to exchange for silver.'[30] This is true in a way, but does also turn the conversion decision and the theory behind it on their head. The very safest way of both bringing the notes up to par and keeping them there was to move towards free conversion of notes into silver at par. But this would naturally restrict—and perhaps eliminate completely—the possibility of issuing loans. This was argued strongly during the Storting debate, where other members of the same Supervisory Council proposed moving rapidly towards the guaranteed exchange rate.

In the end, a small majority resolved to postpone conversion to silver indefinitely. Instead, the Storting agreed on an arrangement whereby a qualified majority of Norges Bank's Executive Board, branch managers, and Supervisory Council would decide when conversion into silver should commence. A first vote on this would be taken in January 1820. If there was not a majority then, the procedure would be repeated quarterly until there was a majority in favour of free conversion to silver at par, which would then commence three months from the vote.

It is tempting to see this as the last of a series of compromises in the creation of the bank. Leading businessmen had originally opposed the Eidsvoll Guarantee. They had been in favour of the new guaranteed exchange rate in 1816, and none opposed it as the target for monetary policy in 1818. But it went from being a concrete target

---

[30] Storting's proceedings, June 1818, 384.

that would soon be met, to being a long-term guideline that would be realized in a discretionary trade-off where the need for credit (in the debate still specific to the biggest taxpayers who had contributed to the silver reserve) would dictate the tempo of the path towards the promised par. The farmers backed the guarantee on both occasions. The majority, however, was held by the large and complex group of local and central officials from the government, church, and armed forces (Figure 1.1). They were swayed by the political and economic situation. Thus the final compromise was reached—parity, but not right now and not at any cost. It was no mean feat to set up a bullion-backed bank of issue in a new nation, and even harder in a time of crisis and within the bounds of a loose union with a stronger country where the constraints on national independence were not yet clear.

Conclusion

The sequence of monetary policy decisions before, during, and after the founding of Norges Bank give a fragmented impression. The combined decision of the constituent assembly at Eidsvoll to guarantee the value of money, while also printing new money to bankroll the new state, was contradictory, excessively optimistic, and abandoned two years later. The decision to form Norges Bank in 1816 involved a series of compromises, but with set dates for establishing a bank of issue with conversion to silver at a fixed rate. The decision to delay this in 1818 undermined perhaps the most important pillar of its creation, by postponing conversion without any set timetable. Numerous different proposals were tabled throughout this process, far more than there is room for here, with loose and speculative ideas about how a new monetary

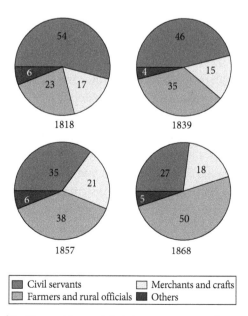

Figure 1.1 Member of Parliament by social status, percentage shares

system might be established without great cost—at least for the groups represented by those putting them forward.

If we view the creation of the bank as part of a broader nation-building process, other factors come to the fore, together painting a more positive picture. There was a relatively broad consensus from Eidsvoll onwards that the bank should be essentially private, separated from the executive's financing needs. Its notes were to be backed by silver. These two elements were intended to ensure, *mutatis mutandis*, a stable monetary value with which neither king nor government could interfere. This principle stood throughout the process. The bank was indeed private, as recommended in the most authoritative proposals. The solution adopted did, however, make concessions to calls from below for a 'national' bank that was not solely in the hands of an economic elite. Although the bank's owners were private, through compulsory contributions, the Storting was awarded control of the bank's governing bodies and, as we will see, of the speed at which the bank moved towards parity.

The decisions with the weakest footing in theory were driven by the challenging circumstances. The Eidsvoll Guarantee was perhaps reckless, but no better way of financing a new nation keen to assert its independence was at hand. The proposal to postpone conversion to silver in 1818 could and probably should have been avoided. But the economic and political situation was incredibly demanding, and the economic burden of moving rapidly to par value would be carried by the group that was hit hardest by the crisis and made the biggest contributions to the new silver fund. All in all, the result was a series of compromises, which were not always elegant from a theoretical viewpoint, but which melded views, interests, and opinions in an overall solution that nobody would consider ideal, but at least left nobody completely high and dry.

Widespread protests followed the collection of the silver tax in 1818. Farmers' marches from the provinces, following the pattern of the old Danish-Norwegian era, threatened the new central power. But the authorities handled these demonstrations relatively judiciously. No shots were fired, and no lives were lost. They also turned out to be the last major farmers' marches the country would see. Subsequent dissatisfaction among the farmers was channelled into the political system, into institutionalized political debate, of which the creation of Norges Bank was an early and direct expression. In the cities too, many protested strongly against perceived injustices in the assessment of taxes. These protests were handled within the new state's systems, through appeals and, in some places, new assessments. Some formal disputes were resolved in the legal system. In this sense, the new state system passed the test. The collection of taxes was to a great extent based on discretionary powers. The actors of the time could not be reassured by econometric analyses two centuries later finding no indications of an elite systematically enriching itself through its control of decisions on the distribution of taxes between regions, communities, and individuals. Interpreting these events today, we have access to much more information—information that suggests that the personal interests of specific individuals and groups were effectively corralled by a will to put the interests of the nation, the intentions of the law, and impartiality in the driving seat when acting in a public capacity.

The broad parliamentary debate and numerous decisions did not pave the way for entirely stringent solutions either organisationally or in terms of monetary policy. But the monetary reforms and creation of a bank of issue were, as mentioned above, about so much more than mere monetary policy in the years after 1814. Here, and especially here, the issues of state powers, tax burdens, state consolidation, and national independence came to the fore. And the bank was put in place without any group getting entirely what it wanted, but also without any group being entirely sidelined. As part of the building of a nation without strong institutions and with very little in the way of democratic traditions, the formation of the bank was about as successful as it could have been.

Henrik Wergeland (1808–45)—poet, historian, cultural celebrity, and later almost iconified as a pioneer of culturally oriented nation building—singled out the bank's protracted birth as a magnificent and necessary sacrifice for this young, impoverished nation. In a famous speech in 1834, he argued that it was the spirit of the nation that demanded and created the bank: 'It gave the people the energy of the weary, who leap up from their rest to get something done, and on whom the sun then smiles most favourably.'[31]

This idealistic-prosaic image undoubtedly paints a romanticized picture of the many conflicts around the bank's formation. Nevertheless, the speech vocalized and, taking into account Wergeland's position, helped create a picture of the bank's formation as a necessary and important sacrifice in the birth of the new nation.

---

[31] Henrik Wergeland's speech 'Til Forfædrenes Minde', given at Eidsvoll 1834, see Henrik Wergeland, *Avhandlinger Oplysningsskrifter 1834–1837*, vol. 2, Samlede Skrifter: trykt og utrykt (Steenske forlag, 1924), 105.

2

A Bank with a Divided Mandate

In autumn 1818, Norges Bank began providing ordinary services to the public, discounting bills and lending directly against real estate. The institution was now both the nation's bank of issue and its sole bank. Expectations of what the bank was to achieve pulled in two diametrically opposed directions. On the one hand, the bank was to take control of the inflated monetary system and bring the value of money back to par, namely the silver value guarantee issued when the Storting established the bank in 1816. Based on both contemporary and modern wisdom, this would speak in favour of tightening the money supply. On the other hand, the bank was to meet the country's considerable need for credit, which would speak in favour of adding liquidity.

Around the time the bank commenced operations, the Storting abandoned a set timetable for converting notes to silver at the promised rate. While convertibility would be pushed further and further into the future, it was always the objective. Conversion at par was eventually introduced in 1842. In the meantime, a desire to supply more credit to farmers, merchants, timber traders, and others competed with the long-term goal of returning money to par. The whole policy was full of contradictions and paradoxes. Liberal, equitable values favoured silver conversion at the guaranteed rate in order to be fair to those who had their assets in banknotes. As time passed, however, the notes changed hands many times. As a result, political decisions leading to a rapid increase in the value of money towards par would effectively redistribute assets between debtors and creditors. This thinking contributed to a 'passive' road to par, where economic growth and development gradually and automatically should strengthen the value of the speciedaler against silver-backed currencies such as the Hamburg banco. The reason why this road became so long and winding has to do with the desire to supply the nation with credit: both the money supply and credit volumes were expanded repeatedly to meet the country's borrowing needs.

For it to take a quarter of a century to reach par was a clear breach of the intentions and principles behind the formation of Norges Bank. Another equally clear breach of these principles was the form that the bank's lending would take. The intention was for the bank to put its notes to work through liquid short-term loans, primarily bills of exchange, which were the main instrument for transactions between merchants and financial institutions abroad. This was in keeping with both economic theory and practice at leading central banks such as the Bank of England and Banque de France. Almost immediately, however, Norges Bank took a different route and systematically packed its balance sheet with long-term mortgages. This restricted its freedom of action and flexibility, and its horizon and attentions became focused on land

Norges Bank 1816–2016. Einar Lie, Oxford University Press (2020). © Norges Bank.
DOI: 10.1093/oso/9780198860013.001.0001

and property rather than the merchant bourgeoisie and the financial circles of which they were part.

A Regional Bank in a Regional Nation

The credit issued by Norges Bank's branches from autumn 1818 onwards was a scarce commodity and in great demand. The allocation of banknotes to the branches—and hence their capacity to extend loans—was determined by how much each region had contributed in silver as part of the compulsory share subscription process. Within each region, money was to be distributed similarly between the different towns and districts. After this, the bank's shareholders—those who had contributed personally to the silver reserve—were to be given priority for loans. The dual motivation behind this principle was to reward those who had contributed to the nation-building effort and to encourage the remainder of the silver to be paid in.

During this early period, Norges Bank's structure and governance system meant that the institution's autonomy was greatly restricted in practice—it was subject to unusually close political control. But it would be slightly misleading to talk about Norges Bank as a single entity under close political control. 'Norges Bank' was in many ways a network of more or less independent banks working under guidelines from the Storting.

To understand Norges Bank's structure and characteristics—not only in the early decades but for most of the nineteenth century—we need to consider Norway's political geography. For three centuries, Norway had been an integrated part of Denmark. There was no administrative centre outside Copenhagen and Denmark. Nor was there any real population centre or transport hub in the country. The southern part of Norway is divided by large mountainous areas that mark a clear east–west watershed. The central region of Mid-Norway is separated from the south-east in turn by more mountains. As things stood in the early nineteenth century, there were four main regions: Østlandet in the south-east, with the city of Kristiania (today's Oslo) at the head of the fjord; Sørlandet in the south, with the city of Kristiansand at its centre; Vestlandet in the west, home to the country's largest city, the trading centre of Bergen; and Midt-Norge, which included the important city of Trondheim, then around the same size as Kristiania (see Figure 2.1). To the north of Trondheim lay another thousand miles of Norwegian territory in the sparsely populated region of Nord-Norge, but even excluding the far north, the Norway of 1816 was a country without a natural centre and little in the way of communications. There were, of course, no railways. The roads were poor and almost impassable in winter. Ships offered the fastest mode of transport between the regions. But documents show that, for example, the Oslo fjord would often freeze over during the winter (which has come to happen less and less often since). Until the arrival of the telegraph in the 1850s, not only goods and people, but also information, became snowed in during the harshest winters.

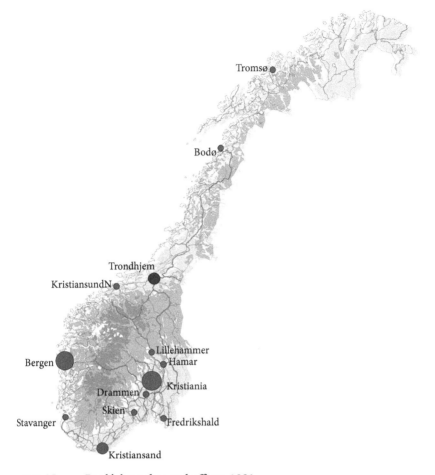

Figure 2.1 Norges Bank's branches and offices, 1881

Kristiania was chosen as the nation's capital in 1814. It was the most south-easterly city and the closest to Stockholm, Copenhagen, and the north German twin cities of Altona and Hamburg which served as a financial centre for the Nordic and Baltic countries. The matter of where Norges Bank should have its head office was discussed repeatedly by the Storting. Kristiania, Bergen, and Trondheim all had their advocates. Eventually, the Storting decided in 1816 that the bank should be located in Kristiania if voluntary subscription succeeded, but in Trondheim if compulsory subscription became necessary, as indeed it did. The recent consensus among historians is that the compulsory bank was to be located as far away from the Storting as possible in order to safeguard its autonomy. This explanation has a natural appeal, especially in the context of a modern discussion of central bank independence. But matters of principle and regional arguments intermingled in the debates on the issue, and the outcome was the result of several rounds of voting under complex rules.

The importance of the head office should not be exaggerated, however. There were four branch offices from the very beginning. The managers of all of the branches were chosen by the Storting in a similar way to the members of the Executive Board and

Supervisory Council. The branch managers were hired on a part-time basis, and all had other jobs. The entire structure, and the fact that the Storting rather than the head office in Trondheim appointed the branch managers, meant that the regional branches were less likely to comply with instructions from head office. On a very concrete level, the mortgage rate was laid down in law by the Storting right up until 1888, despite extensive liberalization of the Norwegian economy in the 1840s and 1850s—fear of usury and 'speculation' was rife in the financial area. The discount rate was set by Norges Bank, but not by head office. Each branch set its own discount rate. Only with the new Norges Bank Act of 1892 was it decided that Norges Bank should have a single discount rate. The regional discount rates were determined on the basis of regional conditions, which varied. In addition, for the reasons mentioned above, it was difficult in practice to coordinate frequent changes to interest rates at short notice, especially in winter. When it came to credit volumes, each branch was given a quota for how much it should lend. If they exceeded these quotas, head office could issue a letter of protest. But that was the extent of its powers.

Conversion at Par Becomes a Distant Goal

The volume of notes in circulation increased in 1818 and 1819 as a result of loans within the limits laid down in law. The Storting had chosen a 'proportionality principle' for Norges Bank, which meant that the amount of money in circulation was to be capped on the basis of a fixed ratio between the bank's silver holdings and the money supply. This ratio was set at 1:2—in other words, the bank could lend twice the value of its silver reserve. There was no particularly exact justification for this, other than that it should eventually be possible to convert these notes into silver. Some notes would be kept for long periods, while others would circulate between private and public players. The conclusion, therefore, was that this ratio would result in a money supply that would permit convertibility without eating away at the silver reserve.

In practice, this cap was used as a limit for lending in Norges Bank's system: the amount of notes put into circulation through legislation was precisely twice its registered silver holdings. At the end of 1818, the value of notes in circulation was 2.5 million speciedaler. By the following year, it had risen to 3.1 million speciedaler. Meanwhile, the market value of the notes had fallen against silver. In spring 1819, the going rate on the Kristiania exchange was 125 speciedaler notes for 100 speciedaler in silver. By the end of the year, this had risen to 155 notes.

As mentioned earlier, the Storting decided in 1818 that conversion to silver at par would commence in January 1820. Formally, it was now up to Norges Bank's governing bodies to make the decisions to honour this promise. This decision would require support from a qualified majority of the members of the Executive Board and branch managers, and then at least ten of the fifteen members of the Supervisory Council. There was not, however, a qualified majority of the bank's governing bodies to implement the Storting's express will. None of the directors voted in favour at the first vote.

All agreed that the value of money was so far from par that the economic consequences of establishing a radically higher value would be dramatic.

This conclusion did not come as a surprise. It also explains the notes' low value when traded on the exchange relative to pure silver-backed currencies, dominated by the Hamburg banco. There is an obvious flaw in a promise that it will soon be possible to sell notes with a low market value at a much higher value. The logic here is so straightforward as to be clear even to those without a theoretical background. If most people in 1819 really believed that the speciedaler would be worth 50 per cent more the following year, they would keep hold of as many of these notes as possible, and ideally get their hands on more, right up until the exchange rate approached par.

During the course of 1820, Norges Bank allowed the money supply to continue to grow slowly through loans and discounting. In November, an important question arose: what advice should Norges Bank give the Storting at its next meeting in 1821? The majority on Norges Bank's governing bodies wanted the Storting to commit the bank to a concrete conversion timetable. The recommendation from the majority of the Executive Board and Supervisory Council was that conversion at par should take place no later than April 1823. The chairman of the Executive Board, Jacob Oxholm, who held this position from the bank's formation until his death in 1832, was generally an avid proponent of moving towards early conversion. Like many around him, Oxholm wore a number of different hats. He came from an old, Danish, civil service family, but lived and worked as a businessman in Trondheim. He was also a member of the Storting from 1821 to 1832. This was not a full-time job. The Storting met only for a couple of months every third year, apart from various extraordinary meetings stemming partly from the money issue itself. At the bank's meetings, he was the one who spoke with scholarly authority, quoting economists such as Adam Smith and Jean-Baptiste Say on matters of banking and monetary theory. A number of subsequent governors have written about Norges Bank's early history. Nicolai Rygg, governor from 1920 to 1946, wrote two large volumes before taking the helm at Norges Bank. Gunnar Jahn, who succeeded Rygg and remained in place until 1954, edited a new book in 1966. In both cases, Oxholm is a favourite, with his clear reasoning and strong, pragmatic arguments for establishing a fixed timetable for free conversion to silver.

The debate in the Storting again proved painful and personal. Arguments would normally refer to general, 'national' interests. But it was easy to suspect that members' positions were rooted in their own private interests rather than those of the nation.[1] And what actually was the national interest in this case?

When the Storting convened in spring 1821, paper money was worth around 60 per cent of its par silver value. Members knew perfectly well who stood to gain and lose from an increase in the value of notes. It would benefit those who held notes or were owed amounts denominated in speciedaler, and those whose income consisted mostly

---

[1] Cf. Jacob Aall, 'Om Bank- og Pengevæsenet, og sammes Indflydelse paa de viktigste Næringsveie i Norge', Nutid og Fortid, et Hæfteskrift (J. Aall, 1832), 157-0.

or entirely of a salary agreed in speciedaler. On the other hand, those who made their living from exporting goods and services had no interest in seeing the value of paper money rise. Their income in foreign currency would then be worth less in Norwegian notes, which they used to make payments in Norway. There was equally little interest in raising the value of paper money among the now relatively large number of people who had taken out loans from Norges Bank. They did not want to have to pay interest and repay principal with notes worth more than those they had originally borrowed.

For borrowers, and those who wanted to borrow from the country's sole bank, the issue of silver conversion also had another aspect. If notes were converted into silver, Norges Bank would end up with notes in exchange. Since the law stated that the value of notes in circulation must never be more than twice that of the bank's silver, conversion could lead to the bank having to restrict the money supply even further, on top of the reduction resulting from conversion itself. This would not just mean a reduction in new lending. Under its charter, the bank was to concentrate on issuing short-term loans with a term of no more than six months. This was not the case, as we will discuss shortly. Many loans were simply rolled over as they fell due, if the borrower so wished. A contraction of credit volumes would obviously put this practice under pressure.

Those advocating silver convertibility had some clear advantages in the debate. The issue was fundamentally about the country keeping its word. Given the recent history of inflation and broken promises, this became an important point. It was a matter of both economics and politics. By keeping its word and keeping its own house in order, the new nation would be able to establish its creditworthiness and cement its autonomy within the union with Sweden. Achieving convertibility at par therefore became a question of statesmanship.

On the other hand, it could be claimed that it was just as much a question of statesmanship to ensure that the promise was kept in a way that the population could live with. What good would it do the nation to uphold its honour and enhance its credibility if the necessary increase in the value of money drove Norwegian timber exporters out of the market? And this did not just apply to the wealthy few. A slide in timber exports would hit everyone along the entire value chain.

In addition, there was a general fear that Norges Bank's silver holdings would be lost if it established a fixed exchange rate—that 'the silver will leave the country', as it was often put. This became an important argument when the timetable for conversion was put back in 1818, and would also come up in subsequent debates. There was a deep and, one is tempted to say, irrational fear that the silver reserve would be weakened. Irrational because the silver reserve was, after all, a reserve. As with later fixed-rate regimes, the bank had to be willing, at least in principle, to use its reserves to defend the value of money. With modern fixed-rate regimes, it is fairly obvious that a bank needs to build its currency reserves up or down to stabilize the currency.

But the silver reserve of 1818 had a special status. 'The silver reserve had become a fetish', wrote Gunnar Jahn in 1966 when he reflected on the debate of 1818, 'and remained so for much of the 19th century.'[2] This observation has a great deal going for it, and it is easy to understand how such a situation came about. The silver was not just any reserve—it had been built up forcibly by means of distraint, and in spite of appeals and tears. Much of it was uncoined bullion in the form of vases, candelabras, dinner sets—quite literally the family silver. Nevertheless, it was a bank of issue's reserve, and it is understandable that there was a greater fear of losing it through bad decisions than there was for the equivalent reserves of foreign currencies when Gunnar Jahn himself was governor.

Oxholm argued during the Storting debate of 1821 that the fears about silver conversion were unfounded so long as the decision on parity was clear and unambiguous, and the bank adjusted its money supply. The big swings in the exchange rate were partly due to uncertainty about what would be the official line, and partly to speculation based on this. A fixed policy would put a damper on these fluctuations—and therein lay the real gain. At the same time, he was clear that the silver needed to be used to implement such a policy. A fixed rate would be established if the players knew that they would be able to convert notes into silver. But it would then also need to be possible to sell silver for speciedaler.[3]

Oxholm won meagre support. It was now explicitly decided that no specific date for conversion at par would be set during this Storting.[4] The exchange rate plummeted. The nadir came the following year, with a closing rate of 222 for 100 speciedaler silver in July 1822. A solution had to be found. The time had come for new compromises.

The Storting now decided that Norges Bank should exchange notes for silver from January, but the amount of silver paid for each note would be within an interval that was well below par (175–190).[5] The principles for the road beyond that were laid down by the Storting the following year. Norges Bank was to pursue a contractionary monetary policy to push up the exchange rate—the currency was to be strengthened by what a contemporary observer referred to as a 'passive' approach. The notes were to be taken to parity by awaiting 'favourable trading conditions and a stronger economy'.[6] In 1824, the Supervisory Council assured the Storting that Norges Bank was continuing to lend in line with the silver coverage ratio.[7] The volume of notes may have been large, but the economy would grow into it.[8] The bank's governing bodies now abandoned their call for a fixed timetable for conversion at par, and asked instead to be given the freedom to bring the bank rate down to 130 during the coming parliamentary term.[9]

The Storting's banking committee followed this up with a complex specification of how the new policy should be understood. Norges Bank was to run with events by setting the bank rate on the basis of the notes' market value. This would ensure that 'the Bank does not by extreme or sudden means bring about a rate that is not a result

---

[2] Gunnar Jahn, Alf Eriksen, and Preben Munthe, *Norges Bank gjennom 150 År* (Norges Bank, 1966), 29.
[3] Proceedings in the Odelsting, 28 June 1821, 488, Storting's proceedings.
[4] Proceedings in the Odelsting, 28 June 1821, 545, Storting's proceedings.
[5] Proceedings in the Odelsting, 11 November 1822, 404, Storting's Proceeding.
[6] Aall, 'Om Bank- og Pengevæsenet, og sammes Indflydelse paa de viktigste Næringsveie i Norge', 160.
[7] Proceedings in the Storting, 29 June 1924, 164, Storting's Proceedings.   [8] Ibid., 180f.
[9] Supervisory Council's letter of 24 December 1823, printed in ibid., 473–93.

of the natural course of things and abruptly distort asset values'.[10] Within the liberal norms championed by at least parts of the Storting, the assembly avoided taking a position on the problem that arises when a political body makes decisions that redistribute wealth between private players. It was the economy itself—the natural course of things—that was to bring the value of money up to what had once been promised. A clear line of action was thus expressed. Norges Bank was to carefully adjust the bank rate when the market provided appreciation. All on the understanding that this was a one-way journey—any adjustment of the bank rate was to be towards parity.

During the Storting of 1824, the bank rate was adjusted to 150. This was done directly by the Storting through a statutory resolution and royal sanction. Norges Bank was authorized to improve the rate to 135, which would remain the limit until the Storting passed a new resolution.[11] In practice, therefore, a band was defined within which the bank could adjust the bank rate—no higher than the defined rate, and no lower than the limit set by the Storting. The rate on the exchange at the time the Storting made these decisions was 145. However, the economic upturn behind this appreciation, attributable in part to international factors, proved stronger than anyone had predicted. The bank rate reached the limit of 135 as early as April 1825,[12] but this was far from the present rate on the exchange, which was 110 at the time. In March, the closing price had even dropped as low as 103, practically par, and the rate on the exchange remained below 110 throughout 1825 (Figure 2.2).

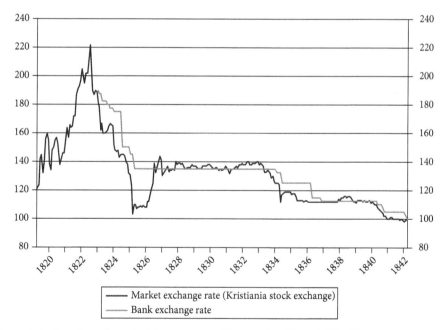

Figure 2.2 Number of speciedaler notes per 100 species silver, 1819–42

---

[10] Ibid., 496.
[11] Cf. Proceedings in the Storting 1824, *Storthings-Efterretninger 1814–1833*, vol. 2 (Jacob Dybwads Forlag, 1878), 495, 98.
[12] Cf. Proceedings in the Storting, April 1827, 46, Storting's proceedings.

Had the Storting given Norges Bank greater freedom of action in 1824, it is likely that speciedaler notes would have been locked into a higher value than was actually the case. Instead, there was an abrupt downturn at the end of 1825, bringing a sudden fall in the value of the notes. In the fourth quarter of 1826, the exchange rate for speciedaler against the silver-backed Hamburg banco was actually worse than the bank rate. This made it profitable to exchange notes for silver, leading to significant conversion activity. In 1824 and 1825, Norges Bank paid out just 715 speciedaler in silver. In the fourth quarter of 1826, the market rate for speciedaler was above 140, and Norges Bank paid out 90,700 speciedaler in silver.[13] In the first quarter of 1827, the exchange rate was back between 130 and 134. The stabilizing elements in the silver standard system had done their job.

In 1827, Oxholm made a strong case for the Storting to permit Norges Bank to take the bank rate to 115. He wanted more freedom to follow the market in order to achieve parity as quickly as possible, pointing out—as he had argued before—that there would have been less short-term volatility and less uncertainty for exporters and merchants if stabilization at a higher silver value had been achieved two years earlier.[14] His proposal was rejected, attracting little support. The Storting adjusted the limit moderately to 125, which was the trade-off that the majority considered most appropriate.[15] Few wanted to rush towards the promise of 1816.

At this time, Sweden was in the process of linking the silver value of the Riksbank's notes to their market price, thus ignoring the formal silver value the notes had been given in 1803. In Sweden, it was the king who was holding things up and wanting to honour the historical guarantee. Although this process must have been known in Norway, it had surprisingly little impact on the domestic debate. A compromise had been found in 1822, and it was defended against calls for adjustments from different quarters. Part of the picture perhaps is that the exporters had much stronger political representation in Sweden than in Norway. The most important difference preventing a transfer of principles and arguments was probably the two countries' starting positions and credibility when the monetary system was reconstructed after the Napoleonic Wars. The Swedish monetary system was never as chaotic as that of Denmark-Norway. Denmark, to an even greater extent than Norway, had a history of currency collapses and broken promises. The argument then is that these two had to pay a higher price to regain market confidence.[16] Through to the 1840s, both Denmark and Norway chose to stand by the promises that they had made back in 1813 and 1816 respectively. Sweden had greater credibility and could therefore afford to take a different route.

In Norway, the waters were muddied by fears of losing silver, of exporters failing, and of partisan economic motives. While different groups did have different interests,

[13] Cf. ibid., 46f.

[14] Cf. Oxholm's proposal, printed in *Storting Proceedings*, June 1827, 572–7.

[15] *Storthings-Efterretninger 1814–1833*, 2, 659f.

[16] Øyvind Eitrheim, Jan Tore Klovland, and Lars Fredrik Øksendal, *A Monetary History of Norway, 1816–2016* (Cambridge University Press, 2016), 95ff.

this should not be given too much weight in explaining the length of the road to parity. Civil servants had a clear personal interest in a rapid return to parity. They received fixed salaries which were not much affected by movements in the exchange rate. This group dominated the Storting, accounting for around half of its members in the period up to 1830, and was also the dominant recruitment base for ministerial posts, other than in the first few years after 1814 when parts of the old *grande bourgeoisie* were still intact.[17] We should add here, for readers unfamiliar with Norwegian history, that this position was not due to formal privileges or narrowly defined voting rights. Civil servants were a small class and largely elected in their districts by voters with a different social background. To some extent, this was because of the class's clearly expressed commitment to working selflessly for progress in the national interest, but there was also clear social pressure not to stand against civil servants in elections.[18]

Criticism of the Failure to Achieve Parity

While it was technically correct for Norges Bank to allow the economy to determine the exchange rate, and adjust the bank rate accordingly, this paints a misleading picture of events. With given reserves and lending rules, the idea was that a gradual increase in economic activity, population, and money supply would grow into the supply of paper money and strengthen the notes' purchasing power.

It was not that simple. Norges Bank's reserves and lending capacity increased through the return on its capital, and both were expanded through other operations, most notably and—in principle—most problematically in 1828. That year, the Swedish king called an extraordinary meeting of the Storting. One of the matters raised by Karl Johan was a desire to improve the availability of credit to the public. It was again the south of the country that was suffering most, while the situation was much better in the areas around Bergen and Trondheim. There was no question that demand for credit exceeded supply under the prevailing interest rate regime. In the Kristiania area, Norges Bank had turned down loan applications for 600,000 speciedaler since the beginning of 1825, even though the applicants could offer full collateral. But was this reason enough for the Storting to take action—and, if so, what action?

In 1828, the Storting wanted to be as amenable as possible towards Karl Johan, without unduly compromising sound principles for the nation's monetary system. Agreement was reached that the government would use its improved creditworthiness to raise a foreign loan of 300,000 speciedaler in silver. This money would then be lent to the public. A proposal that Norges Bank should administer the lending of the money borrowed by the government was rejected. Governor Oxholm believed that it would undermine confidence in Norges Bank if it was given this new role.

---

[17] Jens Arup Seip, *Utsikt over Norges historie*, vol. 1 (Gyldendal Norsk Forlag, 1974), 86ff.
[18] Ibid., 116–23.

The solution instead was to lend 100,000 speciedaler directly through state-owned Discount Commissions. The remaining 200,000 was, by law, deposited at Norges Bank as a contribution to the bank's silver holdings. It had previously been decided that the silver reserve could be expanded, and that notes could continue to be put into circulation at a ratio of 2:1 based on this fresh supply of silver. This principle was now used by the state in a separate statutory resolution to transform its loan into an additional credit base for lending to a hard-pressed business sector.

This relationship was emphasized by Anton Martin Schweigaard, one of the leading professor-politicians of the era, who was active as a theorist, standard setter, and practitioner in a wide range of areas, not least monetary policy. Schweigaard made his entry into the monetary policy debate with a minor work in 1832.[19] This attracted limited political attention at the time, but has subsequently been singled out as particularly clear-sighted and incisive.[20] His recommendation was intended to put an end to fluctuations in the market value of paper money by freezing it, through conversion to silver, at the levels it had now been at for a number of years. The varying value of banknotes created uncertainty in the business sector and would, if parity were to be implemented, lead to a considerable redistribution of wealth. This final argument was at the heart of the promise that those holding the notes would one day get what they were promised in 1816. Schweigaard's position was that notes and wealth had already changed hands and position so many times that the road ahead was more important than everything behind. The advantages of a fixed value through silver convertibility were clear. The promise of 1816 should have been honoured in line with the original schedule—the fall from grace came with the postponement of 1818—but as things now stood, all pragmatic considerations favoured establishing a new par value with a lower silver content.

In a major series of articles in the journal *Den Constitutionelle* four years later, in 1836, Schweigaard castigated Norges Bank and in particular the Storting for the policy pursued since 1818. At this point, the bank rate had been reduced with only ten points (from 135 to 125) since 1825, and the Storting's limits on Norges Bank's freedom of action had been unchanged since 1827. Schweigaard noted that, in reality, the promise of parity had been postponed not only through the 'passive' approach, but also through state-driven expansion of the money supply. The loan transaction of 1828 when the state injected silver into Norges Bank was an example of this. Expansions of the bank's share capital had made the state the single largest shareholder in Norges Bank.[21] But this led immediately—and more permanently—to an increase in the money supply, because Norges Bank always stayed close to the statutory limit on paper money lending relative to the silver fund. This gave the passive approach to parity a longer road to follow.

In principle, Schweigaard's arguments about the supply and value of money reflect the quantity theory of money. There was no place here for the view of the majority of

---

[19] Anton Martin Schweigaard, 'Anmeldelse av Jacob Aalls Bok 'Nutid og Fortid', *Vidar* 1, nos. 21 and 22 (1832).
[20] Nicolai Rygg, *Norges Banks historie*, vol. 1 (Norges Bank, 1918), 206.
[21] Cf. Ibid., 213.

the Storting that more credit would prevent bankruptcies and pave the way for economic growth in Norway.[22] It was not the case that Norges Bank was lending to the nation, Schweigaard argued: 'It has borrowed from the collective and distributed to the individual'.[23] Nor was there any stabilization policy. The bank's silver reserve was supplemented with its own surpluses and deposits from the state. And its only policy was to multiply this reserve by two, which gave the money supply. In the scales where notes were to be balanced with silver, the bank had replaced the silver with a sponge that was sometimes dry and sometimes saturated with water, Schweigaard summed up with his usual incisive and intelligent use of metaphor. Few things could be further from the intended function of silver than a sponge, whether wet or dry.

Norges Bank as Mortgage Bank

The absence of conversion to metal—sponge for silver—was the first anomaly that Schweigaard noted in Norges Bank's principal activity. The second, closely related to the first, had to do with the bank's asset mix: how notes were put into circulation through lending. Following the example of foreign banks of issue—the Banque de France, Bank of England, and Scottish banks—Norges Bank should, he argued, lend money against good, liquid instruments. This would in the first instance mean bills of exchange from businesses. Until the modern payment system of the twentieth century, bills of exchange were a key instrument in the financial system. A bill was normally issued by a buyer, normally for a consignment of goods, as payment to the seller. The seller could then sell (discount) the bill to a third party, often a bank or finance house, and so get the value of the bill in cash, normally with a small deduction for the work and risk involved.

Norges Bank, however, provided very little commercial credit. The bulk of its lending took the form of mortgages, i.e. loans secured against real estate. Schweigaard believed that the legislation establishing Norges Bank should not have permitted this. Referring to foreign models and ideals, it was decided that the bank should provide liquid, short-term loans with a maximum term of six months. Providing long-term mortgages was technically against the law, and he believed that the limited weight attached to discounting bills went against the intentions of the bank's charter. In addition, these long-term loans committed and tied up the bank of issue in such a way that it was technically challenging to pursue an effective policy to stabilize the exchange rate.

Schweigaard argued here for the real bills doctrine as formulated by Adam Smith and later economists. Smith argued that a bank of issue's priority activity should be providing short-term commercial credit. This would make it easy to regulate the bank's balance sheet and the money supply. To use Smith's term, real bills were also

---

[22] Discussed and critiqued in Wilhelm Keilhau, *Den norske pengehistorie* (Aschehoug, 1952), 87f.

[23] Anton Martin Schweigaard, *Ungdomsarbeider* (Aschehoug, 1904), 143.

self-liquidating. Once the transaction financed by the bill was completed, it would generate a cash sum that made it possible to repay the loan when it fell due.

This mechanism was taken further in the British debate early in the nineteenth century by the anti-bullionists, who claimed that the relationship between an underlying real transaction and bill issuance meant that free conversion of real bills to notes could never lead to note-induced inflation. The volume of notes was created and controlled by an underlying real growth in transactions. This understanding was used by the advocates of the Bank of England's policy, during the period when the pound was not convertible into gold, as an argument that the inflation of the time could not have been created by the bank's issue of banknotes against real bills. The most common understanding of the real bills doctrine in the literature relates to this relationship between discounting, note issuance, and inflation.[24]

Smith, on the other hand, recommended this doctrine within the constraints of a system with established conversion of notes into specie. It was this connection to specie—gold—that secured the value of the notes. The principle of discounting bills insured smooth issuance of notes that could be tailored to demand for means of payment and ensured that the bank of issue was liquid and flexible. Schweigaard's argument that Norges Bank should have concentrated on short-term lending, ideally against bills, went along the same lines as Smith's: Silver conversion would protect the value of the bank's notes, while the bills would provide liquidity and supply the business sector with sufficient credit instruments.

Schweigaard's ideals for a bank of issue were established through British-inspired theory and examples from Britain and France. But the composition of Norges Bank's loan portfolio was not as unique as he and many later observers would have it. Juha Tarkka has noted that countries in the Baltic region, which all developed note-issuing banks at a relatively early stage, generally favoured mortgage lending.[25] In principle, all of these countries operated a bullion standard—silver—and were then linked to Hamburg as a financial centre. The Riksbank in Sweden, considered the world's oldest central bank, had the bulk of its lending in long-term mortgages up until the mid-nineteenth century. The same applied to the Bank of Finland. The Nationalbank in Denmark was, in principle, to focus on short-term credit, but assumed substantial mortgages from its share of the Dano-Norwegian Rigsbanken. When the Danish krone was made convertible into silver in 1845, it was decided that only one-sixth of lending could be secured against real estate. This took the bank towards the British— or 'modern'—model for a bank of issue, with liquid, short-term loans. The Prussian model departs somewhat from that further north, but this can be explained largely by landowners having an alternative source of credit in the form of rural credit cooperatives.

---

[24] Thomas M. Humphrey, 'The Real Bills Doctrine', *FRB Richmond Economic Review* 68, no. 5 (1982).

[25] Juha Tarkka, 'The North European Model of Early Central Banking', in *Designing Central Banks* (Routledge, 2009); 'Investment Doctrines for Banks, from Real Bills to Post-Crisis Reforms', in *Preparing for the Next Financial Crisis: Policies, Tools and Models*, ed. Esa Jokivuolle and Radu Tunaru (Cambridge University Press, 2017).

So Norges Bank was not alone. But it did demonstrate a particularly strong tendency towards the mortgage model, especially since the decision to establish the bank pointed in a different direction, and the share of mortgages was particularly high. In the early 1830s, mortgages accounted for more than 90 per cent of total lending. The portfolio mix had headed in this direction from the outset. When the bank commenced operations in 1818, a quarter of its notes were reserved for discounting. The remainder were to be used for mortgages, albeit with a maximum term of six months. These loans could, however, be rolled over, but a new bond was to be issued on the collateral at each renewal. This meant that the effective interest rate climbed from 5 to 8 per cent. To avoid passing these costs onto the borrower, the bank waived this bond requirement. This made it easier to roll over the loans, effectively making them long-term mortgages.[26]

In practice, however, the share used for discounting fell to much lower levels. The Executive Board in Trondheim discounted bills corresponding to exactly 25 per cent of total lending in its first quarter of operation. But in the following six quarters, every last speciedaler went into mortgages. This established the pattern, although some bills were also discounted. Why was this so? It has been claimed (by Rygg) that this was due to pressure from property owners. There was obvious pressure to obtain credit from many landowners, but this was far from a homogenous group, and they were not well represented on the boards of the bank's branches. Another explanation is that Norges Bank had little contact with men of business, since the Executive Board was based in Trondheim, far from the commercial centres of the south-east. The bank's boards were mainly populated with merchants and wholesalers, and to varying degrees we find a similar breakdown of lending at all of the branches. The branches had considerable scope to use their own discretion. The most recent and compelling explanation is that there was most demand for such loans.[27] Presumably, demand from this varied group also increased in the 1830s and 1840s, since many farmers became more closely integrated into the monetary economy, and the number of freeholders who could borrow against their own property increased. This explanation also corresponds to some extent to Tarkka's tentative explanation for the general trend in lending by banks of issue in north-western Europe, namely that 'the agricultural periphery around the Baltic Sea was [...] a fertile ground for the ideas of land banks and mortgage based lending'.[28]

One argument against this explanation is that at times there was clearly (also) an unmet demand for commercial credit. In practice, the bank only discounted domestic bills. On the few occasions the bank traded notes internationally, this was done to add to its silver reserve. Even with commercial credit not related to overseas trade, much credit had to be provided by others, including private domestic lenders and, in

[26] Jahn, Eriksen, and Munthe, *Norges Bank Gjennom 150 År*, 32.

[27] Francis Sejersted, 'Norges Bank og høykonjunkturen i 1840-årene', Universitetsforlaget 1968; Eitrheim, Klovland, and Øksendal, *A Monetary History of Norway 1816–2016*.

[28] Juha Tarkka, 'Investment Doctrines for Banks, from Real Bills to Post-Crisis Reforms', in *Preparing for the Next Financial Crisis*, ed. E. Jokivuolle and R. Tunaru (Cambridge University Press, 2017), 33.

particular, foreign houses, primarily in Hamburg. Interest rates varied, but contemporary observers (such as finance minister Herman Wedel Jarlsberg) reported rates of 1.5–2 per cent per month in the late 1820s, which then seem to have fallen somewhat in the following decade. Early on, Norges Bank was discounting bills at an annual rate of 8 per cent, and there would undoubtedly have been sufficient demand to increase the share of bills considerably.[29]

Early on, the Executive Board gave its explanation for the increase in mortgage lending: mortgages were considered to offer better protection against losses than commercial credit did. They were therefore better suited to safeguarding the interests of shareholders, and to preventing erosion of the silver reserve acquired at such great cost. The board in Trondheim also noted early on that it was in fact easier to distribute loans between areas and individuals according to silver contributed when issuing mortgages rather than commercial credit, which resulted in shorter and more volatile loans. Technically, this is probably correct, but it is difficult to gauge how important it really was. Either way, the loan portfolio ended up tied to land and illiquid. We will return to this in Chapter 3, when Norges Bank's judgement and flexibility were put to the test during the international political and financial crisis of 1848.

A Conclusion of the Road to Parity

Let us return to Anton Martin Schweigaard's series of articles from 1836 criticizing the failure to provide convertibility to silver and the illiquid loan portfolio. While Schweigaard had a few years earlier supported a de facto devaluation and commencing silver conversion at the prevailing rate, he had now accepted that there was no appetite for breaking the parity promise of 1816. Consistently enough, his advice was therefore to move as quickly as possible towards the promised parity. The articles were published just before the Storting returned to the issue of changing the bank rate. It was proposed that the Storting should postpone its debate. The matters were now being dealt with in 'a scientific manner as ingenious as it is interesting' in an official journal.[30] Those behind the proposal thus wanted to see Schweigaard's closing arguments before the decisions were taken.

Interest is one thing, impact quite another. Schweigaard's time had not yet come. After a long debate, the Storting opted for a predictable compromise between the advocates of parity and those who still wanted a lower rate. In 1836, Norges Bank was authorized to adjust the bank rate to 112.5,[31] bringing it in line with the rate on the exchange. A fresh economic boom in the early 1840s caused the speciedaler to appreciate. Between May and October 1840, Norges Bank adjusted the bank rate in three steps from 112.5 to 105.[32] In October 1841, its value on the Kristiania exchange closed below 100 for the first time. The passive road to parity had reached its destination.

---

[29] According to Keilhau, *Den norske pengehistorie*, 100f.
[30] *Storthings-Efterretninger 1836–1854*, vol. 1 (Jacob Dybwads Forlag, 1888), 96.   [31] Cf. Ibid., 503.
[32] Cf. *Storting's Proceedings*, September 1842, 148.

Now nobody could protest against taking the final legal step. The Storting of 1842 assembled in February. A bill proposing changes to the legislation on Norges Bank was tabled in March. Section 1 gave Norges Bank a duty to exchange its notes for silver at par.[33] After twenty-six years, the nation's institutions had finally honoured the promise of 1816. Commitment to this promise survived numerous Storting meetings and changes of personnel at the bank of issue—for example, the most consistent advocate of rapidly honouring the promise of 1816, the bank's first governor, Jacob Oxholm, would never see the promised land. He died in 1832 at the age of fifty-one after fifteen years at the helm and just ten years before the promise was finally honoured.

This slow, 'passive' policy can be given an economic interpretation, with the politicians of the Storting opting to weigh the nation's need for banknotes and credit against a more contractionary line that would have led to a more rapid rise in their value. Politically, the decision was probably as much about trading off different vested interests and viewpoints, as seen during the very formation of Norges Bank. Strongly opposing interests and opinions were at play. The Storting first opted for compromises, where nobody quite got what they wanted, and then the maxim of a 'passive' approach of unknown length, where the destination and to some extent the route were subject to ongoing discussion. Thus a kind of consensus was built around one of the most divisive and demanding issues of the 1820s.

---

[33] *Storthings-Efterretninger 1836–1854*, vol. 2 (Jacob Dybwads Forlag, 1893), 318f.

3

A Relieved Norges Bank

The promise from 1816 was finally honoured in 1842. The notes could now be converted into silver, and the metal-based monetary system prevailed until the First World War broke out.

Norges Bank was still a hybrid bank, as a decentralized institution with locally based long-term loans secured on property. The resulting structure and institutional self-perception made it difficult to perform the true core functions of a bank of issue, i.e. maintain a stable value of notes against metal and liquidity in the thin Norwegian financial market. The situation improved as Norges Bank was gradually relieved of some of its tasks thanks to the emergence of financial institutions that would cater to individuals and businesses. Both private banks and government lending institutions were established, within a framework of close cooperation between government officials and private operators. The same type of cooperation also took place in other areas, such as transport and physical infrastructure, where private and public capital joined to develop systems that would foster growth and modernization.

At the same time as new institutions were born, the dividing lines between Norges Bank and the government's role in financial markets became clearer. We will here look at developments up to 1857, a year that was dominated by a deep crisis in Western economies. The crisis was handled in a relatively successful manner by Norwegian financial institutions, and the crisis was resolved quite differently from the crisis that took place merely ten years earlier. The downturn in 1848 was amplified rather than alleviated by the response of the institutions—in particular Norges Bank.

The crisis in 1857 was in many ways more complex. The telegraph had come to Kristiania, and financial news and rumours were spread rapidly from the main financial centres. Norges Bank's head office was located in Trondheim, not yet connected to the new, state-of-the-art information network. Institutions outside of Norges Bank relieved the central bank of many of its tasks, for example by providing short-term business credit and long-term mortgage loans. Norges Bank had also established broad contact directly with international finance houses and was better equipped structurally and intellectually to cope with external crises that spilled over into the Norwegian economy. The year 1857 marked a important step in a gradual shift away from Hamburg and the Danish twin city Altona, as external financial centres, towards London, which over the next three-quarters of a century would be the undisputed source of standards and liquidity for Norges Bank and the Norwegian financial system.

Norges Bank 1816–2016. Einar Lie, Oxford University Press (2020). © Norges Bank.
DOI: 10.1093/oso/9780198860013.001.0001

The Government and the Bank of Issue

The legislation pertaining to Norges Bank is a long and complicated affair. Through the 1800s, views on the central bank changed, and solutions were found for situation-dependent problems, which were later modified or addressed on an ad hoc basis.

State ownership of Norges Bank was part of this picture. The support measures introduced to address the economic problems in 1828, where Norges Bank received silver from the state, made the government a shareholder in the bank. This diverged from the original conception from 1816; with the diverse ownership the government also became the bank's largest shareholder. In the long term, the government did not want to remain in this position. The draft central government budget in 1839 proposed a partial sell-off of its shares at a price of 140 per cent of the shares' nominal value, but met with the unanimous rejection of the Storting. Why should the state dispose of safe and liquid securities, which also generated a decent return? The same came to pass at the next parliamentary meeting.[1] The opinion held by the majority was that the Norwegian state was just as good a passive owner as private investors, and the Storting had after all become the bank's general meeting as the bank was established through compulsory deposits.

In the resolution establishing a compulsory bank, the Storting's role as general meeting substitute was described as temporary. The main proposals had initially conceived of Norges Bank as an ordinary private limited company with independent bodies, which functioned with a regulatory framework adopted by the Storting. Because of the long road to parity, and not least the fact that Norges Bank was the country's only large bank for a long time, the framework included a multitude of rules and was subject to frequent revisions. When the question arose in the 1830s as to whether the bank should be fully transferred to its shareholders, the king, the government, and the Storting found no valid reason to do so. An act from 1839, unanimously adopted, stated that the possibility should 'unless otherwise decided' be retained, and it has been since that time.[2]

In 1842, the act was extensively amended, in a favourable economic environment. Cyclical upturns and economic growth had brought the notes to parity. The statutory defined size of Norges Bank's silver fund placed absolute limits on how many notes Norges Bank could issue. That was changed by an important amendment adopted in 1842. The general public was given the right to receive one speciedaler note for each silverdaler delivered to Norges Bank. This was meant to increase the supply of notes and eliminate the use of heavy silver in settling payments.

This complicated the relationship between silver and notes with regard to Norges Bank practices and legislation, which was also the subject of debate at that time. There

---

[1] *Storthings-Efterretninger 1836–1854*, vol. 1, 531f.; *Storthings-Efterretninger 1836–1854*, vol. 2, 239.
[2] Proposition, setting, and Odelsting decision (Odelsting's negotiations from March, pp. 260–84; Lagtinget's decision in Lagtinget's negotiations from March, pp. 370, 372), all in *Storting's proceedings*, vol. 9, no. 1, 1839.

were no natural law or sound calculations that dictated a proportion of 2:1 between notes and silver, as decided in 1816. The overriding consideration was that the bank should at all times be able to redeem metal. The proportion rule was simply an aid to self-discipline. It was clearly possible to do without it, as exemplified by the Banque de France, which functioned well without one. But such a daring venture was inconceivable when the issue was discussed in 1842. Parity had only prevailed for a month and a half. The government was still of the view that it was unnecessary to have such large amounts of silver in store without paying interest as demanded by the foundation. Norges Bank's board agreed, and was of the opinion that a proportion of 5:2 was acceptable rather than 4:2, which was applied at the time. If sustained, the bank could then lend more notes—without having to invest in more silver. An increase in lending implies an increase in interest income. But who should be the beneficiary of that income?

The Ministry of Finance's view in 1842 was that note issuance was a privilege of the state. Some of the privilege had fallen to Norges Bank, and its shareholders, upon its establishment in 1816. But a gradual broadening of the authorization to issue required separate policy resolutions, and the return generated by these resolutions was not viewed as a right of shareholders. Income associated with note issuance at a higher proportionality should benefit the state. The solution found was to give the bank a 25 per cent share of the income increase as a remuneration of the additional work in producing and issuing more notes.

Norges Bank's board accepted that the shareholders were not given a right to the additional income, but proposed that it should be placed in the bank's reserve fund. This was an odd construction, established by the Storting in 1827.[3] Earnings derived from sources not mentioned in the foundation had been credited this fund. An example is interest income from the so-called annexed loan arrangement, an ad hoc solution where individuals could borrow money in the bank's first year against direct silver deposits in excess of the compulsory deposits made. Norges Bank could use the reserve fund's silver stock as backing to lend notes at a ratio of 1:1. The shareholders did not have a claim on the profits made in these loans, which was transferred to the reserve fund in the form of silver.[4]

The discussions in 1842, which led to several correctives, were clever but undoubtedly complex. However, the underlying premise was clear in that the owners were to receive the return on the loans against the 'real' silver stock according to the original note cover rules, but the net gains through subsequent policy resolutions in an expansionary direction must benefit the state. However, the state's share of new incomes would be retained in Norges Bank and used to increase the silver stock. When the total sum of income accumulated reached a certain amount (625,000 speciedaler), the state would receive a share certificate for that amount. This arrangement would, consequently, make the state an even larger owner of Norges Bank.

---

[3] *Storthings-Efterretninger 1814–1833*, vol. 2 (Jacob Dybwads Forlag, 1878), 656 ff.
[4] Ref. 'Lov af 24de Juli 1827 angaaende Oprettelse af et Reservefond', § 4.

Sixteen years later this culminated in a new legislative proposal, drawn up by the Kristiania Norges Bank branch, whose importance had increased. It was the branch's strongman, Anton Martin Schweigaard, who was behind the initiative. The proposal aimed at preventing the state from becoming an even larger owner of the central bank. The decision from 1842, by which the state should to be given shares when their accumulated income had reach a certain level, should be revised before being implemented. Since 1842, over 400,000 speciedaler had been accumulated in government bank interest savings. This silver should be disbursed to the government as fast as possible. The government interest income made possible under the amendment to the 1842 law should then be paid out together with the government's ordinary share dividends. A decision took time—the national assembly did not share the liberal academics' fear of government ownership.

The same legislative proposal also extended the thinking from 1842 that an excessive portion of the silver reserves lay idle. According to the Kristiania branch, the growing funds made the bank overly solid, and it should therefore be permitted to issue notes at a ratio of 1.5:1 on the silver in the extra fund and the reserve fund. Norges Bank was now given the opportunity to issue notes from government's bank interest savings at a 1.5:1 ratio. Increased interest income would be distributed according to the established model with 75–25 per cent to government and the reserve fund respectively. This amendment gave Norges Bank the right to lend just over a million more speciedaler, by means of a resolution taken right before the 1857 crisis broke out, without having one more gram of silver in reserve.

Setting aside the complicated matters relating to the right to issue notes, the 1842 law made Norges Bank more apt to accomplish the mission of guaranteeing a fixed note value *in practice*. Up until 1842, it was only the head office that exchanged silver. As a consequence, even though the speciedaler was the same, there were some rate variations between regions. First, the government decided that silver would not only be exchanged at the head office, but elsewhere as well. The bank supported this with enthusiasm. According to the board, combined with the parity exchange, this would be 'the final building block in our legislation on the bank and monetary system'.[5] Domestic rate variations would then become negligible. When the right to exchange silver was introduced, Norges Bank was of the conviction that this could be the only road forward; it was also believed that trust would be damaged if the right to redeem silver was reversed once it had been established.

During the committee's work on the bill in the Storting, a provision was tabled giving Norges Bank the right to keep up to 500,000 speciedaler of its silver reserves in foreign financial institutions. Nonetheless, this foreign silver would still be counted as a legal cover for the notes in circulation. The purpose of holding silver in foreign financial institutions was to give Norges Bank the opportunity make claims on these institutions. This meant that the public did not have to exchange notes for silver in Norway in order to ship the silver towards the place of settlement. Now Norges Bank

---

[5] The Executive Board's submission is printed in the newspaper *Morgenbladet*, 18 June 1841, first addendum.

could sell bills of exchange denominated in speciedaler. The bill of exchange gave the buyer the right to this amount of silver with a third party, a person or an institution that was called drawee in this transaction. The drawee could then be a financial institution in Hamburg, Copenhagen, or wherever Norges Bank chose to keep silver. When the bill of exchange was accepted by the drawee, it could be settled against other payments, in order to limit the physical silver transfers. This arrangement offered a smooth system for payment transfers.

The proposal did not come from Norges Bank's governing bodies, which were, in fact, opposed to the entire arrangement.[6] At the time, the bank did not see any reason to keep funds abroad apart from supplementing the silver reserve. Oxholm, now deceased, was no longer an influence in the bank. For a long time ahead, the bank's leaders in Trondheim maintained a conservative attitude to new proposals, which were mainly driven forward in Kristiania, by the government, Storting officials and the leaders at Norges Bank's Kristiania branch office.

The king had modified one point in the bill that the government presented in 1842.[7] The government wished to move the head office from Trondheim to the rapidly growing capital of Kristiania. A massive fire had just engulfed Trondheim, and the ageing and patriarchal Karl Johan believed that it would be unreasonable for Trondheim to lose the head office during this difficult situation. The government complied in this matter of lesser importance. However, the arguments in favour of moving to the growing political and economic centre remained a theme. Up until 1860, proposals to move the office were still made, in vain, at each Storting meeting, either by Storting representatives or by the government.[8]

More Banks

To a certain extent, the government itself relieved Norges Bank of its role as a lending institution, in the form of state discount commissions, which were directly under the Ministry of Finance. As mentioned in Chapter 2, these discount commissions saw the light in 1828, when the king wished to expand Norges Bank's credit provision possibilities by means of government foreign silver loans. The loan would then be placed in Norges Bank. Norges Bank director Oxholm refused on principle; the bank of issue should not be assigned the task of resolving private businesses' challenges. The establishment of individual loan offices in the largest cites, in order to offer direct lending, became the solution. As mentioned earlier, part of the silver was placed as primary capital in Norges Bank, from where it was lent to the government, which in turn

[6] Gunnar Jahn, Alf Eriksen, and Preben Munthe, *Norges Bank gjennom 150 år* (Norges Bank, 1966), 57.

[7] The proposition is printed in *Storting's proceedings*, vol. 10, no. 3, 261–302; for the deliberations at the Storting, see *Storthings-Efterretninger 1836–1854*, vol. 2, 319–43.

[8] Ref. Jan Thomas Kobberrød, 'Christiania er, som Hovedstad betragtet, Rigets vigtigste Stad', in *Riket og regionene: Grunnlovens regionale forutsetninger og konsekvenser*, ed. Ida Bull and Jakob Maliks (Akademika, 2014); Lars Fredrik Øksendal, *Trondhjem som hovedsete for Norges Bank—noen faktiske og kontrafaktiske betraktninger*, Staff Memo no. 8 (Norges Bank, 2008).

transferred the money to the new loan arrangements. This integrated Norges Bank into the process of financing the new institutions. A division of labour was still created, where the government assumed direct responsibility for direct supply of credit in situations involving businesses with a special need for loans.

The development of a banking establishment outside of Norges Bank had begun before 1828. A savings bank had been established in the capital of Kristiania as early as 1822. The following year, these types of banks started operating in Trondheim and Bergen. This would be the beginning of a wave of new savings banks, generally small and locally based. By 1855, 115 savings banks were in business. Ten years later, the number of banks had risen to 223, and in the period to the 1920s, over 600 savings banks had been established.

In certain places, the establishment of a savings bank was linked to a requirement for Norges Bank to expand its regional branch network in order to widen its geographical presence. A regional branch network was expected to offer cities and their surroundings greater access to a still scarce public good, i.e. bank loans. The savings banks became a conduit, which went via primary capital fund and a gradual expansion of activities. Norges Bank did not lack provisions for its available loanable funds, and the bank could not raise the price on mortgage loans, which had become the most common form of credit. Hence, commercial considerations did not warrant the establishment of new branches. This would only add to administrative costs, without increasing earnings. Characteristically enough, Norges Bank first chose to establish new branches in those places where it seemed rational to do so from an internal banking perspective, and not in the places located at the longest distances from a branch. Akershus was to have half of the loans, with a corresponding increase in work for the three administrators in the capital city. When branches were opened in the relatively nearby cities of Skien in 1835 and Drammen in 1837, the Kristiania branch benefited from a welcome reduction in its workload.

The bank deferred at length, establishing a branch north of Trondheim. Northern Tromsø requested a branch as early as 1826. The Storting and the county governor´s suggestions failed to influence the bank. Since this pertained to the bank's business operations, the viewpoint was tolerated for a long time. Nonetheless, the government gradually started losing patience. In 1851, a compromise was made between the requirement to establish new remotely located branches and Norges Bank's resistance. Norges Bank was given the legal right to establish banking offices with a simplified and more affordable administration than the bank's branches. That idea came from the bank itself, as a concession to the steadily heavier requirements. In practice, there was only a minor difference between a branch and office, and this difference disappeared in 1892 as a result of major revision of the law in that year.

Consequently, in 1852 branch offices were established in Stavanger and Tromsø, with a lending capital of 185,000 and 80,000 speciedaler, respectively. These bank offices were much smaller in size than those of Skien and Drammen, which had administered a lending capital of respectively 447,000 and 733,000 speciedaler when they were founded. Later on, bank offices were also established in Halden (1854),

Lillehammer (1860), and Bodø (1874). They were also opened in Kristiansund (1880) and in Hamar (1881), which was the last one in the 1880s.

The savings banks supplemented Norges Bank as a source of credit, even though the purpose and client base was fairly different from the beginning. The savings banks became a crucial component of the Norwegian financial structure. Government officials participated in establishing the first banks, but the chosen model was still 'private'. While the numerous German savings banks had a public and collective aspect, with municipalities and, eventually, federal states acting as initiative-takers and depositors, the individual citizens' initiative and financial deposits were the basis of the Norwegian savings banks, along the lines of the British model. The motives were essentially philanthropic. Securing old age and providing a sickness and disability protection for workers was an important objective. Ordinary people needed secure safekeeping for their money, and generally, diligence and saving were to be encouraged.[9]

The fact that savings banks paid interest on deposits was a significant motivating factor. Until then, one had to pay to deposit money in the country's only bank. Nevertheless, secure safekeeping and the possibility to transfer between account holders and branches provided deposits for Norges Bank from the very beginning. Norges Bank first started paying interest on deposits in 1842, initially at fixed rates of as high as 4 per cent, which was possible as government-licensed savings banks, under the 1842 savings bank act, were permitted to charge 5 per cent interest rate on their loans. In the strictly regulated Norwegian interest rate structure, which pertained to loans secured on property, the maximum statutory interest rate was 4 per cent. From the outset, Norges Bank was permitted to charge a slightly higher rate of 5 per cent, and savings banks were also given this privilege. Thus, a rather peculiar situation arose where there was a maximum interest rate that the only banks in the country were exempt from applying.

Norges Bank in the Shadow of the February Revolution

On 20 July 1847, Norges Bank sent a document to all its branches.[10] The document illustrates both the board's thinking and approach to administering the bank. The document stated that the silver reserves had been depleted. Hence, the branches were given a general order to discontinue operations. The law was indisputable. In fact, 100,000 speciedaler banknotes were now circulating without legal cover. However, the board was of the view that active withdrawal of an equivalent amount of banknotes would be too strong an instrument. Therefore, the bank was not to terminate loans that were expected to be long term, even though one had a legal right to do so. If the branches now just refrained from issuing new loans until the head office issued new orders, normal reimbursement of the loans issued would return conditions to normal.

---

[9] Based on Lars Thue, *Forandring og forankring: Sparebankene i Norge 1822–2014* (Oslo: Universitetsforl., 2014).
[10] Circular from the Executive Board, 20 July 1847, Alf Eriksen's Papers (AEP), Folder 2, Norges Bank, 499 a–b.

The run on the silver reserve was a crisis symptom. The 1847 crisis was not specific to Norway, but pan-European, reflecting the transition from a rapid boom and later the sharp decline in the British stock market, mainly owing to railroad and manufacturing developments.[11] Norway was probably less affected than many other countries in 1847, but higher import demand and an increase in import prices put pressure on Norges Bank's funds. Around the turn of the year, the crisis in Norway seemed to be blowing over. The banknote/silver ratio was again in keeping with the law. Then, in February 1848, revolution broke out in Paris. France was now Norway's most important lumber market, and the market was promptly hit by the Paris events. A reduction in exports led to a decline in foreign exchange revenues, which increased pressure on the bank's silver fund and reduced Norges Bank's capacity to provide domestic credit. What next?

Coincidentally, the Storting was assembled when the effects of the crisis became noticeable.[12] At the end of March, it was suggested that Norges Bank should be given access to raise a foreign loan to strengthen its silver fund. Such an authorization from the Storting almost had to be interpreted as an instruction to the bank. The suggestion was referred to a Storting committee for examination. Schweigaard was appointed to head the committee, and the final outcome was apparent already at the time of his appointment. According to Schweigaard, Norges Bank's mission was clearly confined to exchanging banknotes for silver at parity. Now, Norges Bank was not, in any sense, threatened, but it was argued that it should raise a loan to help the public. Schweigaard did not consider that to be a task for Norges Bank.

If a loan was to be raised to help business and industry, it was to be a matter for the state. However, according to Schweigaard, it was not the government's task to rescue the business sector from problems due to domestic speculation and imprudence. But now the situation was different; the problems were rooted in completely unpredictable events unfolding abroad. Once again, the state's discount commissions were charged with providing foreign-funded liquidity to business and industry.

As expected, the pressure on Norges Bank's silver reserves increased, and there was yet another violation of the regulation of banknotes issuance. While the Storting discussed plans of action, Norges Bank again requested its branches to stop extending new credit. This was a direct consequence of the central bank's heavy, long-term asset structure. William Bagehot's book *Lombard Street* famously advises to 'lend freely at a penalty rate', as a recipe for how a note-issuing bank should react during a crisis. This was a recipe for a *liquid* bank of issue, which Norges Bank's was not. When the illegal amount of banknotes had exceeded 1.2 million, the Supervisory Council took new decisions.[13] In Hamburg, Norges Bank's draft prices were raised, which would make it more expensive to buy silver there. The discount rate in Trondheim was raised to 6 per cent, bringing the discount rate at the head office on par with that of Kristiania,

---

[11] The Storting's handling of the possibility for a 'probable forthcoming monetary crisis' is best explained in *Storthings-Efterretninger 1836–1854*, vol. 3 (Jacob Dybwad Forlag, 1904), 75–86.

[12] Ref. the Executive Board's epistles to the departments, 21 July 1848, AEP, Folder 3, Norges Bank, 505f.

[13] Letter from the Executive Board to the Supervisory Council, 23 June 1848, AEP, Folder 3, Norges Bank, 500–3.

Drammen, and Skien. The Bergen and Kristiansand branches were asked to *consider* doing the same. This was the only action the head office could take with regard to the discount rate. The setting of the discount rate lay in the hands of Norges Bank's branches. The board had to remind the Supervisory Council of this in a letter sent in June.[14] However, the price increase was more a signal that action was being taken. The discount rate lay clearly below that offered in Hamburg. In response to the crisis, Norges Bank's action consisted of rationing credit and discontinuing provision of new loans.

However, the measure attracting the most attention was the termination of silver redemption in the Kristiania and Bergen branches. The consequence of confining silver redemption to Trondheim was that the public was faced with increased difficulties and costs in redeeming notes for silver. Thus, fewer people would go on to do so, and the breach of the coverage ratio would be less noticeable. At the same time, the notes would be worth more in Trondheim than any other place. Yet this was exactly what one had attempted to prevent under the 1842 law. In 1848, in the country's capital, the speciedaler notes ended up being worth only 117 silver skilling, not 120 as planned.[15] Consequently, Norges Bank was not performing its task in practice, and this was what Schweigaard reacted to. In strict terms, it would have been better if the Supervisory Council had refrained from taking an active role. The decision did not in any event contribute to strengthening the head office's good standing outside of Trondheim.

During late summer, the Storting directed harsh words at Norges Bank, which was criticized for not providing credit when most needed. As a Storting member, however, Schweigaard did not have anything negative to say about the bank's *lending policy*, given the bank's actual room for manoeuvre.[16] The logic behind Schweigaard's reasoning was that it was of no help to manipulate banknote redemption or the appurtenant laws and regulations once a crisis had already erupted. In the long run, this would only make matters worse. Schweigaard's adamant opposition to stop silver redemption in Kristiania is an altogether different matter. When the order was given, Schweigaard, as a bank administrator, strongly protested to the head office. Later, the Storting was also informed of the fact that the Kristiania branch had continued exchanging drafts for foreign funds, even though this was clearly prohibited according to the head office's decision.[17]

What truly went on between the Supervisory Council and the board during the summer of 1848 is barely mentioned in the minutes. We have seen that, in 1842, the board had firmly advocated unconditional silver redemption at the branches. Yet, it appears that the board did not oppose the Supervisory Council's decision to discontinue silver redemption in Kristiania and Bergen in 1848. With the exception of one

---

[14] *Storthings-Efterretninger 1836–1854*, vol. 3, 787.

[15] Ibid., 327, with the full debate on 23–8.

[16] Concerning the establishment of Christiania Kreditkasse, see Erling Engebretsen, *Christiania Bank og Kreditkasse 1848–1948* (Aschehoug, 1948).

[17] Concerning a Credit Bank in Kristiania, see *Morgenbladet*, 15 December 1855. Unknown author. Loose speculations about the origin can be found in literature, but will not be examined here.

man, the board was then composed of the same men as in 1841. The Supervisory Council, as Norges Bank's highest body, probably felt a strong need to actively engage in remedying the obvious breach of the law's provision pertaining to the allowed amount of banknotes in circulation. The regulation did not actually prohibit suspending silver redemption at the regional branches. As mentioned, it was implicit in 1842 that, in principle, a resolution providing for silver redemption at the regional branches would be irreversible. Back-pedalling on that would be viewed as a failure. And it was— but the alternative was continued breach of the law pertaining to Norges Bank. From a formal viewpoint, that was a heavier burden to bear for the responsible authorities.

Commercial Banks Emerge

The credit crunch during the crisis spawned a new bank, regarded as Norway's first commercial bank. The bank, Kristiania Kreditkasse, was established as an instrument to mobilize credit under the crisis, for those whose needs could not be accommodated by Norges Bank. The bank opened with share capital of 40,000 speciedaler. The business concept, built on contemporary Danish models, was that the Kreditkasse would extend loans secured on goods.[18] Norges Bank did not offer loans secured on such assets, even though the original intention had indeed been for that to be a main business of the central bank. The Kreditkasse was to disburse the loans as bills of exchange on the Kreditkasse itself, which did not conflict with Norges Bank's note issuance monopoly. The borrowers could freely use the bills of exchange, and discount them with a third party if so desired. However, after a short period, the Kreditkasse offered interest-bearing deposits, and used the deposits for lending and discounting. This would soon become the core of its business, and the Kreditkasse eventually also added 'bank' to its name: Kristiania Bank and Kreditkasse.

About ten years later, the establishment of what was to become a truly big bank took place. Throughout the 1850s lofty ideas concerning the Norwegian banking market circulated; some ideas were also expressed in the daily press. An article from the newspaper *Morgenbladet* illustrates this mindset.[19] The source of inspiration was the large French bank Crédit Mobilier, established in 1852. The credit conditions in Norway were 'just as complicated and burdensome as our roads and ferry ports', according to the author of the article, who wanted to mobilize available capital. A 'Central Bank that was to contribute to Norway's 'rapid rise and industrial development' should be established in Kristiania. The share capital should be 2 million speciedaler, which was the same amount as in Norges Bank's initial silver fund.

Both the timing of the initiative and the way in which the bank came to be deserves more context. The fact that extensive, concrete proposals to establish a big commercial

---

[18] The establishment of the Norwegian Creditbank is described in Ebbe Hertzberg and Niels Rygg, *Den norske Creditbank, 1857–1907* (Den Norske Creditbank, 1907).

[19] 'Om en Kreditbank i Christiania', *Morgenbladet*, 15 December 1855.

bank were made during the mid-1850s is, to a certain extent, linked to economic and financial developments. After overcoming the 1848 crisis, Norway entered a period of rapid growth, especially with regard to industries in need of substantial capital. At the same time, the Norwegian economy experienced a period of intense liberalization, where past privileges linked to trade and lumber mills were removed. The cotton industry and mechanical engineering were seeing the light of day, even though the great industrial revolution came later, linked to the use of hydropower particularly in the electrochemical industry. Shipping increased rapidly and international conditions were of significance in this context. The British Navigation Acts, meant to reserve transport from England and the colonies for English ships, were revoked. The subsequent Crimean War resulted in a significant increase in international freight rates, and in the Norwegian merchant fleet. Growth was also sustained throughout the 1850s: the Norwegian merchant fleet was the world's eighth largest in 1850, and the third largest twenty-five years later.[20]

The manner in which Norges Bank was organized more or less matches a pattern observed in other areas of society, where private capitalists and public officials worked together. Several of the capital's most important bankers, who had been engaged in private credit provision, were persuaded to join the project. It was preferable to join the new bank being established than to compete with it. Ole Jacob Broch, an omnipresent professor-politician, acted as a force for order. Broch was a mathematics professor, Storting member, and minister who had served several terms. He was also an initiative-taker pushing for the establishment and reform of a number of public institutions. In 1847, Broch was a central actor in the establishment of a large national life insurance company, Gjensidige. In 1851, he was also involved in the establishment of the public bank, the Hypotekbank.[21] The idea behind the Hypotekbank was that it would be financed through long-term government-guaranteed bonds, which were essentially to be sold abroad in order to provide long-term loans secured on real estate. Broch was heavily influenced by French economists and scientists, and was among those who brought home impulses from ideas behind Crédit Mobilier when the new big bank was founded in 1857. After the establishment of this bank, Broch remained a member of the executive three-man strong board. Torkel Aschehoug, also a professor and politician, lawyer and government economist, was among the bank's founding fathers. The professor-politicians were provided with international impulses and national legitimacy, and contributed to the bank's broad foundation; in the context of that time, they also provided decisive and valuable knowledge.

Den norske Creditbank was established in October 1857. A central task for the Creditbank was to provide the business sector with short-term and medium-term credit by discounting bills of exchange and bonds. The Kreditkasse, established in 1848, was operating in the same market, which expanded to a large extent the

---

[20] Trond Bergh, *Norge fra u-land til i-land: vekst og utviklingslinjer 1830–1980* (Gyldendal, 1983), 111.
[21] The establishment of the Hypotekbank is described in Alf Kaartvedt and Leif Christian Hartsang, *Kongeriket Norges Hypotekbank 1852–1952* (Hypotekbanken, 1952).

business sector's financing possibilities. Founded in 1851, the state bank Hypotekbank was more relevant to Norges Bank's activities, offering considerable and welcome relief for Norges Bank. The establishment of the Hypotekbank must be seen in the light of the persistent pressure coming from rural regions for sources of mortgage loans. The need for a new institution grew as Norges Bank gradually reduced its mortgage loan provision in response to strong, theoretically founded criticism. The young Schweigaard's powerful 1836 discourse is mentioned in Chapter 2, and his colleague Broch was among the many people sharing that same idea, and who in the early 1850s had affirmed that the Storting itself must 'bring an end to this monstrosity'.[22]

In parallel to the mortgage loan shift in the balance sheet, an early and more active discount policy emerged. As mentioned, the mortgage rate was set by the Storting, while the setting of the discount rate was left to Norges Bank's regional branches. In practice, up until 1850, the discount interest rate was not used much—the ineffective raising of the discount interest rate in 1848 was an exception. In 1850, the Kristiania regional branch lowered the discount rate to 5 per cent, and the head office followed suit a few months later. During the five subsequent years the head office's interest rate remained unchanged, while Kristiania's interest rate was adjusted from 4 to 6 per cent, mainly as a result of the increase in loanable funds made available through increased deposits. In this context, ordinary banking considerations prevailed over monetary policy in the modern sense—increased deposits had to be converted to interest-bearing loans. Norges Bank was hardly equipped to conduct a national monetary policy, with its loose network of semi-autonomous regional branches established in rural Norway to provide credit within its delimited areas.

1857: Bad News Travels Fast

When we read about how coincidences play a role ahead of crises, coincidences contributing to the manifestation of the crisis, or to its magnitude, are almost always part of the picture. However, in all regards, the Norwegian handling of the 1857 financial crisis reveals a contrary process.

The 1857 financial crisis erupted in United States in early October. The first problems were reported the day after Creditbank had opened, and only a week after Norges Bank had changed by law its metal to banknote reserve ratio, which suddenly endowed Norges Bank with substantial banknote reserves.[23]

In fact, despite the growth of the Norwegian bank market, Norwegian businessmen were tightly integrated into a network extending beyond Norway's borders. Some had receivables outstanding. Others were dependent on unsecured credit from foreign finance houses to operate, especially from the finance houses of Hamburg. Norwegians

---

[22] Jens Arup Seip, *Ole Jacob Broch og hans samtid* (Gyldendal, 1971), 188.
[23] The course of the crisis is well described by Hertzberg and Rygg, *Den norske Creditbank, 1857–1907*, 42–79; it is also elaborately discussed in Åsmund Egge, 'Statens diskonteringskommisjoner: Finansdepartementet som statsbank i det 19. århundre', doctoral thesis, University of Oslo (1988).

could routinely draw on the foreign finance houses to meet their international obligations. Consequently, suspensions by finance houses abroad would have repercussive effects in Norway, entailing liquidity problems and losses on receivables outstanding.

With respect to access of information and the response to events, the difference between the two crises of 1848 and 1857 is striking: The 1847–8 crisis can essentially be understood through the prism of the financial and economic system, marked by imbalances and dwindling credit and silver reserves. Information about the 1857 crisis was received telegraphically from London and Hamburg, and was eagerly received, whether it was true or false. When the Bank of England raised its discount rate to 6, 7, and 8 per cent in October, and later to as high as 12 per cent in November, the news reached Kristiania at the latest the next day.

The effects of a rumour that spread in the capital on Friday, 20 November are illustrative. According to the rumour, Sewell & Neck, the London institutions that were most involved in Norway, had closed its businesses. Already the following day, the Norwegian consulate in London was convinced that the information was erroneous and promptly sent a corrective telegraph to the interior ministry. The minister did not comprehend the importance and urgency of the corrective and did not share it until the following Monday. 'Throughout Sunday the 22nd Kristiania's merchant community found itself in an indescribable state of frenzy', one of the capital's newspapers wrote some time after the event.

When bankers and merchants learned that the rumour was no more than a rumour, the board of the recently established Creditbank had already organized a meeting to deal with the crisis, also attended by representatives of Norges Bank's Kristiania branch. The Kristiania branch explained that it would actively use the silver reserve by shipping a considerable amount of the hard currency to its foreign correspondent banks to enable them to meet their obligations and bolster confidence in them. The speed of information has increased since then, culminating in today's real-time information in global financial markets. However, the information leap has hardly ever been as big as during the period between 1848 and 1857, when trains and steamboats were replaced by the telegraph.

The silver reserve demand in Hamburg had already been increasing before the crisis became full-blown. The Kristiania branch sent 160,000 speciedaler in silver from Kristiania to Hamburg already in September. Then, they moved 50,000 silver daler from Norges Bank's stock in Copenhagen to Hamburg and Altona, where there would likely be a greater need for the funds.[24] Now the Kristiania branch assured that Norges Bank's bills of exchange would still be accepted in Hamburg, even though it entailed a reduction of silver for the bank—1857 was not 1848. The idea that discussions would once again be held about silver redemption in Kristiania was now utterly inconceivable.

---

[24] Norges Bank's transactions under the 1857–8 crisis are explained in Document number 2, Storting's proceedings 1858.

The first crisis atmosphere in Kristiania passed. Then on 2 December information was received concerning the fact that several Hamburg institutions really had suspended payments, and that several were experiencing acute liquidity problems. This was no longer simply a rumour. The same day, a meeting was held at the Kristiania stock exchange attended by about a hundred businessmen. The meeting elected a nine-man committee, chaired by the omnipresent Schweigaard, in order to preserve Norwegian interests now that the foreign institutions had failed. At the time, Schweigaard was a professor of law and state economics and a Storting member—and considered to be the most influential member of the assembly, due to his intellect, oratory skills, and general trust. As mentioned, Schweigaard was also a member of the board of Norges Bank's Kristiania branch. The committee was otherwise made up of the city's most successful bankers and businessmen. Most of them represented several institutions, partly overlapping each other, including Norges Bank's Kristiania branch, Kreditkassen, and the state discount commission in the capital—but a conspicuously large number of the nine men on the committee had participated in founding the Den norske Creditbank.

When the conversion of bills of exchange and bonds came to a halt, many of the businessmen with claims on foreign importers experienced acute liquidity problems. Those who had bills of exchange debt abroad, which they had planned to roll over, were faced with financial institutions' requests for immediate payment to resolve their liquidity problems. The nine-man committee orchestrated a solution by defining the different roles that government, private capital, and Norges Bank would play. The committee expected that Norges Bank would not be able to guarantee as much liquidity support as needed. Government was the only authority that could do so. Therefore, a government loan had to be raised. The government acted in accordance with the business sector's expectations. Already on 5 December, it was decided to raise a loan in the amount of 1 million speciedaler.[25] The loan would be used as liquidity support. This was the background for the government discount commission's final great effort.

A private loan and guarantee arrangement was also established, by means of funds from private persons and institutions. Alongside the liquidity support, an arrangement was designed to prevent foreign creditors from reacting severely against their Norwegian debtors until order was restored with regard to payments. Now a number of bills of exchange would be rejected. It was on this occasion that the Norwegian Creditbank made its first mark. First by inducing foreign creditors to accept collateral for the amounts rather than demanding immediate settlement, and then by administering the entire arrangement.

In this situation, Norge Bank concentrated on its core mission. On 30 October, the head office had decided for the first time to 'make reasonable use' of the new banknotes that became legal on 28 September. A total of 477,000 speciedaler were made available, and distributed to branches and offices as the need for discounting was on

---

[25] Cf. 'Statens diskonteringskommisjoner: Finansdepartementet som statsbank i det 19. århundre', 501 f.

the rise.[26] This liquidity supply probably delayed the crisis sentiment in Norway considerably. Throughout November and the first half of December, Norges Bank lent funds in a normal manner. As long as there was legal room to do so, Norges Bank provided credit to the business sector, including banks in need of liquidity.

It was obvious that the silver reserves were dwindling, something the board could not ignore. On 21 December, the head office decided to revoke the authorization to lend the abovementioned 477,000 speciedaler. At that time they were already lent, so the decision pertained to the fact that the funds should not be lent out again after reimbursement. The banknote reserves were now in strong decline, and Norges Bank responded by ensuring that the statutory ratio was met. When the crisis, for the most part, had passed, the bank mobilized some of the new funds again in July 1858.[27]

Due to the important size of the banknote reserves since the amendment to the law in September 1857, Norges Bank made it through the 1857-8 crisis with no statutory breach. However, faced with a dramatic liquidity crisis, the bank would still stay true to the law pertaining to credit provision. The bank could do so because the government intervened by lending borrowed foreign currency. In contrast with 1848, there was no discussion about reducing access to the bank's silver reserves.

On 8 December, the Kristiania branch sent about 125,000 speciedaler in silver by ship to Hamburg. One of Norges Bank's own correspondents was among the Hamburg institutions that had experienced a liquidity squeeze. Therefore, in the worst case, it could become difficult to obtain silver on Norges Bank's own bills, and that should be avoided. This action illustrated a problem with the decentralized Norges Bank. Strictly speaking, the head office should respond to the dramatic notifications from Hamburg. The head office had also formally concluded an agreement with the liquidity-squeezed Hamburg institutions. However, the main office was located in Trondheim, to which no telegraph line was connected. During the crisis, Hamburg turned to Kristiania for help, and the Kristiania administration chose to send silver on its own responsibility. Strengthening trust in Norges Bank's banknotes was an urgent matter.

The head office later supported that decision. Some time later, the head office in Trondheim sent larger amounts of silver to Hamburg. A total of 500,000 speciedaler were sent via the extraordinary government-established winter shipping lane to Kiel. The issue was that the head office had *not* made the initial decision. Throughout the entire 1857-8 crisis Norges Bank never broke the law's provision relating to silver redemption. Norges Bank still did its job, not only by respecting the law's minimum requirements by redeeming banknotes at parity in Trondheim, as it had in 1848, but also by doing so without interruption in Bergen and Kristiania as well. Silver was even redeemed for Norges Bank's bills in Hamburg. It was not the bank's obligation to do so, but it had the right to. In contrast, providing liquidity directly to the businesses was neither Norges Bank's obligation nor right, if this conflicted with the laws protecting the bank's core task. Norges Bank's contribution to resolving the crisis

[26] Dokument No. 2, 2, Storting's proceedings 1858.
[27] Dokument No. 11, 2, Storting's proceedings 1860.

was to ensure that there would be no doubt that Norwegian banknotes kept their promised value in silver.

Otherwise, Norway's solution to the crisis solution bore clear similarities with that of Sweden and Denmark. In all three countries, governments intervened directly with the bank, providing substantial loans to the business sector. The Swedish account on the crisis policy are in their main structure virtually identical to the Norwegian one: the Riksbank's lending policy was also marked by the crisis, without becoming a main vehicle for channelling government loans to the economy. However, central actors, who held offices both in the central bank and the private sector, contributed to organizing a private credit association with the aim of ensuring access to liquidity for business owners who were affected by the financial crisis. In Denmark, direct government lending was supplemented by loans from the government to Denmark's Nationalbank, which enabled the central bank to increase lending volume.

When Norges Bank followed the lead of the much older and more established Riksbank in 1857 and addressed the crisis by means of its lending and discount policy within the bank's established framework, it should not be construed to mean that Norges Bank had a particularly strong position in the institutional landscape. It was rather the contrary. Norway was not favourable to the Danish approach to the crisis— elements of it were observed in 1828 when the government supplemented Norges Bank's silver reserves, increased its lending capacity, and became an important owner itself. The bank had also been strongly criticized after its handling of the 1848 crisis, with a sudden freeze on lending and suspension of silver redemption at the cyclically exposed branches in Kristiania and Bergen. This was not to be repeated. Moreover, the Norwegian situation was logistically very different from the Danish, where the Nationalbank, parliament, and branches were at a short walking distance from one another. Norges Bank's head office was situated at a long distance from the capital, which hardly facilitated an exchange of views and concerted efforts. The Executive Board of Norges Bank was thus little involved in orchestrating the solutions to the crisis that were essentially devised and implemented by the Kristiania branch.

Conclusion

Two lines of developments have been followed in this chapter. Another important difference with the credit crunch of 1848 was the fact that Norges Bank became part of a better-functioning financial system in 1857, and was relieved of some of its long-term obligations as a result of the establishment and development of a credit intermediation system that provided long-term loans secured on real estate. From the end of the 1840s the theoretical principles advocated by the capital's professor-politicians were effective, through Storting debates and, later on, purposeful practice aimed at a gradual increase of the share of shorter loans in the form of bills of exchange. At the same time, Norges Bank was designed to hold large reserves. In the bank's complicated cover rules concerning the original silver fund, the reserve fund, and the extra fund, the proportionality principle applied. This implied that the bank produced an amount of banknotes based on a spread determined by fixed ratios between different types of metal reserves. Schweigaard had condescendingly described Norges Bank's lending policy as a consequence of a passive rule: one had an amount of silver, multiplied by two, that was then placed in a long-term mortgage loan. However, when he himself joined the bank's board, he became the strongest advocate of a continuation and strengthening of the proportionality system. The bank's provision and capital were mobilized as a part of the metallic basic capital. That capital could through a simple multiplication—albeit with at a lower ratio—generate a larger volume of circulating banknotes.

A very limited degree of flexibility when facing liquidity problems was therefore the norm for Norges Bank. In 1857, the banknote to silver ratio had by coincidence been increased just prior to the eruption of the crisis, increasing Norges Bank's flexibility above normal, which proved to be a serendipitous event for Norges Bank.

4

Gold and Coins in the Age
of Standardization

On 8 May 1873, after a long and heated debate, the Storting decided to establish a new metal basis for the Norwegian monetary system, by transitioning from silver to gold. In the same resolution the Storting rejected the proposal to join Sweden and Denmark in a currency union.

The primary driving force in Norway was Ole Jacob Broch, one of the nation's important professor-politicians. Broch played a role as a man of action, but his influence is of particular interest as an example of the powerful enthusiasm for modernization and standardization, characterizing many of the world citizens in large and small countries. Broch was an apostle of progress and rationality, his ambitions went beyond Scandinavia, and he worked persistently to tie the Norwegian monetary system to one of the existing European systems. The gold standard eventually prevailed, thanks to Great Britain's financial weight and pragmatic arguments with regard to gold's superiority to silver as a basis for metal-based monetary systems. But the truly big dream, partly forgotten because it did not materialize, was the establishment of a universal coin (universal coinage), intended to give all people access to the same monetary unit for cross-border payments.

In its first round, this initiative to form a Scandinavian currency union was aborted as a result of international events and national politics. National resistance against any form of 'Scandinavianism' hindered a membership in the union, and the sentiments created by the German-Danish war made a solution based on German standards unfeasible. Two years later, as a strictly regional solution, Norway finally joined its two neighbouring countries in the Scandinavian Currency Union.

When the dust from the political storm had finally settled, the currency union was realized in well-functioning forms. Along with the two other national banks, Norges Bank contributed to the ever-expanding currency union in its area of influence and improved it with new and efficient ways of settling payments, the main objective being the promotion of trade. The Scandinavian Currency Union is referred to as an unconditional success in the period up to the First World War. Cooperation between the Scandinavian central banks increased as a result of the cooperation in the north-west corner of Europe, featuring a number of common traits, of a cultural, political, religious, and not least linguistic nature. Central bank cooperation also became a supplement to a host of regular meetings in the field of economics, *inter alia* between specialist economists and statistical agencies.

Norges Bank 1816–2016. Einar Lie, Oxford University Press (2020). © Norges Bank.
DOI: 10.1093/oso/9780198860013.001.0001

Norges Bank and Silver in the International System

Chapter 3 showed how the Norwegian financial system was in various ways closely integrated into global finance. A small, export-oriented, and import-dependent economy was reliant on transnational financing sources. At this point, Norges Bank's role grew from being relatively insignificant around the year 1840, to playing a steadily more active role in trading bills of exchange across borders and investment of metal reserves abroad. Through global finance companies, Norges Bank could easily provide funds for trade with Norway. On the downside, Norges Bank also became more directly exposed to global financial crises.

In global trade, means of payment were not primarily made up of metal or bank-notes. Silver was essentially untouchable, apart from during crisis periods and final settlements. The most common means of payment available—between providers and buyers of goods, importers and exporters, financial institutions and trading companies—were various types of bills of exchange, circulating freely within and across national borders, and which could be used in a nearly unlimited number of trades and business transactions up to the expiry date.[1] In addition, banks and financial institutions could discount—buy—bills of exchange; this was an advance of ready money against an interest rate premium, i.e. the discount rate. The banks could then sell the bill of exchange to a tradesman in need of foreign currency.[2]

The bills of exchange were backed by silver and were easily converted into other silver currencies. When Norges Bank bought or sold bills of exchange from foreign companies, the bank decreased or increased silver reserves indirectly abroad.[3] This part of the silver reserve was placed with commissioners in the trade and finance centres where Norwegian foreign trade was most important. In the mid-1800s this was, as already mentioned, more or less synonymous with the system in the Prussian river city of Hamburg, including the neighbouring Danish city of Altona.[4] Here Norwegian tradesmen sold and re-exported fish and timber products to the rest of Europe, and Norwegian tradesmen purchased goods for import, mainly grain, although grocery and textile goods were also important in the Norwegian market.[5]

In addition to facilitating foreign trade by giving Norwegian tradesmen ready access to credit in the most important markets, the placement of silver reserves and trade in bills of exchange had another important function. It prevented foreign trade

---

[1] This paragraph is mainly based on the thorough introduction in Markus A. Denzel, *Handbook of World Exchange Rates, 1590–1914* (Ashgate Publishing, 2010); and Hans Christian Johansen, 'Om at skrive bankhistorie', *Historisk tidsskrift (DK)* 15, no. 5 (1990).

[2] Debt and outstanding funds from tradesmen and financial institutions were often offset through clearing houses, and precious metals would, if needed, be transferred first after these important clearing institutions had balanced all settlements.

[3] Nicolai Rygg, *Norges Banks historie*, vol. 2 (Emil Moestue, 1954), 77.

[4] Hamburg was, up until German unification in 1817, an independent German state, while Altona, which is now a district in Hamburg, was a separate city in the very south in Danish Holstein up until 1864.

[5] An overview of Norwegian import and export values divided into groups of goods from 1866 can be found in Statistisk Sentralbyrå, 'Norges Offisielle Statistikk, Historisk Statistikk 1968', *Utenrikshandel 1975* (1970): table 153.

from having an impact on the Norwegian economy through substantial claims on Norwegian notes and unnecessary inflows and outflows of silver. For example, there could be wide seasonal fluctuations between the different industries that could have a considerable impact. An evident advantage for Norges Bank was the fact that these bills of exchange, unlike the domestic and real portion of silver reserves, were interest bearing and generated additional income.[6]

The Norwegian speciedaler's tie to silver was thus not only important because it provided internal stability and involved payments in a precious metal, but also because the silver standard connected the domestic and international money markets. In the age of bills of exchange, the tie to silver was particularly important as it provided stability between different currencies, and in Europe most of the currencies had some sort of tie to silver during the first half of the 1800s. More stable exchange rates facilitated trade transactions between countries; the fixed silver weight made it easier to convert and calculate prices between currencies. The silver standard was therefore, in many ways, already an international system. The view that gold should constitute the basis for a more complete, universal monetary system nevertheless gained ground through the 1860s.

Gold and Universal Coin

The changeover from a silver standard to a gold standard, and the many technical changes introduced at the same time, connected two schools of thought. One was the prevailing and partly British-inspired liberal economic thinking in Europe. The state was to play a lesser role, but could contribute to promoting private initiatives and free trade. This implied the establishment of a functioning payment system, and in some places, organizing investment in infrastructure and communication.[7] Within the latter area, the British government played a relatively limited role. Alexander Gerschenkrohn's influential interpretation of the government's role in modernization had pointed to the fact that countries whose industrial development lagged behind to a relatively large extent saw government take on a prominent role when industrialization and modernization first gained pace. As a first mover, the British government in Great Britain played a limited role, while in countries like Norway there was a stronger element of government intervention at certain levels. Liberal premises entailed a preference for private forces taking initiatives and raising capital, for example when railroads were to be developed. However, the government intervened considerably during the building phases, which were very costly given the country's expanse and demanding topography. The Norwegian solution for infrastructure development took on a special flavour, because leading public officials were to such a large extent

---

[6] Rygg, *Norges Banks historie*, 2, 76–8.

[7] Francis Sejersted, *Historisk introduksjon til økonomien* (Cappelen, 1985), 55 ff; Albert George Kenwood and Alan Leslie Lougheed, *The Growth of the International Economy 1820–1980* (George Allen & Unwin, 1983), 77ff.

attached to, and legitimized, their role as representatives of ideals of domestic growth and modernization.[8]

The other school of thought was inherited from the Age of Reason and the strong belief in establishing rational and efficient systems for social interaction, an ideal that was strengthened by a number of technological innovations and possibilities later in the 1800s.[9] After the French Revolution, French scientists had constructed the metre, the litre, and the kilo. The units of measurement was based on a decimal system. Even though it broke with many established local variants and systems, it had the clear advantage of being mathematically logical and simple in its use.

From mid-century, we can see a clearly intensified movement in favour of synchronization and standardization. The metric system was promoted in international fora, its use was legally protected in the Unites States in 1866, and it saw a major breakthrough with the *Treaty of the Meter* in 1875.[10] This was a period of extremely high activity in standardization within communication, time, and space. The development of railroads required a global twenty-four-hour clock. British railroads introduced Greenwich Mean Time (GMT) in 1840, and in other countries there was a gradual, stepwise standardization of domestic time, and later the adoption of GMT. The telegraph, which took over in Europe during the 1850s and was developed throughout the two decades that followed, required extensive standardization, physically, technically, pricewise, and to some extent linguistically—and not least in the form of common time standards.[11] In that respect, transnational standardization and cooperation became a driving force behind this broad internationalization wave, or the first wave of globalization, as some choose to call it.

Common standards of measurement and monetary units were a natural outcome of these efforts. The development of the gold standard has often been described 'from within', attributed to forces inherent to the monetary system, and represented by figures or described by lines of reasoning familiar to its historians.[12] There is nothing wrong with this; telegraph, time, measures, and weights can be described in similar ways, through the efficiency and benefits of new systems, set in motion by actors in favour of standardization. But it is—especially in our context—difficult to consider the coordinated coin and metal standardization independently from the widespread enthusiasm for standardization.

All the novelty led to obvious rewards—and for success to be achieved, work, persuasion, and investment were required. This was also true concerning the early 1870s,

---

[8] Trond Bergh, *Jernbanen i Norge: 1854–2004. Nye spor og nye muligheter: 1854–1940* (Vigmostad & Bjørke, 2004).

[9] Jens Arup Seip, *Ole Jakob Broch og hans samtid* (Gyldendal, 1971), 535ff.

[10] Edward Franklin Cox, 'The Metric System: A Quarter-Century of Acceptance (1851–1876)', *Osiris* 13 (1958).

[11] Roland Wenzlhuemer, 'The History of Standardisation in Europe', *European History Online* (2010).

[12] Exceptions exist; Gallarotti 1995 presents a broader image of standardization within post and measuring units (kilo and metre) as an entry to his introduction during the international meetings of 1867 about the expansion of the Latin Monetary Union and further standardization of the global monetary systems. See Giulio M Gallarotti, *The Anatomy of an International Monetary Regime: The Classical Gold Standard, 1880–1914* (Oxford University Press, 1995).

with a shift to gold as the metal reserve.[13] The silver basis was more unstable than desired, as the silver price was subject to wider fluctuations than gold. None of the metals constituted any stable value basis for payment means, but silver much less so than gold. At the same time, the gold standard country, Great Britain, played a dominant role in the international system. For nations that desired growth and development, or simply as a standard for what was modern and civilized, Britain was a role model. The British pound's basis in gold made the standard more attractive. Britain was the world's leading trading power, and much of global trade was settled in pounds. Gold was also superior to silver on a purely practical level—a final settlement in gold required much less weight in precious metal. These aspects were emphasized in the international debate at the time, and indeed later, and were central in the Norwegian and Scandinavian discussions about the choice of metal standard.

The Norwegian view on internationalization and standardization was introduced at the Nordic meetings of national economists in the 1860s.[14] During the 1860s the discussions were primarily of scientific interest and involved the academic elite. In the early 1870s, the discussions suddenly became highly politicized. Both aspects hindered the participation of Norges Bank, whose leaders found themselves, as mentioned, at a considerable distance from the intelligentsia of the capital. Up until the new 1892 bank legislation—which is discussed in Chapter 5—the leaders must also be described as practitioners in the field of banking, remote from general economic reasoning on standardization and system design.

At the very first Nordic meeting of national economists in 1863, in Gothenburg, Sweden, the experts suggested a common monetary system for the three Scandinavian countries. The currencies were already easily convertible. One Swedish riksdaler and a half Danish riksdaler contained about as much silver as a quarter Norwegian speciedaler.[15] This meant that the different silver coins were already accepted in trade happening mainly in the border regions. Now the economists wished to conform to a future international system, and the proposed common coin weight unit—five grams of silver—was adapted to what was expected to be an international unit. This not only corresponded to the French 5 franc, but it also converged towards the decimal system.[16]

A feature of the Norwegian, and partly also the Scandinavian, monetary system, must be underlined: the Norwegian and Scandinavian economies were based on

[13] See for example Marc Flandreau, 'The French Crime of 1873: An Essay on the Emergence of the International Gold Standard, 1870-1880', The Journal of Economic History 56, no. 4 (1996); see also James Foreman-Peck, A History of the World Economy (Pearson Education, 1995), 158ff; including Barry Eichengreen and Marc Flandreau, The Gold Standard in Theory and History (Routledge, 1997), 4–7.

[14] On the Scandinavian discussion, see Ingrid Henriksen and Niels Kærgård, 'The Scandinavian Currency Union 1875-1914', in International Monetary Systems in Historical Perspective, ed. Jaime Reis (Palgrave Macmillian, 1995); Ingrid Henriksen, Niels Kærgård, and Christen Sørensen, 'Den skandinaviske møntunion', Den jyske historiker, nos. 69–70 (1994); Rygg, Norges Banks historie, 2; Seip, Ole Jakob Broch og hans samtid; Krim Talia, 'The Scandinavian Currency Union 1873-1924: Studies in Monetary Integration and Disintegration', doctoral dissertation, Stockholm School of Economics (2004); Lars Fredrik Øksendal, 'Essays in Norwegian Monetary History, 1869-1914', doctoral dissertation, Norges Handelshøyskole (2007).

[15] Respectively 6.376, 6.320, and 6.324 grams fine silver.

[16] The proposal was silver with 90 per cent fineness. See Henriksen, Kærgård, and Sørensen, 'Den skandinaviske møntunion', 6–7; Axel Nielsen, Den skandinaviske møntunion (Børsens forlag, 1917), 6–7.

notes, as evidenced by the ratio of coins and notes in circulation. The amount of coins decreased heavily throughout the 1800s, and after a while made up only a modest portion of money in circulation. In 1873, when the currency union was a burning political issue, the amount of coins did not account for more than about 10 per cent of notes in circulation. Banknotes were printed in small denominations. The lowest bank note was one speciedaler, corresponding to 25.28 grams of silver. Sweden had, at that time and later, banknotes of a much lower value. Many of the small coins did not contain any precious metal. In practice, there was therefore little silver (or gold) in circulation. This differs from what was practised by most of the larger countries. According to Giulio Gallarotti, as much as 80 per cent of payments in France in 1856 were settled in precious metal, only 20 per cent in of banknotes, and the lowest bank note was 50 francs. In Italy in 1865, only 10 per cent of the monetary base was made up of banknotes, the rest consisted of coins. The United States and Great Britain also had large amounts of precious metal in circulation—the lowest bank note from the Bank of England was a 5 pounds sterling. This is ninety times the value of the lowest Swedish banknote after 1873 and 22.5 times the lowest Norwegian note.

This ratio was also a concern in Norway, and at times, the subject of debate. The theoretically conscious and British-oriented Schweigaard had long supported the idea of removing the lowest banknotes to bring more silver coins into circulation. Norges Bank had the monopoly on banknotes, not on coin issue. A stronger incorporation of the silver coin was intended to plant the idea that banknotes 'really' were silver; they were concrete tokens of claim on metal in a vault. A greater amount of silver coins in circulation would, in normative and real terms, strengthen people's perception that money was tied to silver.[17] The question concerning the withdrawal of the lower banknotes and bringing more silver and gold into circulation was also raised at a later date.

The proposal did not win support at this time, however. The most important argument used against more coins was that banknotes were practical. Fishermen and farmers travelling long distances, and with expensive cargo, travelled lighter and more easily with notes than with silver, according to the government and the Storting. This explanation does not say much in a wider context; a given amount of precious metal weighed exactly the same in countries that used more metal coins. Another and more general reason behind the rejection of the proposal was the excessive cost of this solution. The idea was for coins to replace banknotes. In the proportionality system employed for note issuing, silver in the vault was converted, as mentioned, to bank-notes, first at the ratio of 2:1, and from 1842 at 5:2. The idea was, admittedly, that the government, not the central bank, should ensure the amount of coins in circulation. However, the state would incur a 'new' cost in ensuring a permanent, circulating stock of silver, a cost the government was unwilling to take on.

The Norwegian speciedaler was divided into 120 skilling, which could again be divided into 5 ort, each with 24 skilling. This division made calculating somewhat

---

[17] *Lov indeholdende Forandringer i Lovgivningen om Norges Bank*, 28 September 1857.

difficult. These difficulties, and the simplicity of the French system, were the reasons behind two simultaneous Storting proposals to reform the Norwegian monetary system by introducing a decimal system based on daler and skilling.[18]

However, the idea of abandoning silver had not yet been raised, neither at a Scandinavian level, nor at a national level. In the meantime, important events were taking place abroad. In 1865 France had joined Belgium, Switzerland, and Italy in the Latin Monetary Union.[19] It was agreed to use the gold franc as the common coin. This resulted in the decision taken during the second Nordic meeting of national economists in 1866 to adopt the gold coin standard; the future gold coin unit should be the gold franc. But the fact that the Latin Monetary Union was a bimetallic monetary system created problems. The 5 franc silver coin was still circulating alongside different gold franc coins, and both silver and gold were legal means of payment and tied to each other at a fixed value. France wanted more countries to join, and in 1867 all European countries and the United Sates were invited to Paris to discuss the universal coin.

The Norwegian Ministry of Finance was sceptical about joining the Latin Monetary Union, but accepted that the joint Swedish-Norwegian foreign ministry sent a separate Norwegian delegation to Paris.[20] That is when Ole Jacob Broch makes his entrance into coin history. Earlier, Broch was mentioned as one of the founders of the country's first insurance companies and the big bank Den norske Creditbank. The mathematics professor, Storting member, and minister of many years was a prominent figure during the numerous modernization and standardization campaigns, and was a key player in the country's telegraph and railway expansion. Academically and professionally, he was highly engaged in the reform of the Norwegian and international measurement and weight system, and in close contact with French intellectuals.[21]

Among his many initiatives was the *Statistisk årbok for Norge* (*Statistical Yearbook for Norway*), which he published in Norwegian and French in 1871. The book is a study of Norway, naturally, but also an example of Broch's affinity with precision, the concrete, and standards. His description of the country itself, for example, is introduced through a long, detailed explanation of how Norway was thoroughly recorded and measured with the most advanced triangulation techniques, from the icy surfaces of the Kristiania fiord in 1836, all the way up to the north around the Russian border in 1847, after having been pointwise connected to triangular points established in the neighbouring countries. This is how the geographical Norway was established, and how it became connected to the surrounding world, all recorded with the same

---

[18] See Document no. 3 1862 and Innstilling O. no. 62 1863, Storting's proceedings. The new daler unit was to be equivalent to half a speciedaler and be divided into 100 skilling.

[19] Greece joined in 1867. In addition to this, many other governments took, as for example the Austro-Hungarian Empire, a step in the direction of the Latin or rather the 'French' system. See Marc Flandreau, 'The Economics and Politics of Monetary Unions: A Reassessment of the Latin Monetary Union, 1865-71', *Financial History Review* 7, no. 1 (2000).

[20] See the Norwegian prime ministers' government approaches from 5 April and 28 April 1867 concerning foreign affairs, in Ot. no. 45 1869, Storting's proceedings.

[21] Most importantly, see Seip's monumental biography of Broch: Seip, *Ole Jakob Broch og hans samtid*; Another work, also emphasizing Broch's importance, is *Et regime foran undergangen* (Tanum, 1945).

scientific precision.[22] After ten years of work promoting modernization on scientific premises, Broch, characteristically enough, ended his career as director of the International Bureau of Weights and Measures in Paris from 1883, from which the metre's and the kilo's gospel was spread and administered.

After participating in the international monetary conference in Paris in 1867, Broch became passionately preoccupied with the coin. One of his proclaimed sources of inspiration was Michael Chevalier, Saint-Simonist and professor at the Collège de France, who with his involvement in the railroad and Crédit Mobilier had fields of interest that overlapped with Broch's to an astounding degree. The two maintained regular contact through lectures, letters, and personal meetings when Broch was in Paris.[23]

In 1867, Broch argued in favour of a universal monetary system based on the decimal system. This also became Broch's favoured position in the Scandinavian debate. Broch put particular emphasis on the practical advantages of a universal monetary system. Recoinage costs could be avoided, exchange rate fluctuations would be reduced, and prices could more easily be compared. If this type of coin additionally was based on gold, transport costs would be reduced and travel simplified.[24] Gold was simply superior to silver as a measure of value. Broch also had faith in the Latin system because it was already implemented in four states comprising 70 million people, in addition to the fact that the 20 franc was accepted at full value in other countries. At the same time, the Latin coin went hand in hand with the simple metric and weight system. In Norway, both coin and weight could relatively easily be converted to the French-dominated system. Broch affirmed that Norway should use the metre, the litre, the gram, and therefore—along with its neighbours—the gold 10 franc.[25]

Broch's priority was, however, to tie Norwegian money to gold. He argued that delaying a decision to do so would undermine the basis for the speciedaler and increase costs given the growing movement towards a gold standard. The silver price would plummet, and it was now important to take a precautionary approach.

Without much debate steps were then taken also in this direction in Norway, at least in theory. In 1869, the Storting gave Norges Bank the opportunity to hold as much gold reserves as it deemed necessary. The board of the bank did not embrace this opportunity. In mid-1872 less than 1/11 of Norges Bank's metal reserves consisted of gold. At the same time, both Sweden's Riksbank and Denmark's Nationalbanken had a gold share of more than a third, after they had in 1868 and 1871, respectively, started preparing the transition to gold.

In the immediate years following the Paris meeting, there was little movement on the universal coin issue internationally. Great Britain used gold, but wished neither to adapt coin weight to the French system, nor to modify their own specific measure and

---

[22] Ole Jacob Broch, *Statistisk Årbog for Kongeriget Norge 1867–71* (C.C. Werner, 1871).

[23] Seip, *Ole Jakob Broch og hans samtid*, 180 and 556.

[24] See Ole Jacob Broch, 'Beretning Angaaende Den I Paris Afholdte Internationale Myntkonferents', O. no. 45 1869 (Stortinget, 1869). Moreover, Broch believed that the gold coin system would lead to the end of banknotes.

[25] Ibid., 19.

weight units. The many German states did not have a coordinated system and still used the silver standard. As Scandinavian trade was generally with Great Britain and the German states, this was far from optimal. However, in 1871, France lost the war against Prussia. Once unified, Germany introduced a new, common coin system based on gold. The only problem was that the mark's gold content was not compatible with the gold franc.[26] Future prospects for the franc as a universal coin promptly vanished.

This clearly dealt a blow to internationalists like Broch. On the other hand, the new German system had grown more attractive. From a Scandinavian perspective, this was a favourable development in light of the prevailing trade ties. As the three Scandinavian countries, in addition to Finland and the Netherlands, were now the only states using the silver standard—the transition from silver to gold was no longer pressing, but imperative.[27]

Towards a Distinctive Scandinavian System

With the developments in Germany, matters took a quick turn. In 1872, Denmark proposed that the Scandinavian countries coordinate policy to introduce a gold standard. Norway wavered. The head of government, Fredrik Stang, declared he had insufficient insight into the matter to take a position, while the finance minister was uncertain.[28] In principle, the Ministry of Finance deemed it preferable to join one of the international systems. Nonetheless, both the Norwegian and the Swedish finance ministries supported a common Scandinavian stance.

Thus the gold standard and coin system became the key issue at the third meeting of national economists in Copenhagen in July 1872. Broch gave the introductory lecture, advocating that the three countries should join the German system. He attempted to convert sceptics with a veritable deluge of factual information; his introduction was four hours long—according to his own report on the meeting he took a short break halfway through to drink some mineral water—the next day he mercifully let his audience rest after two hours.[29] But Broch's proposal to join the German gold mark was inadmissible for the Danish government, due to the strong anti-German sentiment enveloping the country after the loss of Schleswig-Holstein in the Second Schleswig War in 1864. Being on home ground, Denmark benefited from a powerful voting majority.[30] The German system was thus rejected.[31] The meeting came to the

---

[26] A German gold mark contained 0.345842 grams of fine gold, while a gold franc contained 0.29032 grams of gold. Ref. Ole Jacob Broch, 'Om Myntforandring I De Tre Skandinaviske Riger', in *Tids-Tavler*, ed. Ludvig Kristensen Daa (Cammermeyer, 1872), 98; Seip, *Ole Jacob Broch og hans samtid*, 537ff.

[27] Rygg, *Norges Banks historie*, 2, 51.

[28] Jens Arup Seip, *Ole Jacob Broch og hans samtid* (Gyldendal, 1971), 534–5.   [29] Ibid., 539–41.

[30] As many as 235 participants attended the meeting, while Norway and Sweden combined did not have more than ninety.

[31] At the same time, an alternative for the elaboration of a completely new system based on a new five gram 90 per cent gold coin was abandoned because of the substantial restructuring that would have been required. See Henriksen, Kærgård, and Sørensen, 'Den skandinaviske møntunion', 90.

conclusion that Scandinavia would be best served with the gold standard and the decimal system. But the new gold coins were simply based on a recalculation from the weight of Scandinavian silverdalers, which entailed an alignment with current practice and a smooth transition. The problem was the fact that it was a Scandinavian-specific system, as the gold weight was difficult to convert to other coin systems, and therefore it could not become part of any international system of coinage.

The Norwegian government now promptly endorsed a Scandinavian solution.[32] After a joint Scandinavian commission presented its opinion at the end of September, there was swift move towards the decimal system and a Scandinavian gold coin union based on the weight in former silverdaler system.[33] The coin would only be indirectly tied to an international system. On 18 December 1872 the three Scandinavian governments signed the Scandinavian coin convention, which was essentially based on the commission's proposal, and with it the speciedaler, the ort, and the skilling disappeared. The new unit was to be called krone, divided into 100 øre and based on conversion from the Swedish daler. The main coins were the 10 and 20 krone in gold, and their gold content meant that one kilo of gold would be equivalent to 2,480 kroner. However, the agreement required ratification by the three countries' national assemblies.

In 1873 the coin issue was the subject of one of the biggest political controversies in Norwegian history. The coin issue was used against the government by an aggressive opposition at the Storting.[34] Up to that point, Norway had enjoyed a long period of political stability. The 1840–70 period is often described as the 'civil service state's' (*embetsmannstatens*) time of glory.[35] Civil servants dominated political life, not only in bureaucracy, local administration, and education but also in parliament. The cabinet was filled with civil servants, and it had partly become a self-recruiting body for learned men suitable for the highest offices. The opposition paved the way for the formation of a party system, the precursor to modern parliamentarianism. Until the 1880s Storting members were, in principle, free-floating individuals, elected district by district, based on a perception of suitability for public posts. This was core to maintaining the existing regime.

However, towards the end of the 1860s a farmer and liberal opposition emerged against *embetsmann* governance, against the union king, and against the Norwegian government in Kristiania.[36] In 1869, when the decision was taken to hold annual meetings of the Storting—not merely a few months, every third year—a major shift in the power balance between the Storting and government occurred. The tension and

---

[32] Seip, *Ole Jacob Broch og hans samtid*, 541ff.

[33] Krondaler was the unit, and a gold krone was to consist of 10 krondaler, that in turn were to be divided into 100 øre. Henriksen and Kaergaard, 'The Scandinavian Currency Union 1875–1914', 94; Rygg, *Norges Banks historie*, 2, 52–3; Nielsen, *Den skandinaviske møntunion*, 18ff. See designation from 20 September 1872 and the convention proposal from the Scandinavian joint committee in Ot. prp. no. 1 1873: 19–35, Storting's proceedings.

[34] Jens Arup Seip, *Et regime foran undergangen* (Tanum, 1945), 8.

[35] Seip uses, for example, the designation and 'offsprings' of this on several occasions in *Ole Jakob Broch og hans samtid*; and in *Et regime foran undergangen*.

[36] The following is largely based on the first chapter of Seip, *Et regime foran undergangen*.

power play between government and assembly intensified, with one of the most important clashes taking place in 1872. With a large majority, the Storting passed a controversial amendment to the constitution—minsters had to meet in the Storting, which had not been required earlier. The decision would represent one of the most important steps in the direction of parliamentarianism, which would prevail in Norway twelve years later.

The fact that ministers could be summoned among the people elected meant, in extremis, that government was accountable to the national assembly, and greater political power for the Storting. The government rejected it in full: it refused to approve the decision and the union king used his veto. The political tensions permeating the government culminated in a dramatic act; alongside the army minister, Broch stepped down in protest.[37] The meeting obligation and the king's veto would influence Norwegian political life for the next twelve years, until 1884. When, for the third time, the government refused to approve the Storting's resolution to meet at the national assembly, the government was impeached for having failed to implement a Storting resolution. A new government composed of the Storting majority was then established.

The coin issue was raised in this extremely uncertain aftermath. Broch lost much of his influence after leaving the cabinet. He had a falling out with head of government Stang's entourage and withdrew as the Norwegian delegate to the joint Scandinavian Commission.[38] To the surprise of many, he was still invited to sit in the seven-man commission that would prepare the final Storting bill.[39] The motive was probably to avoid Broch's contribution to an alternative suggestion from the opposition, characterized by his intractable academic authority.[40] However, Broch chose to write a separate statement. He argued, as expected, in favour of the gold standard. But the Scandinavian Currency Union and a new calculation/accounting unit based on the decimal system was discarded, ironically enough. Behind the resistance to change was the fact that Broch did not wish to give up the grand idea of a universal system by using a compromise solution. Broch also argued that the main gold coin was too big, and that the average Norwegian would find it difficult to deal with such a rapid and big difference in the calculation unit.[41] This argument was obviously adapted to the situation; if one managed to create an ideal system—a universal coin—major changes had to be tolerated.

---

[37] Ibid., 8.

[38] Torkel H. Aschehoug was a law professor and Storting politician closely linked to Stang's entourage between 1868 and 1882. Aschehoug became particularly meaningful in the field of economy with his three-volume *Socialøkonomik*.

[39] Prime Minister Stang had probably wished to stop Broch and presumed that as a well-known Scandinavia expert at this time he would no longer work towards a Scandinavian Currency Union, see Seip, *Ole Jakob Broch og hans samtid*, 545.

[40] From a correspondence between Manthey and Broch, taken from Seip, *Ole Jakob Broch og hans samtid*, 545–6. Broch's 'special vote' from 11 January 1873 and a draft of the law are attached Ot. prp. no. I 1873. See above, the majority vote 'Betenkning fra den ved Kongelig resolution af 9de Desember 1872 nedsatte Komission om Myntvaesenet', from 4 Februrary 1873, in Ot. prp. I 1873, 71–106, Storting's proceedings.

[41] Brochs 'special vote', 1–3 and 14–15. He had indeed not given as much weight to this consideration in 1867.

Broch ended up standing alone in the seven-man commission that decided on a Scandinavian solution.[42] At this point, Broch steps out of history as an actor. Nevertheless, his dissent would be decisive.

The Coin Issue and Politics

By the end of 1872 the government had got wind of the leftist opposition's plans to undermine any government proposal.[43] With the initiatives and guidelines from Copenhagen and Stockholm the coin issue featured many aspects that would stir up Norwegians' patriotic feelings. The opposition was probably further triggered when reports came in confirming that the coin matter would first be handled by the Swedish and Danish national assemblies. This was a game deliberately played by the three governments, which communicated closely and cooperated on pushing the issue through. The idea was that by having Sweden and Denmark deal with the issue first, Norway, where opposition was expected to be greatest, would come under pressure[44]—a similar strategy to the one used during the Norwegian referendum on EU membership in 1994. This was scheduled to take place directly after the referendums in Finland and Sweden, where the likelihood of a yes vote were seen as far higher.

The question of the coin's national character also features an identity component devoid of the economic functions of money. In the research on shaping and developing national identity, emphasis has increasingly been placed on the function of money, undoubtedly motivated by the interest in how national identity is shaped and changed, and more concretely by the debate on the introduction of, and in some places opposition to, the euro.[45] Money is everywhere in society, and it creates concrete and perceived connections between government and individuals. Its symbols are often deeply linked to the nation's most treasured values and institutions.

These insights were not entirely new. William Bagehot, author of the iconic book *Lombard Street* and founding editor of *The Economist*, was among the advocates of a universal coin. His main economic arguments were the same as those used by Broch and other Scandinavian universal coin advocates: a common coin system would facilitate trade between countries, promote an orderly monetary system, and enhance international statistics. The numerous monetary systems, with their various designations and denominations, were only completely understood and known by specialists

---

[42] Seip, *Ole Jakob Broch og hans samtid*, 547.

[43] See August Christian Manthey, *Dagbøger for Aarene 1856–1874*, vol. 2 (Den norske historiske forening, 1919), 346; Seip, *Ole Jakob Broch Og Hans Samtid*, 544.

[44] Ludvig Daae, *Politiske Dagbøker og Minner*, vol. 2 (Den norske historiske forening, 1938), 81–2; Seip, *Ole Jakob Broch og hans samtid*, 550.

[45] Jan Penrose, 'Designing the Nation: Banknotes, Banal Nationalism and Alternative Conceptions of the State', *Political Geography* 30, no. 8 (2011); Emily Gilbert, ' "Ornamenting the Facade of Hell": Iconographies of 19th-Century Canadian Paper Money', *Environment and Planning D: Society and Space* 16, no. 1 (1998); Emily Gilbert and Eric Helleiner, 'Nation-States and Money', *The Past, Present and Future of National Currencies* (1999); Eric Helleiner, 'National Currencies and National Identities', *American Behavioral Scientist* 41, no. 10 (1998); Anders Ravn Sørensen, 'Monetary Organization and National Identity: A Review and Considerations', *Journal of Cultural Economy* 9, no. 2 (2016).

in banking and trade. 'Unquestionably great forms employ skilled clerks, who translate these difficulties—whether of Norway, or Australia, or India—very rapidly, but ordinary traders cannot keep such clerks.'[46]

The resistance to change associated him with other conditions, a national sentiment, where money and banknotes appeared as the elected symbols of orderly governance and citizens' attachment to this—and not least, a potent 'image and superscription' of the attachment to a common head of government.[47]

The Norwegian opposition to a Scandinavian Currency Union played a slightly different melody on the same national strings. There was no strong defence of the well-established national banknotes and coins. This was probably because the main image on the banknotes was loosely tied to national symbols and institutions. Up until the 1870s the banknotes depicted stylized figures identifying the country's 'main industries', agriculture, fishing, mining, and shipping. The coat of arms existed, but without a portrait of the king. The coins, minted by the government institution the Royal Mint, admittedly bore a portrait of the king, but the portrait was of the Swedish king, who hardly served as a national symbol.

The problem was that the Scandinavian krone was perceived as Swedish by many. In this concrete situation, the physical expression was of less importance than the fact that those opposed to closer Scandinavian cooperation associated it with Swedish dominance.[48]

The name of this new monetary unit itself, 'krone', underlined this. The direct English translation of krone is crown, which has the same concrete, personal, and institutional meaning in the Scandinavian languages as in English. The Danish had their own personified krone, while the Norwegian krone was Swedish. The speciedaler, which was to be replaced, was introduced in the 1500s. Its etymology was forgotten by many; it originated from the German thaler, which was later adopted in national variations such as the 'daler' in the Netherlands and the United States with 'dollar'.

In the period leading up the Storting debate in May 1873, positions also changed considerably. At the time, Sverdrup was working closely with the national poet Bjørnstjerne Bjørnson and those threatened farmer representatives who had flagged the 'wrong' position on the coin issue, suggesting that they should abstain from presenting themselves for re-election in that summer's forthcoming Storting election.[49]

During the whole debate, Norges Bank's leadership took a passive attitude, while experts and politicians defined the conditions and framework for its work. The bank did not chime in until it was called to duty by the Ministry of Finance in February

[46] Walter Bagehot, *A Practical Plan for Assimilating the English and American Money: As a Step Towards a Universal Money* (Longmans, Green, 1889 [1869]), 14.

[47] The foreword in ibid.

[48] In this context some people believed one was relinquishing the constitution's paragraph 110 that secured a separate national coin and monetary system that was independent from Sweden, see for example Indst. S. 2. 1873, 9, Storting's proceedings.

[49] Daae, *Politiske Dagbøker og Minner*, 2, 74; Manthey, *Dagbøger for Aarene 1856–1874*, vol. 2, 388, 92.

1873.[50] The Executive Board decided to endorse the seven-man commission's draft. In a relatively short statement, Norges Bank did not have anything else to say about the important monetary system reform besides a few objections of a technical and administrative nature.[51] However, when the time to decide was approaching, some of the leaders stepped out of the shadows—not as representatives of the bank, but as elected Storting members: two Norges Bank directors, Strøm and Gram, as representatives from Trondheim and nearby Levanger respectively. Strøm, who at the time was described as 'the most conservative member of the Storting', had been a member of both the seven-man commission and the Storting's expanded bank committee. Despite his attachment to the existing order, he had reluctantly come to the conclusion that the currency union was the correct course.[52]

In the Storting debate, the undisputed leader of the loose leftist opposition, Johan Sverdrup, argued vociferously—using ammunition from Broch's 'special vote'.[53] He claimed that the transition to the decimal system would involve major practical problems, that measure and weight reforms should come first, and that a Scandinavian solution would entail turning one's back on a universal coin. Nevertheless, the government's supporters—especially professor of state finances Torkel Aschehoug—argued that the union would promote Scandinavian trade and economic integration. In spite of the widely differing opinions, it was agreed that a transition to gold was necessary—it was the coin convention that was the moot point.[54]

When the votes were finally cast, the proposal to join the Scandinavian Currency Union was rejected, with fifty-eight against fifty votes.[55] Clearly, the government was surprised at the outcome. Broch was also baffled that his position won the vote.[56] Sverdrup was delighted: 'I have kept my word. The coin convention fell, inflicting a wound on "monarchical" Scandinavianism which will not easily heal. [...] it was a great political victory.'[57] Hence, the Scandinavian Currency Union commenced without Norway.

The government now set out to save what could be saved. Three days after the defeat, professor Aschehoug asked one of the more centre-oriented opposition leaders for help in coming up with an alternative.[58] He took hold of what had been agreed on: a swift transition to gold. Aschehoug quickly drafted a bill for the Odelsting (Lower Chamber) where he included the elements of the original proposal that he assumed

---

[50] The call did not come until 5 February 1873. However, it should be mentioned that on 7 November 1872 the Ministry of Finance asked Norges Bank's leadership to issue a brief opinion on a transitional period for this monetary system reform. The leadership answered on 22 November. See letter from Norges Bank to the Ministry of Finance on 22 November 1872, in FD/FKC/D/Dc/Dca/L009.

[51] See document no. 57 from the Bank Committee, 1873: 'Skrivelse til Finantsdepartementet fra Direktionen for Norges Bank angaaende den Kgl. Prp. om Overgang til Guldmyntfod', Storting's proceedings.

[52] Indst.S.II. From the 29 April 1873 expanded Bank Committee; Storting's proceedings

[53] Øksendal, 'Essays in Norwegian Monetary History, 1869–1914', 29ff.

[54] Stortingstidende 1873, 554–60, Storting's proceedings.

[55] Only one of these was a municipal representative, see Manthey, *Dagbøger for Aarene 1856–1874*, 2, 392. The vote during Storting negotiations 1873, 640.

[56] Daae, *Politiske Dagbøker og Minner*, 2, 82; Seip, *Ole Jakob Broch og hans samtid*, 553.

[57] Halvdan Koht, *Johan Sverdrup 1870–1880*, vol. 2 (Aschehoug, 1922), 118.

[58] Daae, *Politiske Dagbøker og Minner*, 2, 83–4.

would be passed by the two chambers.[59] He assumed correctly, as the majority in the expanded bank committee, and eventually the Storting, subsequently voted in favour of Norway's transition to the gold standard. However, it was a gold coin based on Broch's proposal, where both the speciedaler and skilling were retained. The speciedaler was divided into four kroner instead of five ort. It was a broad middle way, but at least it was paved with gold.

Aschehoug's proposal was passed by the Storting. But with the combination of speciedaler, krone, and skilling, the result was an artificial hybrid. The practical side of the conversion of silver to gold was rapidly implemented. Before the end of the year most of the silver reserves had been converted to gold. The silver in Hamburg was converted at parity, while Norge Bank's minted silver was mainly Danish speciedalers that could be converted to gold kroner, almost without fees. Expenses were limited to transport costs.[60] Furthermore, this was a favourable time for conversion to gold. The price of silver fell in late 1873, and the price gap between silver and gold gradually increased throughout the decade. This created considerable problems for bimetallic systems (combined gold and silver standards) such as the Latin Monetary Union. The problems created by the fluctuating price gap of various metal standards would overshadow the question of the universal coin during subsequent international conferences.

Even though silver was still used in coins along with copper, the change in coin basis entailed the severing of some strong ties. As a symbol of the 1814 heritage and the heavy road to convertibility at par value in 1842, the silver treasure now belonged to the past.

The Coinage Union

The hybrid that was chosen in 1873 was strongly criticized during the following years for hampering trade between the Scandinavian countries. Even though all three countries were using the gold standard, only the Norwegian means of payment were given a lower rate in cross-border trade.[61] Important problems arose, especially in transactions with Sweden, and deliberately so. 'In Sweden the screws were tightened, and it was with their friendly help that the Norwegian government finally got its way in the matter', Broch's biographer later wrote.[62]

In the spring of 1875, a new Storting started its efforts to join the currency union. The debate was relatively brief. The result was already known beforehand, when Sverdrup failed to oppose the government's proposal. With eighty-two against

[59] Manthey, *Dagbøger for Aarene 1856–1874*, 2, 392–3. The Bank Committee used the term middle way, see Indst. O. III 1873, 1, Storting's proceedings.

[60] Alf Eriksen, 'Omkring Norges Bank', *Statsøkonomisk Tidsskrift* 55 (1941), 199–253, 228–9; Rygg, *Norges Banks historie*, 56. Over the following couple of years the remaining silver stock was converted and total losses were estimated at around 24,000 speciedalers, according to Rygg, *Norges Banks historie*, 57.

[61] Øksendal, 'Essays in Norwegian Monetary History, 1869–1914', 33.

[62] Seip, *Ole Jakob Broch og hans samtid*, 560.

twenty-eight votes, the Storting endorsed the government's proposal to join. During the short debate, Norges Bank's men sat silent, both voting with the majority.[63]

After the Storting had made its decision, the institution Norges Bank finally entered the scene. The currency union also implied that Norges Bank would become part of early central bank cooperation with the Riksbank in Stockholm and the Nationalbanken in Copenhagen.[64] Up until the mid-1880s, there was hardly any contact between the three central banks. Subsequently, the central banks not only exchanged means of payment and netted positions, but information and views.[65]

From the beginning, the activities of the Scandinavian Currency Union were limited. There were the two main coins—the 20 and 10 krone in gold—that were to circulate freely between the three countries. Thus, the other countries' gold coins were legal tender at full value without any costs. The right to deposit gold for monetization was available to all, and only the cost of producing the coins was deducted. Nevertheless, the three central banks were obliged to accept the banknotes issued by the two others, which circulated in trade. Admittedly, the Riksbank did so without costs from 1880. The leadership in Trondheim exchanged Swedish banknotes with a 0.25 per cent fee. The fee was introduced because there was a net supply of Swedish notes, which required the transport of notes from Stockholm and then transport of gold back to Sweden. On the other hand, one opened the way for free monetization and circulation of coins. It rapidly transpired that the main coins had a low degree of circulation—they were probably, just as the speciedaler had been, too large for daily use.

In the beginning, on a practical level, the Scandinavian Currency Union was a coinage union. Nevertheless, what started out as coinage union evolved and expanded in the forty years leading up to First World War. In 1881, a first move towards expanded activity took place when the 5 krone coin was introduced as the main coin.[66] However, the most important event took place in 1888, when Norges Bank entered into the agreement between the two other banks. They could draw on each others' newly established sight deposit accounts, without any fees or interest paid. The idea was to facilitate trade and reduce gold transport between the countries. A few years later, in 1897, a common Scandinavian cheque legislation was adopted.[67] Finally, in the beginning of the twentieth century, the three central banks agreed to accept each others' banknotes at parity. Accordingly, since 1901, the Scandinavian Currency Union has been referred to as a comprehensive payment system in the international literature on historical monetary systems and currency unions. The steadily increasing

[63] Stortingstidende 1875, 74–97, Storting's proceedings.

[64] On the currency union see, for example, Henriksen, Kærgård, and Sørensen, 'Den skandinaviske møntunion'; Nielsen, Den skandinaviske møntunion; Gjermund Forfang Rongved, 'Money Talks', in Scandinavia in the First World War, ed. Claes Ahlund (Nordic Academic Press, 2012); Talia, 'The Scandinavian Currency Union 1873–1924: Studies in Monetary Integration and Disintegration'.

[65] Axel Rubow, Nationalbankens Historie: 1878–1908, vol. 2 (I kommission hos Gyldendal, 1920), 113–15.

[66] Nevertheless, this only happened in Sweden.

[67] Henriksen, Kærgård, and Sørensen, 'Den skandinaviske møntunion', 91; Rygg, Norges Banks Historie, 2, 60.

integration has also led to the union being characterized as 'the most successful of all European currency unions' in subsequent literature.[68]

A few years later, the comprehensive system seemed to be short-lived. In June 1905, the Riksbank suddenly rescinded the agreement on fee-exempt drawings on the cooperating bank's accounts. The reason seems to have been that the Riksbank felt justified in receiving payment. The total amount increased considerably from 1888 onwards.[69] But again, not only was this agreement established to be used, the Riksbanken profited from it.[70] The true explanation can probably be found in the political arena; the Riksbank rescinded the agreement precisely a week after Norway left the personal union with Sweden.[71] This was, however, nothing more than a small slap in the face from the Swedish Riksbank. Before the end of September both Nationalbanken and Norges Bank had concluded new bilateral agreements with the Riksbank.[72]

The minor problems created around the dissolution of the Swedish-Norwegian union must be seen as an expression of the robustness of the currency union. The currency union obviously created a number of advantages for financial and economic life. An integrated money market was made, the need for expensive gold transport was minimized, and communication between the three banks steadily improved. It has also been pointed that an effect of the Scandinavian Currency Union was the establishment of a market for short-term financing.[73] A problem when evaluating the effects of the union is that it was created essentially to increase cross-border trade. Yet it is well known that trade between the Scandinavian countries actually diminished in the period.[74] This was to some extent acknowledged at the time, for example when the Riksbank terminated the agreement in 1905, even though the agreement was never blamed for the disappointing development in intra-Scandinavian trade.[75] It was widely believed that the union promoted trade, and consequently that the overall

---

[68] Robert J. Bartel, 'International Monetary Unions: The XIX-Century Experience', *The Journal of European Economic History* 3 (1974): 703. Also see Marcel de Cecco, 'European Monetary and Financial Cooperation before the First World War', *Rivista di storia economica* 9, no. 1–2 (1992), 67, where the Scandinavian Currency Union is referred to as 'the most successful of all European currency unions'. The basis of comparison is narrow. In addition to the Latin Monetary Union it is often only German-Austria in the period between 1857 and 1866 that is discussed in Bartel and de Cecco. Some others also set up national currency unions, such as the Italian Monetary Union from 1861 and that referred to as the currency union in the US from 1789, see Michael D. Bordo and Lars Jonung, 'The History of Monetary Regimes: Some Lessons for Sweden and the EMU', *Swedish Economic Policy Review* 4 (1997).

[69] Nielsen, *Den skandinaviske møntunion*, 54ff.; Henriksen, Kærgård, and Sørensen, 'Den skandinaviske møntunion', 93–4.

[70] This is based on monthly statistics for the period 1892–1905 in Norges Bank's accounts.

[71] See the letter from the Riksbank to Norges Bank 14 June 1905, in NB/DIR2/D/L0641. See material above in NB/DIR2/D/L0642.

[72] The maximum level of interest-free debt possible between the banks before being able to demand settlement in gold was set. The three banks were also given permission to receive payment if customer requested *anvisninger* (drawings) on one of the other banks. However, before the First World War broke out, the Riksbank never seized this opportunity.

[73] Øksendal, 'Essays in Norwegian Monetary History, 1869–1914'.

[74] Scandinavian trade did not decrease solely in real terms; it also declined as a share of the Scandinavian countries' foreign trade. Henriksen, Kærgård, and Sørensen, 'Den skandinaviske møntunion', 101–3.

[75] Talia, 'The Scandinavian Currency Union 1873–1924: Studies in Monetary Integration and Disintegration', 109–10.

trend was caused by other factors. The perceived success of the union explains the attempts to maintain it in the face of mounting difficulties during the First World War and the attempts to re-establish it during the interwar period.

The Global Gold Standard

The fact that the currency union was part of the international gold standard was possibly of far greater importance. What is regarded as the golden age for the classic gold standard, most of the forty-year period from around 1875 to the outbreak of the First World War, coincided with a period of rapid growth and prosperity in the Western world[76]—the second industrial revolution featuring iron, coal, and railroads, as well as tremendous technological advances. On the global level, Germany and the United States, thanks to innovation and large markets, were on the path to outcompeting the British. After many decades of social upheaval and harrowing wars, Europe entered a period of optimism and relative harmony, which was to be designated as *La Belle Époque* in France. The earlier national or regional labour markets turned global. Science not only brought new products and simplified production processes, it also facilitated communication between previously separated regions of the world.

Despite tendencies towards increased protectionism at the end of the century, the period was dominated by economic growth, expanding transnational businesses, and an emerging, global big capitalism. One can object that the highly positive view of the classic gold standard—especially seen in the context of the crisis-ridden interwar years—was in many ways an effect of the general developments in *La Belle Époque*. There was certainly also an interaction in which the global monetary regime contributed to growth and trade by tying all the gold currencies together, thus simplifying investments, money transfers, and trade transactions.

A period of exceptional growth also occurred in Norway, especially after independence from Sweden was gained in 1905. Much was based on the recent establishment of the new electrochemical industry. But this is also a story of globalization; a country poor in capital was dependent on foreign investment. Especially from the mid-1870s and in the beginning of the new century, Norway had accumulated foreign debt in order to finance communications and railways.[77] Foreign investment and government borrowed funds mainly came from the big countries in the gold standard core: France, Great Britain, and Germany.[78] Investments were made in Norway mainly because

---

[76] See for example Foreman-Peck, *A History of the World Economy*; or the first part of Stephen Broadberry and Kevin O'Rourke, *The Cambridge Economic History of Modern Europe*, vol. 2 (Cambridge University Press, 2010).

[77] Øyvind Eitrheim and Lie Einar, *Noen riktig lange linjer: statens inntekter, utgifter og gjeld* (Finansdepartementet, 2014).

[78] Jan Tore Klovland, 'Monetary Aggregates in Norway 1819–2003', in *Historical Monetary Statistics for Norway 1819–2003*, ed. Øyvind Eitrheim and Norges Bank Skriftserie (Norges Bank, 2004), 102ff.; Rygg, *Norges Banks historie*, 2, 158, 329. Sweden also contributed with substantial foreign investments, in particular from the Wallenberg family, see for example Wilhelm Keilhau, *Det norske folks liv og historie i vår egen tid* (Aschehoug, 1938), 103ff.

investors saw the opportunity to make money. But there is reason to believe that both foreign investments and loans were made more accessible and on better terms thanks to Norway's joining the gold standard during the same period.

In the international economics history literature, the tie to gold is seen as a promise of a reliable and stable national economy, from the capital-exporting countries' perspective.[79] The fact that smaller, peripheral countries like Norway had maintained the gold regime and a stable monetary regime made it possible for them to attract capital to a much greater extent than countries outside of the gold standard system. Foreign investments were essential for Norwegian growth after the turn of the century. It can therefore be said that Norway's tie to gold up until the First World War made a contribution to the country's substantial economic expansion, in addition to the fixed exchange rates' positive effect on trade.

The management of Norges Bank's foreign exchange reserves also provides some information about the changes after 1873 (see Figure 4.1). As we recall, Norges Bank's foreign exchange reserves were, in the mid-century, held in Hamburg and Altona. An increasing share of the reserves were also held in Copenhagen, when the Danish capital was the link to these cities.[80] Hamburg and Altona were intermediate

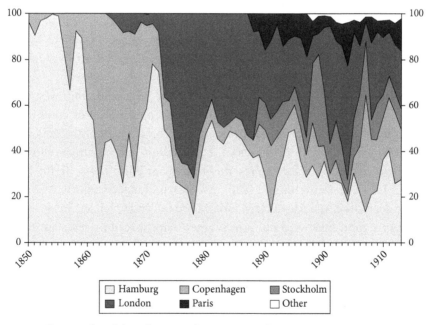

Figure 4.1 Geographical distribution of international reserves, 1850–1913, percentage shares

Source: Norges Bank's accounts, 1850–1913.

[79] Michael D Bordo and Hugh Rockoff, 'The Gold Standard as a "Good Housekeeping Seal of Approval"', *The Journal of Economic History* 56, no. 2 (1996).

[80] Above all, demand for the Danish daler in these cities resulted in the coin often being quoted at a premium. Thomas Johannessen Heftye, *Om Norges Myntcirkulation* (Cappelen, 1873); Rygg, *Norges Banks Historie*, 2, 76ff.

stations for most of the Norwegian transactions with the European continent, Russia, and South America.

After the transition to gold, a major change occurred. Abruptly, about half of the reserves were in sterling, placed with Norges Bank's commissioning agent in London. The share in Great Britain varied and decreased somewhat from the 1890s, and for many years the largest share of reserves were in Reichsmarks. Nevertheless, in a relative sense, western Europe grew more important between 1873 and 1914. This evolution not only illustrates that Norwegian foreign trade was gradually shifting westwards, but that Norges Bank operated using so-called reserve currencies, like many central banks, under the gold standard.[81] As during the time of silver, when Hamburg played a dominant role, the use of reserve currencies was a way of avoiding costly metal shipments and supporting trade interests.

However, gold was a scarcer resource than silver and more expensive to mobilize. Reserve currencies' tie rendered them highly convertible—they were, as the saying goes, 'good as gold'. It is not surprising that Norges Bank kept as much foreign currency as was permitted by the law, and even a little bit more, as it provided interest income. Norges Bank's currency reserves otherwise fall into an international pattern in which especially three currencies were important during the period, i.e. pounds sterling, Reichsmarks, and francs.[82] In the Norwegian context, the dominant British and German position is a consequence of these countries' crucial role in foreign trade. Between 1900 and 1913 more than 55 per cent, on average, of annual Norwegian imports came from these two countries, and they accounted for over half of the export market.[83]

An interesting parallel can be drawn between the geographic shift westward and the process of Norges Bank acquiring an increasing number of commissioning agents in other countries after the turn of the century. Not all of the holdings were large enough to be shown in the chart, but through new commissioning agents, Norges Bank extended its foreign reserves to more Swedish cities, Berlin, Helsinki, Brussels, Antwerp, Amsterdam, Milan, the Austro-Hungarian port city of Trieste, and even across the Atlantic to New York, Montreal, and Quebec. The development is not only a good illustration of how Norges Bank spread its reserves in parallel with the geographic expansion of Norwegian trade, but also reflects the rise in world trade.

In light of the relatively broad discussion of the extent of central bank cooperation before the First World War,[84] it is interesting to note that Norges Bank's dealings with countries like Germany, France, Great Britain, the Netherlands, and Italy were done directly with larger financial institutions in these countries, without the involvement

---

[81] Foreman-Peck, *A History of the World Economy*, 162–4.
[82] Ibid.   [83] Based on calculations from SSB 1968, charts 164 and 165.
[84] See for example Barry Eichengreen, *Gold Fetters: The Gold Standard and the Great Depression 1919–1939* (Oxford University Press, 1995); Marc Flandreau, 'Central Bank Cooperation in Historical Perpsectives: A Sceptical View', *Economic History Review* 50, no. 4 (1997); Kenneth Mouré, *The Gold Standard Illusion* (Oxford University Press, 2009).

of central banks. Furthermore, archive material does not reveal any form of direct contact between Norges Bank and central banks outside of Scandinavia before or during the First World War, and very limited contact in the interwar period. Rather than the Reichsbank, Banque de France, and Bank of England, Norges Bank's business relations were with Behrens & Söhne, Crédit Lyonnais, and C.J Hambro & Son.[85]

Norges Bank in the International System

Norges Bank was already part of an international finance system around the mid-1800s. The changes from the 1870s still ushered in something new. The most important trading partners used the same system, national and international banking evolved considerably during the period, and international trade expanded rapidly.

For Norges Bank, the currency union was important especially because it created an early, active framework for central bank cooperation. Yet its implications for economic development and integration should not be exaggerated, even though trade costs would certainly have been higher without the change in coin metal base in 1873, and shortly after with the simplified calculation method using the decimal system. But the choice of metal standard was, viewed in isolation, probably of greater importance than the union in the long term.

Even though the union contributed to drawing Norges Bank closer into broader global discussions, the bank was barely involved in the discussions about metal standards and cooperation. It was through the efforts of a number of experts and professor-politicians, foremost among them Ole Jacob Broch, that the big coin issue was brought to the table. The desire for common standards and measure was strong, driven forward and inspired by a broader enthusiasm for standardization. The currency union was born out of all this grand thinking; successful, but so limited that the greatest supporter of standardization, Broch, turned his back on it in the first rounds of discussions. During later international congresses in 1878 and 1881, Broch was once again asked to represent Norway, despite his international position as a leader of the International Institute of Weights and Measures in Paris. The belief in a universal coin had now definitively wilted, and Broch's contribution was, symptomatically enough, to argue in favour of a further study of a pure gold standard. However, Norges Bank played a limited role in the process of driving forth a new, Norwegian coin system. The leaders, lacking in expertise, consisting of practical men selected from among Trondheim's middle-class businessmen, did not dare venture into the scientific, international discussions on the system choice.

Norges Bank expanded to a large extent its international network through the Scandinavian Currency Union, especially after 1905. By keeping large metal reserves

---

[85] This is based on an overview of Norges Bank's communication throughout the period, see DIR 1/D, NB, including that which appears throughout the archives as Norges Bank's lack of communication with the central bank outside of Scandinavia before the First World War.

abroad, the bank facilitated trade and finance for internationally oriented Norwegian business. Still, Norges Bank's contact with other central banks were meagre, and basically Nordic. In this respect, Norges Bank's global network was still marked by the same relations one could expect to find in a big bank in a small, peripheral economy, but supplemented by closer contact and agreements on the conversion of notes and coins with the central banks in neighbouring countries within their regional currency union.

5

A Bankers' Bank

In 1892, the Storting passed a law that superseded all former laws pertaining to Norges Bank. As with the bank's foundations of 1816, the 1892 act reflected its era and responded to the perceptions and needs of that period. The new law facilitated the transformation of the regionalized bank of issue into an institution more closely resembling central banks elsewhere. Discussions on the legal framework were held with varying intensity from the 1870s and onwards. Three conditions, in particular, influenced the process and the final character of the law.

The first is the international context the law itself was a part of. Norges Bank's evolution brings to mind the development of comparable institutions in other countries. Similar challenges tend to engender similar solutions. Also, examples from abroad were actively used in preparations and debates as finished models that could be applied, rejected, or adjusted. The term 'central bank' began appearing in various Norwegian sources at the time, with references made to foreign models. The framers of the new law followed world affairs. Whether the leadership at Norges Bank did the same is unknown. As during work on the gold standard and the monetary reform, the way was paved by intellectuals and politicians in the capital. Norges Bank's response was specific, detail-oriented, and resistant to change. If the regionalized leadership at the bank was informed about organizational structures of comparable institutions elsewhere in the world, these seem, for a long time, to have made no great impression.

The second condition was the integration and centralization process already underway in Norway. Norwegian regions were still directly linked to foreign markets in trade and finance. With steamship lanes, channels, telegraph lines, and the railway, national market integration became more effective and self-perpetuating, with the capital as the central hub. A national economy was underway. In 1892 there were forty-seven commercial banks and 362 savings banks.[1] In practice, they were all oriented towards locally delimited markets. As a formal institution, Norges Bank was present throughout the whole country. However, Norges Bank was an association of small banks, each with its separate management and discount rate, and with considerable decision-making autonomy. Would this situation prevail?

The third significant condition is the conflict between the government authorities that, as shown in Chapter 4, framed Norway's entry into the Scandinavian Currency Union. The resolution establishing Norges Bank in 1816 had created a strong

---

[1] Øyvind Eitrheim, Jan Tore Klovland, and Jan F. Qvigstad (ed.): Historical Monetary Statistics for Norway 1819-2003', *Norges Bank's Occasional Papers*, no. 35 (2004).

Norges Bank 1816–2016. Einar Lie, Oxford University Press (2020). © Norges Bank.
DOI: 10.1093/oso/9780198860013.001.0001

connection to the Storting. This was partly to protect against the executive power and the Swedish krone, but also a consequence of the forced subscription with which the bank had been created. When a new legislation in line with foreign models was prepared, the time might have come to give some of the Storting's control over Norges Bank to the government. However, the political context surrounding the legislative work limited the will to pass control of the bank to the executive power considerably.

Gold Reserves and Note Reserves in an Expanding State

In the decades before the new act of 1892 was prepared, the regulations around metal coverages and note issuing were frequently discussed. Earlier, we observed how legislative amendments during the 1800s gave Norges Bank the right to lend an increasing number of notes on the basis of the bank's silver reserves. However, after 1857, the bank chose not to use the maximum scope for lending, instead keeping a considerable reserve of banknotes. This provided a flexibility from the constraints of the metal standard that would prove important. As the bank also shifted its lending practice towards discounting, interest rate setting could now be used more efficiently to regulate the flow of liquidity to the business sector.

The new-found flexibility should not be overemphasized, however. The so-called strangulation mechanism of the metal standard—described in the classic literature from David Hume and onwards, and briefly and critically summarized as 'the rules of the game' by J.M. Keynes in 1925[2]—became apparent during periods of difficult times and pressure on the gold reserves. This was especially true in the demanding 1870s, with a boom in the early decade and the subsequent setback that hit in 1877–8. Eitrheim, Klovland, and Øksendal (2016) have compared the Scandinavian banks of issue interest rate setting from 1870 to 1892, and show how Norges Bank's rate setting had a somewhat greater impact than that of Sweden's Riksbank and Nationalbanken in Denmark. In the 1870s, interest rates were relatively low during the boom, and they were set at a higher level when the downturn hit and gold reserves were diminished and had to be protected. Nevertheless, the degree of tightening was limited in that Norges Bank provided credit throughout this phase of the downturn.[3]

The continued lending was made possible by government's ongoing and extensive import of capital. In the second half of the nineteenth century, the state took up long-term loans in order to finance large investments in infrastructure, especially railways. A relatively strict fiscal discipline was maintained at the same time. Detailed overviews were drawn up on how government revenues should be structured over time to service the loans. Customs revenues bore the brunt of the burden. When import and customs revenues fell after 1876, government spending was quickly adapted to the new revenue level.[4] In this situation, the government was left with sizeable foreign

---

[2] Barry Eichengreen, *The Gold Standard in Theory and History* (Psychology Press, 1997), 14.
[3] Øyvind Eitrheim, Jan Tore Klovland, and Lars Fredrik Øksendal, *A Monetary History of Norway, 1816–2016* (Cambridge University Press, 2016), 199–201.
[4] Fritz Hodne, 'Norsk økonomisk historie 1815–1970', *Oslo, Norway: Cappelen* (1981), 281.

loans that were not converted to investment activity. At this point, Norges Bank's gold reserves were decimated, and the bank was on the verge of having to tighten credit severely. The foreign loan was exchanged into gold that was temporarily transferred to Norges Bank. This was kept on the bank's accounts, providing greater legal leeway for discounting during the crisis. Altogether, the process became a coherent operation, in which the government's direct spending was reduced at the same time as the pressure on Norges Bank's ability to supply liquidity was alleviated.

Much of the discussion around new bank legislation was centred on the metal-backing requirements and the bank's ability to supply credit under varying economic conditions. This is a complex and somewhat technical subject, but underlying the technicalities were decisive differences in principles and interests on monetary and credit policy. The numerous and intense debates between the two professor-politicians, Schweigaard and Broch, in the 1850s and 1860s and prior to the official legal debate, are an instructive introduction to the subject. This is because both participants wanted clear mechanisms for note issuance, and formulated their principles and positions explicitly. As described earlier, Schweigaard became a key actor behind the law revisions of the 1840s and 1850s. He wanted to move away from collateralized lending and turn Norges Bank into a more efficient tool for supplying business activities with short-term credit. Broch fully agreed with him on this point.

However, Schweigaard was a firm believer in the so-called proportionality principle, which Norges Bank had pursued from the beginning. This implied that the number of notes should be proportional to the gold reserves. Schweigaard had supported an increase in the ratio from 2:1 to 5:2, and the issuance of notes against the reserve fund using a proportionality principle. This provided room for note and credit expansion as the possibilities to increase the metal reserves were utilized. For Schweigaard, this was an advantageous instrument for the development of economic activity and society as a whole.

'Schweigaard [...] thinks good years still lie ahead, and that conditions will constantly improve', Broch explained, who contemptuously characterized his colleague, a sworn proponent of a metallistic view of money, as a 'money creator'.[5] Nevertheless, Broch did not primarily criticize the total volume of notes. His criticism was essentially linked to the metal standard's tightening mechanism. This mechanism had a strong impact when the volume of banknotes needed to be reduced overproportionally when gold reserves declined. Broch affirmed that the Bank of England's cover rules, as regulated in the Peel Banking Act of 1844, was better suited to handle cyclical fluctuations, which it was the bank of issue's job to smooth, rather than amplify.[6] In addition to volume of notes entirely covered by the gold reserves, one could operate with a quota of notes within a clearly fixed limit. The quota would normally be met in good periods, and could be reduced when liquidity problems appeared. And if the

---

[5] Jens Arup Seip, *Ole Jacob Broch og hans samtid* (Gyldendal, 1971), 191.
[6] This system is described in detail in J. Keith Horsefield, 'The Origins of the Bank Charter Act, 1844', *Economica* 11, no. 44 (1944).

quota was exhausted, a system without a high proportionality factor between notes and gold would result in less tightening than under the existing system.

Schweigaard's arguments in favour of a large and growing volume of banknotes gained strong support among the emerging popular opposition in the Storting—more so than Broch's, who apparently benefited from the support of the merchant middle class. Their access to discounting was more strongly reduced than others, when the volume of banknotes had to be limited, according to given proportionalities in the system. In 1863, during a particularly fiery Storting debate on law revisions, Broch and Schweigaard were the only two speakers who took the floor—Broch six times and Schweigaard eight—steadily raising their voices while waiving scholarly papers in the air.[7]

The proportionality system was, on that appeal, retained by the Storting. Banknote reserves involved costs. Under the interest rate regulation regime, the credit-hungry public had, with strong spokesmen among elected representatives, a tendency to perceive any bank note reserve as wasted bank credit. It is symptomatic that Broch's support seems to have come from the merchant class—who had access to long-term credit from multiple sources, but feared severe credit contractions with a higher interest rate on discounting during periods of crisis. A defeated Broch found comfort in the fact that he received support from a highly respected Storting representative, the civil servant Henrik Helliesen. We shall return to Helliesen later, as he became minister of finance shortly thereafter, remaining so for twenty years and overseeing much of the preparatory legislative work.

A cover system, indirectly introducing elements of a hybrid solution, was established by resolution, early in the 1870s. The system had a complex character—which might explain why the experts Schweigaard and Broch were the only speakers during the debate. It has earlier been mentioned that Norges Bank could, from 1857, issue banknotes on the reserve fund and the extra fund at a ratio of 3:2—the latter fund was established as a consequence of Norges Bank's obligation to issue banknotes against precious metal. In 1873—a year characterized by a boom and relatively reassuring reserves—access was reduced. Now the extra fund could only exchange banknotes against gold at a ratio of 1:1. At this point, the banknote cover system took on a more mixed aspect. As long as one had an extra fund, the gold tapping would only reduce the volume of banknotes by the same amount. However, when the extra fund was empty, one began to draw from the ordinary metal fund. Consequently, the volume of banknotes had to be reduced at a 5:2 ratio.[8]

Legislative Work in a Period Marked by Political Party Conflict

The 1814 constitution established a constitutional triangle in Norway.[9] The state had a parliament and an independent royal authority, but also a government. During the

[7] Seip, *Ole Jacob Broch og hans samtid.*
[8] Rygg, *Norges Banks historie,* 2 (Emil Moestue, 1954), 119.
[9] Jens Arup Seip, *Utsikt over Norges historie,* vol. 1 (Gyldendal Norsk Forlag, 1974), 69–85.

1800s, the government had brought the personal royal authority under their control. By 1870, the government, now a virtually self-recruiting body, administered the independent executive government authority. As mentioned in the discussion on the coin issue, the principal question in Norwegian politics, from the early 1870s and onwards, became whether or not the government should have such independence or be accountable to the Storting. The question polarized the Storting in an unprecedented manner, and the representatives eventually divided into two groups, liberals and conservatives, remaining so even after the Storting opposition (Liberal Party) brought down the government by impeachment in 1884.

The Liberal Party ('Venstre') was a coalition maintained by the desire to bring the government under Storting control, and became victorious in 1884 with the introduction of the principle of parliamentarian-based executive power. The Conservative Party ('Høyre') was a proponent of the principle of separation of power, as framed in the constitution. At the same time, the party represented the old merchant and administration elites—present in Norges Bank's many branches. This explains why, at the beginning of the 1870s, the representatives that critically engaged the discussion with Norges Bank were those who were Liberal-oriented. In 1876, the Storting asked the government to examine a law revision.[10] The Ministry of Finance took the opportunity to suggest a modification of the banknote cover rules. The finance minister, Henrik Helliesen, who had applauded Broch when he lost the debate on banknote cover in the early 1870s, pointed to the shortcomings of the hybrid solution described above. The system can be said 'to combine the shortcomings of both systems rather than their advantages', Helliesen summarized when addressing the Storting.

Three global models could be drawn on to design a new system. The French model was to give the bank of issue free hands, as long as the bank could always exchange banknotes into gold if the banknote owners so desired. On a theoretical level, this was considered by everyone involved in the reform to be the best system. However, no one dared to suggest the French model be adopted in Norway. The ministry wrote that the public considered having a clear *rule* for banknote issuance as an important security.

The Bank of England's system has already been mentioned: here a volume of banknotes was set that could be circulated without having gold in reserves, with the value of banknotes upheld by confidence in the system as a whole. For each banknote above this set volume, the central bank had to hold a corresponding quantity of gold in reserve. Advocates of this system placed emphasis on the fact that keeping a reserve offered flexibility. This is true, of course, but it presupposed that the reserves were actually in place. In England, during critical situations after 1844, Parliament had to grant the Bank of England permission to go beyond the set limits in order to meet sudden liquidity needs.

---

[10] Stortingstidende 1876, 561, Storting's proceedings.

Eventually a third model appeared: the German Bank Act of 1875.[11] The central bank could exceed its banknote issuance right temporarily by paying a levy to the government. Consequently, extraordinary events could be handled with flexibility. At the same time, if the levy was high enough, the bank would be deterred from printing and lending banknotes in excess for its own benefit. The ministry now proposed a transition towards a largely British system, combined with the German safety valve. In addition, the ministry wanted to place a full-time governor at the summit of the central bank. It was unreasonable for the central bank to be run less professionally than most of the country's commercial banks. Besides, Helliesen wanted to move away from a regional bank system where each branch could set its own interest rate—there would be only one discount rate at Norges Bank.

Norges Bank's Executive Board reacted conservatively. Apart from the safety valve, which was perceived as an improvement, the proposal was frowned upon. The leadership wanted neither a system with a fixed banknote quota nor a centrally set discount rate as proposed by the ministry. The main reason was simply that the existing system had served the country and the bank well. The mechanism is hardly enigmatic. The five members of the board were all between sixty-one and sixty-five years of age. Three of them had been members for about twenty years.

Otherwise, conservatism among Trondheim's older gentlemen went beyond purely organizational and business-related conditions. In Chapter 3, we pointed to how modern communication, first via the telegraph, modified the financial market's character through the rapid spread of news and rumours, increasing demands for swift decisions. Nevertheless, Norges Bank's board in Trondheim refused to go with the tide. Throughout the 1860s, branches rejected the approval of telegraphic requests for liquidity transfers to big banks (those big banks were based on telegraphy) until requests in traditional letter form was submitted. In 1864, the board supported this policy as a principle. When the matter was brought before the highest body, the Supervisory Council, it was divided with five against five, and the decision not to transfer by telegraph was chosen by lot (one exception was made for telegrams sent by the Ministry of Finance). Only in 1888 did the board approve the use of telegraphy at Norges Bank. Around this time a discussion was also taking place concerning the use of a new device, the telephone. Alexander Graham Bell's new invention in 1876 quickly arrived in modernization-friendly Norway. The apparatus was demonstrated in Bergen, Drammen, and Kristiania in 1877. In 1880, the International Bell Telephone Company entered the Norwegian market, and switchboards were rapidly set up.[12] However, in 1882, the Kristiansand branch's request for the purchase of a telephone was rejected. In 1891, when a new inquiry was made from the northern city of Bodø, the board explained that it did not find it to be appropriate to install telephones on the bank's premises.[13]

---

[11] Paul McGouldrick, 'Operations of the German Central Bank and the Rules of the Game, 1879–1913', in *A Retrospective on the Classical Gold Standard, 1821–1931* (University of Chicago Press, 1984).

[12] Ibid.; Evert Bistrop, *Oslotelefonen 1880–1985* (Oslo Teledistrikt, 1990).

[13] Rygg, *Norges Banks historie*, 2, 27–8.

Finance Minister Henrik Helliesen was unconvinced by the Executive Board's objections to the legislative proposals presented. In 1882, he endorsed a bill of law that essentially followed the draft, but also emphasized the bank's structure as a privately owned corporation. The proposal gave private shareholders owning shares of at least 1,000 kroner the right to choose six of the fifteen members of the Supervisory Council. Abroad, the shareholders in privately owned banks of issue often had a certain influence. Helliesen also referred to a request made by a group of shareholders the year before.

This was also the opportunity for Helliesen to limit the Storting's power over the bank. According to the proposal, government was now to appoint three of the members of the Supervisory Council. If Helliesen's proposal was adopted, the main shareholders and government would together be given the right to appoint a majority of the council's members, which would then have greater powers. They were to hire a full-time director and choose one of the other four. Furthermore, the council was to choose one of the three in charge of various regional branches. Other bank officials would still be chosen by the Storting.

The Storting blankly rejected Helliesen's configuration. Indeed, they refused to even take the proposal into account. Instead it was expected that the ministry would now submit a codification proposal in accordance with the Storting's will.[14] The finance minister must have understood that this would be the outcome. Two conflicting views now reigned in the Storting, and the issue would remain unresolved until 1884.

The Liberal Party Tightens its Grip on Government and Norges Bank

With the Liberal Party's overall victory in 1884, Helliesen and his cabinet colleagues lost their positions. The Liberal Party took over the government during that summer. Only a few days later, the Liberal majority at the Storting implemented a large replacement of elected officials at Norges Bank. The process had been introduced in 1881; now it went further and all the way to the top. The bank appointments included eighty-six names. A rather bitter representative from the Conservative Party concluded that no sure conservative could be counted among those who had been replaced.[15] The Storting majority placed three new people on the bank's board. Their academic expertise was indisputable, but they were all liberals, and they brought notable rejuvenation. The oldest, a Supreme Court lawyer, was fifty years old, and the two others were in their forties. A few years later, Karl Gether Bomhoff, a factory owner, was one of youngest appointed when he became governor of the reformed Norges Bank, a position he held until 1920.

---

[14] Stortingtidende 1882, 571–5, Storting's proceedings.
[15] Stortingstidende,1884, 731, Storting's proceedings.

The substitution of bank representatives was not solely a political act. All throughout its existence, through its many branches, Norges Bank had been deeply infiltrated into the local elites' complicated interaction. Therefore, within several of the branches, a good amount of behind-the-scenes crafting had been performed. The locally elected civil servants were often linked to loan applicants in their region, either through kinship, friendship, or business interests. This was accentuated by the existing rules giving certain districts and old depositors an advantage in obtaining loans. The original depositors had departed a long time ago, but references made to this privilege still reappeared in the preparatory work, as a normative tie that needed to be severed. The close local connections, strengthened by the generally long civil servant mandate, made it difficult to refuse to discount a bill of exchange, which in practice meant granting a medium-term loan against nominal security alone. The consequences were exposed to the public in the years preceding the adoption of the new law. Between 1870 and 1889, Norges Bank had to write off just over 3.9 million kroner as losses from their discounting business. Towards the end of the 1880s, substantial sums were involved, as the bank's gold reserves amounted to 40 million kroner.

A number of small and medium-sized branches suffered the greatest losses. Well-secured loans were safe, but the discounting business oriented towards businesses in crisis had suffered large losses. The northern city of Tromsø found itself in the worst situation, with truly threatening losses on loans that were not secured on property. Double-digit percentage points in losses on such loans had to be recorded at other branches too. The head office in Trondheim had lost 5 per cent, while the Kristiania branch had lost 1 per cent. In the city of Lillehammer such loans hardly involved any losses at all.[16]

Large variations could be seen, and the head office had virtually no influence over credit provision by the other branches. The bank's organizational set-up had made few provisions for board control. In many places, the losses were due to poor banking, but some loans were also granted to a small circle of acquaintances. In one incident, prosecution authorities were informed of the credit scheme, but they refused to take it to court. The large losses and lack of control drew substantial public attention and were discussed at the fiscally prudent Storting, which devoted substantial time to working on monetary matters, especially when there was suspicion of mismanagement of government funds.

The long-term consequence of the impeachment in 1884 must have been reasonably obvious, although developing the constitutional consequences was a lengthy process. Government could only conduct policies with the overall approval of the Storting. On the other hand, government needed enough room to manoeuvre. The implications for the organization of Norges Bank were unclear. If the government was

---

[16] According to a series of newspaper articles in *Morgenbladet* in April and May 1889 (nos. 194, 200, 202, 217, 230, 233, 235, 240, 243, 245, 247). The articles were not signed but Rygg ascribes them to Prof. Torkel Aschehoug, cf. Rygg, *Norges Banks historie*, 2, 133–5.

now, per definition, dependent on the Storting's support and confidence, perhaps government could be given a stronger and more direct role in overseeing Norges Bank.

In November 1884, the government set up a commission chaired by the leader of the Liberal Party at the Storting. The commission, set to propose a new act on Norges Bank, was composed of a majority of active liberals. Its report was presented in 1886, and included much of Helliesen's work on updating the bank's monetary policy tools. The cover rules proposal based on the British model was adopted. Further discussions did not take place. Relevant to this may have been that Schweigaard, the towering political and theoretical authority, as well as the number one advocate of the proportionality principle, had forsaken his earthly existence a long time ago, leaving monetary policy debates behind.

The commission was fundamentally sceptical to the idea of returning to a more private bank model. The commission concluded, correctly, that the original idea of a private bank was a consequence of the 1816 men's fear of government abuse of the bank of issue. By 1886, such fears had dissipated. Given the colour of the party in the commission, that is not surprising. In 1884, the Liberal Party had taken control over both the bank and government, and the commission was aiming for a government takeover of the bank, of one kind or another, some time in the future.[17]

Norges Bank's Executive Board, which drafted the commission's consultation response in 1887, included four liberals. They were apparently more change-oriented than their predecessors, but they were at least as preoccupied with defending the bank's independence. The liberal-dominated board agreed with essential elements of the proposal made by government, some years earlier. The Executive Board affirmed that the commission's proposal for government to appoint the head of the Executive Board was unfortunate; then one could experience that 'the governor might lack the desperately needed firmness vis-à-vis government'.[18] The central bank and government were, and should be, two different and clearly separate bodies. On one of the more sensitive topics, for instance, they felt the position of governor should be appointed by the Supervisory Council, and not by any political body.

A Central Bank?

The process of establishing the new law dragged out. The Storting obviously felt no urgency, and the matter was deferred at several Storting sessions. In Sweden, legislative work advanced just as slowly. New and extensive legislation on the Riksbank was not adopted until 1897. It had then been the subject of numerous studies and debates since work began in the early 1880s.

---

[17] 'Indstilling fra den ved Kongelig Resolution af 6te December 1884 til Revision af Lovgivningen om Norges Bank nedsatte Kommission', 14, jf s. 13.
[18] Ot. prp. no. 8, App. 34, 1988, Storting's proceedings.

The Liberal government in Norway was replaced in 1889. The new finance minister from the Conservative Party, Evald Rygh—a lawyer, mayor of Kristiania, and later governor of Kristiania Savings Bank—was thus able to present the Storting with a new law proposal on Norges Bank. The finance minister made a statement asserting that the time had come for new requirements.[19] With reference to the bank's historical context, Rygh declared that the issuance of long-term mortgage loans must cease entirely. During the bank's early years, such loans had been necessary, both politically and financially. Those times had now passed. The public had alternative sources of loans. Shareholders could no longer claim they had specific demands on loans from the bank. Instead, Norges Bank needed to embrace a new role as the bank of banks. By doing so it could also regulate the economy. The regulatory function was the 'Central Bank's most important' task, Rygh explained. The commission report had also employed the term 'the Central Bank'. However, this failed to prevail as a dominant term for Norges Bank's role. In this context, it is interesting to note how, already in 1889, a series of commercial banks outside of Kristiania could merge, and as a coalition, establish an institution called the 'Central Bank for Norway'.

The finance minister's reasoning implied that Norges Bank should withdraw from direct contact with the business sector, apart from the banks. Norges Bank should guarantee the banks' liquidity. Combined, this would produce a twofold effect. The banks would be able to exploit their capital more efficiently if they had the assurance of Norges Bank's permanent liquidity support—and hence, Norges Bank could become a regulator of the economy.

Norges Bank would always be tied by its obligation to exchange banknotes for gold at par value, but had some room for action within this fixed-rate regime room for action. If Norges Bank judged economic activity to be excessive, the central bank could raise the discount rate. Consequently, the price of liquidity would increase. The banks would then limit their lending directly, hoping to avoid Norges Bank's support for rediscounting or forced price increases on their loans. This was the approach used by France and England's emerging central banks, but was new concept in Norway. Traditionally, Norges Bank had been a bank among banks, not a bankers' bank.

This does not mean Norges Bank was far behind in its policy approach. A striking parallel can be observed between Norway and Sweden, an expression of the direct influence these two countries had on one another. In 1886, the extensive Norwegian report referred to a Swedish counterpart, produced three years earlier. Long passages were translated word for word, and overall the Norwegian report adopted the Swedish model.[20] The Swedish banknote and central bank history clearly differ from Norway's, in that Sweden had a more developed financial sector and private banking system, the Riksbank did not have a monopoly on banknote issuance, and Sweden had a well-established financial elite. It is no coincidence that when Norwegian and Swedish

---

[19] Rygh in the Proceedings in Odelstinget 1890, 200–5, Storting's proceedings.
[20] *Indstilling fra den ved Kongelig Resolution af 6te December 1884 til Revision af Lovgivningen om Norges Bank nedsatte Kommission*, 20f.; cf. Gunnar Wetterberg, *Pengarna och makten: Riksbankens historia* (Atlantis, 2009).

governments chose emissaries to discuss the gold standard and a universal coin, Norway sent civil servant and professor-politician Broch, while the Swedes sent A.O. Wallenberg, a banker and politician—but mainly a banker.[21]

The Riksbank was also engaged in direct lending. The Swedish reform gave the Riksbank a monopoly on banknote issuance, and reduced the Riksbank's direct contact with the public.[22] A clear parallel existed between the manner in which the banks of issue were to be established, as a central, coordinated institution: a bankers' bank.

The Act of 1892

In 1892, a new act finally saw the light. The bank's right to issue notes was subjected to a quota system, and a new safety valve was created legislatively. If Norges Bank exceeded the note-issuing right, the bank had to immediately explain its reasons to the Ministry of Finance, and correct the ratio by the end of the following month. Moreover, the bank was to pay a 6 per cent annual fee on the excess to government.

Norges Bank remained a joint-stock company, and the rules for income distribution and dividend payment were revised and clarified. Of the bank's future profits, 6 per cent of nominal share value, after operating expenses and loss provisions, was first to be paid to shareholders. The remainder was then to be transferred to the reserve fund, the state, and shareholders. Against its will and without compensation, Norges Bank became the government's cashier. Paragraph 19 obliged the bank to take over government money transactions, 'albeit without advance payment', as specified. What did this addendum imply? At the very minimum it implied that the government could not overdraw its accounts in Norges Bank. Another interpretation could be that Norges Bank was not permitted to lend money to the government. An initial premise was that Norges Bank should not be a tool for funding the government. In certain situations, this provision was not given a strict interpretation, however.[23] As we shall see in Chapter 6, during the Great War, twenty years later, interpretations and truths with regard to the paragraph's real implications came under strong pressure.

The law clearly weakened the regional guarantees that had built the foundation. The removal of the branches' right to set their own discount rate was the most significant element. This authority now lay with the head office, and the bank's internal rules gave the responsibility to the Executive Board.[24] The bank's highest body was still the Supervisory Council, which was now transformed into a country representation. The idea was that when one removed the regional legislative guarantees, one needed to compensate by giving the whole country influence over the board.

---

[21] Krim Talia, *The Scandinavian Currency Union 1873–1924: Studies in Monetary Integration and Disintegration* (Economic Research Institute at the Stockholm School of Economics, 2004), 234–6.

[22] Wetterberg, *Pengarna och makten: Riksbankens historia*, 236–9.

[23] As explained in Chapter 4, the government had borrowed from Norges Bank in 1828, under special circumstances. Around 1830 Stortinget had at several occasions given the government a proxy to borrow in Norges Bank, at ordinary commercial conditions. *Storthings-Efterretninger 1814–1833*, vol. 3, 467.

[24] Cf. 'Reglement for Norges Bank', printed as appendix 3 til Dokument No. 50, Storting's proceedings 1893.

Nevertheless, as in the past, the Storting would choose all the bank's trustees directly, with one exception.

The strengthening of the board, personified by an appointed governor, was the most important practical consequence of the law. Formally, the new chairman of the board was at the same level as other governors. With powers to prepare matters for Executive Board meetings and conduct daily business, he rapidly became the head office's dominant figure. The position still held only one out of five votes in the board meetings, and neither the whole board nor he would gain automatic control over the branch network's credit provision.

Government would appoint the head of the board in consultation with the Supervisory Council. As long as Norges Bank remained a limited company, the governor could not be considered a civil servant. A fixed limit for employment conditions was not specified. On the contrary, he could be dismissed with a notice of six months or be immediately removed against severance pay, as specified by law. Thus, the position relied on government trust. On the other hand, such a removal would be a highly drastic step—and it was never taken. The 1892 act thus created a position for an independent central bank governor, including a salary in accordance with the responsibility involved.

Various parameters have been used to discuss 'central bank independence', historically and in our time: whether or not the bank can be instructed as to its interest rate setting or lending, who employs and dismisses the governor of the central bank, and the financial relationship between Norges Bank and the government—whether the state can instruct or pressure the bank to finance its activities. The last parameter came under pressure during the First World War. The first, not until new politicians and economists established the low interest rate policy as a permanent dogma after the Second World War. During the 1890s, alternative solutions were not seriously considered, apart from the idea that Norges Bank should set the interest rate on its loans, determine the terms and conditions for extending loans, and engage in lending without external interference.

Why not? Explaining the absence of a theme is always more difficult than explaining its presence. Considering the general political and administrative context, the idea that government should intervene in daily decisions seems out of place. Academic expertise played an important role in Norwegian administration and politics. The frequent presence of central professor-politicians was an expression of this under a civil service government. But academic expertise also played a notable role in public administration at later times, especially in entirely or partly independent agencies exercising authority within health, education, transport, agriculture, and much else. Various formal and normative limits on areas of government intervention also applied in those areas. Admittedly, Norges Bank, in a formal sense, was another type of business. Norges Bank was a limited company with a large number of private owners and its own executive management body and legislation, not an agency. Nevertheless, this would tend to strengthen the arguments in favour of institutional autonomy rather than weaken them. The bank's entire organization was structured to give it ample ability to make professionally sound decisions (executive management) with its own control body (the Supervisory Council). It must have seemed almost unfathomable that this type of framework could allow government to intervene in the bank's business, such as interest rate setting. The best and most relevant expertise was considered to be found in Norges Bank, not in the ministries.

One matter remains. In 1892, relocation of the head office to Kristiania became too much for a Storting sceptical towards centralization. After much debate, it was decided to keep the office in Trondheim. A new round followed in 1896, when what amounted to a backbencher proposal was adopted with the lowest possible margin—it was carried by one vote in the second round.[25] The weight of the capital had finally tipped the scales. From 1897, the head office was located in Kristiania, but the governor of Norges Bank was the same as in 1893.

Employment Requires Professional Expertise

During the years of its breakthrough, the Liberal Party's majority resulted in their men occupying all vacant positions appointed by the Storting. The tradition would soon become that positions were to reflect various parties' parliamentarian strength. Professionalism was of course a preferable quality in those elected, but for employees, it had to be an unconditional requirement. But what professional qualities should be required of the governor of Norges Bank?

There were three applicants for consideration when the Liberal government was to appoint the country's first central bank governor in 1892: head of office Groot from the Privatbanken in Copenhagen, the Conservative Party's former finance minister, Evald Rygh, and Karl Gether Bomhoff. As mentioned, Bomhoff had been appointed to Norges Bank's board by the Liberal Party majority in 1884. He was re-elected by the Storting six years later.[26] In 1892, the remaining board members, certainly not all of them Liberals, encouraged Bomhoff to apply. The Supervisory Council was divided in its advice to the government. Nine were in favour of Bomhoff, and five in favour of Rygh. The rather unknown Groot was not taken into account.[27]

Bomhoff and Rygh were of the same age, but had chosen different paths. Rygh had the classical background for a leader in the 1800s: a law degree, which was also the closest you could get to a degree in economics at the time (basic economics was part of their curriculum). He had benefited from a stipend to study economics in France and England, and had civil service experience in the Ministry of Finance and the capital's municipal administration. In 1883, he was one of the drivers behind the

---

[25] Lars Fredrik Øksendal, *Trondhjem som hovedsete for Norges Bank—noen faktiske og kontrafaktiske betrakt-ninger*, Staff Memo No. 8 (Norges Bank, 2008).

[26] Stortingstidende 1890, 1924, 1928, Storting's proceedings.

[27] Information about the applicants and the following process in 'Dokumenter vedkommende Karl Gether Bomhoffs Ansættelse som Formand i Direktionen for Norges Bank', NAN, FD/FKC, D/Da/435, cf. also *Farmand* 1892, 469 (17.9).

establishment of an 'association of state economists' in Kristiania, which was intended to bring together the city's 'theoretical economists, personalities from the business sector and leaders of government business entities', to discuss subjects of common interest.[28] Bomhoff lived in Trondheim, and did not meet the members of the ministry in the 'association of state economists'. Nor was he a lawyer, but he had passed the pharmacist exam. While Rygh had studied economics abroad, Bomhoff had spent his years abroad studying and working in the field of pharmacy and chemistry. Rygh was a civil servant, Bomhoff a business entrepreneur and manager.

The government chose Bomhoff. The business newspaper *Farmand*, founded in 1891, perceived this as a party nomination, and affirmed that it was grossly unreasonable to spurn Rygh. *Farmand* is an interesting source. The weekly newspaper was written and run by Einar Sundt, who was son of Eilert Sundt, a cutting-edge statistician and social scientist during the mid-1800s.[29] The model was the British *Economist*, edited by Sundt's hero, Walter Bagehot, most famous for his book *Lombard Street*, a classic of central bank literature from 1873.

Rygh's publicly known vision for Norges Bank initially found favour with Sundt. After having travelled to Trondheim and participated in lengthy conversations with Bomhoff, Sundt flip-flopped and expressed absolute trust in the newly employed central bank governor.[30] The two would eventually develop a relationship of trust and confidence—which did not hinder *Farmand* from sharply criticizing Norges Bank in given situations. However, they had a mutual need for one another, especially in 1897, after the head office was moved to Kristiania. Bomhoff provided Sundt with information, while receiving a channel to the public through *Farmand*'s columns. With *Farmand* and Sundt the public economic arena was expanded and professionalized, and with Bomhoff Norges Bank became a more integral part of that arena.

Along with a new board and law, Norges Bank also gained a new self-perception. In the 1890s, the leadership considered Norges Bank to be the country's central bank, without employing that term. The annual report for the first year of operations under the new law delivered a clear message to the Storting.[31] The leadership defined a division of roles in the credit market. Norges Bank was not to engage in 'excessive competition' with the private banks, to which it certainly did not wish to be compared. It was acceptable to be in the market for direct lending to the business sector, but not to hold on to relative positions. Norges Bank was to be compared to other 'public banks of issue'.[32]

The Executive Board was now of the opinion that additional branches were not needed. Engaging in activities that private banks could perform just as efficiently would spread Norges Bank's energy unnecessarily. That idea was difficult to swallow

[28] Wilhelm Keilhau, 'Menn og tanker i Statsøkonomisk Forening', in *Den Statsøkonomiske Forening 1833–1933*, ed. Statsøkonomisk forening (Aschehoug, 1933), 33.

[29] Einar Lie, 'Statistical Thinking in Norway in the Nineteenth Century', *Scandinavian Economic History Review* 49, no. 1 (2001).

[30] *Farmand* 1892, 469 (17 September), 545 (29 October); *Farmand* 1893, 374 (15 July).

[31] The annual report. Printed in Dok. 74, 1894, 9–34, Storting's proceedings.   [32] Ibid.

for those who believed Norges Bank should be in charge of ordinary banking business, and therefore wanted a branch in their proximity. Some new branches were opened in the decades that followed, but mainly to support lending in areas without proper bank coverage. In those areas, Norges Bank remained a direct lender to support business life.[33]

Back in 1894, the Executive Board had argued that the new bank act had given the central management new powers, and it was their intention to use them. Admittedly, if it wished, the Executive Board could apply different discount rates around the country, but this was never done. Unlike before, the many branches would not receive funds from the bank, which would be lent out to the maximum, at a reduced discount rate if necessary. The setting of the discount rate should now be based on the conditions prevailing in the national money market.

The Kristiania Boom and Norges Bank's Foot Dragging

In 1898, the painter and writer Christian Krogh returned to Kristiania after a year in Paris. In a delightful essay, Krogh described the complete transformation the Norwegian capital had undergone. Everything seemed different; the city's main street was reminiscent of Parisian boulevards, with new shops, cafés, and restaurants. The streets were buzzing with more people, veiled in a metropolitan busyness that he had not experienced in the past. In his former habitual café, Krogh was drawn into conversations about real estate speculation and the business start-ups with old and new acquaintances explaining how to earn quick cash. He had been away for a year, but it felt like a lifetime.[34]

Krogh had returned home in the middle of the so-called Kristiania boom, preceding what has later been labelled as the Kristiania crash. Norges Bank both observed and commented on the boom as it was unfolding—but for a long without doing anything to contain it. In its 1898 annual report, written during spring of 1899, the Executive Board pointed to the fact that current figures revealed the presence of vigorous economic activity in Norway. The good times had, however, also resulted in 'excessive speculation'.[35] Speculation in shares and real estate was widespread, especially in Kristiania, whose population was now growing rapidly. In the course of 1897–8, six new banks were established in the capital. The board wrote that market competition had become unhealthy.

Norges Bank considered the problem to be related to the new banking establishments. An influx of capital from neighbouring countries, at times with large investment opportunities, was nothing new, especially after the establishment of the Scandinavian Currency Union. The newly established banks represented more of a

---

[33] Rygg, *Norges Banks historie*, 2, 338–40.
[34] Christian Krogh, *Kampen for tilværelsen*, (Gyldendal, 1952), 439–40.
[35] Document no. 96, 34, 1898–9, Storting's proceedings.

headache. They were given access to foreign credit, and could, to the extent it was based on foreign supply of gold, contribute to a swift expansion of the money supply.[36] Nevertheless, the expansion was fragile and unstable, and Norges Bank did not have at its disposable the instruments to regulate or moderate the upturn.

The newspaper *Farmand* was convinced that Norges Bank had failed to fulfil its role, and believed that their main instrument should have been used. The editor Sundt had, since the outbreak of the Spanish-American War in April 1898, encouraged Norges Bank to be vigilant.[37] In August, Sundt affirmed the wrong turn of events when Norges Bank reduced the discount rate from 4.5 to 4 per cent. The discount rate should rather be raised, possibly up to 6 per cent. Nonetheless, the discount rate was not raised until December 1898, when it reached 5.5 per cent in two steps.[38] *Farmand* held that Norges Bank should have taken action long before in order to both regulate the credit market and secure a solid reserve for providing liquidity support. Indeed, in practice those two conditions were connected. Now the discount rate increase came so late that Norges Bank was obliged to issue a warning concerning credit restrictions. The private banks that Norges Bank had rediscounted could expect no more support for the time being. While this did not trigger a crisis, *Farmand* was scathing in its criticism: 'This is poor leadership; a National Bank should never refuse to discount for its customers, neither banks nor private customers.' If the bank had raised the discount rate in time, this would have been avoided.

Bomhoff was, however, exposed to a cross-pressure. All calls for a discount rate increase were met with 'an outcry from Bergen, Porsgrund, and the former head office, pleading not to punish the whole country for the local Kristiania speculators' errors'. In this sense, it is not surprising that a certain relief in the market in the beginning of 1899 was used to bring the discount rate down to 5 per cent from early February (see Figure 5.1). It proved an unfortunate move. A month and a half later, it had to be increased again to 6 per cent in two steps during the course of a week. The figures indicated that Norges Bank's banknote reserve was abnormally and dangerously low.[39] Shares and real estate prices in Kristiania had risen over several years. A number of banks had toxic portfolios and Norges Bank was heavily exposed.

The calamities began on Monday 12 June 1899. One of the largest companies in the country, Ch. Christophersen & Co, heavily involved in the lumber industry, brought all their bank creditors together and announced that the company was facing acute payment problems. The problems were instantly made known in Kristiania and abroad, through rumours and other channels.[40] Most of the banks in the capital had claims on Christophersen. If Christophersen went bankrupt, the banks' funds would be frozen. Already on the same Monday, the Norwegian Discontobanken had found its way to Norges Bank, and put its cards on the table. This newly founded bank's share

---

[36] Eitrheim, Klovland, and Øksendal, *A Monetary History of Norway, 1816–2016*, 240.
[37] *Farmand* 1898, 332 (24 April).   [38] *Farmand* 1898, 667 (6 August); 1027 (10 December).
[39] *Farmand* 1899, 9 (7 January).
[40] *Farmand* 1902, 1046 (6 December). See also Eitrheim, Klovland, and Øksendal, *A Monetary History of Norway, 1816–2016*, ch. 6.6.

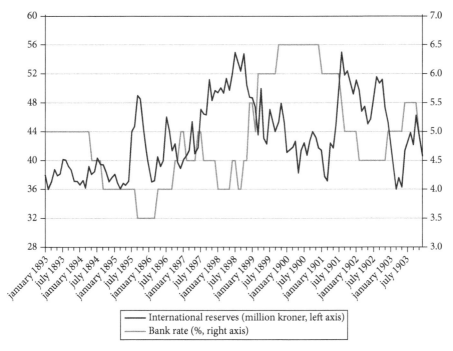

Figure 5.1 International reserves and bank rates, January 1893–December 1903

capital had recently been expanded from 3 to 6 million kroner, and it had claims of 3.25 million kroner on Christophersen.

Discontobanken did not hold considerable deposits from the general public, so perhaps it should be allowed to steer its own course towards a deserved bankruptcy. The other new banks, all of them untested, might not fare well in a run on the banks. If they were dragged down by the fall of Discontobanken, even healthy banks might fail. Based on a fear of widespread consequences, Bomhoff chose to save the Diskontobanken from a sudden collapse, a decision that was met with *Farmand's* highest praise.[41]

Strictly speaking, there were two men who should be praised. After having received the unpleasant news from Diskontobanken, Bomhoff contacted the finance minister. Together, they drew up a plan and let *Farmand* appease the readers of both the Norwegian and English editions on 17 June.[42] *Farmand* reported, rather diffusely, that a quick examination had indicated that Diskontobanken's assets covered its obligations. Therefore, the bank would receive the needed liquidity support. A week after the first crisis signals, Christophersen went bankrupt, and Diskontobanken's close implication in the collapse was made public. Diskontobanken's two general managers were suspended, and a principal officer from the Ministry of Finance was employed to administer the bank. It was announced that Diskontobanken's depositors and lenders would probably receive full coverage, however, whether or not shareholders would

[41] *Farmand* 1902, 1045 (6 December).   [42] *Farmand* 1899, 467–8 (17 June).

recover anything was more uncertain.[43] During the summer of 1898, hardly anyone could seriously have imagined that Diskontobanken could resume normal operations. The whole point was that it did not have to be wound up immediately, and then Norges Bank did what needed to be done.

Norges Bank's balance on 22 June revealed an overshoot of the note issuance right. Complying with the law, Norges Bank sent an explanation to the Ministry of Finance. The overshoot had to occur to 'avert, or at least, contain the economic mishap, that a banking crisis and ensuing panic would necessarily entail'.[44] The finance minister was hardly surprised when he received the letter. He had already ensured that the Ministry of Finance could provide support by converting an available foreign state loan into gold. On the same day that Bomhoff wrote that formal letter, *Farmand* gave ample information to the general public about the Ministry of Finance's intention to supply the bank with gold from abroad to strengthen the gold reserves.[45]

The liquidity needs that Norges Bank covered in 1898 were substantial, as evidenced by the bank's overall discount volume, which came to 190 million kroner in 1897. The following year it increased to 227 million kroner, while the 1899 crisis year showed a peak of 344 million kroner.[46] In July 1899, with gold support from the Ministry of Finance, Norges Bank again reached the legal banknote volume. At the end of September, an overshoot occurred again. Now the Ministry of Finance had no available funds for support. Norges Bank had to take responsibility alone for the liquidity provision. The discount rate was increased to 6.5 per cent. It remained at that level until August 1901. Up to that point in time, the law had been amended again, and Norges Bank's board had gained even more room for exercising judgement. By an amendment to the law in May 1900, the confidence quota, the portion of the banknote amount that was not backed by gold, increased. The time limit for reaching the law's limit in the event of an overshoot was removed. Instead, a system where an increasing fee had to be paid to the government in proportion to the increase in the overshoot period was introduced. The amendments had been under preparation since 1895, but the 1899 experience was now another reason to relax the law.[47]

The 1899 crisis reactivated the regional conflict dimension. *Farmand* had lamented the excessively mild discount policy before the crisis, but applauded the crisis management. The contrary was true in the rest of the country, apart from Kristiania. When Norges Bank's funds were tied up in the capital, they could no longer be used in other regions, and the discount rate constrained the rest of the country. In Trondheim, the criticism of Norges Bank had a special flavour: the head office should be moved back to Trondheim, away from the capital's toxic environment.

However, the discount rate policy would hardly have been more appropriate if it had been conducted from Trondheim. Bomhoff most likely acted more resolutely as

[43] *Farmand* 1899, 483–6 (24 June).
[44] Document no. 96, 22, 1899–1900; Document no. 75, 1900–1, 48, Storting's proceedings.
[45] *Farmand*, 1899, 490 (24 June).
[46] Document no. 96, 22, 1899–1900; Document No. 75, 1900–1, 48, Storting's proceedings.
[47] *Farmand* 1899, 804 (7 October).

he sat in the midst of the storm, where he could readily take the temperature and act in consultation with the Ministry of Finance, something he had been unable to do before 1897.

Liquidity Support and Bank Rescue Plans

The regional dissatisfaction with Norges Bank's intervention in 1899 did not immediately take hold in the Storting. In February 1901, the annual report in which the Executive Board explained what had happened was reviewed. Norges Bank unanimously got the best testimonies for having averted a great disaster.[48] In the course of the next years, the perception of the bank's actions changed. In January 1904, the Storting declared that the fame acquired from their 1899 action had puffed Norges Bank up with vanity.[49] The distance between liquidity support and bank rescue plans involving solidity support was short.

In the month of June 1899, Diskontobanken was the main and acute problem. Liquidity support was presented as the solution, but in reality, all the bank's obligations were overtaken. A couple of weeks later, Den Nordiske Aktiebank (Aktiebanken) discovered that its equity was lost. Norges Bank was asked to offer support under a voluntary winding up. Bomhoff did not want Norges Bank to handle this alone. Other private banks had to contribute and provide guarantee since Aktiebanken was hardly completely solvent. The outcome was a guarantee of 1.2 million kroner furnished by three banks and banking institutions, making it possible for Norges Bank to rediscount Aktiebanken's portfolio.[50]

Christophersen's fall, Diskontobanken's collapse, and the liquidation of the Aktiebanken brought the speculation in Kristiania to an abrupt halt. A tight credit market triggered a violent shift in the building and property market. Cessations and bankruptcies followed. It should have been easy to predict that more banks would experience difficulties. What would Norges Bank do in this situation? This was unknown territory. If a bank was solid, but lacked liquidity, it would be granted support. If the bank was facing solvency problems, the solution should, in principle, come from sources other than Norges Bank.

The guideline was clear, but in practice things were more complicated. How should one define liquidity problems and liquidity support? Liquidity support obviously includes rediscounting of sound bills and notes. This type of support was generously granted in 1899 and in subsequent years. However, the liquidity support could easily come at a risk, as the crisis threatened underlying values and the respective banks could move quickly into a position of insolvency.

After the 1899 crash, foreign credit was to a large extent repatriated and the main victims were the new banks. Founded in 1896, Den Norske Industri- og Vexelbank

---

[48] Stortingstidende, 1900–1, 959–68, Storting's proceedings.   [49] Stortingstidende, 817, 1903–4.
[50] *Farmand* 1899, 508 (1 July), 519–21 (8 July), 547 (15 July).

(hereafter referred to as Industribanken) was among those banks. Industribanken's share capital amounted to 6 million kroner, fully paid up. The bank was never perceived as a speculator along the same lines as Diskontobanken or Aktiebanken. Norges Bank supported the bleeding Industribanken over an extended period. The rediscounting credit increased from close to zero towards the end of 1899 up to 3.25 million kroner by November 1901.[51] Earlier in 1901, Industribanken's board had been reshuffled. It was now believed things would change for the better. In December, the Ministry of Finance provided a larger amount of support in the form of deposits in Industribanken. Around the same time, Industribanken's board made it public that half of the share capital had been lost.

In spring 1902, Industribanken asked the government and the city of Kristiania for support in the form of deposits, assuring that all losses had been written off. The deposits were made after Norges Bank and the Ministry of Finance had reviewed Industribanken's accounts. They estimated that a third of the share capital was intact. Since a number of agencies worked to rescue Industribanken, Norges Bank got deeply engaged in the rediscounting. Unlike with Diskontobanken, there were consistent expectations that confidence in Industribanken could be restored. But it turned out that confidence was definitively lost, and capital was locked in real estate that was plunging in value. In November 1902, Industribanken realized that it could not continue operations. An arrangement to wind up its business had to be found. If Industribanken failed, it would harm the credit market, both at home and abroad. Could this be avoided?

A government acquisition of Industribanken was inconceivable. Norges Bank now agreed to guarantee the claims of all creditors and private depositors, if the risk was shared with the state-owned Hypotekbanken, Kristiania municipality, and government. The first two were only to guarantee a limited sum for their deposits in Industribanken, while Norges Bank argued that government should share the remaining risk on the same level as the central bank. The Ministry of Finance agreed. The considerable general interests involved meant that government was obliged to take on a share of the burden.

The matter was brought before the Storting and was heard in December 1902. The idyll from February the year before was shattered.[52] The main argument for Norges Bank and the Ministry of Finance's plan was that Industribanken's report had been serenely accepted, with confidence in the monetary policy authorities' ability to remedy the situation. The plan met with strong opposition that intensified in several quarters. One element was the fact that opposition used the occasion to level general criticism against the ruling Liberal Party. Criticism also came from the regions; again, a bank in the capital was to be accommodated. Some were critical to asking government to take on responsibility in a new field, instead of leaving Norges Bank to deal

---

[51] On Norges Bank's handling of Industribanken, see Document no. 50 B, 1903–4, 15–18, Storting's proceedings. See also Rygg, *Norges Banks historie*, 2, 256–63.

[52] On the winding up of Industribanken St. prp. no. 43, 1902–3; Indst. S. nr. 71, 1902–3; Stortingstidende 1902–3, 482–596, Storting's proceedings.

with the matter on its own. In the eyes of many parliamentarians, that would have been the appropriate response. Norges Bank itself had engaged in business with Industribanken and profited from the substantial rediscounting operation. It was therefore only fair and reasonable that Norges Bank assumed responsibility for cleaning up.

Nonetheless, the most significant aspect was a rather strong reaction to providing support to banks in difficulty. It was easy to applaud Norges Bank's action in 1899. At the time, many had feared a system collapse, and it appeared that the operation would entail little cost. A couple of years had passed since the great summer panic of 1899. One had discovered that the Diskontobanken's portfolio would show losses for Norges Bank, and losses would also likely incur if Industribanken were to be wound up. Consequently, criticism of the Diskontobanken operation also arose, with growing support for letting the rotten fruits fall and leaving the good. It was now argued that such a healthy approach would best serve the country's creditworthiness in the long run, both domestically and abroad.

After a long debate, the Storting adopted a limited government guarantee (700,000 kroner) for the liquidation of Industribanken. But, for the operation to have an impact, an unconditional guarantee for Industribanken's obligation was needed, or the impending bankruptcy threat would remain. This now became Norges Bank's responsibility. The Supervisory Council gave its approval, even though it was believed the state held an equal share in the social responsibility.[53] The outcome was that Norges Bank took over Industribanken and wound up the bank. Norges Bank, always with reference to societal consequences (*samfunnshensyn*), had thus gone far beyond that implied by the central bank's function as the banks' liquidity guarantor, and beyond measures the government itself wished to take to guarantee solvency.

If Bomhoff late in 1904 had attempted to define some general guidelines based on elements the Storting had communicated about the central bank's role with regard to banks in difficulty the past years, he would probably have made a conclusion along the following lines. First, liquidity support to solid banks against good security is unproblematic and should be unlimited. Second, Norges Bank can and should take the necessary action to prevent a bank failure and panic that could entail systemic failure, irrespective of the bank's position. Third, a bank with solidity problems should be allowed to fail, provided failure does not cause general panic. If a bank has solidity problems that are not critical, then other actors must contribute, preferably municipal authorities or other banks. In such instances, the government should not be expected to contribute.

This was the lesson Norges Bank could learn, which could shape the response to the next bank crisis, in the 1920s. However, as practical rules they never fully came into play. The political situation was different: the banks did not want to play by old rules, and not least the crisis ran so deep that a systemic collapse and panic could hardly be

---

[53] Dokument no. 51b, 15, 1903–4, Storting's proceedings.

avoided. The next crisis also followed a world war, which had rendered many old experiences irrelevant even in a neutral Norway.

The New Central Bank

The 1890s transformed Norges Bank from being a regional system of semi-autonomous branches with a note issuance monopoly, into an organization bearing clear similarities with modern central banks. The head office was equipped with a strong leadership, and it gained greater authority over the branches, which lost some of their privileges, especially regarding setting the interest rate deemed appropriate for local conditions. The new law also clarified that direct credit provision to the public was at best a subordinate task. Norges Bank was to be a bankers' bank with responsibility for maintaining a stable and functioning financial system.

Underlying the transformation was a dissatisfaction with the existing legislation, with its amendments and ad hoc solutions after the bank's establishment in 1816. The regionally oriented system functioned poorly; the substantial loans losses in the 1870s, and especially in the 1880s, implied a strong need for change. The long economic and political development of Norway is of greater importance. New communication and infrastructure had gradually unified a country that had lacked a centre and was clearly diverse in terms of culture, with demanding geographical conditions. The capital Kristiania, a small city in 1814, was now decidedly the country's political, economic, and communication centre. The law was a result of, and strengthened, the ongoing unification and nation building, as the bank got a clearly defined centre with a coherent policy and one, national discount rate. International reforms also played a part, particularly the fairly similar developments in Sweden, where motives, principles, and a number of concrete solutions were read and copied.

The breakthrough of parliamentarianism influenced the long legislative process, and the nomination of the representatives. This breakthrough probably contributed to making the Storting's control stronger than it would have been if the old regime's men had undertaken the modernization. However, in the bigger picture, the political shift did not have such a great impact; the long-term developments, experience of existing legislation and organization, and foreign impulses were dominant factors.

Norges Bank was put to the test during the crisis at the end of the century. It gradually grew into its role. In close cooperation with the Ministry of Finance, Norges Bank organized rescue operations for the banks. Norges Bank was intended to play the role of a liquidity guarantor, and the loans issued should be well secured. Several of the operations, particularly with regard to the widely referenced Industribanken, obviously stretched beyond the limits of the law.

'Societal considerations', a loosely defined term, motivated the bank's intervention. The meaning was defined through concrete interventions. The law said nothing about what the banker's bank should do if private banks needed rescuing. Nor, for that matter, did the law say anything about 'societal considerations', a term with political and moral appeal, absent from the law's concrete and technical formulations. The interpretations and actions met both with doubt and approval by those concerned. Whatever the view, the debate contributed to building Norges Bank's informal position in the landscape of economic politics, within and beyond the framework that the 1892 act had given the new leadership.

6

Blurring the Borders

The Bank During the First World War

Exhausted after a long celebration in his honour, an ageing Karl Gether Bomhoff entered the car sent to collect him outside the Grand Hotel in central Oslo on Saturday evening at the end of October 1920. After serving on the board of Norges Bank for most of his working life, with close to twenty-eight years as its chairman, he could finally put his feet up. Bomhoff's service had been showered with tributes from the king and the entire political establishment in Norway, and during the celebratory dinner he was lauded by both the chair of the Supervisory Council of Norges Bank and Director Moll of the Swedish Riksbank. Even *Farmand*, the critical business weekly, paid tribute to the elderly honoree, and shortly thereafter he received from his successor, Nicolai Rygg, a letter in which Norges Bank saluted him for his notable contribution. The Ministry of Finance chimed in with its 'unreserved recognition of the way in which Mr Bomhoff has performed his responsibilities and services for our country under his highly competent and enlightened leadership of Norges Bank'.[1]

In all the praise, there was a certain emptiness and punctiliousness. It was obvious to Bomhoff that the reluctant praise reflected the contemporary view of his efforts in the critical years leading up to his retirement. Everyone was aware that the Norwegian monetary system was in a shambles after the First World War and that his successor would face daunting challenges mopping up after the slippages of the preceding years. Rygg had already expressed his deep concern at an improvised meeting when representatives of the regional branches were assembled on the occasion of the farewell dinner for Bomhoff.[2] Severe criticism was also voiced at the meeting of the Association of State Economists.[3]

The criticism of Norges Bank's role during the war intensified from the mid-1920s, mainly because the influential Exchange Rate Commission headed by the SSB (Statistics Norway) director, and later central bank governor, Gunnar Jahn, no longer spared Bomhoff and his deputy, Haakon Monsen.[4] Nor did historian and economist Wilhelm Keilhau. In his comprehensive review of economic policy during the First

---

[1] Karl G. Bomhoff, 'Erindringer [unpublished memoirs]' (Norges Bank, 1923), 73.
[2] Nicolai Rygg, *Norges Bank i mellomkrigstiden* (Gyldendal, 1950), 23–5.
[3] E.g. meetings in the Economists' Association, minutes printed in *Statsøkonomisk tidsskrift* 1916, 203, 211; *Statsøkonomisk tidsskrift* 1919, 139–40.
[4] Harald Pedersen's diaries 2, part IV, 24t. November 1925, NAN, PA-0368, E/0001.

Norges Bank 1816–2016. Einar Lie, Oxford University Press (2020). © Norges Bank.
DOI: 10.1093/oso/9780198860013.001.0001

World War, Norges Bank was severely criticized.[5] Together with the captains of finance, the central bank contributed to 'the destruction of the Norwegian monetary system, which the first generation after 1814 had made tremendous sacrifices to establish and which had been in pristine order for 62 years', Keilhau commented.[6] By suspending the banks' obligation to redeem banknotes for gold, and then issuing massive amounts of notes, in addition to the financing of and integration into government activities, Norges Bank's monetary policy has been largely held responsible for the sharp rise in inflation and krone depreciation—and by implication for the strongly criticized parity policy of the 1920s.

Norges Bank followed a pattern observed in surrounding countries in the years 1914–18. War and central bank independence tend not to go hand in hand. Capie, Goodhart, and Schnadt have pointed out that deep national crises, of which war is the most extreme, makes the protection of the independence of central banks less meaningful.[7] It is difficult to protect the resources of a particular institution from the state, if the state's survival and the central bank's social role are at stake. Still, as a non-belligerent country, one would have thought that the mandate for Norges Bank's activities would have remained more or less intact. We shall have a closer look at why that did not come to be.

Panic and Central Bank Independence

When the war broke out on 28 July 1914, the month after the gunshots in Sarajevo, Norway was taken by surprise. Prime Minister Gunnar Knudsen (V) had addressed the Storting in the spring, an address that has taken an inglorious place in the history books: 'This is a time when the horizon in world politics is free of clouds to a degree that it has not been for many years.'[8]

The unprepared government quickly introduced a range of crisis-related measured in cooperation with the Storting. One of the most important crisis-related measures was the establishment of the Provisioning Commission.[9] Norway was an import-dependent country, and for the Knudsen government a primordial mission was to ensure that the people were provided with basic necessities such as food and coal. The task of procuring these necessities was given to the Provisioning Commission. Its establishment underlines one of the main goals of the Knudsen government: as far as possible, normal economic activity was to be maintained, and unemployment avoided.

---

[5] Wilhelm Keilhau, *Norge og verdenskrigen*, vol. 2 (H. Aschehoug & Company (W. Nygaard), 1927), Wilhelm Keilhau, *Den norske pengehistorie* (Aschehoug, 1952).

[6] Wilhelm Keilhau, *Det norske folks liv og historie: i vår egen tid* (H. Aschehoug, 1938), 249.

[7] Forrest H Capie, Charles Goodhart, and Norbert Schnadt, *The Development of Central Banking* (Bank of England, 1994).

[8] Per Fuglum, *Én skute–én skipper: Gunnar Knudsen som statsminister 1908–10 og 1913–20* (Tapir Forl., 1989), 196–9.

[9] See Keilhau, *Norge og verdenskrigen*, 26–8.

During the war, the government stretched the limits, with government activities and spending soaring to unprecedented levels. The Provisioning Commission is invoked here as it was an ad hoc institution that has been held responsible for contributing to what has later been described as the fiscal decline in those years. The commission had been given broad spending authority, and was in principle not subject to any budget limits. This had particular implications for Norges Bank.

The commission was also a response to the panic that prevailed during the first days of August. When rumours of an export ban on grain and flour in Germany started to spread, importers' flour inventories quickly dwindled. Long queues formed outside shops long before opening hours. Prices skyrocketed, and many shops had to close as their shelves were emptied. The uncertainty also affected the banking industry when people queued to withdraw their savings. The turbulence spread to Norges Bank, under growing pressure from private banks that wanted to rediscount to procure liquidity and from the general public that wanted to exchange notes for gold.[10]

It was widely believed that the world war would be a short-lived affair and the board, as well as the government, wanted to maintain normal economic activity as far as possible. Private banks were accommodated; Norges Bank's rediscounting of the banks' bills of exchange increased substantially. The discount rate for such loans was increased from 5 to 6 per cent on 1 August. Liquidity in and from the private banks was sustained, and the cost of holding metal increased. The public was also accommodated when Norges Bank began exchanging notes for gold on 27 July, but due to dwindling money supply and the risk of emptying the bank's vaults, certain tactics called 'small drops' were used. Only one cashier was available and was told to count the gold coins slowly, which drew out the redemption process. The private banks also joined in by restricting withdrawals to a maximum of 100 kroner per day.[11] It was also agreed to introduce a general temporary deferral of all payments.

But when Norges Bank's head office in Kristiania opened on Monday 3 August—referred to as the day of the great panic in Norway—there were long queues of people in front of the bank waiting to exchange their notes for gold. Despite a police presence at each entrance to calm the crowds, Bankplassen was littered with broken umbrellas and torn-off shirt collars.[12] More and more gold standard countries were suspending gold redemption, and the previous consensus on the issue in Norway was starting to weaken. The first move was merely to increase the discount rate further. But on 5 August Norges Bank's obligation to redeem notes for gold was suspended. We lack precise sources on who made the decision, but it would appear that it was the government's decision to revoke the redemption obligation in order to safeguard the stock of gold.[13] The krone consequently started to float and its value was solely determined by

---

[10] Ibid., Bomhoff, 'Erindringer [unpublished memoirs]', 66–7; Nicolai Rygg, *Norges Banks historie*, vol. 2 (Emil Moestue, 1954), 353–5.

[11] Keilhau, *Norge og verdenskrigen*, 11–13.   [12] Ibid.

[13] Gjermund Forfang Rongved, 'The Slide from Stability: Monetary and Fiscal Policy in Norway 1914–1920', Faculty of Humanities, University of Oslo (2014), 90.

supply and demand. A whole fourteen years were to pass before the return to a fixed exchange rate and gold peg.

It was probably because the war was expected to be temporary that certain direct-ors saw no reason to suspend gold redemption, and until the suspension little gold had left the central bank.[14] However, it can be argued that the same reasoning was behind the decision to remove the volume of banknotes' tie to the metal stock. Since the war was expected to be short-lived, a swift and easy return to normal conditions was expected. A good number of crisis-related measures were taken based on an expectation that would not be realized.

One of the measures that proved unfortunate, as the war dragged on, was the deci-sion to reduce—in practice, remove—the penalty fee on the overshoot of the bank-note issuance right. As we saw in Chapter 5, the 1892 Central Bank Act stated that Norges Bank had to pay a 6 per cent fee to government if it issued more notes than permitted. This was meant to balance Norges Bank's role as the bankers' bank with the responsibility for stabilizing the monetary system, with the bank playing the role of a private corporation intended to generate profit for its shareholders. The fee would make it costly to expand the volume of banknotes beyond the fixed limits. Norges Bank advanced arguments against the high and constraining fee in the new situation that had appeared in August 1914. The Ministry of Finance was sceptical about Norges Bank's proposal of a reduction; there could be a 'temptation to use the note issuance for the Bank's profit'.[15] In the end, the Ministry still accepted the proposal.

During the first year of the war, Norges Bank managed to maintain a clear dividing line in relation to the government and its financial needs. Other countries' central banks were rapidly obliged to finance government operations, or its banknote monopoly would weaken.[16] By early August 1914, taking up a loan from the central bank by drawing on the government's deposit account was discussed internally in the Norwegian Ministry of Finance.[17] Governor Bomhoff's curtly dismissed that option. In November, he publicly declared that a loan to the government would constitute 'a vast error'; it was 'unhealthy to push the bank to issue as many notes as possible' and that was something one should have recourse to only in the 'most extreme case'.[18] The government therefore had to turn to the private banks. Norges Bank became an important support for government during the next months. As part of the provision-ing policy, grain imports from North America had to be secured, and here Norges Bank's foreign exchange holdings abroad were of great help.[19] Norges Bank also helped the government raise loans both in London and New York, but the bank did not in any of these cases grant direct loans to the government. Its task was clearly

---

[14] Letter from Bomhoff to Prof. Jæger, 21 November 1914, NB/DIR1/B/Bb/L0001.
[15] Handwritten comments on memo of 25 August 1914, FD/FKC/D/Da/L0456.
[16] Rongved, 'The Slide from Stability: Monetary and Fiscal Policy in Norway 1914–1920', 107–14.
[17] Handwritten comments on draft of Parliament Bill, 14 August 1914, FD/FKC/D/Da/L0456.
[18] Discussion in Economist Association, referred to in *Statsøkonomisk tidsskrift* 1914, 186.
[19] Rygg, *Norges Banks historie*, 2, 365–7, Gunnar Jahn, Alf Eriksen, and Preben Munthe, *Norges Bank gjennom 150 år* (Norges Bank, 1966), 182.

within the role of a coordinating bankers' bank in a situation where the government needed loans from private banks.

If Norges Bank's management were to have taken stock in summer of 1915, it would probably have been reasonably satisfied. The central bank had helped diffuse the crisis sentiment prevailing in August. Despite certain hindrances, the Norwegian economy was faring well. The central bank had provided important assistance to the government, albeit without going beyond the framework of independence, as defined in the legislation and the preparatory work. The financial market had not yet neared the excesses that would characterize most of the war period; on the contrary, through rate cuts, Norges Bank had supported the private banking system. Favourable trading conditions had led to rapid growth in the gold reserves. Norges Bank no longer exceeded banknote cover rules. Towards the end of May 1915, the discount rate was brought down to what was perceived at the time as a 'neutral' level: 5 per cent. The rate cuts helped businesses that Norges Bank took into particular consideration during the war period: those who suffered from price increases, import difficulties, and disturbances that businesses in general were facing. The bank could also take note of the fact that cooperation within the Scandinavian Currency Union seemed to have passed the test so far.

Into the Government's Fold

The belief that the war would soon end was strong and persistent—but so was the war. The government endeavoured to maintain neutrality, and for a long time the Norwegian economy benefited from trade with both sides. Both Germany and Great Britain, both among the country's most important trading partners, had a growing interest in securing Norwegian commodities. Prices for fish, lumber, but also ore and manufactured products increased at a rapid pace. There was soaring demand for war inputs such as copper, pyrite, nitrates, and glycerine. Moreover, these would be central in the demanding tugs of war between the belligerent nations. Not least, the large Norwegian merchant fleet would benefit from exceptional income.[20]

When the war was locked into the trenches on the Western Front, warfare also started taking on the characteristics of economic warfare. The main powers on each side of the trenches were not only focusing on securing resources for themselves, but were also seeking to prevent the enemy from procuring them. Consequently, warfare on the seas became more important. This combination had a significant impact on the Norwegian economy. Some export sectors, such as fisheries and commodities, benefited from rising prices and substantial earnings. The war created a strong international market, flush in money willing to pay high prices. Transport difficulties also

---

[20] Einar Lie, *Norsk økonomisk politikk etter 1905* (Universitetsforl., 2012), 32–4, Monica Værholm and Lars Frederik Øksendal, 'Letting the Anchor Go: Monetary Policy in Neutral Norway during World War I' (Norges Bank, 2010).

pushed up prices. This was the cause behind the strong growth in Norges Bank's gold and currency reserves. Demand for Norwegian goods and services also led to the strong appreciation of the Norwegian krone during the spring of 1915. This was to be expected under a floating exchange rate regime, which in practice was the operating framework at the time.[21]

Rapidly rising prices, in combination with increased government activity, had consequences for government financing needs. Finance minister Anton Omholt wanted to finance increased spending with a range of temporary taxes, but it took time to establish the system and it took even longer for the tax revenues to materialize.[22] Provisioning spending was on the rise, and the civil service knew that financing temporary purchases of grain and other necessity goods using long-term government loans was an expensive proposition.

The Ministry of Finance now launched a new solution.[23] This involved Norges Bank taking responsibility for government advances for provisioning by giving the commission an overdraft account in the bank where advances were reimbursed as soon as the goods were sold. Only one obstacle stood in the way: the 1892 Central Bank Act. Article 19 of the act on Norges Bank gave the basis for a well-established practice: the bank could not give an advance to the government.[24] The ministry's interpretation of this was that the central bank could not give an advance to government *without* compensation—albeit *with* compensation there was no obstacle to an advance. It was also perceived as 'entirely reasonable' that the government had an exceptional relationship with Norges Bank.[25]

In August 1915, Norges Bank showed signs of yielding, accepting the responsibility of providing credit for the Provisioning Commission.[26] The central bank's position was likely a reflection of the belief that war would soon end and that the loan would therefore be limited in size. Sound collateral and rapid repayment justified a one-off loan to a government in need. Norges Bank had also already granted loans to municipal provisioning commissions.[27] The local authorities were not mentioned in the act, and ordinary credit assessments were applied when granting loans to local government.

Central bank financing of the government was initially foiled, however, due to strong protests from the Storting. The leader of the Conservative Party gained wide support when he ascertained that if 'Norges Bank, even at relatively good days, is used to cover the government's current spending, then we are on the wrong path'.[28] Despite the government's majority in the Storting, the protests helped avoid a new path in this round.

[21] Ibid.

[22] Rongved, 'The Slide from Stability: Monetary and Fiscal Policy in Norway 1914–1920', 120–2.

[23] Internal note in Ministry of Finance, 27 July 1915, FD/FKC/D/Da/L0456.

[24] See e.g. Keilhau, *Den norske pengehistorie*, 135, Oscar Jæger, 'Udsigt over de forandringer som Norges Banks virksomhet har undergået ved den nye banklov', *Statsøkonomisk tidsskrift* 8, no. 1 (1894).

[25] Internal note in the Ministry of Finance, 27 July 1915, FD/FKC/D/Da/L0456.

[26] Letter from Norges Bank to the Ministry of Finance, 11 August 1915, FD/FKC/D/Da/L0586.

[27] Norges Banks annual report, 1914.   [28] Stortingstidende, 1915, 2647, Storting' s proceedings.

The reservations proved to be temporary. In January 1916, the Provisioning Commission received a small loan from Norges Bank for grain purchases.[29] During the budget debate two months later the government simply decreed that it would use the central bank to finance provisioning.[30] All protests were ignored; the minister of finance claimed that the government's authority in this case was indisputable, while Prime Minister Knudsen attacked a critical budget committee for attempting 'to bind the government's hands'.[31] Throughout 1916 the Provisioning Commission overdrafts also increased in Norges Bank, and the following year the commission overdrew NOK 178 million.[32] In the period between 1916 and 1917, Norges Bank became an integral part of the Norwegian government's provisions trade.

Important trade agreements made with Great Britain also gave Norges Bank a prominent role, but in an unclear territory with regard to the central bank's formal framework. Britain had a vital position in Norway's external economic and political situation. Norway was, and is, a small and very open economy. A substantial share of production, especially in the capital-intensive manufacturing and mining industries, was export-oriented. The large shipping sector was, by nature, international. This was a privileged position with the freedom to sell to either side during the first phase of the war. For obvious reasons, the warring parties did not want the enemy to get their hands on the goods. Neutral Norway increasingly leaned towards the Western powers, especially Great Britain, with whom economic ties were strongest. The British blockade during the Napoleonic Wars, richly represented in historical and literary writings, clearly reflected the dependence on Great Britain. 'The poor people starved, and the wealthy went short', Henrik Ibsen writes in his famous poem about Terje Vigen, the seafarer who rowed to Denmark to bring grain home to his starving family. According to the long epic poem, printed over and over in schoolbooks for generations, Terje Vigen never came home with his load—a British corvette seized him and, returning home after five years of captivity, he found his family in a 'poor people's grave'.[33]

Dependence on Great Britain was just as apparent in the years 1914–18, with the British and American influence in overseas trade and the Grand Fleets' dominance over adjacent seas. During a negotiation round, Mansfeldt Finlay, the British minister in Norway, reminded the Norwegian prime minister that 'Norway's future as a seafaring nation [...] depended upon British and American trade, bunkers, and ports'.[34] The prime minister knew that Finlay was right. The warning was linked to Norway's role after the end of the war. However, there was also a strong, short-term aspect: When the British, before July 1916, were dissatisfied with Norway's compliance with agreements about deliveries to Great Britain and interception of exports to Germany, coal

---

[29] Internal memo, Ministry of Finance, 19 January 1916, FD/FKC/D/Da/L0590, and undated memo in the same file.

[30] Stortingstidende, 1916, 429, Storting's proceeding.

[31] Stortingstidende , 1916, 440, 449, Storting's proceeding.   [32] Rygg, Norges Banks historie, 2, 513.

[33] Jens Rahbek Rasmussen, 'Love and Hate Among Nations: Britain in the Scandinavian Mirror, 1800–1920', European Journal of English Studies 8, no. 2 (2004).

[34] Quoted from Roald Berg, Norge på egen hånd 1905–1920, vol. 2 (Universitetsforlaget, 1995), 237.

exports to Norway were suspended. This had considerable, tangible consequences for the population during an ice-cold winter.

'The neutral ally', coined by the Norwegian historian Olav Riste, has remained a brief and apt summary of Norway's attitude during the First World War: formally, the country was neutral, but was increasingly drawn into the Triple Entente supply and blockade policy, somewhat out of political orientation, mostly out of necessity.[35] In the public arena, the full-fledged submarine war, which dramatically reduced Norwegian tonnage and caused the death of a great number of seafarers, fuelled strong anti-German sentiment. Britain's needs became decisive for Norwegian trade policy in ever more areas. Trade was at the time regulated to an unprecedented extent by national agreements. For a few of the agreements, financing was also coordinated by the government, with Norges Bank becoming a key instrument.

The central bank's involvement was most clearly reflected in the so-called fishery agreement, which was of significant importance for both Norway and Great Britain, and which illustrates the war economy's complex, intertwined character. In 1915, after German agents had begun large-scale purchases of Norwegian fish, Great Britain sought to obstruct German access to the resources. That process resulted in a surge in Norwegian fish prices, which entailed substantial costs for the warring parties, and Great Britain put intensive pressure on Norway to establish arrangements to circumvent the open market. As the fishing fleet was dependent on external input and the main inputs came from the British Isles, the government feared that the social and economic impact of a blockade would have dire consequences for the many Norwegians dependent on fisheries.

The fishery agreement, concluded in late summer of 1916, determined that the British would secretly obtain 85 per cent of Norway's total fish catch in exchange for necessary supplies. A loan in the Norwegian market was the precondition for the British. Norges Bank was willing to help the government establish the loan—based on the consideration that it was in the nation's interest to secure supplies of important goods, and that the bank's participation was necessary to achieve this. The bank was now more accommodating than earlier, and the fishery agreement has been described as a watershed in the relationship between the central bank and the government.[36]

Quite early during the Norwegian–British negotiations, two British delegates came to Norges Bank at Prime Minister Knudsen's recommendation. Deputy Governor Haakon Monsen received the delegation on behalf of management, largely absent on holiday. He was informed that a loan of about NOK 40 million directly from Norges Bank was necessary to conclude an agreement. If the bank did not contribute, it would entail 'difficulties or cessation of necessity goods imports to one of our most significant industry avenues', according to Monsen's account of the situation.[37] Consequently,

[35] Olav Riste, *The Neutral Ally: Norway's Relations with Belligerent Powers in the First World War* (Universitetsforlaget, 1965).

[36] Værholm and Øksendal, 'Letting the Anchor Go: Monetary Policy in Neutral Norway during World War I'.

[37] Monsen's undated memo, NB/DIR1/E/L0014, cf. the meetings at the bank's board, 7 September 1916, NB/DIR1/A/L0045.

Norges Bank quickly agreed to provide credit, the condition being that necessary imports would be secured.

Formally, this was not a loan to the Norwegian government. It was a loan to the British government, which the Norwegian government had promised Norges Bank would provide. The letter of the law was not violated, but the intention of the law clearly was. Norges Bank was already on its way to becoming the government's credit provider, after having accepted to lend to the provisioning system. By accepting the government's demands for a large loan to a foreign power for buying consumer goods in Norway, Norges Bank contributed to an increase in liquidity supply and hence to higher inflation in a situation where this should evidently have been avoided. The credit granted to Great Britain and the NOK 61 million extended to Germany in the following years, which Norges Bank provided to maintain a semblance of neutrality, and partly in response to German pressure, are significant one-off events leading to the surge in the money supply and inflation during the war years.[38]

It has been argued that the private banks, holding considerable deposits during the summer 1916, should have provided the loan.[39] One reason the option was not explored may have been that the government wanted a prompt resolution, and simply put pressure on Norges Bank to achieve this. The central bank had now taken on part of the responsibility for underpinning economic activity and securing imports in a time of crisis. Credit provision to warring parties shows how focus on 'healthy' monetary policy had decidedly been abandoned in favour of a broader central bank policy. Bomhoff pointed out that the loans to warring parties had been granted because it was in 'the country's interest'.[40] Even though the fishery agreement is often put forth as a prime example of an unfortunate mix between government and central bank, it is by no means unique in an international context. Other central banks in neutral countries supported nation and government by issuing loans to the warring parties.[41] The alternative was a halt in trade, increased import difficulties, and fears of more direct reprisals.

The demanding conditions during the First World War gave rise to new priorities and thereby also contributed to failing central bank cooperation in the Scandinavian Currency Union.[42] For a period, central banks had attempted to counter the effects of divergent movements in the three currencies. To a certain degree, they had also managed to find solutions to avoid excessively adverse effects of law-bound parity under the coin convention. One of these measures was the previously mentioned gold blockade from spring 1916. The Riksbank was under the influence of a series of prominent Swedish economists who feared that the central bank's gold purchases would generate inflation and lead to goods shortages. However, even though the three central banks were able to coordinate policy, they failed to reach a true agreement. Neither the

[38] Hermod Skånland, *Det norske kredittmarked siden 1900*, vol. 19 (Statistisk sentralbyrå, 1967), 145.
[39] Keilhau, *Norge og verdenskrigen*, 310.
[40] Letter from Bomhoff to Moll, 4 July 1917, DIR1/B/Bb/L0001, .
[41] Rongved, 'The Slide from Stability: Monetary and Fiscal Policy in Norway 1914–1920', 75–8.
[42] Gjermund Forfang Rongved, 'Money Talks: Failed Cooperation Over the Gold Problem of the Scandinavian Monetary Union During the First World War', in *Scandinavia in the First World War: Studies in the War Experience of the Northern Neutrals*, ed. Claes Ahlund (Nordic Academic Press, 2012).

Nationalbanken nor Norges Bank wanted to give up the opportunity to cover trade deficits with Scandinavian gold coins. In the course of 1917 in particular, Bomhoff and his Riksbank colleague, Moll, ended up in a bitter conflict; Norges Bank constantly insisted on making claims on the Riksbank and settled the trade imbalance using undesirable gold shipments. The correspondence between them is a chapter in itself and clearly shows how national considerations also affected long-term cooperation during the crisis period.[43] The war dealt a final blow to the Scandinavian Currency Union.

Easy Money and a Difficult Balancing Act

In the course of 1916, a shift in sources of liquidity supply to the Norwegian market occurred. So far, foreign trade had fuelled monetary growth and inflation.[44] Import difficulties had only slightly affected the Norwegian export sector's need for intermediate goods, and the value of export and shipping services had soared. Gold and foreign currency flowed into the Norwegian economy and was exchanged into banknotes in Norges Bank. Up to the middle of 1916, foreign exchange reserves, owing to a favourable external economy, and the volume of banknotes had grown virtually in parallel, but thereafter domestic impulses were mainly behind monetary growth and rising inflation. In this last phase, Norges Bank played an important role; the consequence of the central bank loans to the Norwegian government and the warring parties was a sharp increase in the supply of liquidity and mounting inflationary pressures.

By the end of 1916, the volume of banknotes had risen by 130 per cent over the three preceding years. Now growth accelerated further. In the course of the next two years, the volume of banknotes grew by 300 per cent. When growth finally flattened towards the end of 1920, the volume of banknotes was around 350 per cent higher than its pre-war level. In the course of these years, Norway experienced faster monetary growth than any other neutral country. Developments in this country can easily be compared to those of the belligerent nations.

The general rise in prices, easy money, and prospects for considerable gains through speculation in some industries had consequences for financial market developments in Norway throughout the war years. Anecdotes about the nouveaux riches, flush in money living the high-life, abounded at the time and have been illustrated in vital contributions to popular culture.[45] Speculators benefited from easy access to credit. The number of commercial banks increased by 65 per cent to 193 between 1913 and 1918, especially from 1916. The nominal loans to these commercial banks rose by 360 per cent up to 1918 and by 450 per cent in the period to the end of 1920.[46]

---

[43] The correspondence is found in NB/DIR2/D/L0642.

[44] Øyvind Eitrheim, Jan Tore Klovland, and Lars Fredrik Øksendal, *A Monetary History of Norway, 1816–2016* (Cambridge University Press, 2016), ch. 7.

[45] Lie, *Norsk økonomisk politikk etter 1905*, 34–6.

[46] Øyvind Eitrheim and Jan T Klovland, and Jan F. Qvigstad (ed.): Historical Monetary Statistics for Norway 1819–2003', *Norges Bank's Occasional Papers*, no. 35 (2004).

This substantial expansion in the banking sector stimulated monetary growth in that period. Obviously, a large number of these banks were founded on speculation, with loans backed by risky securities at inflated prices. Nevertheless, as long as prices climbed, banks' lending and expansion persisted, and the bubble in the Norwegian financial sector grew ever bigger.

Norges Bank was aware of these developments at an early stage. For example, Bomhoff was gravely concerned by the stock market frenzy and speculation in October 1915, affirming that one would 'undoubtedly experience ruin both hither and tither', even though he was not yet expecting an ordinary depression like the one in the 1890s. He warned, 'if we don't rein in now, the ruins may prove greater'.[47] A steady course was nevertheless maintained, and the bank's management seemed unable to find effective instruments to curb the expansion. The board's measures consisted mainly of admonishing the private banks. Exhortations to avoid speculative lending were sent out at irregular intervals from 1915.[48]

Even though the private banks must take responsibility for their own lack of lending restraint, the heavy involvement of Norges Bank's branches was a problem. Certain branches increased their lending to such a degree that they enabled speculation. Internal control was severely deficient, and when management finally took action, it mainly consisted of admonishments. The scope for effective intervention was limited by the fact that the government itself had removed its most significant means of control. Before 1914, management had distributed Norges Bank's total lending resources to the branches, and withdrawn or delivered additional funds based on arbitrary assessments. But when the upper limits on central bank lending were removed along with the fee for banknote overshoots, Norges Bank ceased to regulate overall lending. Branches were given, as Rygg later stated, free rein to 'sail their own ship'.[49]

The government did little to counter the bubble building up in the financial system. Admittedly, a supervisory authority for savings banks existed as early as 1900, and did important work during the war, but no such body existed for commercial banks. In 1918, worries had intensified to the point that the Ministry of Finance, with Norges Bank's complicity, drew up legislation requiring all newly opened banks to apply for a licence. The same year, the stockbroker law was adopted, intended to tighten requirements for stockbrokers. A financial council was also established, comprising experts under Bomhoff's leadership in an attempt to engage in a higher-level discussion about the Norwegian money, foreign exchange, and banking markets.[50] But these measures, to the extent they had any effect at all, were taken too late to roll back the wave of speculation.

Much of the criticism of Norges Bank, both at that time and later, has focused on the central bank's failure to use the discount rate to counter speculation and monetary growth.[51] After the discount rate had been raised in August 1914, it was rapidly

---

[47] *Aftenposten*, 11 November 1915. See also Norges Bank's annual report 1915.
[48] Rygg, *Norges Banks historie*, 2, 567.
[49] Ibid., 570–2.   [50] Ibid., 503–5,–530–2, 559–61.
[51] E.g. Keilhau, *Den norske pengehistorie*, 153–4; Rygg, *Norges Banks historie*, 2, 523–4.

lowered to what was considered a normal level—between 5 and 5.5 per cent—where it generally stayed until the end of 1917. Between May and October 1916, it was even as low as 4.5 per cent.[52]

It is possible that Norges Bank was, to some extent, influenced by the British banking school's theory on the relationship between the money supply and inflation. The theory held that an increase in the money supply used for sound economic projects did not generate inflation because the economy expanded at the same pace as the increase in the money supply.[53] The school had its spokesmen in Norway, but the sources from Norges Bank are not entirely convincing and assessments are not linked tightly enough to macroeconomic conditions for it to be possible to draw any safe conclusions. On the contrary, it is obvious that Norges Bank's concern over the effects of a high discount rate on ordinary, less cyclically exposed sectors strongly motivated Norges Bank's 'deficient' interest rate policy.[54] Even though some earned good money and greatly benefited from high inflation, others only experienced the darker side. Attempts to restrain the relatively few speculators with a 'normal' interest raise increase would intensify the strain on the larger number of struggling economic actors and businesses.

At the same time, a 'normal' crisis discount rate of 7 per cent was not considered effective in limiting the most important development, namely speculative activity; earnings were simply too good. This was a point of view shared by the other Scandinavian central banks, which were caught in the same balancing act. If the objective was to influence speculators, the discount rate had to be set at a level of perhaps 15 per cent.[55] None of the central banks was willing to risk the economic consequences of an extremely high interest rate. Consequently, Norges Bank maintained the discount rate at the level it would have in normal times. However, owing to inflation, this led to highly negative real interest rates.

As one may suspect, Norges Bank hardly believed that it was the interest rate, through the supply-side channel, that drove the money supply and inflation. As in Sweden and Denmark, the central bank argued that it almost exclusively met demand for money. The increase in banknotes was due to the 'abnormal conditions' created by the war: it was a result of the loans provided to the warring parties, the increase in goods prices due to the war, soaring profits, and rising wages.[56] Norges Bank seems to have been aware of the relationship between an increase in the money supply and inflation, and thus that the central bank had indirectly contributed to the developments. However, Norges Bank washed its hands of any responsibility, arguing that its actions were exclusively a consequence of external needs and demand that the central bank could not leave unaccommodated.

---

[52] Norges Bank's annual reports.
[53] Værholm and Øksendal, 'Letting the Anchor Go: Monetary Policy in Neutral Norway during World War I'.
[54] The dilemmas created by the dual character of the economy is a recurrent theme in the annual reports.
[55] E.g. the presentation from the governor of the Danish Nationalbanken at the Scandinavian meeting between central bankers in Copenhagen in May 1918, NB/DIR2/D/L0643.
[56] Norges Bank's annual report, 1918.

Failed Attempts at Retrenchment

Danger signals in the financial market were evident, and towards the end of 1917, Norges Bank made a first attempt at tightening. The discount rate was raised to 6 per cent, and was held at that level for a year and a half. Under normal conditions, this was a high discount rate, but the move proved ineffective in an environment of surging credit explosion and rampant inflation. In 1917 and 1918, Norges Bank attempted to regain control over the money supply and avoid being used as the government's wallet, but attempts to regain control produced virtually the opposite effect.

In 1917, a formal dividing line between the government and central bank was clearly and deliberately crossed: government revenues had been small, but spending had soared during the first two years of the war. Gradually, the extraordinary tax revenues began to flow into government coffers, but government revenues were subject to substantial seasonal swings. In autumn 1917, the Ministry of Finance expected large tax revenues and wanted to receive interest on these up until payment.[57] Under the 1892 Central Bank Act, Norges Bank was charged with handling government transactions using the government's deposit account with Norges Bank, but it had never been clarified whether Norges Bank should pay interest on government deposits. Consequently, the government used private banks to boost its interest revenues, but the ministry did not consider the interest sufficient.[58] The Ministry of Finance again turned to Norges Bank, without really expecting a positive response. To the ministry's surprise, the deputy chairman of Norges Bank, Monsen, was positively inclined towards the arrangement. The bank tried to lower the significant banknote overshoot, and the board wanted to prevent private banks from gaining access to more lending for 'less advisable purposes'.[59]

Money swiftly flowed into the government's deposit account, and in the beginning of 1918, deposits amounted to well over NOK 30 million.[60] Nonetheless, they quickly dropped during spring. In late summer, the first monthly balance was in the red. Though it was not deep in the red, it was deep in symbolism: the government had begun overdrawing its account in Norges Bank.

It may seem peculiar to place emphasis on this aspect given the central bank's considerable credit provision for government provisioning. But when Norges Bank had acceded to finance provisioning in 1915, it was specified that loans could only be used for necessary purchases of food and intermediate goods, and that the loans should not reach large amounts. In December 1916, Bomhoff sent a sharp reprimand to the Ministry of Finance because of a weekly report showing an account deficit. The civil servants at the ministry were also, well into the war, opposed to such types of overdrafts. Eivind Olaf Bødtker, director general of the finance division of the ministry, told Bomhoff privately that if he received an expenditure order from the government,

---

[57] Memo entitled, 'Foliet', 4 October 1917, FD/FKC/D/Da/L0456.   [58] Ibid.
[59] Letter from Norges Bank to the Ministry of Finance, 5 October 1917, FD/FKC/D/Da/L0456.
[60] This is based on information in the annual national budgets, printed each year as St. prp. 1, in the Storting's proceedings.

even with Bødtker's own signature, he should overlook it.[61] Bødtker left the Ministry of Finance in 1918, however, and towards the end of the year overdrafts were again requested. In subsequent years, monthly reports indicate considerable overdrafts from summer and throughout the years 1919 and 1920. Bomhoff protested using financial and pragmatic arguments.[62] It took Gunnar Knudsen, now also finance minister, months to answer—before dismissing the objections.[63]

In the course of 1917, Norges Bank advanced, in the form of loans, all of NOK 178 million to the Norwegian provisioning authorities. The repayments took longer and longer. The many different provisioning authorities, and possibly above all the Provisioning Directorate, lived lives of their own. Indeed, during the last years of the war those demands were considered to have strongly contributed to the rise in prices and banknotes.[64] Up until summer of 1918, total overdrafts in Norges Bank were steadily increasing.

In June 1918, Norges Bank put on the brakes, demanding an explanation from the Ministry of Finance.[65] Internal communications revealed Bomhoff's view to be that the central bank had taken on a new role in the nation's interest, and that the bank had been willing to do so for a long period.[66] However, the provisioning authorities' use of the bank had substantially increased, and short-term loans were not reimbursed as scheduled. The Ministry of Finance's solution was to let private banks take over the responsibility for the expenditures. In summer of 1918, negotiations began on what would be known as the big provisioning loan. This loan, organized as sales of Treasury bills, would cover outstanding credit in Norges Bank, and also included Knudsen's government expenditure for fishery acquisitions after the British had terminated the fishery agreement towards the end of 1917.

Private banks were favourably inclined, but problematically demanded the right to rediscount the Treasury bills in Norges Bank.[67] For the central bank this was an obvious dilemma, as it opened a back door to central bank money. Bomhoff was reluctant to promise any rediscounting, but the private banks were unrelenting, with the political authorities' support. Another aspect is that the Storting, which in 1915 loudly protested any infringements on Norges Bank's independence, seemed less attached to such principles in 1918. Now taking the opposite approach, representatives stressed the importance of assuring private banks that the central bank would be accommodating.[68] Norges Bank yielded.

It was soon revealed that private banks, to a large extent, would use the rediscounting right. The year after it had been granted, the loan was also considerably increased,

[61] Bødtker statement, recorded during the impeachment of Prime Minister A. Berge, *Riksrettssaken mot statsminister Berge m. fl. 1926–1927: (Dokumentasjonshefter I–VI)* (Centraltrykkeriet, 1927), 652–3.

[62] Letter from Norges Bank to the Ministry of Finance, 10 October 1919, FD/FKC/D/Da/L0456.

[63] Letter from the Ministry of Finance to Norges Bank, 2 March 1920, FD/FKC/D/Da/L0456.

[64] Rygg, *Norges Banks historie*, 2, 512.

[65] Protocol from the Executive Board, 18 June 1918, NB/DIR1/A/L0047.

[66] Letter from the Executive Board to the Supervisory Council, 7 September 1918, NB/DIR1/E/L0037.

[67] See e.g. letter from the Ministry of Finance to Norges Bank, 17 August 1918, NB/DIR1/E/L0037; 'Direksjonens protokoll' 21 August 1918, NB/DIR1/A/L0047.

[68] Stortingstidende 1918, 2793ff, Storting's's proceedings.

and repeatedly renewed.[69] All through this period, Norges Bank was obliged to meet private banks' demands with an accommodating attitude. Even though a good overview of the extent to which rediscounting was used has not been found, it undoubtedly contributed to the sharp increase in the money supply. The irony of the matter was that government now found it easier to raise loans for its growing expenditure. As these loans were freely discounted in Norges Bank, the central bank also lost all control over lending to private banks, which it had sought to control for a long time. Norges Bank's two attempts at tightening were marked by utter failure.

We find similar developments, though with a number of national differences, in many central banks. The Bank of England, the very model for Western central banks, has a long history of contributing to government funding in difficult situations—when Norges Bank was established a century before, this model and role had been warned against. Nevertheless, Great Britain, France, and Germany are not the most relevant points of comparison here. Capie, Goodhart, and Schnadt rightly pointed out that a given social institution's 'independence' is necessarily subordinate when the nation's existence, autonomy, and central institutions are at stake.[70] But in principle the other Scandinavian countries took the same path.[71] The Norwegian provisioning loan, for example, was designed as a carbon copy of a corresponding operation involving the Riksbank. Beyond the Nordic countries, a similar development can be found in Switzerland and the Netherlands—and in neutral Switzerland the central bank was already engaged in government financing as early as 1914. Distinctive aspects in Norway were perhaps that the increase in liquidity was so large that the government had limited control over its activities and borrowing, and that the speculative bubble built up in the last years of the war to the extent that the decline would be all the greater when the time came to remedy the situation when conditions normalized around 1920.

When the Party is Over

The thoughts Karl Gether Bomhoff entertained on his way home from his grand farewell dinner at the Grand Hotel, with words of homage, speeches, and summaries, are unknown to us. Already before the farewell dinner, signs of a hangover from the war times' excesses had manifested themselves, and events of the previous years must have taken up Bomhoff's attention at the end of his tenure. The Norwegian monetary system was in an utter shambles. The money supply had increased 3.5 times since the outbreak of the war, and consumer prices had tripled.[72] After having peaked towards the end of 1917, the Norwegian krone's value had been in free fall. The krone had fallen below its earlier par value in spring 1919, and was now worth around half of its

---

[69] See material in, FD/FKC/D/Da/L0597 og L0598.
[70] Capie, Goodhart, and Schnadt, *The Development of Central Banking*.
[71] Gjermund Rongved, 'Blurring the Borders: How the Central Banks of the European Neutrals during the First World War Became Part of the State Machinery: Examining the Case of Norway', *The International History Review* (2018).
[72] Statistics Norway, 'Historisk statistikk 1968', *Statistics Norway, Oslo* (1978), tables 246, 247, and 282.

pre-war value. Norges Bank's independence from government had come into play. The stability of the financial system had been undermined and cooperation within the currency union had failed. Bomhoff left behind him a fragile institution, faced with serious challenges.

During the war's early phase, no one, especially not Norges Bank's leadership, had imagined such an outcome. The early crisis-related measures were deployed in a period where everyone expected a short war and a rapid return to normal conditions. The central bank was nevertheless worried, as a central bank often is. Norges Bank was concerned about pressured business sectors unable to share in the substantial war profits. This made the central bank less inclined to raise the discount rate as a tightening measure. The central bank's concerns were evident in the handling of provisioning loans to the Norwegian government and associated loans to the warring parties. Fear of a fatal outcome for the Norwegian population and economy left the bank obliged to contribute. The lay of the land overshadowed the letter of the law.

The latter was not entirely new: 'social considerations' were also used to justify actions stretching beyond the letter of the law in the wake of the Kristiania crash. As mentioned, the law said nothing about rescuing banks or about 'social considerations'; it did not say anything about emergency provisioning or 'national considerations' either, which became the normative concept during the war years. The difference between those two episodes is not first and foremost the nature of the formal rules applied, but the consequences and posterity's perception of them. During the Kristiania crash, Bomhoff acted in a manner many future economists and politicians (and indeed historians) would look favourably upon. Banks are social institutions that should often be rescued if they are solvent, sometimes even if they are not. In addition, the operation as a whole was rather successful on that occasion.

In retrospect, however, monetary policy during the First World War has been considered fundamentally unsuccessful. This was due to the sum of numerous small decisions, taken over a long period. Norges Bank took a day-to-day approach in addressing many acute and often conflicting needs, and attempted to strike a balance as best it could. Later generations of economists and historians have criticized a lack of principles, control, and overview over the entire financial household, with which Norges Bank became increasingly intertwined.

Bomhoff could be content that unemployment and distress had been lowered and that Norway had succeeded in maintaining its neutrality. It is symptomatic that this was also the Knudsen government's main objective during the crisis years. Indeed, attempts to bring about balance underline Norges Bank's importance for and coincident objectives with the state apparatus. Hence, the experiences of the First World War point further on in time towards the central bank's subjugation to government authority following the next world war.

However, before that time, the efforts to regain independence and return to pre-war normalcy, by means of the prolonged and costly parity policy, would contribute to placing Norges Bank at the centre of power in economic life.

7

The Pyrrhic Victories of the 1920s

The 1920s began with wild fluctuations in output and employment and a yearning for radical change that penetrated to the heart of the political establishment, combined with social upheaval and labour conflicts. The Liberal government appointed committees to examine the possibility of introducing workers' councils and profit sharing in business and industry and future state ownership of present private enterprises. 'It is not easy today to enter fully into the conditions of the time in 1917, 1918 and 1919. World empires had been seen to collapse. Anything could happen',[1] the professor of economics, Erling Petersen, wrote in a historical account of the period.

Nevertheless, in all this turbulence there is no doubt that, all in all, the established order emerged supreme that decade. The issue that more than any other marks the continuity with pre-war thinking is the strict and drawn-out monetary policy that re-established the value of the krone at pre-1914 parity. Despite the high social and economic costs, established fundamental principles of the liberal order were restored to the Norwegian monetary system.

When studying the making of economic and monetary policies, it is tempting to believe that the restoration of the krone to its pre-war value was a victory for politics, chosen by Norway's political institutions, despite the ongoing pain that pursuing this policy had caused. However, the Storting and the government withdrew to the side-lines in vital phases of the parity policy, forgoing any assessment of ends or means. Economic policy issues were important to the policy-makers of the day, though less so than many historians would like to believe. The church controversy and prohibition were probably more prominent contemporary political issues; the latter leading to three changes of government in that decade. Following the chaotic years during and after the First World War, politics ceded the economic realm to institutional technocrats, represented especially by the governor of Norges Bank, Nicolai Rygg (1920–46). For good or ill, Rygg was the strongman the situation set the stage for.

Rygg started out with strong support from the political and intellectual milieus in his programme for restoring the pre-war value of the krone. Gradually, the support eroded. Concerns and doubts spread among economists, especially after the devastating banking crises in the years 1923–4 and the declining profitability and heavy real debt burden in vital parts of the domestic economy. The growing labour movement and Labour Party—on a socialist programme, hostile to the vital institutions of

---

[1] Erling Petersen, *Norsk Arbeidsgiverforening gjennom 50 år* (Grøndahl, 1950), 337.

Norges Bank 1816–2016. Einar Lie, Oxford University Press (2020). © Norges Bank.
DOI: 10.1093/oso/9780198860013.001.0001

capitalism, which Rygg personalized in the eye of the critics—came to represent the most important threat to Norges Bank's policies in its final stage.

Labour came out as the winner of the parliamentary election in 1927 and formed a new, short-lived government in early 1928. When the government was overthrown after a few weeks in office, the parity policy could be completed and 'normalcy' restored. However, Rygg and Norges Bank won a costly victory. In the aftermath, the parity policy was mainly seen as erroneous and misguided. Rygg's active role in overthrowing the Labour government in 1928 became a formative element in the labour movement's perceptions of Norges Bank's and its governor's past—and future—role in Norwegian society.

Rationale for Parity

Around 1920, all participants in the ongoing public debate seemed to agree that the fiscal and monetary policies during the war had been mismanaged. However, in the early phase of the war, there was, as mentioned, a debate among economists on the role monetary expansion played in the sharp rise in prices. The adherents of the so-called 'banking school' believed that expanding the money supply by extending loans to sound, profitable projects did not necessarily create higher inflation.

Opposing the banking school was the 'quantity theory', which had deep historical roots. It maintained that there was a relatively fixed correlation between money growth and price inflation. Supporters of the theory saw the price inflation also in the early phase mainly as a result of strong expansion of liquidity and credits.

In 1920, Nicolai Rygg, whose monetary policy views largely coincided with the quantity theory, became governor of Norges Bank.[2] However, this theoretical basis explains only a part of the reason for the strongly felt desire of the time on the part of Rygg and most commentators to return to pre-war monetary values. The pre-war *status quo ante* beckoned. And it beckoned even more intensely in 1920 than during the war. Economists with somewhat different views on the relation between monetary expansion and inflation seemed to agree that the monetary system should be restored on familiar grounds. This change can be illustrated by the views of the professor of economics Oscar Jæger, who in a lecture in 1916 had clearly distanced himself from the orthodox 'metallic' views on the relation between gold and money held by many economists and not least of the general public. Jæger pragmatically pointed out that money performed its task as a means of payment or store of value as long as it was legal tender and universally accepted. He also pointed out that the money supply and price levels were strongly influenced by major gold strikes, such as in the Transvaal and in Alaska, and by new industrial processes (e.g. cyanide leaching) which made it

---

[2] Rygg's first account of the relationship between prices and money, cf. Gunnar Jahn, Alf Eriksen, and Preben Munthe, *Norges Bank gjennom 150 år* (Norges Bank, 1966). The following paragraphs are largely based on Einar Lie, *Norsk økonomisk politikk etter 1905* (Universitetsforlaget, 2012), ch. 2.

easier to extract gold from ore. More gold meant more money in circulation. Of course, the value of money was fixed in relation to gold, but *all other* values were affected by how much gold could be mined and panned for in the various gold rushes, so that more money could be put into circulation. Jæger argued that such randomness in determination of the money supply made gold less rational as a 'fixed' measure of value in a modern economy.[3]

In 1919, the same Jæger said something different. His fundamental views on money had not turned towards the dedicated metallists. And he joined the chorus that called for restoring order to the inflated and neglected Norwegian economy. 'On the whole, these matters could not have been managed more poorly', he explained in reference to monetary and fiscal policy. 'We need to return to full gold redeemability', he demanded. Interest rates had to be raised sharply to push down the money supply. 'This increase is certain to be quite substantial and will probably meet with vociferous protest by businesses, but nevertheless, prices must be forced down.'[4] Here Jæger was speaking at a debate before a meeting in the Economists' Association, which a number of prominent economists, businessmen, and politicians attended. His comments followed a lecture by another professor of economics, professor Thorvald Aarum, who declared that 'all thinking people' had now understood that the destruction of the monetary system was the fault of the policies that had been pursued during the war and were still being pursued even after the end of hostilities. No dissenting views had been presented at the debate.

At that meeting was Nicolai Rygg. Rygg, a professor of economics, previously a director of what is now Statistics Norway, and a short time later governor of Norges Bank. In Norges Bank, the second in command after Bomhoff had resigned and taken up a position in Den norske Creditbank—the large commercial bank established in 1857, right before the deep financial crises. A new deputy governor, Erling Sandberg, had entered office. Bomhoff had hoped that Sandberg would succeed him after his retirement. However, Sandberg left office for a position in the management of Christiania Bank og Kreditkasse, where he soon became chief executive. (To the general Norwegian public, Sandberg's name and reputation is unfavourably tied to his manoeuvring during the war, when he took office in Vidkunn Quisling's cabinet as a minister of finance.) When the position was announced, only two persons applied, both without sufficient weight and experience. The prime minister then turned to Rygg and managed to persuade him to take on the duty as Norges Bank's governor.

By that time, Rygg had produced a sheaf of reports and other publications on economic, social, and historical topics. Rygg has, understandably, been portrayed by later observers as not only the defender of the established order, but also as an authoritarian, conservative figure who stood firm against forces advocating radical systemic change in interwar politics and economic thought. He was all this, perhaps,

---

[3] Oscar Jæger, 'Guldspørgsmaalet', *Statsøkonomisk tidsskrift* 30, no. 2 (1916).
[4] Jæger's statements in the Economists' Association, referred in *Statsøkonomisk tidsskrift* (3) 1919, 140.

but the Nicolai Rygg who was appointed by the financially discredited Gunnar Knudsen government, was also something more—and perhaps something else.

Rygg was not only a well-known expert, but also someone who could act with moral authority. Of the works that he devoted a great deal of effort to and in which posterity has lost interest are comprehensive socio-statistical studies of the disadvantaged. His express ideal was the pioneer social scientist Eilert Sundt, who combined advanced social research with a strong commitment to improving the lot of those living in poverty or dependent on others. Regarding the same Sundt, the historian Jens Arup Seip wrote that as a young man, he 'was searching for a cause to devote himself to'.[5] Perhaps the same applied to Rygg.

Aarum concluded his lecture in 1919 with a comparison with the situation a hundred years earlier, when the young Norwegian nation over many years and at great sacrifice established the monetary system that was now in crisis. Rygg surely understood the comparison; he had published his monumental history of Norges Bank the previous year. In it his sympathy clearly lay with those who had worked vigorously to secure the value of the speciedaler at the legally prescribed parity in the decades leading up to the long-promised convertibility of notes against silver at par value in 1842. Rygg was in no doubt as to how important this effort was for the new nation, and it may be that he saw not only his own cause, but also himself in a broader historical context, not least when an increasing number of parity-adherents were seized by scepticism and uncertainty as the crisis-beset decade wore on.

One of Rygg's frequently quoted justifications for restoring statutory redeemability was uttered during the 1927 annual address, right before the goal was reached:

> It would not be enough to argue that standing by a decision once made entails drawbacks [...] We are speaking about a matter of fundamental importance to the nation over time. The hardships arising from the transition to normal, lawful conditions are transitory. No one is blind to how very serious they are. But the nation is eternal, and what is at issue is a decision with importance down the generations.[6]

This was a decision that Rygg was willing to implement, even though it was unpopular and burdensome.

There were serious misgivings because the high interest rate and tight liquidity made borrowing difficult and expensive. Prices were pushed down, but it was acknowledged early on that wage costs did not fall to the same degree. This gave rise to profitability problems for businesses and farmers. Debts had to be repaid in kroner that were increasing in value. This was a hardship. On the bright side, creditors, often invoked as conscientious 'little guy' savers, saw the value of their savings restored. The rights of savers were one of the principal arguments for parity: it was unfair for those

---

[5] Lie, *Norsk økonomisk politikk etter 1905*, 48.
[6] Quoted from Francis Sejersted, 'Demokrati og rettstat: Et perspektiv på 1800-tallets politiske brytninger', in *Demokrati og rettstat* (Pax Forlag, 2001), 153–99.

who deposited a gold krone in the bank or lent it in 1914 to risk getting it back in the form of a paper krone with less than half the original value only a few years later.

After a number of years, with several rounds of debt restructuring or settlement in the meantime, these 'savers' rights' arguments began to lose their immediate postwar appeal. Wartime profiteering and financial decline were also more pertinent and contrasted with the purifying nature of maintaining a steady course and adhering to principle in the first postwar years. 'Back to gold or the Deluge,' wrote the editor of the business magazine *Farmand* in 1920.[7]

Contraction and Crises in Business and Banking

Parity entailed returning to a situation where a kilogram of gold cost NOK 2,480, compared with around NOK 3,600 in early 1920. The US dollar had remained fixed to gold, so that a return to NOK 2,480 on the international foreign exchange market meant that the krone would have to appreciate from around NOK 5.70 to NOK 3.75 per USD. When prices are pushed down by austerity measures, the krone would by definition be worth more in the domestic market, in turn causing the krone to appreciate against pegged currencies. Norway was not alone in its open pursuit of a deflationary policy, though no country carried it out consistently from such a disadvantaged position.

The path to parity was made longer immediately before the rise in the krone was initiated. In mid-1920, the extremely high price level in Norway was expected to fall, because the expected postwar crisis had already taken hold, resulting in rapid deflation in the US and the UK. The effects of this crisis might have helped to push prices down and the value of the krone up. However, several labour unions demanded compensation for the previous year's price rise. In summer 1920, a court of arbitration awarded them a 23.5 per cent increase in contractual pay rates.[8] This drove prices even higher, at a time when they were supposed to fall. This put the business sector in a profit squeeze, and the arbitration award set the stage for a major labour conflict the following year, when employers would demand substantial wage reductions to compensate for the price decline that the economy and monetary policy was forcing on them. Here a policy that coordinated wages and deflationary policies would have had a far better outcome. But as there was little room, either institutionally or in terms of *realpolitik*, for the government to coordinate wage and price policy, this meant more business failures and exacerbated labour conflicts.

Norges Bank's discount rate, which guided national interest rates, was gradually raised from 5.5 per cent to 7 per cent in 1920. This policy was supplemented by Norges Bank's specific lending activity through its regional offices. This lending was

---

[7] Quoted from Knut Kjeldstadli, *Et splittet samfunn 1905–35*, Aschehougs Norgeshistorie (1994), 86.
[8] Tore Jørgen Hanisch, Espen A. Søilen, and Gunhild J. Ecklund, *Norsk økonomisk politikk i det 20. århundre: verdivalg i en åpen økonomi* (Høyskoleforl., 1999), 68.

curtailed, and domestic liquidity, the quantity of notes in circulation and prices, declined through 1921 and 1922.

The Collapse of the Banking Sector

Rygg was fond of maritime metaphors, especially when the nation's economy was in 'perilous waters' or being 'battered by a powerful gale'. 'There are rough seas dead ahead', he said in late 1921, when signs of a more extensive crisis in the banking sector started to become clear. The first banks were in trouble already in 1920, but it was not until 1923/4 that Norway suffered a full-scale banking crisis, with heavy losses and classic bank runs by anxious customers.

Economists and historians have disagreed about the factors that are most important for explaining the crisis. Some have attached the most importance to the considerable slippage during and after the First World War, which necessarily led to austerity and a higher number of business failures.[9] Others have expressed the opinion that the parity policy's initial phase was important. Austerity came at the same time as the postwar crisis and global deflation took hold, the economic conditions of banks and their customers deteriorated, and the desire to withdraw liquidity acted as a constraint on support measures on the part of the central bank.[10]

Regardless of the ultimate cause, the crisis was extensive, by both contemporary and current standards: 131 banks failed. Some resumed normal operations, others went bankrupt, and most were liquidated by the government after a period under public administration. In the worst year of the crisis, 1923, commercial and savings bank losses amounted to an incredible 7 per cent of GDP (gross domestic product). By comparison, during the decidedly worst year (1991) of the large Norwegian banking crisis of the early 1990s, losses totalled approximately 3 per cent of GDP.[11]

During the banking crisis in the 1990s, the authorities operated with a clear division between the central bank's 'liquidity support' and the government's 'solvency support'. Norges Bank could provide liquidity if it was clear that the recipient bank still had equity capital. However, a decision to inject equity capital would be made by the government following deliberations via the political process. The legislation surrounding Norges Bank's support in the 1920s was broadly similar, as the central bank, as previously mentioned, should only give loans against good collateral. However, we do not find the same clear division of labour between the state and the central bank in

---

[9] This is most clearly expressed by Sverre Knutsen, inter alia in Gunhild J. Ecklund and Sverre Knutsen, *Vern mot kriser? Norsk finanstilsyn gjennom 100 år* (Fagbokforl., 2000), ch. 4; and Sverre Knutsen, 'Kritisk historisk forskning om økonomisk politikk', *Sosialøkonomen*, no. 3 (2000), 10–15; and by Hermod Skånland, 'En skjev historie', *Sosialøkonomen*, no. 8 (1999), 2–5 (cf. also his opinion piece in *Aftenposten*, 30 May 1998).

[10] The most obvious representative of this view in recent literature is Hanisch, Ecklund, and Søilen, *Norsk økonomisk politikk i det 20. århundre: verdivalg i en åpen økonomi*. Somewhere in the middle we find, e.g., Wilhelm Keilhau, *Den norske pengehistorie* (Aschehoug, 1952); and Fritz Hodne and Ola Honningdal Grytten, *Norsk økonomi i det tyvende århundre* (Fagbokforl., 2002).

[11] Hermod Skånland, '*Bankkrise og livet etterpå*', in Penger og kreditt (1990).

concrete rescue operations. Norges Bank's actions where mainly constrained by its own judgements of the individual bank's ability to survive in the long run, and of the central bank's financial resources.

In addition, the institutions in place to deal with such a crisis were weak and rudimentary. There were bank examiners for savings banks, but supervision of commercial banks did not come until 1925, as a consequence of the crisis. There was no clear division of responsibility between the government, ministry, and central bank, nor had any clear principles been formulated for how losses arising in a bank would be borne after the shareholders and equity had been wiped out.

Throughout 1921, a total of thirty-five commercial banks turned to Norges Bank for financial support. Rygg and his deputy, Sverre Thorkildsen, worked full time, including Sundays, sometimes through the night to find solutions for banks in financial trouble. Norges Bank looked like an 'operating theatre', Rygg later explained, as one bank after another were brought to the central bank for life-saving treatment. In 1921 and 1922, the authorities pursued a reconstruction and support policy.[12] Troubled banks were encouraged to merge with stronger institutions. In 1922, several banks were given substantial capital injections in order remain open. Among them were the country's two largest banks, Centralbanken and Foreningsbanken. Centralbanken received NOK 50 million in subordinated loan capital. Of this amount, Norges Bank subscribed half, while the government and private interests injected two-sixths and one-sixth, respectively. No complete picture of Centralbanken's financial situation existed when the support was given, and as far as Foreningsbanken was concerned, it was clear that nearly all equity capital had been lost. At large meetings attended by members of the cabinet, the president of the Storting, Norges Bank, and representatives of private banks, fresh funds were placed on the table, but were not as readily forthcoming. Later, Nicolai Rygg gave an account of the urgent plea from the president of the Storting, Otto B. Halvorsen, to rescue the bank. 'We had to stretch ourselves a good deal, since the collapse of banks would be a catastrophe for our country. The private banks as well as Norges Bank conceded this much, but at the same time vociferously asserted the regard for their own position they were obliged to take.'[13] This time, Norges Bank's contribution was NOK 10 million of a total of NOK 50 million. Private contributions were modest, and the government through the Ministry of Finance had to cover the lion's share.

From 1923, the problems became exacerbated owing to new bank runs. During the Kristiania crash, Norges Bank had tried, and to a large extent succeeded, in saving banks of vital systemic importance. With the rapid widening of the crisis, the government and Norges Bank found it impossible to provide enough support to keep the large number of banks in need for financial support running. A new law to deal with

---

[12] The following paragraphs are written in view of Engebretsen, *Norsk Bankvesen*, Rygg, *Norges Banks historie*, and Sverre Knutsen and Gunhild J Ecklund, 'Vern mot kriser? Norsk finanstilsyn gjennom 100 år' (Fagbokforlaget, 2000), in particular.

[13] Quoted from E. Engebretsen, *Norsk bankvesen: et historisk riss med særlig vekt på forholdene etter verdenskrigen* (Tanum, 1939), 83.

the crisis, the Administration Act, was passed in March of that year. The law was targeted mainly at preventing the effects of the widening number of depositor runs on troubled banks. Banks brought under public administration would get a new Executive board, appointed by Norges Bank. Their existing deposits would be frozen so as to make further bank runs impossible. However, the bank could accept new deposits, which had priority over older ones. Pre-administration deposits earned simple interest on the frozen amount; interest was not compounded. As the years passed, the interest foregone was substantial. However, the actual guarantee scheme for new deposits created a self-reinforcing effect, in that banks not (yet) placed under public administration lost depositors to banks that were administered by the government. To use a contemporary simile, the banks fell like dominos, where one bank's collapse knocked the next one over, and so forth. The first major bank forced into public administration was Foreningsbanken. The very next day, Centralbanken asked to be placed under public administration, in order to stop runaway withdrawals.

During the days that followed, Norway's fifth largest bank, Handelsbanken, was (to use a metaphor close to the governor's heart) able to ride out the storm. But after serious difficulties in the face of a new run, the bank implored the government for assistance. The prime minister and minister of finance, Abraham Berge, covertly deposited NOK 25 million in Treasury funds. The following year, Norges Bank provided NOK 15 million. However, Norges Bank demanded and received a government guarantee for this amount, as insurance against a loss. Handelsbanken was quickly put into liquidation. The same fate befell Centralbanken and the vast majority of commercial banks brought under administration, though the winding-up period extended until the mid-1930s. Moreover, political repercussions included impeachment proceedings against Berge and his ministers for spending government funds without obtaining the consent of or informing the Storting. They were acquitted in 1927, with some members of the impeachment tribunal dissenting.

In the years following the crisis, total bank losses were estimated of the order of NOK 1.8–1.9 billion, of which just over NOK 350 million was borne by depositors, whose savings vanished. The government bore a smaller share of these losses. But the real losses on deposits were greater, owing to foregone interest on amounts that had been frozen over a long period.

Back on the Road to Pre-War Parity

The liquidity supplied in the years 1921–3 by Norges Bank to private banks in trouble was fully at odds with Rygg's wishes with regard to the paramount objective of restoring the krone to its former value in gold. During these years, however, the liquidity effects of banking policy were virtually neutralized by the hard line on lending to private individuals and local governments. This line continued in the years 1924–6, during which a substantial portion of loans and deposits was repaid to Norges Bank by commercial and savings banks. Thus, the central bank pursued a policy of contraction until parity was achieved in early 1928, even though the policy was violated by central bank transactions with banks during the central bank's handling of the banking crisis.

Among the ranks of professional economists there was increasing dissent from the parity policy's normative and political arguments. This was partly because the policy's undesirable effects had become apparent and partly because the forcefully expressed need to restore order after the First World War faded. As the years passed, the fairness arguments for parity also began to lose some of their force. A crucial argument for parity advocates was that a gold standard ensured that creditors would not able to settle their obligations in depreciated kroner, or, from other side of the debt transaction, that savers and lenders would actually be guaranteed their money back at the agreed value. When more than ten years had passed since 1914, and depository and debt relationships had shifted sharply among persons and businesses, it became less and less evident just what sort of justice was being served.

Incidentally, this point was also a key part of the British debate, over the choice between deflation and expected unemployment on the one hand, and the depreciation of the value of the assets of large and small savers on the other. 'Of the two perhaps deflation is [...] the worse; because it is worse in an impoverished world, to provoke unemployment than to disappoint the rentier', wrote one of the most noted opponents of parity, the economist John Maynard Keynes, in 1923.[14]

The krone had appreciated from autumn 1920, although a substantial current account deficit caused by the downturn pushed down on the exchange rate in mid-1921 (see Figure 7.1). This was followed by a renewed appreciation, until the banking

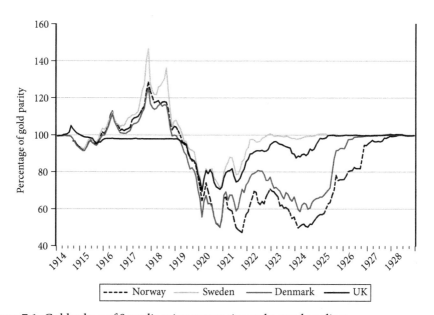

Figure 7.1 Gold values of Scandinavian currencies and pound sterling

[14] John Maynard Keynes, *A Tract of Monetary Reform* (Macmillan, 1923), 40.

crisis hit with full force in 1923. Sweden returned to parity relatively quickly; there had been less slippage there during the previous years, and the problems in the banking industry were more limited in scope. Developments in Denmark paralleled those in Norway to some extent. But the problems in the banking industry were less extensive, and the result of the actions taken was a more rapid return to near normal banking activity. The distance to the pre-war gold price was also less in Denmark, which meant that the implementation of parity policy could be made briefer and less painful.

Towards the middle of the decade, the path to parity appeared to be an impossible and unreasonable goal. In 1924, Wilhelm Keilhau, at the time a university lecturer in political economy, advocated stabilizing the gold price at the current level. His arguments were identical to those of Keynes quoted above: deflation was 'brutal and unjust', inflation 'impaired credit'. What remained was what he perceived to be a middle course, namely reintroducing a gold standard with redeemability, but at a lower price than the one prevailing until 1914.

Through 1925 it was clear that all university economists supported such a course. In 1926, it was endorsed by a government-appointed currency commission. This commission was chaired by Gunnar Jahn, Nicolai Rygg's successor at Statistics Norway. While the currency commission did not explicitly oppose parity policy, it did recommend that the krone be stabilized at the existing gold and dollar value, and to take a possible next step at a later date 'once more experience has been gained'. However, government never made an explicit decision to halt the parity policy. The value of the krone had increased from the middle of 1924. In January 1926, Norge Bank increased its discount rate from 5 to 6 per cent. The external value of the notes continued to increase, relatively sharply early in 1927.

Threat from the Labour Party

The goal was reached in 1928, by which time the krone had long stood close to its pre-war value. Even so, the final six months before the krone was fixed at its earlier parity in terms of gold proved to be among the most dramatic in the history of Norges Bank. Two parties had roundly criticized the parity policy and Norges Bank in the election campaign in 1927, the emergent Labour Party and the Agrarian Party, the latter founded in 1920. The result of the general election on 19 October 1927 came, according to Rygg's memoires, 'as an enormous shock'.[15] Although it was not Norges Bank's reaction he was referring to, the indications are that the election outcome also aroused concern in the bank. The Labour Party progressed from twenty-four to fifty-nine seats, making it the largest party in the Storting. Probably no less surprising was the same party's acceptance of the king's request to form a government once the Storting had convened for a new session at the end of January 1928.

---

[15] Nicolai Rygg, *Norges Bank i mellomkrigstiden* (Gyldendal, 1950), 321.

After a sharp appreciation of the krone and deflation set in during 1925, the Labour Party rallied around harsh criticism of the non-socialist monetary policy.[16] Part of the Labour Party's criticism targeted the substantial executive power over the parity policy that resided in Norges Bank. The fact that a partially privately owned bank could raise the discount rate, apparently without regard to unemployment and the debt situation in rural communities, was tantamount to provocation. Some saw it as evidence that international banking capital in all its ramifications was the true power broker in Norway. After a while the criticism pointedly referred to 'Norges Bank and the economic forces and powers that Norges Bank represents'.[17]

The Labour Party was sharply critical not only of the monetary policy and of Norges Bank's leading role in it, but of the entire non-socialist/capitalist social order and its institutions. Inspired by the Russian revolution, the party had since 1918 turned in a revolutionary direction and a social-democratic wing established itself as a separate party. Although those loyal to Moscow broke away from the party in 1923, and although the party reunited with the Social Democrats in 1927, it retained a distinctly socialist and revolutionary profile throughout the 1920s. This was at about the same time as the labour parties of Sweden, Denmark, and the United Kingdom took the reins of government for the first time. In the Norwegian Labour Party, instances in neighbouring countries of social democrats joining non-socialist coalition governments were referred to with deep contempt.[18]

The landowners, factory managers, and Supreme Court lawyers who made up Norges Bank's Executive board in the 1920s were clearly not supporters of the Labour Party. True, chairman Rygg showed much personal sympathy for parts of the labour movement's cause, but he was at the same time frustrated over the Labour Party's extreme rhetoric and assaults on Norges Bank.[19] Rygg, like others, was evidently worried about 'those forces that are seeking to bring a catastrophe upon us'.[20]

When the Labour Party surprisingly ended up accepting the king's request to form a government in January 1928, the party might naturally be assumed to have taken a step *away* from its hardboiled revolutionary line and thus drawn closer to the stance of labour parties in Norway's neighbours. But not even a Labour Party operating under the parliamentary rules of the game reassured Norges Bank. The moderates in the party's Storting group, in the first instance Christoffer Hornsrud, to whom we will soon return, had right from the start of the 1920s tabled motions in the Storting that in various ways undermined the policy that the bank sought to pursue. At centre stage for the party was the proposal for a Storting-appointed banking council which would not only oversee the private banks and their activities but also have overarching responsibility for the entire monetary policy: interest rate setting, foreign exchange

[16] Quoted from Haakon Meyer, *Den første arbeiderregjering* (Det norske Arbeiderpartis forlag, 1928), 18.
[17] 'Pengemakt eller folkemakt: Arbeiderregjeringen – bankdiktaturet' [pamphlet], (Det norske Arbeiderpartis forlag) 1928: 19.
[18] Ivar A. Roset, Det norske Arbeiderparti og Hornsrud regjeringsdannelse i 1928 (Universitetsforlaget, 1962).
[19] Francis Sejersted, 'Ideal, teori og virkelighet: Nicolai Rygg og pengepolitikken i 1920-årene', in *Demokrati og rettsstat*, ed. Francis Sejersted (Pax, 2001).
[20] Rygg, *Norges Bank i mellomkrigstiden*, 359, see also 78–9.

management, and lending.[21] On a more fundamental level, all the Labour Party proposals pointed in the same direction: the current monetary policy—not only its objectives but also the means chosen—was a matter on which democratically elected politicians should be entitled to have their say. Compared with the preceding period, this was an entirely new departure.[22]

Such concrete proposals had a far wider appeal than rambling plans for revolution and a socialistic social order. They were probably also an important element in the Labour Party's substantial advancement. The fact that the party succeeded in presenting itself as a credible alternative to the present monetary policy was at the time viewed as one of the main explanations behind its election success.[23]

Parity Policy's Rescue and the Organization Securitas

After its success in the general election, the Labour Party was invited to form a government. This task felt Christoffer Hornsrud, who assumed the positions of prime minister and finance minister. The government formation had economic as well as other repercussions—in the currency market and the private banks—which gave rise to just as much, if not more, immediate concern for Norges Bank. True, developments had, viewed from Rygg's vantage point, had already taken a wrong turn a few months prior to the election. Norges Bank had succeeded in raising the krone exchange rate to 98 per cent of par, but the value of the overall foreign currency holdings had fallen from NOK 300 million in January 1927 to about 100 million at the beginning of October. In the period after the election the rate of capital outflow accelerated dramatically. Over the course of just a few weeks in October the bank sold foreign currency worth more than NOK 30 million.[24] In the days prior to and after the formation of the new government the figure reached almost NOK 54 million.[25] 'There was an utter state of emergency in this period', Rygg later asserted.[26] He never doubted that it was the political uncertainty that prompted the capital flight.

To Rygg's mind Norges Bank faced a dual challenge. On the one hand the reserves were almost exhausted, at the same time as the banking crisis was set to flare up anew. One of the two remaining large commercial banks was beset with major solvency and liquidity problems.[27] Both circumstances would undermine confidence in the krone and potentially make it impossible to maintain an exchange rate close to parity. On the other hand, the new, post-election situation, with the Labour Party and the Agrarian Party in the majority, threatened to impair Norges Bank's opportunity to resolve the challenges in a manner that would win confidence in the markets.

---

[21] Egil Nysæter, 'Sosialistene og pengepolitikken 1920–1928', masters thesis, University of Bergen (1972), 54.
[22] This was the Norwegian variant of an international tendency, cf. Barry Eichengreen, *Golden Fetters: The Gold Standard and the Great Depression, 1919–1939* (Oxford University Press, 1992).
[23] Meyer, *Den første arbeiderregjering*.
[24] Norges Bank's annual report 1927, 46 (graphical representation).
[25] The krone rose in the same period by just short of 5 per cent.
[26] Rygg, *Norges Bank i mellomkrigstiden*, 346.   [27] Rygg, *Norges Bank i mellomkrigstiden*, 354.

Rygg's attempted solution was also two-track. Through temporary legislation the government would establish a new, temporary institution, the Deposit Agency. The Deposit Agency would accept voluntary deposits from the private banks and from Norges Bank. The agency would then channel these funds to banks hit by a liquidity crisis. The state would guarantee the deposits. Loans provided by the agency to such banks would be backed by collateral in a guarantee fund established by way of mandatory deposits from all banks. Both the agency and the guarantee fund would be placed under the same management board, drawing members from the relatively recently established Bank Inspectorate and Norges Bank.[28] The proposal was radical, and served in the deepest sense to blur the distinction between Norges Bank's responsibility and that of the state. Norges Bank would have a stronger and freer role in supporting failing banks, while the bill for liquidity support that could not be paid back would end up with the central government. Moreover, Rygg was probably not averse to the fact that the agency would contribute to partially camouflaging the incompatibility of the parity policy and the bank support policy and thus ensure that renewed support to the banks did not sour confidence in the parity objective.

In his work on the Deposit Agency Rygg was to operate in close conjunction with a private company, Securitas, which came to be viewed in a somewhat mythical and highly negative light in the emergent labour movement. Behind Securitas' guarantors stood a long line of captains of business and industry with close links, probably on both the owner and client side, to the three major banks that remained after the banking crisis.[29]

Securitas' mission was to stabilize the prices of the shares of those banks: DnC, Bergen Privatbank, and Kreditkassen. When a share price threatened to fall below its nominal value on the Oslo Stock Exchange, Securitas would come forward as a buyer. So long as no other buyers turned up, Securitas would mop up whatever shares were offered by the three banks in order to pre-empt a further fall in value. In 1925 Norges Bank had granted the company an overdraft facility of just over NOK 20 million to make such purchases, secured by the shares purchased and by personal guarantees from Securitas' backers.

The relief action fitted nicely into Norges Bank's picture of the situation. The market for bank shares was heavily impacted by the banking crisis and deflationary expectations. Like Securitas' initiator, Rygg had noted that the run on Foreningsbanken in 1922 and Handelsbanken in 1924 had followed steep falls in the banks' share prices. In both cases individuals connected to the banks had attempted to defend the banks' share prices through support purchases, to no avail. A coordinated relief action for all three remaining large banks would bring greater calm to the share market and to the banks' situation in general.

The most pressing problem as regards the Securitas agreement was the need for secrecy. Due to the nature of the relief action, the collaboration could not be made

---

[28] Eivind Thomassen, 'Knuten på perlekjedet: Securitas-aksjonen og Norges Bank 1925–1928', masters thesis, University of Oslo (2012), 98 et seq.

[29] This and the following are based on Thomassen, 'Knuten på perlekjedet'.

public. Should it become apparent that a single company was buying up all bank shares at par, it would be an invitation to people holding shares in the banks concerned to dispose of them before Securitas ran out of funds. The need for secrecy prompted the Executive board not to inform the Supervisory Council of the credit line. Reports to the Storting make no mention of the collaboration.[30] Further, Rygg brought the Ministry of Finance and the tax assessment authorities on board in keeping the relief action as secret as possible. At a large meeting with other senior government officials, Rygg lamented all the rules and norms that had to be breached to enable Norges Bank and the central government to help Securitas out. However, all present, according to Rygg's handwritten record of the meeting, were 'aware that because the measure was for the public good, they had to turn a blind eye'.[31]

Norges Bank's involvement in price stabilization was not unique. In Sweden the Riksbank (central bank) supported the private company Moneta's involvement in stabilizing the prices of a wide range of share prices. In Denmark too, the central bank made support available for price stabilization, and supported other forms of extraordinary activity. Support for organized strike-breaking raised the question of how far the central bank could go in a socially and politically heated period without putting its political neutrality at stake.[32]

There is no doubt that Securitas by and by became a useful mainstay for Norges Bank. The company's operations were crucial to maintaining share price stability in 1925, 1926, and 1927. Stable prices appear to have contributed to a calmer setting for the banks in more general terms in these years, as illustrated by the absence of a single run on a major bank in the period. In calm periods, with its large network of guarantors, Securitas also assisted Norges Bank's attempts to pressure individual banks into collaboration and to refinance some regional banks. The collaboration between Securitas and Norges Bank grew ever tighter through 1926 and 1927.

Fall of the Labour Party Government and Fulfilment of the Parity Policy Goal

Norges Bank was prepared for difficulties in defending the krone after the new government was formed. At one his first meetings with Hornsrud in the days before the government took office, Rygg sought to persuade Hornsrud to support his proposal for the establishment of a deposit agency, which was also controversial in the non-socialist camp. He also spoke of the ongoing effort to stabilize share prices on the stock exchange, and of Securitas' role. Rygg explained that Securitas' credit line was almost exhausted, and that the company might soon have to abandon its support buying. He announced that prices would be freed up on the same weekend that the

---

[30] This is described more thoroughly in ibid.
[31] The meeting is recorded in one of Rygg's notes, but the date (apart from the year, 1925) is unclear. However, judging by the order of the notes, the time would be the turn of the month October–November.
[32] Erling Olsen and Erik Hoffmeyer, *Monetary History of Denmark 1914–1960* (Danmarks Nationalbank, 1968).

government took office. To Hornsrud and his cabinet colleagues, it must have seemed that the new government was being exposed to immense pressure. It does not seem entirely unreasonable to speak of a systematic spreading of panic.

Viewed from within, this was pressure to which the government could not possibly give way and which thus set the stage for its fall. Opposition in the party to the government's formation had been vehement. It was warned, in Hornsrud's version, that the government would merely be an administrator of the interests of the bourgeoisie. Little would fulfil this prophecy more unequivocally than tabling a proposal designed to protect the banks' interests, which was the government's very first step.

At the same time, Securitas' decision to cancel buy orders on the stock exchange at twelve noon on 28 January, the very point at which the cabinet was to attend its first council of state, was clearly a hostile act. The halt to buying triggered a dramatic price fall and a run on DnC and Bergens Privatbank, just as Rygg had warned. But if tactics were involved in the timing of the halt to buying, they were certainly not involved in the actual decision to call off the relief action. Securitas *was* rapidly nearing the end of the available credit and had known this for some time. New funds could perhaps have been procured, by the guarantors or by Norges Bank, but why should the company agree to that when the government was unwilling to follow Norges Bank's advice? Also pertinent is the fact that Securitas' managing director, along with the company's initiators, was, in confidential meetings with Rygg and the Liberal leader and shipowner Johan Ludwig Mowinckel, himself a Securitas guarantor, adamant that he desired the government's fall at the earliest opportunity.[33]

For his part, Rygg wished to put himself outside the purely parliamentary struggle. He was asked in the government's first few days of office to put his authority behind the demands to topple the government at the earliest opportunity. But Norges Bank would not engage in party politics, he reportedly said.[34] Besides, Rygg asserted later, 'retaining Hornsrud's government would have been a crucial strength'.[35] Rygg admitted that he tried to pressure the incoming government. He even regretted doing so to Hornsrud. However, Rygg considered it his duty as governor of Norges Bank to warn against the dangers that loomed and their consequences.[36] His approach was in that sense matter-by-matter—and ultimately repressive. He would have been agreeable to a government from the avowedly socialistic Labour Party, if only it cast aside its ideological principles and followed the line Norges Bank considered to be the correct one.

Despite the evident gap in their respective basic views, Norges Bank endeavoured to cooperate with the government. When the proposal for a deposit agency was rejected, Rygg asked the Ministry of Finance to arrange a foreign currency loan that would enable Norges Bank to defend the krone exchange rate. That process was duly initiated. However, it was the bank itself, rather than the government, which took

---

[33] Thomassen, 'Knuten på perlekjedet', 114–15.
[34] Rygg's notes, 'Under the Hornsrud regime', 6.2.1928, S-2948/J/L0001, NAN.
[35] Rygg, *Norges Bank i mellomkrigstiden*, 355.
[36] Eivind Thomassen, 'Nytt blikk på Hornsrud-regjeringens fall? Sentralbanken, sosialistene og securitas', *Historisk tidsskrift* 92, no. 3 (2013).

charge of the collaboration. On 2 February Norges Bank raised the discount rate from 5 to 6 per cent without informing the government. When Hornsrud later asked Norges Bank (albeit while presiding over what was merely a caretaker government) to inform the ministry beforehand next time the Executive board planned an interest rate hike, the directors reportedly intimated that they failed to see the point since they would in no event take any action that was not absolutely crucial for the krone exchange rate.[37] However, a few days later the prime minister announced that the central government's credits were now overstretched. A government loan was out of the question, as was holding the value of the krone. When Liberal leader Johan Ludwig Mowinckel came up to Rygg's office immediately afterwards, Rygg spoke his mind. To Mowinckel's query, Rygg replied 'with hand on heart' that the Labour government had to be brought down. 'If the Labour government remains in office, there will be chaos', he explained. The following day a vote of no confidence was called and passed in the Storting. Mowinckel himself referred to Rygg's assessments at a meeting of his party's Storting group.[38]

With the Liberal Party and Mowinckel back in government, the most important framework conditions needed to return the krone to full parity were in place. The Liberal government rapidly procured a foreign currency loan of USD 30 million.[39] Inasmuch as this too failed to restore confidence, Norges Bank won the government's support for a large, composite relief action for DnC. This appeared to turn sentiment around in the krone market. As early as 20 February, Rygg enlisted the cabinet's support to peg the currency to gold at the earliest opportunity to avoid further speculation.[40] By royal decree of 16 April 1928 the government revoked (with effect from 1 May) the decree from March 1920 which had temporarily suspended Norges Bank's obligation to redeem banknotes.[41]

However, the fall of the Hornsrud government was to cast long shadows over the final stage of restoring the krone to its previous parity. The debate in the Storting on Hornsrud's inaugural address and on Mowinckel's government declaration, and the debates on finance and gold redemption, were all characterized by vehement denunciations of the monetary policy by the Agrarian Party and the Labour Party. The debate was more rancorous than ever. Rygg was described as a dictator who, on behalf of international finance, dictated Norway's political development via his 'lackeys' in the Storting. Rygg had 'long ago been appointed head of government by the gang of exploiters and parasites he represents', asserted the Labour Party's main organ, the *Arbeiderbladet* newspaper.[42] 'It is no longer the people that hold the power, but Rygg at Norges Bank.'[43] Criticism from more neutral quarters was also crass.[44]

The agreement on the DnC rescue was in itself instrumental in reinforcing the criticism of Norges Bank's Executive board and the Mowinckel government. Norges Bank's contribution was primarily to take over a number of DnC's problematic exposures.

---

[37] From NOU 1983: 39, *Lov om Norges Bank og pengevesenet*, 112.
[38] Quoted from Thomassen, 'Knuten på perlekjedet'.   [39] Rygg, *Norges Bank i mellomkrigstiden*, 356.
[40] Ibid., 357.   [41] Ibid., 382.   [42] Quoted from ibid., 374.   [43] Ibid., 377.   [44] Ibid., 378.

That was sensational enough, and the resolution was approved by Norges Bank's Executive board with a majority of just one vote. Most controversial, however, was a sizeable offering of various types of credit from a number of major UK banks which Norges Bank had helped to arrange. At meetings with the representative of the UK banks, Norwegian-born Sir Karl Knudsen, Norges Bank and the government avowed that the authorities were prepared to return to the gold standard.[45] Although the negotiations were secret, rumours trickled out. More vehemently than ever the critics maintained that the Norwegian government was prostrating itself before international capital interests, and behind the Storting's back to boot. The agreement with the large UK banks was, according to the *Arbeiderbladet* newspaper, 'the most shameful outrage that has been perpetrated on democracy in Norway'.[46] Interestingly enough, Norges Bank—and even more clearly Mowinckel—denied that assurances of a return to the gold standard had been given, despite the fact that Rygg's own records suggest the contrary.[47]

A Victory More Costly than Pyrrhus'

At the end of April the Storting voted to re-establish full convertibility. The parity policy of the 1920s was over and done with. The months prior to gold convertibility could be seen as a trial of strength between the prevailing society and its challengers. Norges Bank and the supporters of parity were the victors. It was without doubt a victory not just for the prevailing society, but also for Norges Bank. After years of deflation and censure, the central bank had returned the krone to its earlier parity with gold.

This was possibly the apex of Norges Bank's influence, and of its exercise of influence. But in the long run the political costs were so high that the costs of Pyrrhus' epic victory over the Romans at Asculum pale beside them. Rygg and Norges Bank's goal of parity placed them on the wrong side of the political and theoretical divide that the interwar period brought forth in the view of what was good monetary policy. The strongest means available were deployed to attain that goal, and the bank sank deep into the political ballgame revolving around powers of state and government formations.

There is nothing to indicate that Rygg wished to play the role of the non-socialist/capitalistic society's foremost protagonist. In the same way, in a sense, that Christoffer Hornsrud hardly wished to play the role of subverter of the prevailing society. Rygg preferred to justify his views and his actions in terms of what he perceived to be

---

[45] Rygg's notes, 'Mange konferanser', 28 February 1928, 2; 'Det berettes fra mange kanter…', 3 March 1928; 'Sir Karl returnerte idag…', 9 March 1928, S-3947/E//L002, NAN.

[46] Rygg, *Norges Bank i mellomkrigstiden*, 377.

[47] Mowinckel in the Storting, 27 April 1928, Stortingstidende, 1187–8; Rygg's notes, 'Mange konferanser.', 28 February 1928; 'Det berettes fra mange kanter…', 3 March 1928; 'Sir Karl kom tilbake idag…', 9 March 1928, S-3947/E//L002, NAN.

eternal and objective truths. That was how he justified his own and Norges Bank's conduct and prominent position, in the early phase of the parity policy, when clearing up the chaotic banking crisis and bringing the policy to completion.

The role of enemy of the working class soiled the picture. For all that, the fundamental ideological conflict between Rygg and Hornsrud was clearly genuine. Despite a measure of pragmatism and willingness to collaborate, they gravitated to positions which in the 1920s were very far from each other. Rygg desired, in keeping with what throughout had been the will of the non-socialist majority in the Storting, to save the banks from failure and to keep the krone at par. This put him in league with the most conservative forces in politics and society, but there was more to it than that. It was also a goal which in Rygg's eyes was so superior and sacrosanct that it far and away, at all events when the krone stood at 98–9 per cent of its previous par value, precluded compromise with other considerations. It also made it impossible for Hornsrud to accede fully and unequivocally to the requirements set by Norges Bank.

On a deeper level it was the evident economic and social consequences of the parity policy that had triggered the political conflict in the final six months of the process of returning the krone to parity. The fact that the krone exchange rate was a theme of debate in the Storting at all was a novel feature of the 1920s. The tendency was international. Possibly it proved stronger in Norway due to a heavily polarized parliament and a parity policy that was particularly protracted and painful.

8

The 1930s Crisis

Collapse and Zenith

There is hardly any single year that stands out as prominently in the history of Western central banks as the year 1931—and with good reason. That was the year when the gold standard collapsed. Several countries maintained the gold standard, but Great Britain, the system's creator and advocate, had no choice but to abandon it in September. The severe banking crisis on the continent, negatively impacting the entire Western world and rapidly developing into a deep and widespread international crisis, was the cause of the collapse. In addition to that, problems brought forth by the crisis stretched beyond the sphere of the financial system. The aftermath of the crisis was dominated by bankruptcy and unemployment, with adverse effects that would persist for the entire decade.

The year 1931 was of significance also for Norway and Norges Bank. The gold peg, adopted by the Storting in the 1870s, was abandoned by Norges Bank promptly after Great Britain abandoned the gold standard. This was a major decision. However, considering the concrete situation prevailing in Norway at the time, that decision was rather inevitable. A few weeks later came the first signs of stress at the country's two most important banks. Handling both these banks was a challenge. It was decided that Norges Bank should provide unreserved support for the banks in order to avoid, at all costs, a collapse of the fragile banking system. This decision was as unavoidable as the decision to abandon the gold standard.

The collapse of the gold standard and the banking system's vulnerable position followed shortly after the painful reconstruction of old monetary principles in the previous decade. One can find elements of Greek tragedy in the krone's tie to gold during those years. Through generations in the 1800s, the tie to metal had been an expression of economic stability. That stability needed, in the eyes of Norges Bank and the political establishment, to be restored. However, the pursuit of parity in the 1920s, achieved in 1928, delivered only short-lived stability before the meltdown in 1931. The 1920s crisis had also been severe for the banking system, with substantial costs to owners, the government, depositors, and customers, which had been obliged to relate to banks with ever-changing names and owners. The dawn of a new decade nurtured a belief that banks were on solid ground. Nonetheless, after dramatic global events and new significant losses in 1931, the situation seemed just as dismal yet again.

The year 1931 was one of economic crisis, yet one of the finest moments in Norges Bank's institutional history. The new exchange rate policy prevented a tight policy with high interest rates to defend the value of the krone. This new policy also made room for support measures and a relatively flexible monetary policy, first during the run-up to the new banking crisis, and later as a more general policy throughout the decade.

The 1930s was a watershed for monetary policy in Norway and in other countries, marked by a paradigm shift ensuing from new ideas about currency, money, and credit. In Norway, Norges Bank was not an active proponent of the most experimental ideas—central banks rarely are—but the central bank was still given a key role in the quest to resolve the crisis and restore monetary stability.

Gold is Abandoned

The crash of Wall Street in autumn 1929 was accompanied by a sharp fall in US production, with repercussions for Europe.[1] This also influenced global payment flows. Substantial war reparations were imposed on Germany following the First World War. At the same time, France and Great Britain had accumulated sizeable debt, especially to the United States. For a long period, the system functioned as the losers of the war repaid their debt to the European victors, who in turn paid the United States, and a share of the latter's balance-of-payments surplus was channelled back to European banks, mainly in Germany and Austria.

Credit-Anstalt, Austria's largest bank, was the first major victim of the production and payment crisis. The bank collapsed in spring 1931. The crisis spread to Hungary and Germany—although historians disagree on the extent of that contagion and the extent to which the countries were influenced by the same factors that brought down Credit-Anstalt.[2] During summer 1931 the Bank of England raised the discount rate twice in an attempt to contain capital flight, but the problems only intensified through late summer and autumn. On Saturday, 19 September, the pound's convertibility into gold was discontinued. On Monday morning, the enthusiastic dystopian headline of the Labour Party's main newspaper, *Arbeiderbladet*, read: 'The Very Foundation of Capitalist Society is Shaking'.[3]

This immediately posed a challenge for Norges Bank: was it possible and preferable to maintain a tie to gold in a situation where Great Britain had abandoned pound sterling's tie to the metal? Against the background of the monetary policy experience of the 1920s, when Norway went further than any other country to re-establish the old notes' former gold values, one might have expected strong opposition to abandoning the tie to gold. Instead, Norges Bank adopted a clearly pragmatic attitude in the late September days of 1931.

---

[1] The following is mainly based on Barry Eichengreen, *The European Economy since 1945: Coordinated Capitalism and Beyond* (Princeton University Press, 2008).

[2] See e.g. Harold James, 'The Causes of the German Banking Crisis of 1931', *Economic History Review* (1984).

[3] *Arbeiderbladet*, 21 September 1931.

On 19 September, Nicolai Rygg was on a business trip to Madrid; he immediately headed back home, arriving in Oslo on 22 September. In the meantime, the government held a crisis meeting with Norges Bank's remaining board. According to notes taken by the minister of justice, Norges Bank's directors were not especially surprised about the situation.[4] Norges Bank had, like many other European banks, chosen to shift reserves from pound sterling to the US dollar, out of fear that the Bank of England would be incapable of maintaining the position. Sverre Thorkildsen, Rygg's deputy, had also been in contact with the leaders of the Riksbank in Sweden and the Nationalbank in Denmark. Neither of these two banks had plans to abandon the tie to gold in the near future, but the central banks shared the view that the situation was entirely open. When the prime minister and Finance Minister Peder Kolstad asked what the central bank's plan was, Thorkildsen explained that the situation was changing too rapidly for any plan to be drawn up, but that the government should promptly prepare a royal decree to abolish the gold standard. There was little doubt that Thorkildsen believed the government might need to use it in the not too distant future.

During the few days between the fall of the pound and the Nordic countries' resolution to follow, a heated debate took place in Norway. Parity policy was an underlying issue; at times this policy was also explicitly invoked. Several newspapers expressed fear that the Norwegian authorities would end up locked into an established rate. Business and banking organizations also expressed fear, both publicly and behind closed doors, that Norges Bank would keep the new exchange rate between pound sterling and the krone—after a few days the pound stabilized and then remained around 10 per cent weaker than it had been before 19 September.[5]

The problem that was now expected to arise was that the exchange rate would reduce the competitiveness of Norwegian goods and services, immediately against sterling and in the longer term against other currencies that would follow sterling. There were also fears that the krone would be defended by raising interest rates to a high level. In fact, the discount rate was raised by a whole percentage point, to 6 per cent on 25 September. Rygg's public statements could also clearly be construed to mean that the krone should be defended.[6] However, this was a matter of necessity. The fixed exchange rate regime left the central bank governor with no other choice than to affirm that the existing exchange rate would be defended at any time—if not, all confidence in the exchange rate would immediately vanish.

The openly declared will to defend the krone was short-lived. Developments in the other Nordic countries had triggered the fall in the Norwegian krone. On Sunday, 27 September, the four heads of the Nordic central banks met in Stockholm. Veiled in discretion, the meeting was held in the central bank governor's magnificent home in the city of Karlavagen, in Stockholm, not in the Riksbank's own building. The meeting

---

[4] Asbjørn Lindboe, *Fra de urolige tredveårene: Dagboksnedtegnelser og kommentarer* (Tanum, 1965), 108.
[5] Tine Petersen, 'Da Norge forlot gullet: Norges Bank og kurspolitikken 1931–1933' (2011), 30.
[6] *Aftenposten*, 26 September 1931.

opened with a rather extensive account of the Swedish krone's situation and the Riksbank's reserves. Both were seriously affected by the German banking crisis. This crisis had spread to several Swedish banks, which had financed considerable investments in Germany, and shared a number of important clients with German banks that had collapsed. From June to August 1931, the Riksbank had lost 60 per cent of its reserves, mainly because Swedish banks had exchanged their krona in order to cover their liabilities abroad. It soon became apparent that Governor Ivar Rooth of the Riksbank was not offering an analysis and plan of action but a message to his Nordic colleagues: the only option for the Riksbank was to follow the pound.[7]

The Nordic colleagues gave accounts of slightly simpler situations and somewhat divergent evaluations. The Finnish central bank governor believed Finland did not need to abandon gold immediately. The Danish Nationalbank also believed they could hold firm. Rygg reported that the situation in Norway was less precarious than in Sweden. Nevertheless, he supported Rooth and believed that the tie to gold should be abandoned immediately. Rygg did not see any advantages in waiting, only disadvantages, because banks would lose reserves by defending a currency that would necessarily fall in value. The four concluded the meeting with unanimous support for proposing to revoke the gold redemption obligation in their countries. However, they did not agree on any date for this, nor did they define guidelines for their countries' future exchange rate policy.[8]

Shortly after the meeting ended, the decision to abolish the Swedish krona's tie to gold was taken. By telephone, Rygg told members of the cabinet that Norway must do the same. Just before midnight on Sunday, the decision to abandon the tie to gold was made effective—the sequence reflects with perfect clarity the realities and formalities of the decision. Two days later, Denmark followed suit, and on 13 October Finland became the last Nordic country to take the leap into an unknown future.[9]

Professor William Keilhau—Rygg's greatest antagonist at the time, and competitor in the battle to establish a correct understanding of history—described the episode as a defeat for Rygg and Norges Bank in his book *Den norske pengehistorie* (*The Monetary History of Norway*) (1952). He points to the fact that the central bank had attempted to preserve gold for one week, and that Rygg later described the events of September 1931 as a 'currency disaster'.[10] Internal memos clearly demonstrate that Norges Bank wanted to let go of the gold peg. However, Rygg was a firm believer in maintaining a fixed rate for importers and exporters, which was also supported by other Nordic countries. The events of September 1931 saw not only the collapse of the gold standard but also the dissolving of a system with fixed rates of exchange between a large number of trading partners.

---

[7] A detailed account of the meeting and Governor Rooth's opinion is found in Gösta Rooth, 'Ivar Rooth Riksbankschef 1929–1948', *En autobiografi intalad för och utskriven av Gösta Rooth. Stockholm: Gösta Rooth, eget förlag* (1988). See also Petersen, 'Da Norge forlot gullet: Norges Bank og kurspolitikken 1931–1933', 34f.

[8] Rooth, 'Ivar Rooth Riksbankschef 1929–1948'.

[9] Petersen, 'Da Norge forlot gullet: Norges Bank og kurspolitikken 1931–1933', 36.

[10] Wilhelm Keilhau, *Den norske pengehistorie* (Aschehoug, 1952), 195.

This still does not fully explain why Rygg abruptly came to the conclusion that it was appropriate to follow Great Britain and give up the precious gold peg. The British economy and politics were crucial in the West-oriented Norwegian economy. Exchange rate policy (and also trade policy) had been closely linked to Britain for a long period, as indicated in Chapter 6. The policy of parity in Norway was also built on a British model. When pound sterling disconnected from gold, Norges Bank once again followed the guiding, albeit fading, star of Great Britain and the Bank of England.

Throughout the subsequent two years a discussion took place about how the value of the Norwegian krone should be determined—and by whom. Nevertheless, before this discussion could really start, a new acute and severe situation arose, notably a financial crisis at the country's two largest banks.

Rescue Operation for DnC and Bergen Privatbank

While Norway had been less affected than Sweden by the financial collapse on the continent, a very open Norwegian economy had by no means escaped the ill effects of the global crisis. In addition, the Norwegian economy had to face some homemade problems of their own.

The crisis had already struck the Norwegian economy early in 1930. A fall in production first became evident in the latter half of the year, but prices fell quite rapidly throughout the entire year. In early 1931, when a new round of wage negotiation was starting, wholesale prices had fallen by about 15 per cent since the turn of the year 1929/30.[11] Employers demanded a corresponding salary cut. This was rejected by the employees' main organization, which also demanded reduced working hours.[12] The stalemate ended in a major conflict, lasting from April to August. The work stoppage came on top of the intensifying adverse effects of the global crisis. This generated large losses at commercial banks, and their problems deepened due to a steady decline in deposits, reflecting the growing insecurity among the general public. After the krone was depegged from gold on 28 September, the discount rate was raised sharply from 5 to 8 per cent in order to avoid an excessive fall in the value of the krone. This also increased the burden on banks and their customers in the context of an already demanding situation.

After signals that the country's two largest banks, Den norske Creditbank and Bergen Privatbank, experienced appreciable liquidity problems, Norges Bank held meetings with each of the two banks' boards of directors in the beginning of October 1931. After the 1928 crisis, the two banks had managed fairly well. Still, corporate customers severely hit by the economic downturn and labour conflict weighed heavily on their balance sheet.[13]

---

[11] Statistisk sentralbyrå, *Statistisk-økonomisk oversikt over året 1931* (Statistisk sentralbyrå, 1932).

[12] Finn Olstad, *Med Knyttet Neve: 1899–1935*, vol. B.1 (Pax, 2009), 335.

[13] Nicolai Rygg, *Norges Bank i mellomkrigstiden* (Gyldendal, 1950), 444–5; Petersen, 'Da Norge forlot gullet: Norges Bank og kurspolitikken 1931–1933', 198–9.

The leadership at DnC hoped the liquidity problems would be short-lived.[14] However, on 5 November, the chairman of the board of DnC signalled that the bank also faced a solvency problem.[15] Write-offs and a repair were necessary to build a sufficiently solid basis to continue its business. The rescue proposal, sent to Norges Bank on 19 November, contained numerous measures, among other things a write-down of share capital to NOK 11 million.[16] The measures would obviously lead to insecurity among depositors and shareholders, with a drop in share prices and withdrawals from savings accounts, as witnessed many times in the preceding decade. Wise from experience, DnC asked Norges Bank for a NOK 50 million deposit, without collateral and uncallable for three years, with NOK 10 million to be repaid annually. Moreover, DnC requested a public declaration destined to secure the banks' further operation.[17]

Developments in Bergen Privatbank were somewhat similar, even though the board believed that the bank was essentially dealing with a liquidity crisis.[18] While Privatbank was preparing their annual accounts, Norges Bank asked to review the bank's outstanding loans.[19] Early in November, the Bank Inspection reported losses of about NOK 20 million.[20] Here too, the share capital had to be written down, and new share capital needed to be raised. The board was not optimistic with regard to raising the capital needed, and wanted Norges Bank to guarantee the new subscription. Moreover, an arrangement that could secure sufficient liquidity protection was necessary. This protection would be vital during the looming and widely anticipated confidence crisis.[21]

On 11 December—not particularly early—Prime Minister Peder Kolstad of the Farmers' Party was informed of the problem for the first time. The next day Rygg was present at the government meeting to account for the new crisis the Norwegian banking system was facing. At that point, Norges Bank had already defined the premises for the formal crisis management solution: Bergen Privatbank had requested an immediate response as to how Norges Bank planned to address the crisis. The board was therefore convened at short notice. Rygg's evaluation highlighted that the two banks should be treated in a somewhat similar manner. The requirements for guarantees pertaining to equity and liquidity injection would place a heavy burden upon Norges Bank. In addition, there was no provision for either means of support in the existing legislation—the conventional liquidity support, as a lender of last resort, conditioned solvency in the receiving bank. Thus, the answer should be 'no'. Rygg pointed to a solution based on the act relating to commercial banks, which permitted the

---

[14] Ibid., 318.

[15] Minutes from meeting, 23 December 1931, NB/DIR1 A/boks 96. Separat forhandlingsprotokoll for direksjonen, 1914–40.

[16] Erling Petersen, *Norsk Arbeidsgiverforening, 1900–1950* (Grøndahl, 1950); Helge W Nordvik, 'Bankkrise, bankstruktur og bankpolitikk i Norge i mellomkrigstiden', *Historisk tidsskrift* 2 (1992).

[17] Ibid.   [18] Rygg, *Norges Bank i mellomkrigstiden*, 445.

[19] 'Separat forhandlingsprotokoll for direksjonen, 1914–40. Referat 23 December 1931, 2, NB/DIR1/A/boks 96.

[20] Gunhild J. Ecklund and Sverre Knutsen, *Vern mot kriser? Norsk finanstilsyn gjennom 100 år* (Fagbokforl., 2000), 122.

[21] Rygg, *Norges Bank i mellomkrigstiden*, 446.

government to grant a three-month moratorium for crisis-hit banks, or with only 75 per cent or less of the share capital intact. Under such a moratorium, banks could defer repayment of debt without creditors being allowed to seize the banks' assets and demand that the bank be placed under administration. This would provide breathing room for the banks while they continued their work on a reconstruction plan. The proposal was unanimously accepted. On the same day, both banks were informed that the liquidity support demands were rejected and that they needed to inquire with the government concerning a payment deferral by virtue of a moratorium.[22]

A number of politicians wondered why Norges Bank had not supported the banks earlier, in order to avoid the payment consequences. Prime Minister Kolstad repeated several times that the government should have had greater influence over Norges Bank's economic policy and decisions.[23] The government's frustration is easy to understand. The government was informed late, and their only contribution was to work on a moratorium that now had to be adopted. There was no other alternative, partly because Norges Bank had refused to provide liquidity support and loans, and partly because of a government highly reluctant to assume virtually any responsibility or cost.

In several meetings, Rygg indicated that the two banks together represented a third of all lending from commercial banks. For the country's important corporate customers the two banks were utterly dominant. On their own account, Norges Bank elaborated an overview of customers' identity, their turnover, and the number of jobs in each company. Norges Bank came to the conclusion that bankruptcy, or just a longer cessation of operations, would lead to considerable consequences—or, using Rygg's formulation from a subsequent meeting, be 'extraordinarily distressing' for the economy as a whole.[24] Rygg was also of the view that the banks' difficulties could not necessarily be resolved through a single action. In order to hinder a further weakening of confidence, he believed that Norges Bank needed to offer an unlimited guarantee that the banks would be kept afloat. However, this implied accepting all costs required to compensate for future financial problems.

The government did not disagree with this evaluation of the situation. During a confidential meeting held on 19 December, Prime Minister Kolstad stated his viewpoint. It was 'in the State authorities' interest, at all levels, to render banks operational again'.[25] During new meetings, this was further specified to mean that the government clearly believed that 'State authorities'—a designation that evidently included the parliament and government but not Norges Bank—would not take on any financial burden for the bailout plan.[26] This attitude must be seen in the light of the ongoing saving policy to reduce government expenses. The motive was to reduce the substantial

---

[22] Minutes from 23 December 1931, 'Separat forhandlingsprotokoll for direksjonen 1914–1940', DA I-3160/A/ boks 96, NAN.

[23] Lindboe, *Fra de urolige tredveårene: dagboksnedtegnelser og kommentarer*, 114.

[24] Meeting in the Storting 17 January 1932, see Einar Lie et al., *Norges Bank 1916–2016* (Fagbokforlaget, 2016), 264.

[25] 'Referat fra møte 19.12.1932 kl. 1400', D/Da/L0413, FD/FKC.

[26] Letter from the prime minister to Norges Bank's board, 2 February 1932, NB/DIR2/D/boks 122, NAN.

government debt, which was the legacy of the slippages during the First World War. The policy was at odds with the nascent macroeconomic doctrines, and several of the University of Oslo's economists protested openly against the debt repayment.[27]

The bailout mission therefore had to be assigned to Norges Bank. As mentioned, the law did not impose on Norges Bank to save banks that had lost a share of their equity capital. On the contrary, liquidity protection lay with the central bank, and, under the circumstances, Norges Bank was designated as the saviour. Rygg probably also believed early on that this was the only practical option. At the same time, he realized already in autumn 1931 that the rescue plan might prove costly and controversial. Rygg's approach was therefore to do whatever he could to help rescue the banks. However, he wanted the Storting to adopt an explicit resolution. The purpose of the resolution should be twofold, stipulating that the plan was needed and desirable, and providing Norges Bank with the necessary authority to act. His opening address during a confidential meeting with the prime minister and leaders of parliament at the Storting, on 17 January 1932, clearly described the role of the Storting: if parliament leaders wished the banks to be saved, a formal request had to be made. 'Without it, the matter must be closed forthwith and the banks liquidated'. With a positive resolution, Norges Bank would then see things through with all necessary means—including a year-long supervision of the banks. 'I think I dare say that this control by the banks' Executive board and operation will be exercised with unfailing firmness and resoluteness.' So spoke Nicolai Rygg.[28]

The state authorities heeded this advice. The Farmers' Party declared that one should rescue the banks, underlining once again the importance of withholding government financial support. The Conservative Party shared that view: the banks should be saved, but without government capital. The Liberal Party politician Johan L. Mowinckel adopted the most rescue-oriented position, and proposed that the government guarantee capital if Norges Bank agreed to it. He was also among those who strongly warned against the consequences of not providing support, pointing out that the situation could become even worse. 'But if we don't help these banks, we would be embracing the disaster'. The Labour Party politician Johan Nygaardsvold held beliefs on the matter at the extreme opposite end of the spectrum. He was sceptical of the idea of entrusting Norges Bank with a rescue mission. His reasons were sparse, but he emphasized the risk involved in providing unconditional support, and rightly pointed out that according to regulation this was not the central bank's mandate.

After this meeting, Norges Bank prepared the overall package, which included writing down the share capital of the two banks. On its own initiative, Bergen Privatbank performed its write-down, which corresponded to the loss agreed between Norges Bank and the Bank Inspection. The DnC board's hand was twisted to perform

[27] Jens Christopher Andvig, *Ragnar Frisch and the Great Depression: A Study in the Interwar History of Macroeconomic Theory and Policy* (Norsk utenrikspolitisk institutt, 1986), 317.
[28] Minutes from meeting in the Storting, 17 Jan 1932, NB/DIR1/A, NAN.

the write-down as Norges Bank made it a condition for large, affordable loans. The new share subscription took place while Norges Bank was preparing the rescue operation. To everyone's surprise, the operation was quite successful, particularly in the case of Bergen Privatbank which received the support of Bergen's shipping magnates. Early in February 1932, when Norges Bank had finished elaborating the rescue package, it became obvious that private interests would provide the totality of the equity needed, which Norges Bank required for the two banks. However, the fact that Norges Bank and members of the Storting wholeheartedly supported these two banks was made known, which was also a significant factor.

Consequently, in practice, the bailout plan was actually a form of liquidity support; the banks were freed from their difficulties, and were able to repay the funds. The rescue package was elaborated when the crisis was at its deepest. This was only brought to light at a later time. Besides, when it became clear that support would be offered, the banks gained both confidence and new equity capital. For them, trust and financial stability was embraced by the willingness to rescue the banks.

DnC and Bergen Bank remained under Norges Bank's surveillance for several years. DnC was entitled to terminate the agreement with Norges Bank in 1939. During a ceremony, gratitude was expressed to the Storting and government for allowing Norges Bank to come to the rescue, 'first and foremost, in the best interest of society'.[29] The gratitude was received by the Labour government in place, by its finance minister, Kornelis Bergsvik, who had been a backbencher in the Storting in 1932. No one recalled that little gratitude would have been directed to Bergsvik, had he prevailed at the time, when the Storting voted 102 against the Labour Party's forty-six to allow Norges Bank to save the banks.

On an Autonomous Course

While dealing with the crisis-hit banks, an intense discussion about the new exchange rate issues arising after 19 September 1931 wore on. During the first months, exchange rate movements were as dominant a theme as price movements. The September discount rate increase was aimed at containing large foreign exchange losses. Very rapidly, direct regulation was introduced. On its own initiative, Norges Bank established a Foreign Exchange Council, and the banking organizations and large business organizations were pressured to join. The purpose was to obtain an overview of foreign exchange holdings by Norwegian commercial interests in foreign banks and establish a form of control over currency movements and their use. Banks were soon prohibited from using foreign exchange to pay for 'luxury goods' abroad—this was the initial phase of increasingly extensive foreign exchange regulations. This occurred at the same time as a highly profiled 'buy Norwegian campaign', which dominated the crisis years. In October 1931, the prime minister, finance minister, Storting president,

---

[29] Quoted after Erling Petersen, *Den norske Creditbank, 1857–1957* (Fabritius boktr., 1957), 330.

and the governor of the Norges Bank all signed a petition in Norwegian newspapers to act responsibly and buy Norwegian-produced goods in order to safeguard Norwegian jobs.[30] Later on, the royal family would also actively support the campaign.

Two simple questions arose concerning the exchange rate in the course of the months following 19 September. First, which exchange rate should now be established for the krone? And second, who would be in charge of fixing this exchange rate? Should it be Norges Bank or government authorities?

Both questions degraded the relationship between Norges Bank and the Farmers' Party government, particularly after spring of 1932.[31] Several important commercial interests, such as the export industry and farm and forest owners, wanted a weak krone. They put forth arguments in the press and through their political contacts in favour of Norges Bank, which by means of its interest rate and liquidity policy should establish an exchange rate that would support their foreign trade.

As mentioned, Rygg was a firm advocate of a fixed exchange rate regime, and argued that a new fixed range would have to be determined for the krone. Both Rygg and his Scandinavian colleagues were interested in the possibility of establishing a new gold standard. The pressing concern was Great Britain and pound sterling. As long as the pound failed to be integrated into a higher international order, and fluctuated considerably, Norges Bank did not see any viable path to any new exchange rate regime. On 28 September, Norges Bank communicated that their aim was to stabilize the price level. In practice, that meant increased focus on preventing abrupt exchange rate changes, but otherwise allowing fundamentals to work. Under those conditions, Rygg did not undertake any actions to meet the Famers Party's demands. The government's standpoint mainly reflected the views of exporters, farm owners, and forest owners, who favoured setting a fixed, lower exchange rate range for the krone.

There were two main areas of conflict between Norges Bank and the government. The government first attempted to set up an alternative academic authority to Norges Bank, which took the form of a secret Currency Committee in November 1931, which gave the government an advisory role in monetary policy matters. Attempts were also made to undermine Rygg's authority. Gunnar Jahn, director of Statistics Norway, was chairman of the committee. In the first report of the committee, Norges Bank's handling of the situation right before and after 19 September was mentioned in positive terms. Public criticism of Norges Bank because they had refused to weaken the value of the krone against the stronger pound in late autumn of 1931 was refuted, citing the sharp decline in the krone's gold value.

Subsequently, 'The monetary technical committee' was announced in the king's speech from the throne in April 1932. The committee was immediately set up, again with Gunnar Jahn as chairman. Its mandate explicitly included a role to communicate on 'Norway's monetary policy in relation to gold currencies, the pound, and the price level'—and much more. Rygg had issued strong warnings against this committee, in

---

[30] Petersen, 'Da Norge forlot gullet: Norges Bank og kurspolitikken 1931–1933', 48.
[31] The following paragraphs after ibid.

letters and meetings. He argued that its very establishment would undermine Norges Bank's position and authority in a demanding currency market. This was probably the intention too, but the explicit aim was clearly to create depreciation pressures to push down the krone exchange rate. The prime minister and finance minister repeated those aims in the press when referring to the committee. This resulted in an important weakening of the krone exchange rate, while rumours of the authorities' intervention in fixing the krone exchange rate abounded. Strategically, Rygg then invited the prime minister and finance minister to a meeting with Norges Bank's board. His meeting minutes give the impression of a factual discussion, concluding with a message sent out to NTB (the Norwegian News Agency) the same day. In it the prime minister explained that the new committee would not propose a new exchange rate, that the government was working in close collaboration with Norges Bank, and that the recent days' exchange rate movements were 'unfortunate'. Later, however, the farmers' organizations sharply criticized the government for its retreat. Many years later, Finance Minister Sundby explained that the governor of Norges Bank had 'severely reprimanded him publicly'.[32]

The 'technical committee' also turned out to be a source of de facto support for Norges Bank's approach. Rygg was invited to several committee meetings, and the discussions did not reveal any considerable differences in assessments. The committee also chose to renew criticism of the government's public polemic concerning the krone exchange rate. Moreover, it pointed out that such questions were unsuited for public debate led by persons of authority, especially not by those in authority to determine the exchange rate themselves.[33]

Rygg was also criticized by the prime minister and finance minister. Rygg became the target of a number of rumblings coming from the two politicians, both in the press and at the Storting. They perceived the present exchange rate policy approach as restrictive and inappropriate. The criticism was repeatedly brought forward with clear references to the monetary policy conducted in the preceding decade.[34]

When the attempts to pressure Rygg into taking another direction failed, the government tried, by formal means, to take control of the exchange rate policy. Already in autumn 1931, prominent Farmers' Party politicians had affirmed that the exchange rate policy needed to be a government task now that the gold standard had been abandoned. The issue of the division of tasks between the state and the central bank was raised at numerous meetings. During autumn 1932, Rygg stated that the Storting could formally pass a decree on the principles of the exchange rate policy, however, such a decree would be unfortunate and difficult to implement in the current situation. Furthermore, he argued that if the government were to issue decrees on the exchange rate that were to be implemented by Norges Bank, the result would be an impossible division of tasks. 'If the government decides the exchange rate, it will also

[32] Rolf Bjørnstad, *Jorden og mannen: Jon Sundby* (Bøndenes forlag, 1968), 225–6.
[33] Petersen, 'Da Norge forlot gullet: Norges Bank og kurspolitikken 1931–1933', 65.
[34] Stortingstidende, 1932, 222f, Storting's proceedings.

have decision-making authority over the amounts to be spent in buying and selling foreign exchange, which is utterly unsustainable. Responsibility must rest in one place', Rygg wrote in 1950. These statements were a rather precise reflection of the meeting minutes and letters from the discussion that had been held a mere twenty years earlier.[35]

During autumn 1932, the government asked Professor Wilhelm Keilhau, sitting on the monetary technical committee, to draw up a legal opinion on where the responsibility for exchange rate setting should lie after abolishing the statutory gold redemption obligation the year before. Keilhau's opinion was that 'responsibility for the monetary system' was a government task. Nevertheless, government could not intervene in Norges Bank's daily management, and a decision that explicitly and implicitly set the exchange rate figured among management's tasks. However, the government could draw up exchange rate policy regulations, which would bind the central bank. After the first legal opinion, Sundby wanted to know whether the guidelines for the existing, temporary exchange rate policy could be laid down by the government, or whether decisions that actually determined the exchange rate could be made directly by the government. With these questions on the table, Keilhau retreated from further work. He was not a follower of Rygg. Nonetheless, this probably stretched beyond the limits of the acceptable for a liberally oriented professor.[36]

Into the Sterling Block

At an international level, the years 1931–3 abounded with national variations and attempts to re-establish collective solutions. The most significant joint initiative was the London Economic Conference in summer 1933. Before the conference, Nordic central bank managements gathered in Stockholm, where they discussed the current situation and the path ahead.

The three central banks had taken somewhat different approaches since 1931. Sweden had defined price stabilization as an objective, but practical policy was pragmatic and similar to Norwegian policy.[37] A tug-of-war between the central bank and government also took place in Sweden. Just before the meeting, Denmark had devalued by all of 17 per cent by virtue of the so-called 'Kandlergade compromise', a broad compromise reached by Social Democrats and the agricultural oriented Liberals. An important reason was that New Zealand, the main competitor to the British agricultural market, had devalued sharply just ahead of the compromise. With regard to their attempt to make Norges Bank move towards a lower rate, Denmark's exchange rate policy was a clear motivation behind the Farmers' Party's pressure on Norges Bank to move towards a lower exchange rate.

[35] Rygg, *Norges Bank i mellomkrigstiden*, 478.
[36] Petersen, 'Da Norge forlot gullet: Norges Bank og kurspolitikken 1931–1933', 77.
[37] Tobias Straumann, *Fixed Ideas of Money: Small States and Exchange Rate Regimes in Twentieth-Century Europe* (Cambridge University Press, 2010), 121.

During their preparatory meeting, the Scandinavian countries agreed that a future return to gold would be the optimal move, but that it would not be possible at a practical level. Rygg raised the possibility of stabilizing against the pound for a group of countries. Consensus on a future policy approach was not achieved before the decisive London Economic Conference.[38] The Nordic countries were small fish in a big pond, and they did not overestimate their importance.

The London Economic Conference was a failure. However, it did provide clarification. The dollar had been devalued in April 1933, but the rate that would prevail in the future was uncertain. President Roosevelt stated that he was uninterested in any further stabilization of the dollar. Instead, he affirmed that the dollar's external value must reflect domestic needs. In what was referred to as 'the bombshell message', it was made public that the US government had been given the authority to devalue the dollar to 50 per cent of the initial gold value.[39] And so, the dollar, of steadily growing importance, was in practice circulating abroad as a future anchor currency in a fixed-rate system. A group of countries—France, Belgium, the Netherlands, Luxemburg, Italy, and Switzerland—engaged in discussions that resulted in principles for common defence of a continued gold peg. During these discussions, members of the British delegation privately asked the Nordic countries what their position would be on a pound sterling group, composed of the British Empire and Argentina. Gunnar Jahn, a member of the delegation, received the inquiry as Rygg had already returned home because of the slow progress in the discussions.

It would appear that a formal inquiry was never made. Nor was any resolution passed concerning a tie to pound sterling. Nevertheless, a de facto stabilization against pound sterling occurred in summer 1933. An exchange rate of 19.9 was established in June after a depreciation through the first half-year. In July and August, there were some deviations, but from September Norges Bank intervened in the foreign exchange market in order to counter smaller movements and maintain a fixed exchange rate. The rate of 19.9 was never explained. However, the Farmers' Party had, also when governing, demanded an exchange rate of 20 kroner. Most probably, defiance rather than practical considerations prevented the exchange rate from being set at a rounder 20 kroner. In the course of the same months, Sweden and Denmark undertook the same stabilization, at 22.4 and 19.4 kroner, respectively.

This common tie is not that surprising: the Nordic countries wanted a form of stability, and their connections to Great Britain were closer than to the gold block countries. Some years later, in an internal report from the Bank of England, the relationship with the Scandinavian countries was summarized as follows: 'The already close connections with this country brought the Scandinavian countries into the sterling area, where they have in some ways a privileged position. In trade affairs, they hang on the coat-tail of the dominions; their access to British markets is assured [...]

---

[38]   Petersen, 'Da Norge forlot gullet: Norges Bank og kurspolitikken 1931–1933', 85–6.
[39]   Gianni Toniolo, *Central Bank Cooperation at the Bank for International Settlements, 1930–1973* (Cambridge University Press, 2005), 146–7.

Neither from the point of view of commerce nor finance could we afford to allow Scandinavia to lag behind in general recovery.'[40]

Rygg, His Resources and Network

The Scandinavian countries were fully aware of these mutual advantages. Another significant point is the fact that Norges Bank's formal and informal international contacts were largely with Nordic central banks—and increasingly the Bank of England. This was an important part of Norges Bank's resources and knowledge platform.

The style of many of Rygg's notes and letters is sober, and seldom personal. He was a poor orator and did not possess the ability—or will—to engage in polemics. He was polite and aloof when discussing his opponents. Rygg was equally distant when referring to himself. One exception is a private record from spring 1932. At the time, Rygg found himself involved in the two important banking crises; foreign currency problems, including a reorganization at the bank; and financing of the shipbuilding and canned food industries—along with much else. I 'stand alone, without any help whatsoever', he wrote in one of his notes. Some weeks before, the director general of the finance department in the Ministry of Finance, who was responsible for budget matters, and matters relating to credit policy and Norges Bank, collapsed, never returning to work. In 1928, after a highly demanding period of close interaction with the central bank's management, the big bank DnC's esteemed director fell acutely ill. He would never resume work.[41] The following year, Rygg himself was absent from Norges Bank for four months. His doctor instructed him 'to take a holiday [...] due to illness that is the consequence of the great strain he had experienced over several years', as stated in a letter to the Ministry of Finance.[42]

However, Rygg kept up the pace throughout the tremendously demanding period in the early 1930s. He was certainly not alone in performing the tasks, though his responsibility could not be shared with subordinates. Rygg's deputy, Sverre Thorkildsen, was present throughout the entire period of Rygg's mandate. Thorkildsen was able to perform independently and with authority, in the role of deputy as well as during Rygg's absence. Management was often summoned at short notice to meetings for lengthy discussions—sometimes failing to follow Rygg's instructions to the letter. Alf Eriksen's statistics division produced data and analyses, which were subpar compared with today's standards. However, no one else offered institutional expertise that could compete with theirs.

The Ministry of Finance did not have expertise that could compete with Norges Bank. The two director generals in the influential finance department at the ministry during the interwar period, were lawyers with good knowledge of budget procedures

---

[40] Quoted after Petersen, 'Da Norge forlot gullet: Norges Bank og kurspolitikken 1931–1933', 92.
[41] Petersen, *Den norske Creditbank, 1857–1957*, 344.
[42] Dr V. Fürst's letter to the Ministry of Finance, 21 May 1929, D/Da/L0413, FK/FKC, NAN.

and relevant legal principles. Nonetheless, throughout the entire banking and currency crises, no one in the ministry left behind a single document resembling a technical account of the consequences of various measures. Statistics Norway had competent economists, such as Director Gunnar Jahn, and certain academics had a practical vision. From time to time, the government turned to such personalities to form committees, not only to compete with the central bank's academic authority, but also because it lacked academic expertise.

This expertise was scant because the government was little involved in 'politics' in this field. Monetary policy and exchange rate policy had been under the central bank's responsibility. This was also the case in a good number of other countries. Therefore, in 1932, the central bank's network remained the most relevant element in assessing stabilization options for the pound exchange rate, if Sweden devalued its currency, or if a strong Norwegian weakening of the krone was to be countered by measures on the part of our closest trading partners. In particular, Rygg maintained regular contact with the head of the Riksbank, Ivar Rooth. His numerous and brief notes from many telephone conversations bear testimony.[43] The Nordic central bank governors met on a regular basis, in addition to communication via letters and telephone calls. Rygg also met with other central bank governors in councils and committees in London and Geneva. From 1935 on, the Farmers' Party's John Sundby, or the Labour Party's finance ministers, did not have access to contacts with similar insight and information. Access to information and expertise—academic and administrative bodies' most persistent source of influence[44]—was therefore an important and scarce resource that benefited Norges Bank. Rygg's feeling that he stood alone in dealing with important tasks was actually the consequence of the real and formal skills distribution concerning matters relating to monetary and exchange rate policy, which necessarily put a tremendous onus on Norges Bank.

The temporary expert bodies did nonetheless tend to support Norges Bank when they were faced with criticism. An alternative expertise was established around the Labour Party during the 1932–4 crisis years. Economics professor Ragnar Frisch's meeting with Ole Colbjørnsen and the Labour Party is the most recurrent theme of the 1900s economic-political history. Early in the 1930s, Frisch—a path-breaking economist and econometrician, and later Nobel laureate—wrote several papers in an attempt to understand the crisis and propose solutions. Many of these proposals involved providing liquidity, either directly or indirectly, and increasing purchasing power. In 1934, after the journalist Colbjørnsen at the newspaper *Arbeiderbladet* had connected with Frisch, the Labour Party took direct advantage of Frisch's expertise in the elaboration of its crisis programme. The Labour Party's Johan Nygaardsvold's chastisement of Gunnar Jahn and the bourgeois parties' monetary technical committee was also one of the most important rhetorical victories for the Norwegian Storting.

---

[43] See also Per H. Hansen, 'Cooperate or Free Ride? The Scandinavian Central Banks, Bank for International Settlements and the Austrian Financial Crisis of 1931', *Scandinavian Journal of History* 37, no. 1 (2012).

[44] B. Guy Peters, 'The Politics of Bureaucracy', in *The Politics of Bureaucracy* (Routledge, 2014).

Gunnar Jahn and the bourgeois parties referred to Keynes to explain that the government had to save before investing. By means of Frisch's translations and input, Nygaardsvold could read a letter aloud, written by the same Keynes. In this letter, Keynes explained that the monetary technical committee had misunderstood his works, advising them promptly to take the opposite standpoint.[45]

The contact with Frisch gave the Labour Party's opposition programmes weight and legitimacy. Nevertheless, no evidence suggests that this contact provided with lasting expertise. A document entitled *A Norwegian 3-Year Plan*, compiled by Colbjørnsen and the geographer Axel Sømme, was perceived as a shift in the Labour Party's programme. In this document, a strong, expansionary policy was suggested, involving considerable government budget deficits. The party's crisis plan, launched in 1934, proposed the same. Nonetheless, overwhelming indications reveal that the party's most prominent members had failed to fully comprehend or accept the new ideas: when the Labour Party's expansionary policy proposal was rejected by the Storting, the party remained in favour of the tax increases designed to finance some of the spending increases. Among other reasons, they argued that this would help repay government debt. This approach was diametrically opposed to the new authority's policy; rather than expanding aggregate demand, the tax cuts would have a tightening effect. The following year, the underlying comprehension of the finance policy was specified, when the Labour Party's finance minister, while presenting the budget for 1935, clearly stated that deficit was not a path to take. In 1937, Nygaardsvold joyfully reported in his diary that he could present yet another deficit-free budget. In addition to this, in a speech given two years later at a LO (Norwegian Trade Union Confederation) congress, social minister and party leader Oscar Torp apologized for the fact that government debt had not been further reduced.[46]

The new macroeconomic ideas had certainly empowered and legitimized the opposition's plans and programmes. However, these ideas were discarded when practical politics were needed. The free thinker, Colbjørnsen, was also ignored during those moments. He was important in what one referred to as 'the new orientation' of the Labour Party's economic policy. Nonetheless, he was not given any noteworthy functions when the party came to power.[47] Frisch could not provide continual advice. The strange fact is that the party did not engage in any action to build up other expertise in the central administration after coming to power in 1935. Hence, the administration from 1945 onwards was a clear break with previous policy; this was the time when the government apparatus became equipped to make expert assessments as a basis for a judgement-based economic policy. The expansion of knowledge within ministries—especially the Ministry of Finance—was an important element in the rapid reduction of Norges Bank's de facto influence after the Second World War.

---

[45] Andvig, 'Ragnar Frisch and the Great Depression: A Study in the Interwar History of Macroeconomic Theory and Policy', 387–8.

[46] Ibid., 390.

[47] Einar Lie, 'Norsk økonomisk politikk i det 20. århundret', *Historisk Tidsskrift* 85, no. 4 (2006), 74.

The Nygaardsvold Government and Norges Bank

In 1933, a minority Liberal government took over. In 1934, when Rygg understood that a change was about to occur, the most pressing question for Norges Bank was the Labour Party's future positioning on exchange rate policy. The same year, the Labour Party had suggested buying out Norges Bank's private shareholders. The central bank was opposed to that, and neither the Farmers' Party, nor any of the other parties, were favourably inclined. Nevertheless, the Farmers' Party argued in favour of a lower krone exchange rate, while the government, with Gunnar Jahn as prime minister, supported the exchange rate policy in place.

In this situation, in order to secure support, Gunnar Jahn attended a series of meetings with Nygaardsvold of the Labour Party.[48] LO favoured a fixed exchange rate. During a meeting in January 1934, Rygg succeeded in convincing Nygaardsvold to make a declaration securing the existing policy. To Rygg's disappointment, the declaration called for a fixed exchange rate, but without defining its level. Nygaardsvold did not wish to make any further commitments. Rygg interpreted this to mean that the matter would arise again, and that the Farmers' Party and Labour Party, together making up the majority at the Storting, might propose to reduce the krone exchange rate against the pound. Nevertheless, the exchange rate was not brought up during the crisis debate, which dealt with support measures and budget policy. After the Labour Party, with the support of the Farmers' Party, formed a government in 1935, exchange rate policy was not revisited.

The Nygaardsvold government reigned between the demanding 1920s and the period following the war, during which economists and the party itself took considerable distance from Rygg and Norges Bank. The result should have been stronger confrontations in the course of the years subsequent to 1935. However, it is difficult to discern these contradictions—with one exception, the discount rate increase towards the end of 1936. Activity rose rapidly through that year, with a rise in the wholesale price index of almost 7 per cent. Housing construction increased considerably, in parallel with a sharp rise in share prices. In 1935, Statistics Norway's share index showed an increase of 25 per cent. The first six months of 1936 were calmer; but the autumn months brought the rate of increase to 29 per cent on an annual basis. 'Now is the time to equip ourselves for the next downturn (not act as if the tailwind is here to stay)', Rygg summarized in a note made for his personal use, during the meeting before the discount rate was increased. The low 1933 interest rate had served its purpose. He explained that it was now appropriate to pursue a cautious tightening.

During an early meeting with the finance minister, Rygg received signals that government was opposed to a discount rate rise.[49] The increase was still implemented, provoking instant reactions. The interest rate increase promptly came up in the Storting

---

[48] Rygg, *Norges Bank i mellomkrigstiden*, 600.
[49] Rygg's note 24 November 1936, from meeting with Minister of Finance Bergsvik, 'Notater og brev 1936', S-3947, NAN.

debate, during which the finance minister explained that the government disagreed with the central bank's decision. 'Norges Bank has, as one knows, according to law and regulation, power over and responsibility for the discount rate', he explained.[50] A few days later, when Rygg was summoned to appear before the standing committee of finance to account for the discount rate increase, he was confronted with strong criticism. 'I replied that I would willingly take the burden upon myself', Rygg explained. However, he added that it was 'the actual conditions [...] that determined these things'.[51]

Still, the episode is not an example of sharp contradictions between the new government party and Norges Bank. In terms of practical policy, the Labour politicians were perhaps closer to Rygg than one might expect—Rygg's practical views were surprisingly free from any conservative dogmatic doctrines. The delinking from gold, the relatively low interest rate that followed the period of unrest, and considerable liquidity supply from the central bank are elements of the more general picture. This is also the retrospective view: the countries in the pound bloc fared better than the countries that held on to the gold peg.[52] Norway was among the countries that used liquidity and exchange rate policy to promote economic expansion, although some would argue that committee work in which Rygg took part contributed to opening the way for new credit to the forestry and lumber industry. In spring 1932, he became the leader of a broadly composed committee, which was assigned the task of saving the strained shipbuilding industry. This resulted in cooperation, modernization, and moral pressure on shipbuilders to build in Norway, as well as the establishment of a series of new lending arrangements and credit sources. Norges Bank's direct involvement was limited, but government transfers and credit were given.[53] Rygg was also asked to lead a committee set to evaluate measures for improving profitability in the canned food industry. A sales centre was established, based on an existing fishing and agriculture model. Membership was compulsory, prompting liberals to refer to the enterprise as 'forced cartels'. On this occasion, Norges Bank's branches were directly used to provide credit to producers in difficulty. The work continued almost throughout the entire decade, with a large number of meetings and wide public debate.[54]

In such matters, Rygg was at his best, with great authority and integrity, and strong appeals to find solutions to collective problems. His text and speech contained heavy doses of *pathos* and *ethos*, to use two of the art of classical rhetoric's key concepts: pathos addresses the audience's feelings, and ethos indirectly or directly points to the orator's own authority. All the same, for an economist, the weft of *logos* in the speeches

---

[50] Stortingstidende 1937, 47–9. Storting's proceedings.

[51] Rygg's minutes from the meetings in the Storting's standing committee of finance, 28 November 1935, 'Notater og brev 1937 I', S-3947, NAN.

[52] C. H. Feinstein, Peter Temin, and Gianni Toniolo, *The European Economy between the Wars* (Oxford University Press, 1997), ch. 8.

[53] St.meld. 27, 1936, Storting's proceedings, summarises the preparations and actions taken.

[54] Ot.prop. 55, 1935, laid the formal framework for the regulations of this industry. The preparations done are described in the introduction. The Norges Banks archives have comprehensive records from Norges Bank's engagement in these preparations. This is, however, not examined by the author.

was surprisingly thin. Rygg's line of thought could remain unrelenting over a very long period of time; still, he was not always as sharp and precise when it came to concrete economic relationships and mechanisms. The big words constantly shoved the smaller ones slightly aside.

Indeed, Rygg was not first and foremost an economist. He was a strong independent administrator of the bank and monetary policy, able to remain firm and unyielding in times when the persons and positions in political institutions changed. Succeeding generations have painted a portrait of Rygg as the head of an institution that conducted a policy that was unpopular among politicians, based on an (erroneous) academic foundation, which in postwar years justified the central bank being placed firmly under government control. However, as mentioned, Rygg enjoyed support from the Storting on many of his policies in the 1920s and 1930s. During the later decade, his active role in elaborating crisis solutions was much greater than subsequent generations gave him credit for. The level of explicit economic reasoning was astoundingly lower than what we find in Norges Bank and surrounding government institutions after the watershed in 1945.

Perhaps this is why the Nygaardsvold period passed with such a small number of open conflicts: Rygg did not feel the need to discuss economic policy principles or guidelines that could have given the central bank a firmer basis for its decision, but that could also have created conflicts. The discount rate increase and other unpleasant measures were forced by 'actual conditions' or 'the responsibility we must take for the future'. Disagreeing with that, in principle, is quite difficult.

9

Occupation and Loss of Autonomy

The Second World War came to Norway on 9 April 1940, when a superior German force invaded Norway.[1] This was one of the darkest days in Norwegian history, still one of the finest in Norges Bank's history. In the chaotic morning hours, the large gold reserve was evacuated and, by a long journey in inland Norway and along the coast, finally brought to safety overseas.

The rest of the war, and of the first pre-war years, brought less glory to Norges Bank. Already before the gold had departed Norway, a gradual inflation of the Norwegian monetary system had started because of the Germans' requisitions of legal tender through the central bank. In the following years, large sums of Norwegian kroner were withdrawn from Norges Bank as a part of the financing of the occupational force's activities in Norway. This created a large liquidity surplus, which made monetary policy more or less inefficient, until the surplus was finally eliminated around 1950.

One of the earliest actions of the Norwegian government was to relocate the central bank's formal functions away from the occupied areas, along with the government. A new Executive Board in exile for Norges Bank was appointed, consisting of several opinionated and energetic personalities. This board clashed with the leadership of the former headquarters in Oslo, led by the ageing Nicolai Rygg; it clashed with both the Ministry of Finance and the exiled cabinet in London; and to a certain extent it clashed with other central banks with which Norges Bank traditionally had close ties.

When in spring 1945 the pieces were being put in place for a new division of authority between Norges Bank and the transitional postwar government, the weakened central bank did not participate in any meaningful sense in the negotiations on its own future. New macroeconomic principles downplayed the role of monetary policies, in particular independent monetary policies conducted by the central bank. A new generation of politicians wanted strong and direct control over all important policy means in the hands of elected bodies. And the memories of the parity policies and the strong Norges Bank in the 1920s were omnipresent in the debate on the central bank's future role.

---

[1] Parts of this chapter is previously published in Einar Lie, 'Losing autonomy. The Norwegian central bank during the Second World War', *Economic History Review*, 77, no. 4, 1363-83 (2011). I am grateful for permission granted by Wiley.

The Coming of War

A new, large war broke out in September 1939, when Germany invaded Poland. During the previous weeks, the value of pound sterling had been under pressure. The value of sterling fell and foreign exchange regulation was introduced. Late in August, the Nordic central bank's governors convened in Stockholm, as they did in 1931, when sterling left its gold peg. They agreed that the Nordic countries should leave the pound and tie their respective kroner to a more stable currency, preferably US dollars. In a meeting in the Ministry of Finance in Oslo a few days later, a new exchange rate was settled. Rygg wanted to keep the existing rate. However, the minister of finance wanted to lower the value of the kroner, from 4.27 to 4.40 kroner per dollar. The matter was discussed shortly after in the parliament's standing committee for finance and economy. The decision, announced by Norges Bank and the parliament simultaneously, was that the new rate should aim at keeping the domestic price level as stable as possible, and that a rate of 4.40 was better suited for that purpose.[2]

In the autumn of 1939, Norges Bank had for years prepared for a new war, which its governor had anticipated since the mid-1930s. A large number of preparations had been undertaken. The vault in Oslo had been reinforced and new vaults had been built in some of the branch offices. Detailed emergency plans had been developed, for the main office and branches. Rygg wanted to make the bank's offices safe from bombing; he also contacted the army's command in order to construct a safer subterranean vault outside Oslo. The vault was constructed but never used. From following world events, Rygg no longer believed that a future war would have bombing as a final purpose. He now feared an occupational war, in which no vaults could protect the values of Norges Bank.

From the gold era, Norges Bank had deposited considerable amounts of gold in foreign countries. In 1938, Norges Bank started to transport all foreign reserves, except those in North America, to either the US or Canada, the only two countries the governor perceived to be safe in a coming war. The very last shipment left Cape Town on 9 April 1940, the very same day as Denmark and Norway were invaded by German forces.

The gold that should cover the issued notes could, according to the 1892 act of Norges Bank, not be sent abroad. On Rygg's initiative, Norges Bank's board had asked the government to prepare an amendment of the act. A bill was prepared early in 1940 but still not sent to the parliament when April arrived. As a precautionary measure, the gold, which previously had been stored as glimmering coins and bars in the shelves of Norges Bank's vault in Oslo, was securely packed for fast and long transport. The bars were packed in 1,503 sealed wooden crates, mainly of forty kilos each; the gold coins placed in thirty-nine small barrels, each weighting eighty kilos. Moreover, detailed plans for the evacuation and transport of the gold were made by the leadership. These plans became useful in the morning of 9 April.

---

[2] Nicolai Rygg, *Norges Bank i mellomkrigstiden* (Gyldendal, 1950), 620.

When news of the invasion by sea reached Oslo early in the morning of 9 April, Rygg was alarmed and immediately got down to Norges Bank's building. Here, the pre-planned system for evacuation of the gold reserve was mobilized. Bank clerks were called in and armed with pistols; twenty-seven lorries arrived over a few hours, while the 1,503 crates and thirty-nine barrels of gold—in total around forty-nine tons—were carried up from the deep basements and loaded on to the lorries. When the last crates had been loaded and the lorries drove off, escorted by armed bank clerks, Oslo had already fallen into the hands of the invasion forces. In accordance with the evacuation plans, the gold was initially transported to bank vaults in Lillehammer, where space had been cleared for the gold ahead of time. Then followed an intricate journey through the western towns of Åndalsnes and Molde to the far-north city of Tromsø, where a British cruiser transported the gold out of the country, to the US and Canada.[3]

During the afternoon of 11 April 1940, the headquarters of Norges Bank was surrounded by German soldiers. Shortly thereafter two envoys from the German occupation forces, which had captured Oslo two days previously, visited the bank. Their mission was clearly to secure the bank's gold reserve for German interests, and Norges Bank's second in command, Deputy Governor Sverre Thorkildsen, confirmed that he would not dispose of Norges Bank's gold in a manner that was at odds with the occupier's interests.

This was a golden day in the history of Norges Bank. The gold transport was both exceptionally successful and financially important, and for both these reasons it has become an event that has been chronicled and narrated over and over again, whether in the media, scientific journals, or popular magazines. The relative paucity of other Norwegian highlights from the 9 April invasion—lack of preparedness by the government and armed forces, slow and half-hearted mobilization—has probably also served to increase the relative significance of the event. And not least, in regard to the central bank's role and reputation, the episode was an initial shining moment in a wartime and occupation history that in total seems problematical and unflattering.

Financing the German Occupation

Compared with most other European countries during the Second World War, Norway suffered less during occupation in terms of acts of war and the numbers of killed and wounded. Nevertheless, the economic ramifications were formidable. Norway was strategically important because of its geographical location, and for a long while the Germans feared that Allied forces would land on the Norwegian coast; as a result, numerous fortifications were constructed along the coast. German apprehension concerning a potential second front in Norway also led to the retention of

---

[3] For details on the evacuation of the gold, see Asbjørn Øksendal, *Gulltransporten* (Aschehoug, 1974); Robert Pearson, *Redd gullet! Historien om den norske gulltransporten i 1940* (Dinamo, 2010).

major troop levels in the country, with a peak of 400,000 German soldiers. These soldiers needed food and quarters, and many of them also sent food back to their families in Germany. In addition, many prisoners of war and forced workers were sent to Norway during the final year of the war, totalling roughly 100,000 people. Not only were fortifications built, but also industrial complexes and infrastructure were upgraded in order to deliver inputs to German war production. Even though Norway benefited from many of these latter measures following the war, the overall activity was a major burden on a relatively limited national economy stemming from a population of around 3 million.

In theory there are several ways an occupier can proceed in order to transfer resources from an occupied country to its own activities. Material resources and labour can be confiscated, which is the traditional manner in which military forces obtain provisions in foreign territories. But such a procedure violated the rules of war, and they would incite severe hostility. In particular, the use of civilian forced workers was forbidden. Forced workers were used extensively in Norway to construct railways and industrial complexes, but these workers were exclusively foreigners, hailing mainly from eastern Europe.

In a relatively functional market economy, it is always most expedient to be able to pay for oneself. Not even a sharp increase in taxation could have generated the revenues required by the occupation within a relatively short span of time. The German solution in occupied countries was therefore a type of inflationary taxation. German expenditures were paid for with a special occupation currency, either directly as mandatory legal tender in the economy, or through conversions to the local currency in the central bank.[4] Such conversions were 'requisition forms disguised as money', as one of the German Reichsbank's leaders put it.[5] In reality such conversions served to finance running needs at an expense that limited itself to the paper costs associated with printing the 'requisition forms'.

The German currency that was used in the occupied areas was the so-called *Reichskreditkassenscheine* (Reich's credit Treasury notes, or RKKS). In Belgium, the Netherlands, and especially France, RKKS were used directly as payment by the German occupiers, and the money circulated for a long while alongside the original banknotes. RKKS were withdrawn from circulation in Belgium in 1941 and in France in 1943, through conversions to national currency in the respective central banks.[6] In Norway there was a quicker and less bumpy transition to an inflated national currency, by way of solutions that soon afterwards served as the model for the German arrangements in Denmark.

---

[4] This is based largely on Götz Aly, *Hitler's Beneficiaries: Plunder, Racial War, and the Nazi Welfare State* (Macmillan, 2007); Alan S Milward, *The Fascist Economy in Norway* (Clarendon Press, 1972).

[5] Quoted in Harald Espeli, '"Det gavner ingenting å gjøre store vanskeligheter i små saker. Dette er ikke store saker"—Norges Bank, administrasjonsrådet og etableringen av okkupasjonskontoen i 1940', *Historisk tidsskrift* 90, no. 04 (2011).

[6] Herman Van der Wee and Monique Verbreyt, *A Small Nation in the Turmoil of the Second World War: Money, Finance and Occupation (Belgium, its Enemies, its Friends, 1939–1945)*, vol. 35 (Leuven University Press, 2009); Willem Frans Victor Vanthoor, *The King's Eldest Daughter: A History of the Nederlandsche Bank 1814–1998* (Uitgeverij Boom, 2005).

Already on 10 April 1940, the day after the German invasion of Norway, the Germans announced on NRK (the Norwegian state broadcaster) that the Norwegian population was obliged to accept RKKS as payment for their goods, and the bank-notes were in fact immediately used to pay for goods and services. This created both confusion and certain challenges, partly because the Germans often paid for small amounts with very large bills, with the problems of exchange that this entailed. Firms and individuals soon took the obligatory German banknotes to private banks and to branches of Norges Bank. The historian Harald Espeli has demonstrated how this created a state of confusion and uncertainty. Several branches converted RKKS to Norwegian kroner at the rate determined by the Germans, though other branches were reluctant to do so, among them the branch in Stavanger in south-western Norway. German officers had turned up at the branch with suitcases full of RKKS and demanded the credit notes be exchanged to Norwegian kroner; this was done under protest from the board of the Stavanger branch. A few days later the same board declared that the branch would no longer accept the occupation currency. Fearing reprisals, however, the main office instructed the Stavanger branch to submit to the German demands. A major shipment of money was sent from Oslo with German soldiers as guards, so that the money could subsequently be paid to the German occupiers in Stavanger.[7]

Around 20 April, a German Wehrmacht officer proposed that these issues could rather be resolved by allowing the Germans to pay with Norwegian kroner. If the Wehrmacht could cash in their RKKS at the main office in Oslo, there would no longer be any local frustration or uncertainty regarding the status of the RKKS. Governor Rygg then chose to consult with the Ministry of Finance in regard to the further course of action.

At this point in time, the Norwegian government was retreating from the war zone, and the so-called Administrative Council had been established. The council had been appointed by the Supreme Court on 15 April and served as the leadership of the civilian governance of Norway until it was dissolved by Reichskommissar Josef Terboven on 25 September 1940. In the council, the responsibility for issues sorting under the Ministry of Finance was given to the prominent Liberal Party member Gunnar Jahn, head of the Central Bureau of Statistics and previously the finance minister in Johan L. Mowinckel's Liberal government (1934–5). Jahn's unambiguous assessment was now that Norges Bank should acquiesce to the German demands. When Rygg hesitated, Jahn urged him to take the issue up with the central bank's most authoritative body, the Supervisory Board. But it soon turned out that it was not only cabinet ministers who had fled the city, and only three of the sixteen members could be summoned, with a fourth member joining the discussion on the following day.[8]

[7] Espeli, "'Det gavner ingenting å gjøre store vanskeligheter i små saker. Dette er ikke store saker"—Norges Bank, administrasjonsrådet og etableringen av okkupasjonskontoen i 1940'.

[8] The matter was accounted for in broad strokes in Norges Bank's report on its activities during the war, and in Gunnar Jahn, Alf Eriksen, and Preben Munthe, *Norges Bank gjennom 150 år* (Norges Bank, 1966). The matter is reviewed in detail and critically in Espeli, "'Det gavner ingenting å gjøre store vanskeligheter i små saker. Dette er ikke store saker"—Norges Bank, administrasjonsrådet og etableringen av okkupasjonskontoen i 1940'.

At the outset it was clear that the Supervisory Board sided with the sceptics. The majority thought that it should be possible to cash in RKKS, but without any formal agreement being signed. During the meeting, Rygg's argument in favour of such an agreement was that it might help clarify the situation and perhaps provide greater control. The sceptics for their part were concerned with the moral and political aspects of such an agreement, and it was only at a follow-up meeting, where Jahn himself participated, that the Supervisory Board relented. The meeting took a dramatic turn when Jahn demonstratively walked out because his viewpoints were not winning through, announcing as he left that he would 'inform the German authorities that I did my utmost and that I lay the blame on Norges Bank', according to Rygg's memorandum. The scepticism had abated by the time Jahn returned, and the final vestige of resistance was overcome by a subsequent letter from the Administrative Council, which urgently requested the Supervisory Board to sign an agreement with the Germans in regard to RKKS.

At the end of April, an envoy from the Wehrmacht presented a draft agreement in Jahn's office, with Rygg and Deputy Governor Thorkildsen in attendance. The proposed agreement referred to the RKKS being guaranteed by the German state, although in fact no such guarantee existed. Rygg also stated that there would have to be an overall limit to the amount of money involved, though no exact limit was subsequently determined.

The agreement with the Germans was not criticized by the postwar inquiry commission for Norges Bank, nor did it spark much debate later on, except for in the aforementioned work by Espeli. Espeli is critical on both a formal and a moral basis, pointing out that the agreement provided the Germans with an expedient solution to their financial problems while the military battle for Norway was still ongoing. This is undeniably correct; at the same time, however, the normative and political aspects of the agreement are probably more important than the purely economic and practical consequences. In any event, the Germans were not prevented from making exchanges: what was achieved through the agreement and subsequent practice was that only Norwegian banknotes were in circulation, and that all demands concerning exchanges were centralized. Jahn, and gradually also Rygg, emphasized both aspects. It would have a positive psychological effect that the monetary system was orderly and as intact as possible;[9] furthermore, the new arrangement made the overall German expenditures more transparent. Jahn was clearly preoccupied with how the war—the duration of which no one knew—would affect the economy in its entirety. He repeatedly returned to this point in his journal entries: the need to still consider the whole economic picture, with an eye towards employment, provisions, and much more. In this regard the agreement provided a sturdier foundation than a jumbled system with kroner and RKKS side by side, or suitcases full of German banknotes presented over the counter at the branch offices.

---

[9] Ibid., supplemented by Jahn's journal entries and Rygg's contemporaneous notes.

A more surprising example of adaptation to the occupying power is a statement that Norges Bank asked the private banks to release during the frenzied days of April 1940. The gist of this statement was that the bank in question would be 'loyal' to German demands and not make 'dispositions that would presumably be of direct or indirect benefit to the British Empire or its allies'—allies that at that juncture included the Norwegian government itself. Norges Bank's justification was that the banks could thereby function as prior to the invasion. The statement goes surprisingly far in specifying who 'the enemy' is; however, no preliminary draft of the statement is to be found in the archives, nor is the agreement mentioned in postwar reports or in the papers of the inquiry commission, and it is therefore hard to say whether the statement emerged under duress, was a result of haste, or was in fact a carefully planned document.[10]

The Occupation Account in Practice

The sums of money that were cashed in and registered in the central bank's so-called occupation account are presented in great detail in both Norges Bank's postwar report of its wartime activities and the inquiry commission's report. Already during spring 1940, the Executive Board that had continuously tried to curb the German withdrawals was supplemented with a German member, Rudolf Sattler, who a short while previously had been appointed director of the Reichsbank's Magdeburg branch.[11] Sattler enjoys near universal acclaim in both contemporary and later Norwegian sources, which on numerous occasions underscore that he cooperated throughout the war on a purely 'professional basis'. In consideration of the Norwegian economy and monetary system, he also cooperated in the persistent attempts to curb the withdrawals from the occupation account, though these attempts proved largely unsuccessful.

During a conference with a representative from the Wehrmacht in April 1940, Norges Bank asked the Germans to indicate the size of the sums they wished to cash in, receiving in reply that 80 million kroner should suffice for the upcoming months. The Germans then announced in August that they were making plans for their troops to spend the winter in Norway, and that the construction of barracks and so forth would require roughly 100 million kroner per month for a certain period of time. When it soon afterwards became clear that the Blitz against Great Britain was proving unsuccessful and that a host of fortifications were to be constructed along the Norwegian coast, Norges Bank was informed that the withdrawals would increase further. According to Norges Bank's report on the wartime era, Sattler then travelled to Berlin on behalf of Norges Bank, though without ultimately winning favour for the Norwegian views. During September and October 1940, the withdrawals increased to 175 million kroner per month. In 1941 the withdrawals from the occupation account

---

[10]   Ibid.
[11]   Harald Espeli, 'Central Banks under German Rule during World War II: The Case of Norway', in *Norges Bank Working Papers* (Norges Bank, 2012).

increased even further, as a result of the extensive work being carried out, in particular on fortifications.[12]

Table 9.1 shows the accumulated withdrawals from April 1940 and until Liberation Day in May 1945. Some deposits were made by both German and Norwegian governmental agencies throughout the war, and the column on the right shows the net burden on Norges Bank, which corresponds to roughly 130 per cent of the pre-war gross national product.

Rygg and his closest associates proved largely ineffectual in curbing the German withdrawals, and it is not easy to envision how they could have succeeded. In other, more limited areas they were more successful in curtailing the Germans: for example, the German authorities wanted entrepreneurs who were working for them to have easier access to credit than other companies, an arrangement that Rygg repeatedly managed to prevent. Corresponding discussions were held in regard to companies that undertook hazardous salvage operations of German ships; Rygg refused to accept any guarantees in this area as well, because this lay outside of Norges Bank's mandate.[13]

The bank's governing bodies became increasingly Nazified during the war, as was the case with most public and private enterprises. However, the first new board member was the aforementioned Gunnar Jahn, who was appointed by the Administrative Council, and who served from January 1941 until he was arrested by the Germans in October 1944. Several members of the NS, the pro-German collaborationist party, were subsequently appointed, particularly to the Supervisory Board.[14]

The question of whether the Executive Board, and Rygg in particular, should resign was discussed at several junctures. In May 1941 the Executive Board registered a lengthy statement in its secret protocol, where it accounted for its deliberations on whether the chairman, Rygg, should resign either on his own or together with the entire

Table 9.1 Cumulative sum withdrawn from the occupation account in millions of Norwegian kroner

Date	Cumulative sum withdrawn from the occupation account	Net burden on Norges Bank
June 1940	250	167
Dec. 1940	1,450	1,157
June 1941	2,611	2,132
Dec. 1941	3,958	3,286
June 1942	5,040	3,967
Dec. 1942	6,311	4,552
June 1943	7,499	4,908
Dec. 1943	8,757	6,115
June 1944	9,915	7,195
Dec. 1944	11,077	7,333
May 1945	11,676	8,004

[12] According to Norges Bank, *Norges Bank under okkupasjonen* (Gundersens boktrykkeri, 1945), 29–47.
[13] Ibid., 48.
[14] Jahn, Eriksen, and Munthe, *Norges Bank gjennom 150 år*, 328–30.

board. Their assessment was that the interests of both the nation and the monetary system would be best served if they remained in their positions. A corresponding discussion ensued when Rygg turned seventy early in 1942; though his post was not restricted by an age limit, Rygg considered it natural that he should retire. The Ministry of Finance urged him to remain as governor, however, and Rygg complied.[15] After the war, Rygg explained his decision with his desire to ensure stability in the monetary system; it is a paradox, however, that the finance minister of Quisling's collaborationist government also wanted Rygg to continue, and probably for similar reasons.

In the postwar inquiry commission, one of the members dissented from the otherwise unanimous support for Rygg and his dispositions during the war. Sverre Iversen, who at the time was the director of the Directorate of Labour, pointed out that Rygg's stated wish to retire more or less coincided with the formation of Quisling's collaborationist government on 1 February 1942; had Rygg arrived at a different conclusion, 'all the branches of public life would have taken the same course of action against the aggressor', Iversen contended. His dissenting opinion was also based on an entirely different set of principles than Rygg's and Jahn's desire for orderliness and a functioning monetary system. The underlying problem in occupied Norway, according to Iversen, was that the German projects enjoyed access to workers and companies that were a bit too willing to serve. Furthermore, according to Iversen, this state of affairs was aided rather than hindered by Norges Bank's attempts to maintain as much confidence as possible in the economy and the legal tender.[16]

Ræstad and Keilhau

In the attempts to keep the German withdrawals in check, Rygg acted as though he were still the leader of Norges Bank—formally, however, he was not. As early as 22 April 1940, the Norwegian government decreed that the bank's Executive Board had been 'dismissed', as it was known in the formal language of the day, and that a new Executive Board had been appointed that was to accompany the gold reserve and the government away from the invasion forces and the war zone. The jurist Dr Arnold Ræstad was chosen as the new chairman of the Executive Board in exile; after a brief intermezzo the head of Norges Bank's Gjøvik branch, Jens Nørve, was hired as deputy chairman. The third full-time member was Professor Wilhelm Keilhau, an old adversary of Rygg's. Two additional members of the Executive Board, Ole Colbjørnsen and the shipowner Thomas Olsen, were appointed—it was seldom that these latter two met, however, and their deputies usually attended the formal meetings. It was therefore the three full-time members who became the prevalent voices of the new

---

[15] This is mentioned by both ibid. and Norges Bank, *Norges Bank under okkupasjonen*.
[16] 'Komiteen til gransking av Norges Bank under okkupasjonstiden', *Innstilling fra Komitéen til gransking av Norges Banks virksomhet i okkupasjonstiden* (Finansdepartementet, 1948), 12.

Executive Board.[17] We do not know why exactly these three were appointed; the process was swift, however, and the three of them were all people who were readily available. Furthermore, as a team the three of them constituted a healthy mix of theoretical knowledge and practical experience within the field they were set to manage.

Arnold Ræstad, the new chairman, soon emerged as the strong man of this troika, even though Keilhau also made the most of his new position. Ræstad is among those people who enjoy great prominence during their lifetime, only to fade away completely posthumously. In 1921–2, Ræstad served as the foreign minister in one of the Liberal Party's governments, resigning after a mere eleven months after having come to an impasse in certain important negotiations. Most of his activities took place in other areas of public life, as an author, publicist, and businessman, and his fields of interest included communication and transportation. For example, upon arriving in Åndalsnes during the retreat in April 1940, Ræstad managed to contact the British delegation and the BBC, and on the government's and Norges Bank's authority he secured the assistance of British troops—not to guard the gold reserve, but to set up short-wave and medium-wave transmitters in order to send news bulletins in competition with the state broadcaster NRK, which had fallen into Nazi hands.[18] Soon afterwards the government set him to work on establishing Nortraship, the organization that administered the Norwegian merchant fleet during the war; Ræstad's assessment of the matter soon differed from that of his predecessor, and in an extremely short while he managed to draft the legislation that was subsequently adopted.

Upon establishing itself as part of the Norwegian government in exile in London, the new Executive Board soon found itself at odds with its surroundings. This was partly because both Ræstad's and Keilhau's bearing and work methods were at times provocative, but it was just as much due to their basic outlook on major issues. A recurring challenge was the exile bank's relationship to the Oslo office, which continued to employ the insignia of the country's central bank and which remained in contact with several other central banks. From the very beginning, however, the London-based Executive Board made it clear that *it* represented Norges Bank. An initial written manifestation occurred after one of the bank's employees, who had accompanied the gold reserve on its northward retreat and who later ended up in Stockholm, was ordered by the new Executive Board to present himself in London; at the same time, however, Rygg had instructed the person in question to return to Oslo as soon as possible because his original place of employment, the Foreign Exchange Department, required his efforts. In the London board's letter to the Ministry of Finance—the board never addressed itself, formally or informally, to the Oslo office—the

---

[17] Norges Bank, *Beretning fra direksjonen for Norges Bank om virksomheten i det frie Norge og i London i tiden 22. april 1940 til 13. juli 1945* (Norges Bank, 1946), 2.

[18] Märta Ræstad's journal, 15 April 1940. The diary is available at https://www.norges-bank.no/globalassets/ upload/images/tidslinje/talerartikler/marta-rastads-dagbok-scan.pdf.

matter was tackled head on: 'Mr Rygg, who already on April 26 [*sic*] was relieved of his duties as governor of Norges Bank, is of course in no way authorised to give […] an order on behalf of Norges Bank'.[19]

The formal position of the former main office in Oslo was on numerous occasions clarified by Ræstad and Keilhau. In Ræstad's terminology, the Oslo office had no constitutional foundation, but was to be considered a 'de facto institution'—it existed, but with no formal role. When Norges Bank nonetheless continued to maintain contact with institutions such as the Swedish central bank and the Bank for International Settlements (BIS), so as to settle its ongoing payment obligations, Ræstad and Keilhau deemed it necessary to issue a circular letter to several central banks in July 1942. The letter pointed out that the Oslo office did not represent Norges Bank, that Norges Bank was not obligated by agreements made with the Oslo office, and that payments to Oslo could not be considered valid.[20]

The letter created quite a stir in several countries and resentment in Oslo. Rygg's explicit reaction alluded in particular to the fact that Norges Bank in reality maintained the payment service in order to ensure that a certain amount of provisions were sent to Norway from unoccupied Sweden. But at the core of his endeavours were his attempts to curb the Wehrmacht's withdrawals from the occupation account; this effort was helped by Rygg acting as the central bank's governor, even though it does not seem that he explicitly invoked this function for himself.[21] But a demonstration in the form of a circular letter from London that asserted that Rygg merely led a 'de facto' institution hardly strengthened his authority in relation to the occupying power. Incidentally, the letter was rescinded later on as the result of continuous pressure from several ministers and the leadership of the Ministry of Finance, who were not informed of the letter in advance.[22]

Undoubtedly, the greatest task for the London Executive Board was their extensive plans to relaunch the monetary system after the war. This project lasted continuously from 1942 until 1944/5, by which time it was evident that the proposals from Ræstad and Keilhau had failed to win support from any of the camps. We will not discuss at length the various proposals and their details—suffice to say that a common trait was their aim to reintroduce and restore stability after the war. There are obvious similarities between especially Ræstad's thoughts and the ideas that dominated the Norwegian debates on monetary policy following the First World War, when all the actors wanted to return to a pre-war gold standard. After extensive studies the London-based Executive Board proposed in 1942 to issue a new krone after the war, with a fixed gold value that was based in particular on pre-war currency rates. This krone was to be gradually put into circulation after liberation and be used alongside the already existing kroner.

---

[19] Norges Bank London (NBL) to the Ministry of Finance, 29 August 1940, S-2061/D/L0166, NAN.

[20] The letters exist in both Norwegian and English versions in S-3946/D/Da/L0007, NAN.

[21] Rygg's reaction reached London through various channels, but is most elaborately expressed in *Norges Bank under okkupasjonen* (Gundersens boktrykkeri, 1945).

[22] Johan Melander's note 'Norges Banks rettslige stilling', 26 January 1943, S-3946/D/Da/L0021, NAN.

The proposal was sent to the government's members, several civil servants, the leadership of the Norwegian resistance movement, and the 'de facto institution in Norway', and informally also to certain other actors in Norges Bank's immediate circle. All the elements of the plan—tying the krone to gold, determining its value without taking economic realities into consideration, and circulating the new krone before the old one was withdrawn—were criticized by everyone who reviewed the proposal. 'But this is complete madness!' thundered the head of the Swedish central bank, Ivar Roth, when he laid eyes on the plan.[23]

The Bank of England was equally sceptical. The British pointed out that many occupied countries were currently working on plans for monetary reform after the war, but that none were planning to introduce a new currency and thenceforth use two parallel systems. In particular the Belgian plans to swiftly bind or sterilize a major percentage of the existing amount of money, and then proceed with in principle the same currency, was cited as an interesting example.[24]

Paul Hartmann, the finance minister in Nygaardsvold's national unity government in London, was also among the sceptics. Hartmann had served for many years as the mayor of Oslo, and was one of Ræstad's closest friends. During his exile in London, Hartmann kept a journal that was obviously written with an eye towards publication at some future date. After mentioning his scepticism of the proposed monetary system, Hartmann felt the need to explain his perception of Ræstad to his journal and its readers. 'He often becomes ensconced in his own line of reasoning, and his ideas tend therefore to detach themselves to a worrying degree from the real world. Despite my admiration for him, I have therefore always viewed his conclusions with the utmost scepticism.[25]

Hartmann was probably mostly critical of the protracted discussions on gold and the practical concerns regarding the two different krone standards. For Hartmann's young advisors, the ideas regarding the choice of the krone's value were just as discouraging. The most important of these advisors was the young economist Knut Getz Wold, who graduated in 1939 at the age of twenty-four; despite his relative youth, the dynamic Getz Wold acted with great authority and self-confidence, and his minister granted him a significant amount of leeway. An important forum for the ongoing discussions was a committee that comprised Konrad Nordahl, Erik Brofoss, a pair of the Ministry of Finance's civil servants, and the London-based Executive Board of Norges Bank. Nordahl was attached to the Norwegian Confederation of Trade Unions (LO), and though he had no formal position in the government, he would later become a member of Norges Bank's Executive Board. Brofoss, who became the dominant economic policy-maker in Norway after the war, was at this point in time the bureau chief of the Ministry of Provisioning.

---

[23]   Paul Hartmann, *Bak fronten: fra Oslo og London 1939–1945* (Aschehoug, 1955), 59.
[24]   Christian Brinch's note 'Møte i Bank of England' (Meeting in the Bank of England), 3 September 1942, and Keilhau's minutes from 6 September, 1942, both S-3946/D/D6/L0006, NAN.
[25]   Hartmann, *Bak fronten: fra Oslo og London 1939–1945*, 60.

In regard to the issue of monetary reform, the members of Norges Bank were in a clear minority. For their part, Getz Wold, Brofoss, and Nordahl focused partly on issues of fairness and redistribution, that is, on how the financial burdens of the war were to be placed on the shoulders of those who had profited during the war. In the specific choice of krone rate, however, pragmatic arguments prevailed, in a trade-off between import costs and price pressure on the one hand and cost level and competitiveness on the other.

Ræstad, in contrast, did not think in such terms. His deliberations were largely formal and concerned gold standards, the pre-war rate of exchange between kroner and pounds, and the importance of revaluing the gold reserve, which had last been done in summer 1940. According to this perspective, Ræstad cannot be counted among the many transitional figures from the Second World War and the postwar era who heralded a switch to new ideas in economic policy in general or monetary and interest rate policy in particular. Ræstad's ideas related almost exclusively to experiences from before the First World War, and Getz Wold noted in his journal, with a certain sense of surprise, that 'all his ideas seem to originate from that era'.[26] In any event, Norges Bank's proposal was included in a meeting between Norges Bank and the Ministry of Finance in January 1943, where Erik Brofoss was also present. Brofoss shared the Ministry of Finance's view on Ræstad's gold standard krone, or the 'H7 krone', as it was known in Ræstad's proposal in honour of King Haakon VII.

That the Executive Board viewed matters differently than not only the younger economists, but also their central bank peers, was also explicitly pointed out by the representatives from the Bank of England. In the aforementioned meetings, the Bank of England's representatives explained that they failed to understand how Ræstad and Keilhau could favour a fixed postwar krone value before anyone knew the krone's international value or what the average Norwegian had to pay for 'his bread and his ale'.[27]

A Tightening of the Reins

The January 1943 meeting also demonstrated how Hartmann viewed the relationship between the central bank in exile and the de facto institution at home. In several instances, Ræstad and Keilhau had promoted the central bank's formally autonomous position on lesser issues, frequently gaining the approval of the Ministry of Finance, who accepted that the Norges Bank Act of 1892 continued to regulate the relationship between the government and Norges Bank. After the London-based Executive Board had registered their addresses and accounts as the Norwegian central bank, however, Ræstad argued vigorously that Norway's gold reserve should be formally transferred

---

[26] Knut Getz Wold's journal, 20 January 1943, KGW, 0627/d/Dg/L0055, NAN.
[27] Christian Brinch's note 'Møte i Bank of England' (Meeting in the Bank of England), 3 September 1942, and Keilhau's minutes from 6 September 1942, both S-3946/D/D6/L0006, NAN.

to Norges Bank (London); by that time the Norwegian state had deposited the gold in American and Canadian vaults. Although Ræstad's claim was formally understandable, it clearly breached the pragmatic sense of community that characterized, or at least should have characterized, the exiled government's common endeavour to win the war and create peace.[28] Nor did any transfer of the gold reserve ultimately take place.[29]

During a meeting early in 1943, however, Hartmann stated that he envisioned that Norges Bank in Oslo would be further developed following the liberation, and that it was not prudent to make decisions in London that were to have a long-term effect in the postwar era. According to the official minutes, this view was immediately supported by Nordahl; according to the more unofficial account, as recorded in Getz Wold's journal, Ræstad was 'stunned', 'red-faced and angry'.[30]

From a purely administrative perspective, the Ministry of Finance's view should come as no surprise, as the main office in Oslo had more or less been transformed from a central bank to a de facto institution when the occupying power took over and the Norwegian government retreated from the capital; taking such a perspective one step further, it would seem reasonable to contend that the process should be reversed following the liberation. Underlying Ræstad's outrage, however, was a fundamental antipathy against both the 'de facto institution' and the Germans who occupied the country, coupled with strong ambitions on behalf of the London-based Executive Board. His plans for postwar Norway did not explicitly deal with the relationship between Oslo and London, but the subtext was clear: for postwar Norway, according to Ræstad's notes, there should be an enduring division between Norges Bank and 'the Oslo institution'. He did not want to comment much on the latter's administrative machinery, he wrote in one passage, but presumed that it would be 'used as much as possible for Norges Bank's tasks in the new situation as well'.[31] In both this and other contexts, 'Norges Bank' was clearly the entity that he himself led.

The decision to opt for the 'Oslo institution' as the basis for the Norges Bank of the future did not create problems for the fairly robust Finance Minister Hartmann. What *did* become complicated, however, was when, a few months later, he proposed to the cabinet that Norges Bank's Executive Board should answer directly to the Ministry of Finance. It was first at this juncture that the Norges Bank Act of 1892, which had been

---

[28] But hardly more than formally understandable. Johan Melander (who later served as a director general in the Ministry of Foreign Affairs and as CEO of Norway's largest bank, DnC) was during this period employed as the secretary for Norges Bank's Executive Board. An undated and unsigned note, which in all likelihood was written by Melander, stated that the government's decision to appoint a new Executive Board that was to accompany the government away from the invading forces did not necessarily entail that all the bank's assets were automatically placed under the disposal of this board. 'P.M. om disponeringen av og disposisjonsretten til Norges Banks gullbeholdning under dens transport fra Oslo 9.4.1940 til USA og Canada' (P.M. on the disposal of and right of use to Norges Bank's gold reserve during its transportation from Oslo to the United States and Canada, 9 April 1940), S-3946/D6/L006, NAN.

[29] Cf. Ole Colbjørnsen's undated note, 'Merknader til direktør Ræstads innberetning' (Comments on Director Ræstad's report), FINL S-2061/D/LD166, NAN.

[30] Johan Melander's note dated 21 January 1943, S-6/3946/D/D6/L0016, NAN. Knut Getz Wold's journal 20 January 1943, PA–0627/D/Dg/L0055, NAN.

[31] 'Den norske pengeenhet' (The Norwegian currency), study from the Executive Board of Norges Bank dated 25 August 1942, NBL, S-3946/D/D6/L0016, NAN.

continuously interpreted in the discussions between the ministry the government, was clearly and formally set aside.

Hartmann was vehemently opposed by several of the conservative members of the national unity government, who clearly feared that such a decision would never be reversed were it to be effectuated.[32] After modifying the proposal slightly, Hartmann informed Prime Minister Nygaardsvold that he would resign if his proposal was not adopted. The modification consisted in changing the wording of the section that 'transferred' Norges Bank's activity to the Ministry of Finance, to a phrasing where the king or an entity he authorized could issue 'instructions for the Ministry of Finance's and Norges Bank's areas of activity' without any impediment from the legislation concerning Norges Bank. The ordinance, which was to be in effect until liberation, was approved with dissent.[33] Norges Bank was thereby subject to ongoing instruction from the government, in actuality Hartmann, for the remainder of the London era.

Hartmann was in his own estimation highly conservative, especially in monetary issues. There is no reason to presume that he was opposed to a largely autonomous central bank as a matter of principle. But he was very much opposed to an autonomous Ræstad, and to a certain degree an autonomous Keilhau. At the time, Keilhau was set to travel to Washington to participate in the discussions concerning the international monetary and currency policies that were to inform the postwar era. These discussions promised to be more monumental than those that hitherto had taken place concerning both major plans and minor formalities. Hartmann, and particularly his young associate Getz Wold, clearly felt that the situation demanded that Ræstad and Keilhau be kept under control.

Norges Bank and the Bretton Woods System

The major issue in winter and spring 1943 was discussions concerning Norway's position on the proposal for a new international monetary order, which was to be implemented after the war. On the table were two wide-ranging plans, one drafted by the British economist John Maynard Keynes, the other by Harry Dexter White, a high-ranking official in the American Department of the Treasury. Both plans aimed to establish the stable framework for international trade that had been lacking for quite some time, but the solutions they outlined were markedly dissimilar. The differences stemmed in part from differing theoretical underpinnings, but they were sharpened by the divergent British and American interests in technical and political solutions.

We shall not go into detail here about the plans and their elaboration, but instead focus on their key aspects as seen from the Norwegian perspective. The Keynes Plan entailed the establishment of the International Clearing Union, which was to use a

[32] Hartmann, *Bak fronten: fra Oslo og London 1939–1945*, 109. Keilhau's handwritten letter to Hartmann dated 24 August 1943, FINL, D/L0170, NAN.
[33] Provisional regulation of 3 September 1943, included in Bank, *Beretning fra direksjonen for Norges Bank om virksomheten i det frie Norge og i London i tiden 22. april 1940 til 13. juli 1945*, 116–17.

new unit of account, the bancor. Each participating country would start with a certain amount of bancors that corresponded with their pre-war trade, population, and gold reserve levels—criteria that incidentally favoured Great Britain. If significant imbalances arose, as measured by the bancor reserves, increased interest rates would induce the countries in question to restore the balance. In such a system, the responsibility for maintaining equilibrium would lie with surplus and deficit countries alike.[34]

The White Plan proposed two other institutions: a world bank to provide long-term credit to countries who needed it, and a major stabilization fund to supply more short-term credit; such credit was, however, to be allocated on the basis of commercial criteria. The White Plan was also based on a system of fixed rates of exchange for the various national currencies. Taken as a whole, these two criteria largely laid the responsibility for eliminating imbalances on the deficit countries in the system.

The Ministry of Finance was swift in its reply.[35] The ministry's political assessments shared their underlying principles with those of the Keynes Plan. This plan was considered to be the most flexible one, for instance in regard to national exchange rate policies, and more suitable for meeting what the ministry feared would be the truly monumental challenge after the war: how would it be possible to achieve equilibrium in the payment systems with a financially robust United States, with its strong tradition of protectionism, and a more impoverished Europe with major reconstruction needs? None of the studies expressed any confidence that the United States would follow a trade policy that differed fundamentally from the one the country followed in the wake of the First World War. It was therefore necessary to establish a system that would also impel a major surplus country—namely, the United States—to do its part in reducing trade surpluses.

Norges Bank commented on the matter both formally and informally, and their perspective differed entirely from that of the Ministry of Finance.[36] The Executive Board was primarily sceptical regatding the flexibility and the room for discretion that were intrinsic to both plans, but perhaps primarily in the Keynes Plan. Furthermore, Ræstad and Keilhau pointed out that the plans entailed that elected politicians would assume a greater role at the expense of the central banks, which stood for professional acumen and which did not depend on the fluctuating moods of the people to carry out their chosen courses of action.

Ræstad and Keilhau met with Keynes a few times in London to discuss the matter. At their final meeting, Ræstad and Keilhau brought with them their own proposal, featuring autonomous central banks, full gold convertibility, and formal obstacles that would hinder member countries within an established cooperation from changing their rates of exchange. The ensuing correspondence aptly symbolizes the meeting

---

[34] Herman van der Wee, *Prosperity and Upheaval: The World Economy, 1945–1980* (Penguin Books, 1987), Armand Van Dormael, *Bretton Woods: Birth of a Monetary System* (Springer, 1978).

[35] Knut Getz Wold's note dated 13 May 1943, NBL, S-3946/D/Db/L0009, NAN.

[36] Keilhau, 'Utkast til uttalelse om Keynesplanen og Whiteplanen' (Draft statement concerning the Keynes Plan and the White Plan), 10 May 1943; the Executive Board of Norges Bank, 'Forhandlinger om en internasjonal pengeordning' (Negotiations concerning an international monetary system), 13 May 1943, NBL, S-3946/D/Db/L0010.

between future and past—the far-distant past, even. Keynes quashed the issue of central banks by referring the matter to the governments of the countries in question. In contrast, he was quite explicit when it came to determining monetary values and rates of exchange:

> I appreciate the reasons and the experience which lie behind this. But I cannot believe, after the experience of the period between the wars and of this war itself, that anything so conservative would really meet the needs of the new conditions [...] I shall hope yet to convert you and Dr. Keilhau to looking with not too unfavourable an eye to something more ambitious than you are favouring at the present![37]

However, Keynes proved unable to persuade Ræstad, who defended the use of fixed external gold convertibility in a lengthy reply, using arguments that were virtually identical with those he had promoted during the deflationary policy of the 1920s. His arguments were formal, perhaps even idealistic, and in no way related to concrete economic mechanisms or results:

> a mobile state of the currency as an international economic order is incompatible with an orderly, as opposed to a speculative, economy [...] it can never be justified as an economic, anymore than on any other, ground to sacrifice the fundamental stabilisation of economic life for purposes of contingency and expediency, however important they may be.[38]

Sending Ræstad to the United States for the impending negotiations does not seem to have been considered. The government had decided early on that Keilhau would make the trip, but the Ministry of Finance was reluctant to appoint him as the head of the delegation. Ole Colbjørnsen, who was attached to the Norwegian embassy in Washington, was briefly considered as a potential chairman, but Hartmann ultimately decided to put Keilhau in charge. The final two members of the delegation were to be Colbjørnsen and Norway's trade attaché in Washington, Arne Skaug, who would later serve as the trade minister for many years.

Keilhau was sent to the conference with a written instruction. In its level of detail, and not least in its candid explanations for being so detailed, it was an uncommonly bureaucratic piece of text. Numerous subsections made clear that the Norwegian view was that a flexible international system was called for, also in order to determine the rates of exchange; the rates that would be determined upon the war's conclusion

---

[37] Keynes to Ræstad, 4 July 1943, same file.

[38] Ræstad to Keynes, 16 August 1943, NBL S-3946/D/Db/L0010. Keynes disagreed, as he would have had he met Ræstad twenty years previously. But now it was Keynes who had the backing of the people's representatives: 'When a particular country's wage-policy has got out of step with its neighbours' at the existing rate of exchange, the choice, between deflation in order to create unemployment and a modification of exchange rates, as the best available means to restore equilibrium is a political, as well as an economic and banking, question. And in this country Parliament would be unwilling, I am quite sure, to limit itself beforehand to use only the former alternative' (Keynes to Ræstad, 16 August 1943).

should therefore not bind the rates that were to apply in a more normalized future. The delegation was also instructed not to deal with issues relating to the division of authority between central banks, ministries, and governments. The most exceptional subsection was the seventh, which went as follows:

> The ministry has decided that the delegation should not issue any statements or make any proposals that in any way anticipate decisions concerning the future monetary system in Norway, cf. the Ministry of Finance's and Norges Bank's differing viewpoints on this matter. Nor should any statements be made that may in any way seem to disparage the value of the occupation krone or the status of Norges Bank in Oslo.[39]

The instruction had been drafted by Knut Getz Wold, who attached his own twenty-two-page comment to the Keynes Plan and the White Plan as the backdrop for the ministry's view. It was also Getz Wold who had formulated the proposal to have Norges Bank answer directly to the Ministry of Finance.

Keilhau crossed the Atlantic on the *Queen Mary*, which also lodged the British delegation. Keilhau soon reported that he had held productive discussions with Keynes, and that he had set forth proposals that had gained widespread approval. A short while later he also reported that the British delegation had invited him to attend their preliminary meetings in Atlantic City.[40] It was by no means a given that Keynes and the British delegation would have welcomed Keilhau joining them in Atlantic City, considering Keilhau's previously stated views. But perhaps these views were on the verge of changing. Finance Minister Hartmann's assessment of Keilhau was that despite his impulsive outbursts, he was knowledgeable and sensible, but that he was utterly dominated by Ræstad's overbearing personality. That Keynes wielded a similar influence over Keilhau is certainly a possibility. It is for instance difficult to rediscover Keilhau's and Norges Bank's viewpoints from 1943 and 1944 in the book that Keilhau wrote in 1946 on the genesis of the new international monetary system.[41] Professor Johan Vogt's eulogy for Keilhau upon his death in 1954 also underlined that Keilhau had felt very close to Keynes.[42]

The Ministry of Finance did not pay much heed to the plethora of messages from Keilhau. It was first when the finance minster and his confidantes read in the *Times* and the *Evening Standard* that the Norwegian delegation had proposed the abolition of the BIS, followed by comprehensive interviews with the head of the delegation, that the correspondence began in earnest the other way across the Atlantic. 'This is a major attack against the Bank for International Settlements (BIS), an acute and controversial

---

[39] 'Det britiske forslag om en internasjonal clearingunion og det amerikanske forslag om de forente nasjoners stabiliseringsfond', NBL D/Db/L0010, NAN.

[40] Telegram quoted in a communiqué from the Ministry of Foreign Affairs to the Ministry of Finance, 28 June 1944, NBL D/Db/L0010, NAN.

[41] Wilhelm Keilhau, *Det nye internasjonale pengesystem* (The new international monetary system) (Aschehoug, 1946).

[42] Johan Vogt, 'Wilhelm Keilhau', *Statsøkonomisk Tidsskift* 2 (1954).

issue in foreign policy, one that there isn't the slightest reason for Norway to instigate', an alarmed Getz Wold wrote to Skaug.[43] The BIS issue had not been discussed prior to Keilhau's departure, and the Ministry of Finance's general attitude was that Norway as a small country should not become embroiled in controversial discussions that did not affect its national interests. As it transpired, the BIS proved to be a major and difficult issue at Bretton Woods, even though a toned-down proposal, which was presented later on by the Dutch delegation, won general support.[44]

It is not readily apparent why the Norwegian delegation proposed to abolish the BIS, though it seems likely that general anti-German sentiments played their part. From a technical perspective, it was hard to see in 1944 what role the BIS would play in the future international system of payments, but the question of liquidation came undoubtedly to the fore because of the Basel-based bank's ongoing collaboration with German authorities. That said, there were also several practical reasons to let the matter lie until the war was over. However, such practical considerations did not weigh heavily on Norges Bank London in general and Keilhau in particular. There was also a certain parallelism between, on the one hand, the desire to quickly terminate the BIS, and on the other hand, to either create a 'new' Norwegian unit of currency, undefiled by the German monetary system, or wipe Norges Bank Oslo off the central bank map, such as the circular letter from 1942 had in mind.

For the Ministry of Finance, the episode served in any case to confirm all their prejudices concerning Keilhau. Shortly after he was instructed to return home after the formal negotiations had concluded, even though certain reports remained unfinished.[45]

A New Era

The transition from the London government to the new national unity government in Oslo witnessed a wide-ranging political change in personnel and mood, one that is difficult to comprehend entirely, as moods and mentalities often are.

The young economist Otto Christian Malterud—who for long stretches of time worked for the legation in Oslo and followed much of the planning that took place in London, in Stockholm, and among the leadership of the Norwegian resistance in Oslo—wrote a frank and open letter to Keilhau in September 1943, with a personal reflection on why he thought the ideas from Norges Bank in London seemed outmoded: 'I dare say that we who have lived under German occupation also to a great degree have distanced ourselves from the pre-war lines of reasoning.' The attitudes of both young economists and prominent bankers had changed by this juncture. This

[43] Knut Getz Wold to Arne Skaug, 14 July 1944, NAN-0627/D/Da/L0001.
[44] Gianni Toniolo, *Central Bank Cooperation at the Bank for International Settlements 1930–1967* (Cambridge University Press, 2005), 269ff.; Robert Skidelsky, *John Maynard Keynes*, vol. 3, *Fighting for Britain* (Macmillan, 2000).
[45] Documents in file 'Prof. Keilhau', FINL L0170 64, NAN.

was supposed to serve as a kind of explanation to Keilhau for why key actors in Norway had referred to his and Ræstad's proposals as 'utterly useless and totally insane'. In addition to several technical arguments, Malterud contended that plans that neglected practical consequences and an equitable distribution of the burdens of war, and that only related self-reflexively to monetary theories and legislation, would fall dead to the ground.[46] Getz Wold expressed similar thoughts in a letter to economist Arne Skaug, later cabinet minister for the Labour Party. 'He is completely unable to understand the psychological attitude of those at home, which might have enabled him to view himself and his own endeavours in the proper relief', Getz Wold wrote concerning Keilhau, referring to the time that Keilhau had spent in tandem with Ræstad.[47]

Exactly what sort of moods and attitudes were prevalent? The exile communities in London and partly New York and Stockholm had become hotbeds for new impulses and for planning and politics, especially in the field of economics. The administrative milieus also produced numerous young talents who would subsequently become prominent bureaucrats and politicians—Knut Getz Wold, Arne Skaug, and Erik Brofoss have already been mentioned, and several more could have been added to that list.

Nevertheless, the overall picture is that the 'resistance movement in exile' was dethroned in favour of a broadly defined 'resistance movement at home'. All the political parties, but perhaps the burgeoning Labour Party in particular, witnessed a swift and forceful changing of the guard. Those who were associated with the policies of the interwar period, the deficient defence spending, and the lacklustre mobilization prior to the German invasion had to yield to the next generation. The new leaders included many from the resistance who enjoyed great popularity and who spoke with great moral authority after the war. The first attempt to form a government centred around Chief Justice Pål Berg, the leader of the resistance movement in Norway during the war. When Berg encountered opposition, from among others his Liberal Party colleague Gunnar Jahn, it was the Labour Party's Einar Gerhardsen, who had been incarcerated with Jahn and many others in the prisoner camp at Grini, who formed a unity government. Gerhardsen's government became the youngest in Norwegian history. The average age of the cabinet ministers was forty-four years, which was far more sensational at the time that it would be today. The youngest minister was the thirty-year-old Jens Christian Hauge, who had led the military resistance (Milorg) from 1943.

This generational shift helped reinforce certain changes that were already budding in the 1930s. As a result, both in Norway and in many other countries, a different mood existed in 1944/5 compared with the years following the First World War, when the prevalent political forces wanted to re-establish the pre-war conditions for

---

[46] Malterud to Keilhau, 10 September 1943, S-3946/D/D6/L0019, NAN.
[47] Getz Wold to Skaug, 13 August 1943, Pa-0627/D/Da/L0001, NAN.

prosperity. It was a new future that was to be built in 1945, and this was perhaps particularly evident in the economic sphere.

A common characteristic of the parties' political programmes, and of their joint programme for the immediate postwar years, was a strong belief in planning and governance.[48] This belief was related to a clear mistrust in the forces of the marketplace being as unfettered as during the precarious interwar period. But equally significant was a somewhat indefinable belief in political action and in 'economic democracy'. This was a concept that was variously understood; in practice it actually entailed both a demand for stronger governance by the Storting and the government, and arguments for the establishment of corporative agencies in economic life. Such ideas had been articulated and discussed during the crises of the 1930s, and some had also been incorporated in the parties' political programmes. But across party lines, the Nygaardsvold generation of politicians had been reluctant to carry out those ideas.

Keilhau's lack of understanding for the new 'psychological attitude' is perhaps best seen in his defence of an autonomous central bank. As he wrote in 1943, the sole purpose of a bank of issue should be to take care of the state's monetary needs, without any influence from partisan politics. In contrast, the finance ministers were at the core of political power; they were answerable not only to the national assembly, but also to their party and their programme. A transfer of power to the finance minister would therefore entail an expansion of 'the political sphere of society at the expense of the technical'; this would hardly be beneficial, Keilhau contended, in what was meant as an understatement.[49] But at home in Norway—and in numerous countries that either nominally or in reality were preparing such transfers of power—it was precisely such notions that monetary policy should be protected from 'the political sphere of society' that stood at an all-time low during the conclusion and aftermath of the war.

In domestic circles during and after the war, the issue of an 'autonomous' central bank was hardly discussed; it was taken for granted that an entirely new era was dawning for Norges Bank. When it was suggested in May 1945 that Gunnar Jahn should become governor of Norges Bank, Jahn dejectedly wrote in his journal that someone was trying to 'get rid of' him, as he was by now convinced that Norges Bank would in the future be 'entirely subordinate to the Ministry of Finance'.[50]

This was not only related to views on 'economic democracy' and control by popularly elected representatives, but also the new economic intelligentsia's views on the role of monetary policy. The modern macroeconomic paradigm was in favour of using a coordinated fiscal and monetary policy to influence aggregate demand, and thereby society's economic activity. This was part of the international zeitgeist, inspired by Keynes in particular. The Norwegian variant achieved its particularity through the economic-political thinking of Ragnar Frisch, whose students soon

---

[48] These question is discussed more in depth in Einar Lie, *Ambisjon og tradisjon: Finansdepartementet 1945–65* (Universitetsforlaget, 1995).

[49] 'Utkast til uttalelse om Keynesplanen og Whiteplanen' (Draft statement concerning the Keynes Plan and the White Plan), Keilhau's note dated 10 May 1943, NBL, D/Db/L0010, NAN.

[50] Gunnar Jahn's diary, 25 May 1945, GJ.

dominated both the economic debate and the governmental postwar planning agencies. The generational shift in economic policy coincided here with the graduation of numerous economists from a recently established programme at the University of Oslo that was inspired by Frisch.

In his thinking, Frisch placed scant emphasis on the monetary aspect of the economy. Frisch's statements on the need to restructure the liquidity surplus that had been created in the Norwegian economy during the war also suggest that he was against such a measure, or at best considered it to be inconsequential. During a seminar with several younger economists in 1945, professors Petersen and Frisch discussed this question with their former students, with the two teachers representing the most opposing viewpoints at the seminar. Petersen contended that it was important to bind or eliminate the liquidity surplus; Frisch felt this was largely unimportant, and he was not reluctant to go further in directly regulating the economy.[51]

For the Ministry of Finance and Norges Bank, the summer and autumn of 1945 represented a transitional period, one that paradoxically was both open and settled. In line with Hartmann's decision in 1943, the 73-year-old Rygg was reinstated as the central bank governor in spring 1945. Rygg himself considered the decision to be 'humiliating', as he clearly felt that he had always been the central bank governor and was in no need of being reinstated.[52] Rygg remained in his position while a national unity government was being constituted by Einar Gerhardsen, in spite of efforts to have him quickly removed. Gunnar Jahn supported Rygg and provided him with political cover, since Gerhardsen was keen to include Jahn in the government. Jahn had two non-negotiable demands: the one pertained to the powers of authority for the regulation policy, the other that Rygg was not immediately deposed in 'a mean-spirited manner', as he himself put it in his journal.[53]

How did things turn out for the formal leadership of the central bank in exile? London was London and Oslo was Oslo, and never were the twain to meet—other than in a physical sense one day in July 1945, when Ræstad, Keilhau, and Rygg all convened in Jahn's governmental office. Jahn, who stood firmly in the Oslo camp in his view of the London Executive Board, had received in advance fairly wide-ranging demands from Ræstad concerning how his experience and expertise should be used thenceforth. During the meeting, Ræstad highlighted the extensive network he had gradually acquired among central bankers, while Keilhau pointed to his participation in the Bretton Woods negotiations. After some back and forth, Keilhau made it clear that he and Ræstad merely wished to be of assistance in a brief transition period. According to Rygg's detailed minutes, Jahn replied that 'he had unfortunately not been intelligent enough to perceive that this is what the gentlemen desired'. Ræstad

[51] Tore Jørgen Hanisch, *Kryssløpet mellom vitenskap og politikk: Odd Aukrust og forskningen i Statistisk sentralbyrå'. Innledning til Økonomisk forskning og debatt: utvalgte artikler av Odd Aukrust 1942–1989*, vol. 75, *Økonomisk forskning og debatt. Utvalgte artikler 1942–1989 av Odd Aukrust* (Statistisk sentralbyrå, 1990), 18.
[52] Gunnar Jahn's diary 14 May 1945, GJ; Knut Getz Wold's diary,14 May 1945. KGW.
[53] Gunnar Jahn's diary, 14 June 1945, GJ.

and Keilhau were then placed at Rygg's disposal as advisors.[54] This is the last we hear of Ræstad in Norges Bank's history, and he passed away suddenly a few months later.

New Exchange Rate and Monetary Reform

Extensive studies on both rate determination for the Norwegian krone and reform of the monetary system had been carried out in London, first in Norges Bank and then as replies or alternatives to their study. No clear proposal in any of the areas had been put forth, however, and in-depth studies were instigated in the summer of 1945.

Before the war, it was in practice Norges Bank that determined the exchange rate. However, the extensive studies that were carried out in summer 1945 led to the central bank being divested of any meaningful role in that context. An exchange commission comprising fifteen members was appointed, including the professors Ingvar Wedervang, Ragnar Frisch, and Wilhelm Keilhau. The commission was unanimously in favour of devaluing the Norwegian krone by 20 per cent by increasing the exchange rate for pounds from 20 to 24 kroner. In the exceptional situation following the war, the correct, underlying value of the krone was uncertain; the deciding factor became the export industries' current situation and long-term interests. The conclusion from the Economic Coordination Council (Det økonomiske Samordningsråd), an important and recently established corporative agency, was different. The council was in favour of maintaining a stable domestic price level, so as to avoid sparking off a price–wage spiral; the majority recommended maintaining the rate of exchange for pounds at 20, which also was the government's ultimate decision.

The majority of Norges Bank's Executive Board favoured an exchange rate of 22, while Rygg himself recommended 20, though his opinion was by no means a major factor in the government's decision. Rygg participated in a meeting of the exchange commission in order to account for the central bank's viewpoint. According to a young economist who was a member of the commission, the meeting was overshadowed by the strong animosity between Rygg on the one hand and Frisch and Keilhau on the other. The last two 'did not have much professional respect for Rygg and Norges Bank. During the meeting, Frisch in particular spoke to Rygg in a 'fairly condescending tone.'[55]

It was more difficult not to charge Norges Bank with the task of restructuring the monetary system. However, when the Storting instructed the central bank to draft a reform proposal along with the Ministry of Finance, this provoked strong opposition. The problem was Rygg, who was portrayed as the most prominent of the conservative economists. Several others also expressed their criticism, which was also partially aimed at Jahn, because he had for several years been part of Rygg's Executive Board.[56]

---

[54] Minutes from the meeting in Jahn's office, 13 July 1945, S-3947/E/L0008, NAN.
[55] Petter Jakob Bjerve, *Økonomisk planlegging og politikk* (Norske samlaget, 1989), 30.
[56] 'Odeltingets vedtak om lov om visse finansielle tiltak', meeting in the Lagting 13 July 1945, Storting's proceedings.

The Storting nonetheless passed a unanimous resolution, though a Labour Party spokesman emphasized that this was only so as to avoid dissent regarding the current situation.

Rygg worked on this case throughout the summer of 1945. The plan he elaborated on behalf of Norges Bank consisted of four different measures. The first measure was to register all bank deposits, combined with an exchange of the wartime kroner to a new type of currency. The banknote registration was intended to help determine the postwar assets of both companies and private individuals; the increase of wealth during the war could thereby be determined by comparison with the 1939 tax returns. This was to form the basis for the second and perhaps most vital measure: a one-time tax with a high and severely progressive tax rate that aimed at appropriating large parts of the surplus purchasing power in a manner that placed the burdens on those who had profited most from the war. This proposal was not a novelty from Norges Bank, but had been incorporated in various guises in the proposals and drafts that had been elaborated in the central administration in London. In contrast, the third measure—that the government should take up a sizeable 'liberty loan' domestically— was a new element compared to previous studies. The liberty loan was to be a long-term loan with favourable terms, so that the general public would be strongly encouraged to bind the portion of the surplus purchasing power that had not been appropriated by the one-time tax. Finally, the proposed fourth measure was that the state should have the authority to obligate private banks to place a part of their liquid assets as long-term deposits in Norges Bank.[57]

The final two proposals garnered little public attention and were never followed up. The exchange of banknotes was transacted, though first in September 1945; by then the newspapers had for a long while reported on how people were buying travel cards and trolley passes in large quantities, all types of goods that were not subject to rationing, and unregistered securities at extremely stiff prices. A proposition for a one-time tax, with its combined appeal to economic theory and a sense of justice, had won fairly widespread approval immediately following liberation. But the unanimity had already evaporated before the new postwar government submitted their bill to the Storting. In the bill that the Ministry of Finance had drafted on the basis of Norges Bank's report, all assets were to be treated more or less symmetrically: those who had invested new financial wealth in a house or farm in the latter stage of the war were not to be taxed less than people whose assets were in banknotes and bank deposits. This required fairly realistic evaluations of real estate, however, and such realism by no means typified the Norwegian system of taxation (nor does it to this day); lengthy cabinet discussions concluded with several ministers, including the prime minister himself, dissenting from parts of the proposed legislation.

After a parliamentary election resulted in the formation of a pure Labour Party government late in 1945, Jahn's proposition was withdrawn.[58] During the subsequent

[57] Jahn, Eriksen, and Munthe, *Norges Bank gjennom 150 år*, ch. 24.
[58] The account here is according to Einar Lie, 'Pengesanering og reguleringsøkonomi', *Historisk tidsskrift* 73, no. 1 (1994).

months a new proposal was drafted. Public opinion was now more critical of the proposal. The young economists who had been educated in Frisch's classrooms had argued all along that the liquidity surplus was not really a major factor behind the inflationary pressure, which had primarily been caused by the physical absence of consumer goods. That which around six months before had been referred in abstract terms as a 'restructuring'—one that was to alleviate price control and ensure that those who had become rich from the war would foot most of the bill—was now referred to as a 'a record-high tax' to the state. The business community, which at the outset had been the most vociferous supporter of the measure, became more disapproving and demanded several special arrangements. For this and other reasons, the Conservative Party's attitude to the tax swung from being favourable to being critical and cautious. By the time Finance Minister Erik Brofoss submitted a proposal to the Storting in 1946, the tax rates had been lowered and a number of tax breaks and special arrangements had been introduced.

Not much remained thereby of Norges Bank's initial proposal. Jahn's journal summary was clear and to the point: 'A restructuring is in any case no longer on the cards, that's for certain. That means we will glide into a lengthy period of regulations that hardly will prove effective, but no other path is now available if we are not to let things slide entirely.'[59]

The Recovery that Never Was

In actuality, monetary measures were largely insignificant until the liquidity surplus was eliminated early in the 1950s. Nonetheless, issues pertaining to Norges Bank were still part of the economic debate, but mostly to indicate that the bank played an entirely new role than before. For example, the new finance minister, Erik Brofoss, repeatedly alluded to the central bank and monetary policy in his annual fiscal address to the Storting. His main point was that monetary policy was now an integrated part of a general economic policy; the days were over when separate goals could be set for monetary policy.

The declared, overarching aims for the government's economic policy from 1945 onwards was to maintain full employment, high economic growth, and a 'fair' distribution of income. In the presentation of his first national budget, the new minister of finance, Erik Brofoss, told the Storting that these aims were fundamental in securing the well-being and welfare of the population. Monetary values were subordinate, and mainly means to meet the true ends of economic policy-making.[60] The purchasing power of the krone should indeed be kept stable. However, this should mainly be done by the use of direct price controls, to secure the real value of wages earned.

---

[59] Gunnar Jahn's diary, 18 January 1946, GJ.
[60] Financial adress 19 February 1946, Stortingstidende, 1945–6, Storting's proceedings.

The Labour government declared a new programme for economic planning and policy-making. Policy targets should be met by detailed planning of the different sectors of the economy, and a number of new policy tools, fine-tuned to reach the goals, set up for the different sectors. Public spending, taxes, and duties should be adjusted to economic developments and needs, as should rationing and price controls. All policy means should be centralized in government. Additionally, Brofoss held, in line with contemporary doctrine, that the interest rates should be kept stable at a low level. A key understanding was that a low interest rate would promote high investments and growth in the long run. Low interest rates would also benefit the social distribution aims, as it would lower the costs of housing and living.[61] In the government's view, the advantages of stable, low interest rates were so obvious, and a high interest rate relatively inefficient in regulating economic activities, that the interest rate should be maintained at a low level even in the case of a booming economy.[62]

The main line of thinking was supported and promoted by the influential groups of economists trained at the University of Oslo—the only university in Norway at the time. Finance minister Brofoss had studied economics at Professor Frisch's department at Oslo University in the 1930s. He soon recruited a number of Frisch students to key positions in his ministry.[63] The new intelligentsia underlined that monetary stocks, interest rates, and exchanges rates were distractions from the real economic quantities in the economy—the production of physical goods and services—which were the main aims of policy-making. Traditional monetary policies, especially high interest rates, were seen as imprecise and largely inefficient policy tools. In the early postwar years, Frisch and his proponents saw their public activity as a kind of information campaign against old-fashioned monetary-oriented 'delusions' in economic thinking and politics.[64]

The emphasis on the 'real' economy, a concept central to Norwegian and to some extent Nordic macroeconomic thinking, came to appear in a number of international debates on standards for national accounting, a field where general theory, statistical classifications, and production of numbers for policy-making intercepted. The distinction between the real and financial sphere and the supremacy of the former had a number of impacts on how concrete economic variables were interpreted within a macroeconomic framework. Frisch and his former students in Statistics Norway maintained that the accounts should (in principle) be constructed around physical flows, primarily on the basis of production, investments, and consumption. In the standard of Richard Stone, later Nobel laureate for his work on national accounting, the macroeconomic aggregates were conventionally calculated as the sum of income from production factors, work (wages), and capital (interest, profit, and dividends). This was regarded as a grossly erroneous approach from the Norwegian and Nordic

[61] See Odd Aukrust and Petter Jakob Bjerve, *Hva krigen kostet Norge* (Dreyer, 1945).
[62] See e.g. Eivind Erichsen, *Økonomiske problemer idag, og i tiden framover: artikler skrevet i tiden 14. Mai–25. August i Dagbladet* (Halvorsen & Larsen, 1945).
[63] Trond Bergh, 'Norway: The Powerful Servants', *History of Political Economy* 13, no. 3 (1981).
[64] Petter Jakob Bjerve, *Økonomi og politikk* (Aschehoug, 1971).

side: a concept of aggregate wealth accumulation had to be derived from the 'real sphere'. Interest, profit, and dividends had nothing to do with the real contribution of physical capital but arbitrarily determined by institutional characteristics and decisions. Interest and dividends should rather be treated as transfers in the tables, and not compared with salaries, the remuneration to registered man labour.

This subtle point connects to a more general perception of the value of the financial sector in Norwegian society. Frisch and his young economists represented a break with established traditions, which they themselves were the first to underline. Still, their arguments bear clear similarities with the persistent scepticism regarding the financial sector's role and 'speculation', which has persistently been present in Norwegian economic debate. We find it in the first discussions around the establishment of the bank and new notes in independent Norway (see Chapter 1). We find the same elements in early attempts to classify the population as 'productive' or 'unproductive' by leading statisticians in the late nineteenth century. In the statistical casting of the adult population, the 'productive' were those defined as people who worked—housewives without income were included in the definition. Capitalists, rentiers, and non-managing shipowners were among the 'unproductive', along with children and disabled. Here too, we find a clear preference for perceiving value as something created by hard work (and natural resources), not by accumulated capital and financial institutions.[65]

What consequences did this new political and economic thinking have for Norges Bank? The central bank, with its long-established orientation towards monetary values and policies, was undoubtedly a symbol of past thinking and practices, which had to be reformed and restricted in the new postwar era.

Brofoss' views on Norges Bank followed the same line. In his first fiscal address he also dealt in detail with Rygg's report to the Storting on matters relating to the occupation account. Rygg had argued that the state and not Norges Bank should be responsible for the occupation account, and he made several comments concerning how any war reparations should be channelled through the state and deposited in the account as repayment. In response, Brofoss more or less ridiculed such an exposition of the relationship between Norges Bank and the state. According to Brofoss, it was the economic situation—primarily how the mass of liquidity was to be treated—that had to determine what should be done with these and other payments, and such an assessment had 'nothing whatsoever to do with a quasi-legal question of repayment'. His point was in any case to demonstrate that a formal separation between 'the state' and 'the national bank' was an obsolete notion.[66]

In this situation it was not surprising that the state chose to nationalize Norges Bank, through a proposal in 1949 to acquire the shares that were privately owned. This took place amid an international wave of nationalization; the British authorities

---

[65] This larger topic is discussed in Einar Lie and Hege Roll-Hansen, *Faktisk talt: statistikkens historie i Norge* (Universitetsforl., 2001), 309–40; and Einar Lie, *Den norske Creditbank 1982–1990: en storbank i vekst og krise* (Universitetsforlaget, 1998), 49–51.

[66] Stortingstidende 1946, 283ff, Stortings proceedings.

had undertaken a corresponding operation in regard to the Bank of England in 1946.[67] The shareholders had never exercised any influence on the bank's operations; the shares were more akin to obligations with a predictable dividend. With this in mind, the Executive Board of Norges Bank opposed the proposal, though with a pragmatic economic consideration: though the measure did not affect governance, the purchase of shares would add liquidity to the economy at a time when the opposite was desirable. In the Storting, the centre-right minority opposed the proposal, though their arguments had little to do with professional autonomy; rather, several MPs emphasized the long-term aspects and that Norges Bank was historically the Storting's bank, and that for many the shares had literally been acquired by means of the family silver. Nationalization would break these ties to the past and entail a stronger concentration of power in the hands of the government.

But also this debate seemed to be mostly about settling old scores, both with the autonomous Norges Bank and particularly with Rygg. Several Labour MPs repeatedly invoked the failed monetary policies of the 1920s, as well as Rygg's and Norges Bank's readiness to help depose the first Labour government in 1928. As such, the debate on nationalization served its purpose, providing a new opportunity to renounce the old ways and demonstrate the government's authority and responsibility in the monetary sphere.[68]

Norges Bank's new leadership represented a different view on monetary policies but accepted the superiority of government in its former realm.[69] The governor from 1946, Gunnar Jahn, never challenged the ministry in policy matters, though he firmly believed that the Labour Party and their advisors clearly underestimated the potential of monetary policy.

Conclusion

In total, the immediate postwar years led to a near-absolute loss of status and autonomy for Norges Bank. After the First World Was, the established political milieu wanted to restore the pre-war conditions for growth and prosperity. 'Return to normalcy' was Warren G. Harding's, the US candidate for the presidency, slogan for his campaign in 1920. The same slogan could have applied to many European governments, not least Norwegian politicians and Governor Rygg's effort to restore the old normalcy in the 1920s. In 1945, the weight of the political milieu wanted to build a new and different future. No one wanted a return to the interwar situation, with economic crises, mass unemployment, and social conflicts.

The 1946–50 period is often labelled the 'era of recovery' in the context of economics and politics. For Norges Bank, however, there would be no recovery of its former

---

[67] John Fforde, *The Bank of England and Public Policy, 1941–1958* (Cambridge University Press, 1992).
[68] Odeltingstidende 1949, 382–421, Storting's proceedings.
[69] Governor's annual address, 1948, printed in Norges Bank's annual report.

position. New economic theories and the planned expansion of the role of government in economic life would leave little room for interwar central bank independence. In Norway, references to the parity policy in the 1920s and Rygg's role in defending the financial and political establishment were often referred to in postwar debate. Throughout his career as a central banker, Rygg won almost all the battles he engaged in. However, his costly victories paved the ground for the close to complete loss of autonomy from 1945 onwards.

The conflicts in London, and between Norges Bank London and the home head office, played only a minor role in the transition. In all areas of Norwegian society, the years of world war and the recovery years witnessed a reorientation and to a certain extent a radicalization in the economic and political communities—except in Norges Bank. For this reason, the central bank in exile was not a factor in the new economic-political thinking or in planning the exchange rates and the monetary reform in 1945; this work recommenced after the new Gerhardsen government was formed late in 1945. A new generation of politicians now entered government positions; men who had been through their formative political years during the crises and political struggles in the interwar period, and who were distant from the 'normalcy' of the liberal political order prior to 1914.

The lengthy sojourn in London and the proximity to the Bank of England and several important exile communities, along with the monetary negotiations that led up to Bretton Woods, might, under different circumstances, have benefited Norges Bank and increased its expertise, connections, and internal standing in the central administration. Instead, because of the rapid change in political and economic thinking, supplemented by all the turbulence and quarrelling in and around Norges Bank, the wartime brought about a clean break between the wartime and postwar eras. The debates on future planning, monetary policies, and nationalization of Norges Bank confirmed that the room for independent central bank policies would be radically decreased.

10

The Government's Bank

In June 1951, the central bank governors of the Nordic countries met in Copenhagen. Each year since the war, the five had met in a different capital city, and each time they met, they concluded that the central banks played a small political role compared with the interwar period. Their complaints echoed the sentiments in many European central banks, which had experienced a rapid fall in their economic influence and standing in public life. In a time marked by extensive price and foreign currency regulations, and high governing ambitions of the ministries of finance, traditional monetary policies were of little importance and the central banks had limited influence.

Seen from Copenhagen, change was stirring in the summer of 1951. Deregulation was on the agenda in all countries. The recipients of Marshall Plan aid committed to the gradual liberalization of international trade. When Great Britain devalued the pound sterling in 1949, the Scandinavian countries followed suit. This gave a better rate of exchange between the US dollar and European currencies and contributed to facilitating deregulation.

The discount rate was raised in Denmark, Finland, and Sweden through 1950. At the Copenhagen meeting, Denmark's central bank governor spoke optimistically of 'a clear flourishing of the bank of issue's responsibility and position' at home.[1] The governor of Sweden's central bank, the Riksbank, could relate something similar. When the governor of Norges Bank, Gunnar Jahn, took the floor, he described a different situation. As in previous meetings, Jahn told his colleagues about an interest rate that was 'nailed down' and about a Norwegian central bank that remained without instruments.

The fixed interest rates were part of a broader reorientation in the politics of financial markets. In a few years' time, the term 'credit policy' more or less completely replaced 'monetary policy' as a key concept among experts and politicians. 'Credit' was, in principle, the end product of the financial institutions: the loans given to households and firms. The term implied a shift in focus from aggregates that had previously been at the core of central bank activity—money, liquidity, and interest rates, as a means to control inflation and output—to loans facilitating specific types of economic activities. Credit policy mainly became a process for regulating aggregate lending and allocating the credit to various sector of the economy. When starting to

---

[1] Misc. from the central bank meeting in Copenhagen, 4–5 June 1951, AE/IC, 6 July 1951. File 'PM 1240–1259, 1951', box F 0008, STAT.

Norges Bank 1816–2016. Einar Lie, Oxford University Press (2020). © Norges Bank.
DOI: 10.1093/oso/9780198860013.001.0001

conduct credit policies, the authorities needed both a formal and informal system for regulating and allocation of loans, and some principles for prioritizing between potential credit customers. Both challenges came to engage government ministries, while Norges Bank sought to find a role in the implementation and management of the emerging system.

An expanding system of state banks, created to promote defined political objectives, became a key element in the new credit policy. To ensure that these banks received cheap financing to provide low interest rate loans, an ingenious system for regulation and persuasion was designed to funnel savings from private institutions to the state banks. This system was complex and pervasive. Norges Bank had important duties. However, the principles and policies were solidly anchored in the government apparatus, with less room of manoeuvre than in a number of other European central banks.[2] In practice, Norges Bank became the government's bank, as part of its key policy apparatus. The central bank governor, Gunnar Jahn, wanted another policy and a freer role, but adapted to the new reality that was forced upon Norges Bank. When he stepped down in 1954, Norges Bank was among the least influential of the central banks in western Europe.[3]

Towards a More Open World

In early 1950, Jahn too was optimistic about the central bank's role in Norway. Since about 1947, the United States, the strongest, new superpower of the time, actively sought, with the help of the Marshall Plan, to promote liberalization of international trade and payments. In the summer of 1950, western European countries, with the help of the United States, established the European Payments Union, a multilateral settlement system for western Europe as a replacement for the bilateral agreements.[4] It was unclear when and in what form this liberalization would be implemented, but

---

[2] The situation for other Nordic central banks are mentioned later in these chapter. Eric Monnet, *Controlling Credit: Central Banking and the Planned Economy in Postwar France, 1948 1973* (Cambridge University Press, 2018) goes in detail on the Bank of France role in the postwar credit policy. For other countries, see ibid., ch. 7.

[3] This was undeniably how Gunnar Jahn saw it. An attempt to compare the Scandinavian central banks in this period, Sven Arntzen, *Norges Banks rettslige stilling i forhold til Regjering og Storting* (Norske Bankforening og Forretningsbankenes felleskontor, 1958), suggest the same. Historical accounts of the other Nordic central banks typically describe central banks that exercised stronger influence on economic policy compared with that of Norges Bank. See in particular Erling Olsen and Erik Hoffmeyer, *Dansk pengehistorie* (Danmarks Nationalbank, 1968); Peter Englund and Lars Werin, *Från räntereglering till inflationsnorm: det finansiella systemet och Riksbankens politik 1945-1990* (SNS (Studieförb. Näringsliv och samhälle), 1993); A. Kuusterä and J. Tarkka, *Bank of Finland 200 Years—Parliament's Bank (part II)* (Bank of Finland and Otava Publishing Company, 2012). This impression is also prevalent in recent historical accounts of central banks such as the Federal Reserve and Bank of England, cf. Allan H Meltzer, *A History of the Federal Reserve, Volume 1* (University of Chicago Press, 2003); and Forrest Capie, *The Bank of England: 1950s to 1979* (Cambridge University Press, 2010). Also M. H. De Kock, *Central Banking*, 3rd ed. (Staples Press, 1956). De Kock, in his attempt to describe contemporaneous central banking practices more generally, finds that both monetary policy instruments and practices in other countries, which were absent in Norway, rendered the central banks in those countries more influential than was the case for Norges Bank.

[4] On the European Payments Union in general see Barry Eichengreen, *The European Economy since 1945: Coordinated Capitalism and Beyond* (Princeton University Press, 2008); on Norway's relationship with European Payments Union, see Lars F. Øksendal, 'En fast kurs. Norsk betalingspolitikk 1945-58' (NTNU, 2001).

that it would be pursued was already clear in the Bretton Woods agreement, which the Allied countries had signed in 1944.[5]

Regulating the external economy was, by definition, incompatible with free trade, as was price regulation and rationing. Without direct regulations, it would no longer be possible, as it was during the war, to prevent the money supply from affecting the price level, balance of payments, and exchange rates.

The regulation of prices that had started during the war continued in the years that followed, primarily because there was no effective reform to reduce purchasing power. Price regulation and price subsidies were used to maintain a stable price level in order to avoid a wage–price spiral. But the international price level was steadily increasing and price subsidies were becoming an unreasonably heavy burden on state finances.

The devaluation in September 1949 tore this strained system apart. The devaluation of pound sterling was expected during the International Monetary Fund's (IMF) annual meeting that month, after years of rumours and pressure from the United States. It was on the cards that many western European countries would follow suit. Central bank governor Jahn participated in two of the government's meetings on this issue in late August/early September. It was decided at these meetings that Jahn, as Norway's representative to the IMF, had the authority to devalue the krone as much as pound sterling. This meant that there would be a new, adjusted rate against the dollar as soon as the British decision came into effect. The government estimated a devaluation of approximately 20 per cent. During the dinner in Washington on 16 September, Jahn learned that the devaluation of pound sterling would be 30 per cent. Jahn telegraphed Brofoss and said that he thought the government should stick to the decision to follow the pound, even though the devaluation was higher than expected. Brofoss gave his consent by telegram shortly afterwards. The rest of the government was spread around the country in connection with the election. Brofoss, together with Jahn as his advisor, drafted the decision without any real analysis of the situation.[6]

The devaluation, which ended up at 30.5 per cent against the dollar, made it too expensive to maintain the same level of import subsidy. In the spring of 1950, after the parliamentary elections, the prices were therefore allowed to rise. A following price jump absorbed the remaining surplus liquidity, and a part of the rationing of goods could be ended. The plan was to resume price stability at a new, higher price level. The international price increase during the Korean boom in 1950–1, and frequent price adjustments that followed the boom, undermined the attempts at stability. Even though the regulatory system was not immediately abolished and many individual prices were regulated through the 1950s, it was clear that maintaining price stability and a stable external economy would require new key instruments.

Even though much was written at the time about *other* ways to regulated aggregate demand, those who grew up during the previous political regime would easily believe

---

[5] Harold James, *International Monetary Cooperation since Bretton Woods* (International Monetary Fund, 1996), 27ff.
[6] Einar Lie et al., *Norges Bank 1916–2016* (Fagbokforlaget, 2016), 326.

that monetary policy, which in one way or another regulates the supply of money and the interest rate level, would again become the primary demand-regulating tool of the authorities. In many countries the perception was that central banks would need to have a leading role in the postwar regime. The governments in most of the member countries chose the central bank to be the representative in the newly formed organization to foster global monetary cooperation via the IMF.[7]

Around 1950, the situation seemed relatively open. Would the ongoing process towards a more open economy bring back the key monetary policy instruments, and especially the use of the interest rate? In March 1950, the Foreign Currency Council, with the central bank governor at its head, made a statement that Norway was again approaching a very serious liquidity crisis. Moving towards a more open economy, with direct regulation coming back, it was natural to raise the interest rate from the level it had been at since the war, when an enormous liquidity surplus dominated the financial situation. 'Of course the interest rate must be raised', stated the central bank governor in a conversation with the finance minister, 'it is the most important instrument we have to restore order here at home'.[8]

Raising the interest rate was not on the political agenda. In the years just after the war, the government had established or strengthened several state-owned banks with specialized purposes: the Norwegian State Housing Bank, the Fishing Industry Bank, the Norwegian Industry Bank, the Norwegian state's Educational Loan Fund for students, and many others. These banks quickly expanded during the years of reconstruction and even further during the postwar era (see Figure 10.1). They granted loans to promote political aims, and the price of the loans from these banks was the primary, concrete reflection of the policy of low interest rates.[9]

With access to spare liquidity, it had been easy for these banks to keep interest rates low in the years immediately following the war. The state banks financed their lending by selling low-yield bonds to the private banks that were happy to receive a return on their own large reserves. Around 1950, when the surplus liquidity in the commercial and savings banks had shrivelled and international interest rates were on the rise, it was evident that this method of financing the state banks was no longer viable. Without additional cheap financing, the state banks would either have to increase interest rates or stop lending money. Neither of these options were politically desirable.

The interest rate policy was made in an intersection of theoretical and political principles which claimed that a regulated low interest rate had positive distributive effects and promoted long-term growth in the economy. Let us also underline what was *not* a motive behind the new monetary policy principle: to keep the running cost of public debt at a low level. In many European countries, the handling of huge

---

[7] The descriptions of the Bretton Woods agreement is mainly based on James, *International Monetary Cooperation since Bretton Woods.* and Eichengreen, *The European Economy since 1945: Coordinated Capitalism and Beyond.*

[8] GJ, 13 March 1950.

[9] Einar Lie, *Ambisjon og tradisjon: Finansdepartementet 1945–65* (Universitetsforlaget, 1995), 222.

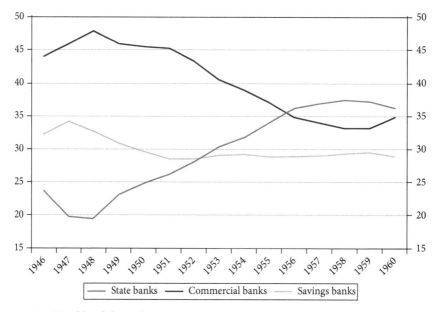

Figure 10.1 Total bank loans by type, 1946–60, percentage shares

government debt was an important motive for maintaining a low level of effective interest rates. The Norwegian postwar public debt was relatively low. The creditors were mainly domestic institutions, and the loans were granted in Norwegian kroner. After repayments on temporary loans in the early postwar years and the price jump following the devaluation in 1949, the real value of the debt was relatively modest.[10] Considerations around the public debt hardly appears in archive sources from the Ministry of Finance and Norges Bank in the late 1940s, 1950s, and 1960s. Where we do find a government's own interest is in providing large amount of cheap money to finance state-owned banks, to fulfil the ambitions following the broader principles of the low interest rates dogma, and the aim to direct credits to selected parts of the economy.

Credit Policy in the Making

The way forward became a complicated process of negotiations with the private credit institutions, to persuade them to restrict their own lending and purchase of state bonds for financing state banks. An integrated part of the system was new legislation in the financial system and, above all, the threat of new legislation if the negotiations did not bring about the desired resolutions.

---

[10] Statistisk Sentralbyrå, *Historisk statistikk, Norges Officielle Statistikk XII 291* (Statistisk Sentralbyrå, 1978), table 242.

In neighbouring Sweden, the central bank itself took initiatives towards regulations, and used a great deal of energy and independence to manage the regulations.[11] As with foreign currency regulation, credit regulation was a natural extension of the Swedish central bank's previous area of expertise. In his book, *Controlling Credit: Central Banking and the Planned Economy in Postwar France, 1948–1973*, Eric Monnet provides a rich analysis of the Bank of France's role in its credit policy, which was more central (and sophisticated) than the lack of orthodox monetary policy would imply. However, in Norway, the Ministry of Finance shaped and managed the new credit policy, after a short period in which the central bank took the initiative.

Just before Christmas 1950, Jahn summoned representatives from the commercial and savings banks unions to find a voluntary way to reduce the private extension of credit and to find a solution to the state bank's financing problem. From January 1951, the Ministry of Finance formalized this group into the Cooperation Committee.[12] In the years that followed, this committee became the most important forum for negotiations between the state and the private banks.

In the early 1950s, it was evident that Norges Bank lacked both the ability and the will to turn the Cooperation Committee into a sufficient regulation tool. Jahn succeeded in getting the committee to reach agreement on the so-called qualitative credit control, where a list of legitimate loan conditions must be met in order to grant a loan. However, the results of these agreements are debatable.[13] The Cooperation Committee's leader also agreed with the commercial and savings banks on a new bill about deposit reserve requirements, which the government sent to parliament who passed it. However, this new regulation toll never become a key instrument in liquidity policy.[14] Norges Bank did not have the power to force the banks any longer, and many indications suggest that Norges Bank did not *wish* to force the banks to completely restrict loans. A total restriction would hinder competition between them and weaken profitability.[15] The Cooperation Committee was not the solution, at least not the only solution, to the credit policy challenges.

At the same time as Norges Bank was perceived as slowing the development of the new regulation regime, the Ministry of Finance was strengthening. Following changes in the cabinet in 1952, a department was established within the ministry to coordinate all aspects of the government's economic policy-making.[16] The department staff were recruited from the group of relatively young candidates from Ragnar Frisch's new study programme in economics at the University of Oslo, who did not have the same reservations about the credit policy regulation as Norges Bank. If the key instruments

---

[11] Englund and Werin, *Från räntereglering till inflationsnorm: det finansiella systemet och Riksbankens politik 1945–1990*.

[12] Marit Graff Hagen, 'Samarbeidsnemnda, en studie i samarbeidet mellom staten og de private kredittinstitusjoner 1951–1965' (Hovedoppgave i historie ved UiO våren, 1977).

[13] The overall effect of these limitations are hard to gauge. According to ibid., the banks characterized this arrangement rather positively. Erling Petersen, *Den norske Creditbank, 1857–1957* (Fabritius boktr., 1957), 144, however, is negative in his evaluation.

[14] Gunhild J. Ecklund, *Creating a New Role for an Old Central Bank: The Bank of Norway 1945–1954* (Handelshøyskolen BI, 2008), 152–3.

[15] Annual speech, 1950, 20.   [16] Lie, *Ambisjon og tradisjon: Finansdepartementet 1945–65*.

were strong and comprehensive enough, they believed it would be possible to reach the interest rate level that the politicians had set.[17] This led them to the relatively extensive development of the legal framework for regulating the banks. The Cooperation Committee saw the preparation of new regulations as mainly a tool of negotiation, a hidden threat, to force banks to grant cheaper loans to the state banks. But there was no doubt also that the ministry *wished* to use its authority to intervene when the committee did not produce satisfying results.[18]

The first law, the *interest rate law*, was passed in 1953, allowing the ministry to regulate the interest rate and commissions.[19] With this law, the ministry had the authority to control, but also to directly intervene and change, the interest and commission rates in the private banks. This was naturally the most controversial part of the law. The law's authority was never invoked, but the very existence of the law contributed to giving the ministry the upper hand in loan negotiations. The government also took control of the bond market. Starting in January 1954, all Norwegian bearer bonds above a certain amount could only be issued with the government's approval. This gave the government control over the issuing and the conditions of all new bond loans, and made sure that the state banks (and other prioritized borrowers) were always given priority. As expected, Norges Bank had a negative reaction to this law.[20]

Key instruments for the monetary and credit area were consequently centralized in the Ministry of Finance. The integration of instruments previously controlled by Norges Bank into central government must be viewed in a wider connection than the implementation of new economic ideas and practices. It was also motivated by advisory principles regarding how the state should be organized, which has changed significantly over time, where Norwegian development, for the most part, has followed international trends. This connection is not highlighted in national and international literature on the central bank. Here independence and association are evaluated and explained mainly by shifting economic doctrines, with the need for timeliness, credibility, and longevity, on one side, and coordination and demand-driven regulation on the other.

The postwar era provided a more active and methodical shaping of the entire central administration, which made it more suitable to carry out policies that actively shape society.[21] The first initiatives came immediately following the war, and several larger ones have since followed. A unifying principle was that the ministries should be in a better position to act as politically formed secretariats for the government. This entailed bringing vital functions connected to planning and policy-making into the ministries, and moving routine duties and decision making to semi-independent bodies reporting to the ministries. Large services, like the Norwegian Customs Service

---

[17] Cf. in particular Ot. prp. 55 1953, Storting's proceedings.

[18] Lie, *Ambisjon og tradisjon: Finansdepartementet 1945–65.*

[19] Ot. prp. 55 1953, Storting's proceedings.

[20] Lie, *Ambisjon og tradisjon: Finansdepartementet 1945–65*, 232.

[21] Tore Grønlie, *Ekspansjonsbyråkratiets tid 1945–1980*, vol. B. 1 (Bergen: Fagbokforl., 2009); Tore Grønlie, 'Norges Bank—og andre 'uavhengige' statsinstitusjoner', *Historisk Tidsskrift* 96, no. 03 (2017); Lie, *Ambisjon og tradisjon: Finansdepartementet 1945–65*, 256–72.

and the Norwegian Tax Administration, which also were under the Ministry of Finance, became independent entities – partially to avoid that a large amount of individual decisions were taken by the ministry itself. This added to the workload of the political leadership, especially with responsibility for the decisions. Key instruments that were deemed politically important, such as fixing tax and customs rates, stayed within the ministry. This was also the case for Norges Bank. The central bank took a series of individual decisions connected to financing and financial institutions, printing of bank notes, and the extensive regulation of foreign currency transactions. The most important political decisions—and the interest rate was highly political—were to be taken by the ministry.

Norges Bank was not affected by the general initiatives, since the bank was regulated by separate legislation. On the outside the situation looked unchanged, but in reality the political control of the bank was now different. The single, main reason for the bank's subordination was the new economic-political principles that emerged from the interwar period. Still, it is worth noting that the principle driving the organization of the ministry and the central bank was in line with the fixed principles for organizing the state, which were discussed in the government and then in the parliament in connection with a series of large reorganizations.

Up until the war, a comparison between Norges Bank and the ordinary state apparatus seems less relevant. The central bank was a company with a large number of private owners, with operations seen as only partly the *state's* activities, as exercising stat authority. Yet with the state's takeover of the stocks and the strong emphasis on the integration of monetary policy with related parts of policy-making, Norges Bank got closer in similarity to semi-autonomous directorates that were politically driven, and took operational decisions in its own name.

Perceptions, Cultures, and Organization

Erik Brofoss's arrival as governor of Norges Bank in the spring of 1954 brought a difference in the understanding that Rygg, and to some degree Jahn, had regarding the role and duties of the central bank.[22] 'I have certainly moved away from the thought that the central bank can be a neutral, objective institution', he summarized in an internal memo in 1966.[23] In Brofoss' opinion, Norges Bank could not set its own goals, for example on a stable krone exchange rate or price stability, that were separate from the goals the politicians set for the entire economic policy.

Several cases showed how the leadership in the central bank was subject to politics, and this principle of subordination was also evident in a number of major and minor

[22] The main sources for Brofoss's views on the central bank's role is 'Sentralbankens statsrettslige og forvaltningsrettslige stilling', presentation held for 'Oslo krets av Den norske sakførerforening', 27 October 1959, and Brofoss's speech at Norges Bank's 150-year jubilee in 1966 (Norges Bank 150 år, appendix 1 Beretning 1966, 137).

[23] 'Skjævelands Post festum-betraktninger', notat EB/LF 4 July 1966, file NB Korr. saker 1966 ang nye lover, box, 164 serie Di, EB.

decisions. For example, in 1956, at Brofoss's initiative, the discretionary decision-making authority regulating the bond market was transferred from Norges Bank to the Ministry of Finance.[24] With a new central bank act, Brofoss was little by little going to recommend that the government be given the right to override the Executive Board by issuing formal instructions.[25]

Another reason supporting Brofoss's particular understanding of the central bank was that, just as when he was finance minister and trade minister, he thought that the discount policy had a restrictive effect when it came to influencing total demand on the economy. In this area, financial policy was the stronger instrument. It also didn't make much economic sense that Norges Bank, with the help of previous instruments, should meet any independent targets. In addition, Brofoss was deeply, personally convinced of the need and the desire for a stable, low interest rate. This gave little space for a conventional monetary policy.

In these areas, Norway clearly differed from Sweden and Denmark. The two neighbouring countries carried out the principle of a low interest rate policy, but with central banks that wished to mark a greater independence than in Norway (it didn't take much). This is particularly evident in Sweden, where the Riksbank, after having raised the interest rate in 1955, raised it again in 1957 without informing the government in advance.[26] This would have been unthinkable in Norway, both in Brofoss' time, and under his predecessor Jahn.

Brofoss gave speeches in Stockholm and Copenhagen when the Riksbank and the Danish Nationalbank celebrated 300 years and 150 years respectively. His lyrical speeches warned his neighbours of their freer roll. In Sweden, he highlighted the age of the Riksbank, as well as the mark of independence, and thought the Swedish national anthem, 'Thou Ancient, Thou Free', was a fitting self-portrait for the institution. For some this could be associated with a new-found independence, but for others, he warned, it was easy to 'see this disastrous interwar era that filled some of the darkest pages in the central banks' history'.[27] In Copenhagen, Brofoss spoke during the dinner party. Here he indirectly touched on the relationship with neighbouring Germany. He had little tolerance for this country to the south and was especially critical of the independent policy of the German central bank (Bundesbank).

> During talks about economic policy at the Nordic central banks' annual meeting, it is evident that parts of Denmark are connected to the Continent. Our Danish friends represent the pure doctrines and belief that our Lord, as an end to the creation story, put the interest rate into the world to keep the economic development in eternal

---

[24] 'Godkjenning av partialobligasjonslån i medhold av rentelovens § 3', letter to the Ministry of Finance from Norges Bank, 26 April 1955, mappe 2 0-1-173, D 0732 NB/DIR2; see also Lie, *Ambisjon og tradisjon: Finansdepartementet 1945–65*, 237.

[25] EB/LF 12 March 1969. Memo to Skjæveland, box 164, EB.

[26] Englund and Werin, *Från räntereglering till inflationsnorm: det finansiella systemet och Riksbankens politik 1945–1990*.

[27] After Ragnar Trøite, *Norges Banks uavhengighet i etterkrigstida: en analyse av sentralbankens uavhengighet fra 1945 til 1970 i et komparativt perspektiv* (R. Trøite, 2010)., 82.

balance. After creation, came the fall, and with that came the finance ministers into the world. Without having climbed very high in the tree of the wisdom of good and evil, they are ready to take the lion's share of the apple harvest. The finance ministers are not included in mercy. Whenever several central bank governors are gathered together, they are served the heads of finance ministers on a platter. As a maladjusted youngster, I have not always been able to enjoy this meal.[28]

Not only during party speeches, but also concretely in practice, in politics and in internal administrative business, Brofoss showed a break from the others.[29] Change was inevitable when 45-year-old Brofoss took over for 71-year-old Gunnar Jahn. With a rare capacity for work, he threw himself immediately into the job of changing his new institution. When Brofoss left the bank in 1970, it had seen quite a transformation.

Norges Bank's own banking services—the former processing, cashier, and deposit functions had previously been carried out in separate departments—were assembled in one processing and accounting department. A new banking and loan department was created for business with other banks. The foreign currency department was strengthened with its own foreign currency policy office. Reporting duties, which had formerly been divided seemingly ad hoc between the general secretariat and the statistics department, were placed in a new economic-statistics department with three offices.[30]

Brofoss wished to raise the bank's profile as economic advisor to the government, and the advisory function was in close connection with competency. With strong personal engagement, he immediately began recruiting young economists, educated under Frisch's 'watchful eye' at the University of Oslo. The number of economists grew rapidly.[31] In 1970, there were more university-educated economists in Norges Bank than in the Ministry of Finance.[32] Many of the Brofoss recruits were promoted to leadership positions during the 1970s and 1980s.

Without a doubt, the most important recruit was Knut Getz Wold, to the position of deputy governor. Brofoss and Getz Wold knew each other from wartime London, when the young Getz Wold, working in the Ministry of Finance, constantly appeared as a critical observer to and tried to reverse the relatively conservative leadership of Norges Bank in London. Around the end of the 1950s, Getz Wold had received the reputation as one of the country's leading economists in his field. After many years as a board member of the European Payments Union, he was the highest authority in

---

[28] Ibid., 83.

[29] Erik Brofoss, *Vår Bank* 3/1970, 71; Per Bang and Jon Petter Holter, *Norges bank 175 år: mennesker og begivenheter* (Norges Bank, 1991), 90.

[30] A presentation of the main organizational changes in Norges Bank's history is presented in Egil Borlaug and Turid Wammer, 'Noregs Bank: Grunntrekk i administrasjon, oppgåver og historie' (2009).

[31] Petter Jakob Bjerve, *Økonomisk planlegging og politikk* (Norske samlaget, 1989).

[32] In 1970 Norges Bank employed twenty-three economists whereas the Ministry of Finance employed twenty-two, Trond Bergh, 'Norway: The Powerful Servants', *History of Political Economy* 13, no. 3 (1981) (author's count).

Norway on international monetary cooperation.[33] Though relatively similar in political opinions, Brofoss and Getz Wold were of different personalities: Brofoss with a direct, at times authoritarian way of handling his organization and surroundings; Getz Wold with a friendlier and more sociable habitus.

Brofoss's arrival and the reforms he led brought about changes in the organizational culture. 'Norges Bank is a hierarchical institution', Wilhelm Thagaard, the high-profile director of the Norwegian Price Directorate, once pointed out to Getz Wold, and meant a conservative, bourgeois hierarchy.[34] Brofoss, himself the son of a farmer from Kongsberg, represented a break from this class system. For example, Brofoss did not like being referred to as 'Chief Director', but preferred, like most members of the Labour Party, an informal title.[35] The bank's image became more similar to other public institutions than to private banks. The 'old' ideal of the civil service was that they should set *examples* for companies and persons in the private sector. Civil servants should, according to a British political science definition, stand like the Jesuit body of a zealous ascetic.[36] A similar ideal was impressed upon Norges Bank's employees in the beginning of the 1950s, in the bank's handbook. Brofoss, who had frugal habits, reinforced these ideals. 'The governor director of Norges Bank sits in a cloister-like environment', reported the Australian central bank after a visit.[37] In this appearance, the break with the future might not have been very sharp; several newspapers commented that Brofoss, with his sober idealism and his high ascetic character, despite it all, was a reminder of his predecessor Rygg.[38]

Many of the newly recruited economists were highly educated young men, often from the districts, who usually, contrary to many senior-level people already in the bank, did not have a background in law, business, or finance. They were given significant responsibility. Neither Brofoss nor the economists showed much respect for the established system or the hierarchy in the bank. The young economists became known as 'the sweater gang'.[39]

The changes created excitement. Sven Viig became deputy governor in 1953 and left the bank in 1958 for a director position in a private, commercial bank. Gabriel Kielland, from the old regime, became the director in the economic-statistics department, but hinted many times that he felt excluded from the camaraderie between Brofoss and the young economists.[40]

---

[33] Getz Wold declined a proposal to become minister of finance in 1963. Kristian Asdahl, 'Kjære Knut Getz Wold', *Penger og kreditt* 15, supplementary issue (1995). He was also asked to enter the cabinet in the same position in 1971 but declined again. KGWM, ch. 24.

[34] KGWM, ch. 11, 5.   [35] Bang and Holter, *Norges Bank 175 år: Mennesker og begivenheter*, 90.

[36] After Christopher Hood, 'The "New Public Management" in the 1980s: Variations on a Theme', *Accounting, Organizations and Society* 20, nos. 2–3 (1995).

[37] Bang and Holter, *Norges Bank 175 år: Mennesker og begivenheter*, 90.

[38] 'Brofoss den gode', *VG* 31 May 1954.

[39] J.P. Holter in interview with B. Klunde og C. Venneslan 6.6.2009; Tilbake til statistikkens verden! Orientering 5 1995, 8.

[40] Eivind Thomassens interviews with Trygve Spildrejorde og Johan Frøland. Kf. also e.g. Økonomisk-statistisk avdeling, notat Stat/BjH/RuL 19 December 1962, mappe 'PM 2050–2139' box F 0012, STAT.

Credit Policy in the Negotiation System

Late in the 1950s, Norges Bank seemed to have considerable influence on monetary policy, partly because of Brofoss's personal influence, and partly due to the concrete economic situation. Brofoss became increasingly involved in the internal party processes, council, and committees, the party's agendas, and much more. Brofoss sat on the Labour Party's Central Board from 1961 to 1964. During this period, it was rumoured that he may be party leader and Prime Minister Gerhardsen's successor.[41] It is not certain this really lifted Norges Bank's position, but it advanced the issues the central bank governor himself deemed important.

In February 1955, the discount rate was increased from 2.5 to 3.5 per cent, as part of the so-called February measures. The government was credited for taking this initiative. Behind the scenes, as stated in a letter and meetings with central members of government, it was clear that Brofoss was a main champion for these measures.[42] In other respects, now as before, Norges Bank took the formal decision. At the same time, the deposit reserve requirements were used for the first time.[43] An Open Market Operations Committee was formed for the Ministry of Finance and Norges Bank to coordinate future open market operations, after advice from Norges Bank. According to many newspapers, it looked as though monetary policy in Norway had been given a delayed rebirth.[44]

However, the background for Norges Bank's council at the beginning of 1955 was not a wish for conventional monetary policy. In the autumn of 1954, Norway was in an acute foreign currency crisis and all investments had to stop. Changing the interest rate also played a tactical role for the government. In part towards the countries that extended credit to Norway, and supported and expected Norway to carry its share of the burden to get the European Payment Union in balance, and in part towards the Norwegian commercial banks that should be pressured to purchase state bonds. These so-called February measures did not bring about large use of the key conventional monetary policy instruments in Norway. For the government, increasing the interest rate was extremely unpopular, and among the economists the results raised doubts.[45] The effects of the imposed reserve requirements were even more unclear. The reserve requirements remained untouched and any new discount rate increase did not come into effect before 1969. Additionally, the open market operations were, after a marginal attempt, put away, and the Open Market Operations Committee was dissolved.[46]

---

[41] This rumour is discussed in Roy Jacobsen, *Trygve Bratteli: en fortelling* (Cappelen, 1995).

[42] The February measures are described in detail in Lie, *Ambisjon og tradisjon: Finansdepartementet 1945–65.* 249–52 and Trøite, *Norges Banks uavhengighet i etterkrigstida: en analyse av sentralbankens uavhengighet fra 1945 til 1970 i et komparativt perspektiv*, 41–4.

[43] Ten per cent of the deposits for banks with a total assets over 100 million NOK, 5 per cent for banks with assets from 10 to 100 million NOK. Norges Bank's annual report 1954, 35.

[44] Trøite, *Norges Banks uavhengighet i etterkrigstida: en analyse av sentralbankens uavhengighet fra 1945 til 1970 i et komparativt perspektiv*, 44.

[45] Trond Bergh, *Storhetstid (1945–1965)*, vol. 5 (Tiden, 1987) and Lie, *Ambisjon og tradisjon: Finansdepartementet 1945–65.*

[46] File 'Markedsoperasjoner 1954–63', D 0779, NB/DIR2.

Norges Bank's lasting contribution under the leadership of Brofoss was the attempt to restrict private loans with the help of voluntary agreements between the authorities and the private credit institutions, and with a more explicit framework than there had been with the Cooperation Committee. The direct effect came in the summer of 1955, when the Ministry of Finance, unsatisfied with the effect of the February measures, proposed a new, more strict reserve requirement law.[47] The proposal was not well received by the unions of the commercial and savings banks. Like Jahn before him, Brofoss, with the consent of the prime minister, went into negotiations in the Cooperation Committee.[48] The outcome was the first credit agreement in December. The banks and the authorities agreed on the conditions for a large state loan. At the same time, the bank unions, on behalf of the members, committed to Brofoss's initiative, to trying to keep the total amount of loans in 1956 and 1957 at the same level as in 1955. In return, the Ministry of Finance's bill was put on ice.

The loan ceiling was a way to stop private creditors without directly threatening the target of a low, politically set interest rate level. The way it was negotiated, as a semi-corporatist agreement with the banks unions, was completely in line with the ideas of the Labour government.[49] Moreover, the agreement about a loan ceiling was the same solution chosen by the social democrat's regime in Sweden.[50]

The agreement 1955 was seen as a temporary measure, but the credit agreements decided by the Cooperation Committee were lasting.[51] The first agreement covered the years 1956 and 1957. A new agreement was entered into in 1957, but was cancelled in August of 1958 due to a short-term international economic downturn. In 1959 and 1960 came agreements without loan ceilings, but with attempts to influence liquidity. In 1960, a new framework was agreed on, which obliged the parties to enter annual agreements each year between 1961 and 1964.

The Active Subordination

The areas where Norges Bank assisted the government expanded between the years 1954 and 1970. Brofoss had always tried to insert his initiatives into a long-term strategy for how Norway should recreate itself into a modern industrial nation.[52] Regional development politics had an important, defined role in Norwegian economic planning and policy. The heavily regionalized Norway had little by little got a centre. However, the wealth created by industry was unevenly divided, with higher incomes

---

[47] Hagen, 'Samarbeidsnemnda, en studie i samarbeidet mellom staten og de private kredittinstitusjoner 1951–1965', 88; Lie, *Ambisjon og tradisjon: Finansdepartementet 1945–65*, 274ff.

[48] Hagen, 'Samarbeidsnemnda, en studie i samarbeidet mellom staten og de private kredittinstitusjoner 1951–1965', 88.

[49] Finn Olstad, *Einar Gerhardsen: en politisk biografi* (Universitetsforlaget, 1999).

[50] Lars Jonung, 'Riksbankens politik 1945–1990', in *Från räntereglering till inflationsnorm: det finansiella systemet och Riksbankens politik 1945–1990*, ed. Peter Englund and Lars Werin (SNS Förlag, 1993).

[51] Hagen, 'Samarbeidsnemnda, en studie i samarbeidet mellom staten og de private kredittinstitusjoner 1951–1965'.

[52] See e.g. Rune Slagstad, *De nasjonale strateger* (Pax, 1998), 281ff.

in south-eastern parts of Norway, and around cities and larger centres. Northern Norway became a focus area from 1950, partly because the Germans systematically burned the most northern part of this region when they moved southward in the autumn of 1944 and partly because of a slower pace of recovery and growth. The Norwegian regional development politics became part of a national obligation; the entire country should be able to take advantage of modernization and wealth. A deep-rooted principle of equality was also evident. Neighbouring Sweden, also with large, open areas, a spread-out population, and relatively low income, chose a centralization strategy. The incomes of the rural population would increase with centralization and relocation to cities. The policy was blessed by the worker's movement and a driving social democracy. Their Norwegian counterpart did not accept the income inequality that the system predicted during the long transition period. Norway took many small steps to establish a policy that created and maintained activity in small towns, which could give the foundation for an acceptable income level on an individual basis.[53]

Several initiatives in regional development policies were weaved into drafts and decisions when Brofoss was present, in the leadership, in the Foreign Currency Council and in the Cooperation Committee in the 1950s and 1960s. At the same time, stricter production requirements were enforced with the continuation of liberalization, and around 1960 Norway's relationship with the various western European free trade agreements was on the agenda. In 1961, the Regional Development Fund was established, based on a previous fund to develop northern Norway. The fund's main responsibility was to contribute to financing projects that corresponded to the intentions of the government's regional development plans. Erik Brofoss was the chairman, and in 1964 the fund entered a formal cooperation agreement with Norges Bank.[54]

With the cooperation agreement, employees at Norges Bank's district branches carried out a commercial and accounting analysis of the companies that applied for or had received aid.[55] Another duty for the fund was to take the initiative for new regional development policy measures, like a regional policy think tank. When Brofoss desired that the fund take the initiative to construct new cities in eastern Norway, like the industrial estates and new towns in Great Britain, the meeting was held in his office at Bankplassen and the notes were taken by bank staff.[56] More striking is how Brofoss used his position as central bank governor to create the role for himself as, quoting one historian, 'the obligatory point of passage' in cases of regional development politics.[57] As Executive Board chairman in Norges Bank, Brofoss was the chairman for the body that recommended to the Ministry of Finance which companies should be able to take out a bond loan in the Norwegian market. As leader of

[53] Einar Lie, *Norsk økonomisk politikk etter 1905* (Universitetsforl., 2012),102ff.

[54] Norges Bank's annual report 1964.

[55] Knut Knutsen, 'Samarbeidet mellom Distriktenes utbyggingsfond og Norges Bank', *Penger og kreditt* 9, no. 3 (1981).

[56] Conversation with Viking Mestad and Knut Knutsen, cf. Jan F. Qvigstad, 'On institutions', speech at the Norwegian Academy of Science and Letters 12 November 2013, available from https://www.norges-bank.no/en/news-events/news-publications/Speeches/2013/12-November-2013-Speech-Jan-F-Qvigstad/.

[57] Øyvind Thomassen, 'Herlege tider: Norsk fysisk planlegging ca. 1930–1965' (NTNU, 1997).

the Foreign Currency Council, he exercised influence on access to international capital. As chairman of the Cooperation Committee, he used the credit agreement to gain understanding from the private banks about prioritizing loans for projects that contributed to the development policy. The Development Fund guaranteed these loans.[58] At times, these positions were used to influence controversial issues in accordance with individual conviction and across various objections.

For many of the district branches, these commitments were important. They were established in part throughout the nineteenth century, at a time when Norges Bank was the country's only bank, and have been maintained despite communications challenges. In 1964, at the request of Norges Bank, the Directorate of Rationalisation introduced a proposal to close down eight of Norges Bank's twenty branches around the country. Norges Bank reasoned that this case had implications on regional politics, and sent it to parliament, where it was decided to give these branches current regional policy duties.[59] Some branches should service other public institutions, for example as secretariat for Folketrygdfondet (National Pension Fund). The Bodø branch became the branch office for the Fishing Industry Bank. For other branches, the most important duty was monitoring and accounting analysis of the companies, often very small, that received aid from the Regional Development Fund. As late as 1989, Norges Bank had carried out 7,354 accounting analyses for the Development Fund.[60] This is how the bank branch network was maintained and how Norges Bank was further integrated into the government's work. From the concept of 'central bank independence', which was used in Norway during this period, this is an expressive supplement to the integration of monetary policy with general economic policy measures in the Ministry of Finance. The administrative support and coordinating tasks made Norges Bank a concrete and direct part of the government's apparatus.

The clearest example of how Norges Bank was a tool for the government was a specific lending scheme, called the 'Hambro Scheme' or the 'Norway Scheme'. The background for this scheme was that the mechanical engineering industry, from the beginning of the 1960s, had begun to struggle with tough competition from foreign shipyards. From 1965 until 1972, Norges Bank placed around 700 million kroner, or 14 per cent of its total foreign exchange reserve (mostly in Hambros Bank in London, but also in two American banks), at very low interest rates.[61] This was an instrument for giving a hidden interest subsidy on long-term loans from the same banks to Norwegian (and eventually to foreign) shipowners who wished to build ships in Norwegian shipyards. The subsidy element eventually became quite significant due to the high British interest rates at the end of the 1960s. Norges Bank estimated in 1970 that Norges Bank had lost at least 100 million kroner in interest payments.[62]

---

[58] Erik Brofoss, *Vekst- og strukturproblemer i norsk økonomi: Forelesninger ved Universitetet i Oslo høstsemestret 1963: 4: Fjerde del*, vol. 4 (1964), 327.

[59] Authority resided at the Supervisory Board.

[60] Harald Bøhn, 'Norges Banks distriktsavdelinger 1983–2001', in *Staff Memo* (Norges Bank, 2012), 15.

[61] Letter to Klassekampen 13 April 1984, Val/Jur HFS/St/AG, file 'Hambro-ordningen' box 463.431 NB.

[62] Letter to Cappelen 13 February 1970. See correspondence between Brofoss and Cappelen in file 'Dokumenter mottatt av direktør Knut Getz Wold under møte 10.1986', file 5–6, box 0014, STGR.

The scheme raised the question about how Norges Bank and the government had the foreign exchange reserve at their disposal at all. Brofoss pointed out in a letter exchange with the head of the supervisory board that the law clearly stated that Norges Bank's Executive Board had the foreign currency reserve at its disposal. There were no legal guidelines for this kind of management.[63] Brofoss also claimed that it must be reasonable to bring the government in. 'As I am sure you realise, I might go farther than other central bank governors in asserting that we are a branch of state administration that the government must have a considerable amount of influence over.'[64] The problem was that there was no doubt that the reserve was meant to be managed as a means to provide good liquidity and high returns, and not for political goals.[65] There was also every reason to think that the case should have been reported to and handled by parliament. According to the constitution, parliament was entitled to have supervision over the nation's monetary system, and over Norges Bank. In addition, subsidies should formally by granted by parliamentary decisions, as a part of the budgetary process or separate propositions prepared by the government.

The scheme first went public in 1984, and it created considerable unrest. The timing couldn't have been worse and Norges Bank's reputation was at an all-time low. When the scheme was revealed, Norges Bank was in the middle of an ongoing liberalization of the credit markets.

Interest Rate War and Downfall of the Negotiation System

The credit ceiling, based on negotiations and voluntary agreements with the life insurance companies and the savings and commercial banks unions in the Cooperation Committee, was never an effective tool for fine-tuning private lending. The bank unions didn't have any means to force members to follow these voluntary agreements. There was also disagreement about how the number of loans and the lending ceiling should really be measured. This is the background for why the Ministry of Finance in the early 1960s opted for developing a broader and more fine-meshed law in the regulation of the credit market.[66]

In Brofoss's and Norge's Banks view, a more direct regulation scheme, managed by the Ministry of Finance, should not replace real negotiations between the authorities and the private credit institutions, as eventually became the case. Norges Bank believed that the use of instruments and regulation in a future law should be decided as part of negotiations. The Cooperation Committee had, after all, succeeded in developing some instruments in the credit policy. Norges Bank had also developed a new short-term lending scheme in the central bank, in cooperation with the banks.

---

[63] Letter to Klassekampen 13 April 1984, Val/Jur HFS/St/AG, mappe 'Hambro-ordningen' box 463.431 NB.
[64] Brofoss to Cappelen 13 February 1970, file 5–6, box 0014, STGR.
[65] Cappelen to Brofoss 14.3.1970, file 5–6, box 0014, STGR.
[66] G. Hagen, 'Samarbeidsnemnda, en studie i samarbeidet mellom staten og de private kredittinstitusjoner 1951–1965'.

The qualitative guidelines were expanded. Agreements were made about interest rate adjustments in 1961 and standardizing central interest rates in 1963.[67]

Around 1960, government decided that a large, public committee, under the leadership of Deputy Governor Getz Wold, should to go through the key instrument apparatus in the credit policy. The general idea in both Norges Bank and the Ministry of Finance was to provide a basis for new legislation but still try to keep basic parts of the system of cooperation intact. However, the committees report in December 1963 was badly received by the banks. In the report, the main political goal about high growth and full employment was taken for granted. The desirability of a low long-term interest rate was repeated.[68] To increase the authorities' ability to allocated credit to prioritized areas and regulate the total supply of credits through the financial institutions, two new tools were suggested: supplementary reserve requirements and obligatory holding of state bonds. Supplementary reserve requirements forced banks to set a certain percentage share of increased lending into an interest-free account. If the reserve requirement levels were high enough, new loans would become extremely expensive for the banks and therefore not granted. Through the obligation holding of state (or state-guaranteed) bonds, the authorities could force the banks to place a certain sum in bonds issued to finance state banks. An obligated placement here—'forced purchase' of state bonds, as this was referred to—would both block the lending capability and ensure financing for state banks at interest rates set by the Ministry of Finance. The proposal was disputed and very unpopular with the banks, but clearly an effective way to move capital out of the private and into the state credit institutions.

The domestic fiscal policy has been kept in the background so far, but it is closely connected with the credit policy and financing of state banks and investments. The fiscal policy had for a long time carried a part of the burden of the expansionary credit policy, with low interest rates and a very high investment level, compared with most Organisation for Economic Co-operation and Development (OECD) countries.[69] The Norwegian state has an equally long history with heavy state financing and high savings levels; the period during and after the First World War, and partially during the 1970s expansionary policy, are exceptions. Throughout the nineteenth century, large infrastructure projects were carried out thanks to foreign loans, which were repaid through the operating surplus in the state's activities. After the war, the investment rate was high in the private sector, partially due to a favourable tax regime for the business sector, which was a similar trend in other Nordic countries, and partly by state banks granting loans at regulated low interest rates.

Throughout the 1950s and into the 1960s, part of the state bank financing came directly from the national budget, through large operating surpluses. (The corporate taxes were low, but Norwegian individual taxes were high in international comparisons.) After the Labour Party lost its clear majority in 1961, public expenses gradually

---

[67] Ibid., 152, 160–1.

[68] Innstilling fra den penge- og kredittpolitiske komité (Finansdepartementet 1964), 156.

[69] Øyvind Eitrheim, Jan Tore Klovland, and Lars Fredrik Øksendal, *A Monetary History of Norway, 1816–2016* (Cambridge University Press, 2016), 458ff.

increased. The operating surplus became smaller. The growth in expenditure also contributed to the underlying pressure on interest rates. However, the most important and concrete result was that it now became more crucial to find a credit policy measure for financing the growth of the state banks, as the available operating surplus was tapped down. This pushed obligation holdings of state and state-guaranteed bonds to the forefront.

In 1965, the four centre/conservative opposition parties won the parliamentary election. These parties had previously debated in parliament for a lower growth of public expenditures, which would have strengthened the financing opportunities for the state banks. A higher interest rate would have been the obvious solution; the entire regulation regime had made efforts to keep the interest rate low, especially from the state banks. The interest rate policy was, however, never taken up for broader discussion by the government. The minister of finance, economist Ole Myrvoll from the Liberal Party, simply declared early on that there would be no discussion about changes to the interest rate policy.[70] As for the credit law, passed right before the change of government, the four coalition parties had voted against the most restrictive paragraphs, like supplementary reserve requirements (that should provide for effective quantity regulation) and investment obligation, before they took office.

The new government's resistance to these requirements made the banks willing to continue negotiations. The hope was that these decisions would not be enforced, as direct measures or as hidden threats, in the negotiations. After several negotiation meetings during the autumn of 1966, Brofoss also succeeded in entering into a new credit agreement with the commercial banks, which committed to not exceed their lending beyond a total fixed amount in 1967. The government committed to not enforcing supplementary reserve requirements and investment obligations.[71] The interest rate conditions on state loans were also adjusted. This was a partial victory for the private banks, and at first glance, also a triumph for Brofoss.

The credit agreement never worked effectively. During the spring of 1967, the number of loans was quickly increasing. In addition, the financial policy weakened considerably. At the end of the 1960s there was no operational surplus available for financing state banks. In this situation, financing the state banks became an acute challenge. In September 1969, the Ministry of Finance presented a powerful package of measures, and the obligation to hold state bonds came into use.[72] The discount rate was also raised by 1 per cent, but this was explained as a one-time phenomenon from the Ministry of Finance's side.[73]

Mistrust and disappointment marked the years 1966–9, and this period would forever ruin what Brofoss called 'the atmosphere of the Cooperation Committee'.[74] The time when the credit policy meant the voluntary purchase of bonds and the voluntary lending restrictions from the private bank's side were the most important

---

[70] Einar Lie and Christian Venneslan, *Over evne: Finansdepartementet 1965–1992* (Pax forlag, 2010), 85.
[71] See Ecklund, *Creating a New Role for an Old Central Bank: The Bank of Norway 1945–1954*, 40.
[72] Ibid., 43–4.   [73] Ibid., 44–5.
[74] 'Åpen post', NRK November 1969. Available from NRK's digital archive.

key instruments, and how these would be used was the outcome of real negotiations with the authorities in Norges Bank, was permanently over.

The credit law, especially after it came into full effect in 1969, contributed to formalizing and institutionalizing credit regulations in an entirely different way than the negotiation and agreement system had done. This, without a doubt, weakened Norges Bank's role in the preparation of monetary policy arrangements. The importance of the governor's personal involvement in Norges Bank changed too. From dependency on individuals with significant authority and close personal connections to central persons in both the banks and the ministry, the credit policy now assumed the overview of vastly complex statistics—over lending, management of capital, liquidity, and securities in the private credit institutions.

The Government's Bank: A Summary

This chapter has highlighted that Norges Bank became the government's bank, mainly because Norges Bank's activities became closely integrated with the government's economic policy. The guidelines for the credit, interest, and foreign currency policies were made by the Ministry of Finance. A number of policy instruments were still under Norges Bank—as we find in a number of other state directorates—but clearly under the government's control. In addition, an administrative integration was being carried out, as Norges Bank took over a number of administrative tasks that were not really connected to central bank duties. These activities came to occupy Norges Bank's large and costly department network, which had the capacity to carry them out.

Being the government's bank meant that Norges Bank was no longer primarily the parliament's bank. Parliament became a rather unimportant arena for Norges Bank. A clear example was that the parliament was not informed of the subsidy scheme established with Hambros Bank, the Norway Scheme. This was a quiet but significant break with past practice. The bank was created by parliament, which controlled the bank and decided on a long series of control questions. Also, during the interwar period, Norges Bank used its close connection to parliament to gain support and legitimacy when big decisions needed to be taken. Throughout the long period when the Labour Party was the majority government, parliament was pushed into the background when it came to major policy issues.

During the entire period, Norges Bank operated without any clear legal framework. The 1892 law was still formally valid, though no longer applied in practice. There was a striking lack of interest in establishing a formal framework for the bank's duties, and it was not until 1985 when a new central bank act was adopted. Prior to that, the bank's operations were characterized by political objectives and demands, and a pragmatic and at times active adaptation of them.

11

The Foreign Currency Exchange Rate
Policy Up Until 1986

Norges Bank came to play a central, technical role in maintaining and defending a stable krone exchange rate during the years 1946–86. This role was reflected in how the bank advised on the basis of a loyal position to the fixed krone exchange rate regime and to binding international exchange rate cooperation.

Throughout the 1970s, both exchange rate stability and exchange rate cooperation came under heavy pressure. This was partly due to the large changes in the value between different currencies, changes that led to the collapse of the Bretton Woods system in 1971–3, and to exchange rate instability in the years that followed. This pressure also came partly from a Norwegian economic policy that gradually drifted further and further away from the economic policy of the countries against which the Norwegian authorities attempted to maintain a stable exchange rate. In balancing consideration of exchange rate stability with other economic and political goals, the political authorities apparently chose to give less priority to exchange rate stability during the 1970s and 1980s. In 1978, Norway backed out of the European fixed exchange rate cooperation, and during 1976–86, the krone was devalued ten times.[1] Even though Norges Bank officially came to contribute to both recommending and carrying out this policy, the policy defied the strong ideals and viewpoints of the organization. The exchange rate policy, and the problems it led to in relation to the central bank, caused the government, in the first half of the 1980s, to push Norges Bank completely aside when it came to the shaping of Norwegian exchange rate policy.

Despite the fact that Norges Bank was, to a large extent, pushed aside when it came to the exchange rate policy, much of the policy was still shaped inside the walls of the institution. Hermod Skånland, the new deputy governor and vice chairman of the board from 1971 onwards, played a key role in developing changes in the krone exchange rate regime and exchange rate adjustments, seeking solutions to the economic and political challenges of the time. Skånland's initiatives on exchange rate policy, and the changes which followed, triggered a deep conflict with other groups in the bank, not least with Skånland's superior, Governor Knut Getz Wold. This conflict lasted until Skånland took over as the central bank governor in 1985. This divide split

---

[1] Jan Fredrik Qvigstad and Arent Skjæveland, 'Valutakursregimer', in *Stabilitet og langsiktighet– festskrift til Hermod Skånland*, ed. Kjell Storvik, Jan Fredrik Qvigstad, and Sigbjørn Atle Berg (Aschehoug Forlag, 1994).

Norges Bank 1816–2016. Einar Lie, Oxford University Press (2020). © Norges Bank.
DOI: 10.1093/oso/9780198860013.001.0001

the organization in two and further contributed to undermine the bank's role as advisor on exchange rate policy.

The Norwegian authorities came through the entire postwar era to operate with an official goal of fixed exchange rates. Compared to other, smaller currencies, the Norwegian krone was among the more stable currencies during the period 1971 to 1986.[2] It is not evident how a different exchange rate policy would have prevented many of the problems that were about to build up in the Norwegian economy, certainly not after 1979 when Norway enjoyed high revenues from oil exports. In hindsight, looking back on the years following the drop in oil prices and major changes in economic policy in 1986, the frequent devaluations that occurred in the decade between 1976 and 1986 stand out as a symbol, and in some way a part of the explanation for what had gone so terribly wrong.

This chapter will look specifically at Norges Bank in relation to the foreign exchange policy from 1973 to 1986. Norges Bank's role in relation to the domestic monetary and credit policy of the same period will be explored in the next chapter. This is a separation of themes that contemporary actors would have recognized. Control of the capital flows contributed to isolating the Norwegian money market from the international market, and made 'foreign exchange policy', the exchange rate question, and the foreign exchange regulations their own specialized area, and to some degree detached from the domestic interest rate and credit policy. This separation of areas that were increasingly interconnected, and which was also reflected in the institutional organization, is one of the reasons that the exchange rate policy became one of the most controversial questions of the time.

The Defender of the Krone Exchange Rate

From 1945 to 1971, when international exchange rate relationships to a reasonably extent seem to have been regulated in line with the Bretton Woods agreement, Norges Bank, on behalf of the Norwegian authorities, played a central role in maintaining an orderly foreign exchange market, as prescribed by the agreement. It did this most directly through the technical work of buying and selling foreign currency to the Norwegian foreign exchange banks at fixed exchange rates, and most pervasively in the bank's work overseeing the extensive regulations of capital flows in and out of the country. Furthermore, Norges Bank managed the Norwegian foreign exchange reserves.[3] By advising the government on foreign exchange questions, Norges Bank took on a role as protector of a fixed and binding exchange rate policy during the postwar era.

---

[2] Tobias Straumann, *Fixed Ideas of Money: Small States and Exchange Rate Regimes in Twentieth-century Europe* (Cambridge University Press, 2010) underlines the fact that the Norwegian krone was among of the most stable small currencies in Western Europe in this period, cf. pp. 198–9.

[3] Erling Børresen, *Norges Banks gullpolitikk etter 1945* (Norges Bank, 1983).

There seems to have been general agreement that Norges Bank was the advisor on exchange rate matters but that it did not have the authority to formally decide the krone exchange rate. Somewhat paradoxically, the practices continued until the new central bank act in 1985 could suggest otherwise. Concerning the devaluation in 1949, it was Norges Bank that acted formally on behalf of the Norwegian government when the decision to change the exchange rate was made, though in reality the decision rested with the government. Also regarding subsequent changes to the exchange rate during the 1970s and 1980s, a practice developed (with one exception) that it was Norges Bank which made the 'formal decision'.[4] However, there is no trace of a conception that Norges Bank could ultimately decide on an exchange rate that differed from the one recommended by the government.[5]

When it came to the exchange rate, the bank's advisory function was key. The technical work in Norges Bank's currency department naturally provided first-hand knowledge on the foreign exchange markets and the technical sides of foreign currency management. The central bank governors (and senior central bank officers) also had intimate and solid international contacts through representation in the IMF, as well as in the meetings of the Nordic central banks and in the BIS in Basel. These were less formal and gave more regular contact with many of the same central bank actors meeting each other year in, year out.[6] Membership in the European Economic Communiy's (EEC) exchange rate cooperation from 1972 to 1978 gave Norges Bank a seat on the so-called central bank governor's committee, and participation in the close technical cooperation with the European central banks.[7]

Throughout the entire Bretton Woods period and well into the 1970s, Norges Bank argued, in its role as the government's advisor, that politicians should be quite cautious regarding adjusting the Norwegian krone exchange rate. The Bretton Woods agreement allowed for such adjustments to occur, but with the important restriction that the exchange rate should only be adjusted to correct so-called 'fundamental imbalances' in the current account. There were hardly any such fundamental imbalances after 1949. Thus, discussions about the krone exchange rate became a relatively marginal topic as long as the international fixed exchange rate cooperation worked. When these kinds of questions arose, Norges Bank always argued against changing the exchange rate. While the background for these discussions, and the kinds of arguments that were used, varied,[8] the attitude regarding the exchange rate was

---

[4] In several of these cases it is not clear, however, how the decision was made. See Carsten Smith, *Bankrett og statsstyre* (Universitetsforlaget, 1980), 511–13.

[5] See e.g. Alice Rostoft, 'Valutauro og valutapolitikk', *Penger og kreditt* 1, no. 1 (1973); Knut Getz Wold, 'Norges Banks samarbeid med statsmaktene, bankene og utlandet' (1972).

[6] Annotations in Gunnar Jahn's diaries and Knut Getz Wold's memoirs, Knut Getz Wold and Jan Thomas Kobberrød , 'I samarbeid' (Norges Bank, 2017) points to this.

[7] See NOU 1983: 39, *Lov om Norges Bank og pengevesenet* (Norges Offentlig Utredninger, 1983). Harold James, *Making the European Monetary Union* (Harvard University Press, 2012), 104, also illustrates this kind of cooperation between central banks.

[8] Statement from the Executive Board to the Ministry of Trade, 24 August 1956, 'Oppskrivning av den norske krone', file 'Kurser, eventuell revaluering/devaluering 1956–7', box D 0249, NB/VAL1; Norges Bank's statement to the Ministry of Trade, 1 September 1967, cited in excerpts from Norges Bank's annual report 1967, 94–6.

characterized by a deeply rooted ideal of international cooperation, which can be seen as a natural consequence of the extensive international contact and cooperation.

After the multilateral fixed exchange rate cooperation finally collapsed between the years 1971 and 1973—first with the suspension of gold exchange in the United States in the summer of 1971, and thereafter with the collapse of the new exchange rate agreement in the winter of 1973—Norges Bank attempted to integrate these view-points into the exchange rate policy. In theory, from 1973, the Norwegian authorities could have chosen to let the supply and demand of the Norwegian krone decide the exchange rates in relation to another currency, and let the krone 'float', as it does today. A floating exchange rate was, however, considered completely unrealistic for a small open economy like Norway. Norwegian economists feared that a floating exchange rate would bring about too much volatility in import and export prices.[9] Instead, Norges Bank argued, from 1972 onwards, for Norwegian participation in the European fixed exchange rate cooperation, the so-called 'snake'. The enthusiasm for the European exchange rate cooperation would remain strong in Norges Bank through the 1970s.

The European exchange rate cooperation, in the form of the European Monetary System (EMS) from 1979, was based, like the entire EEC system that it was a part of (and which both Brofoss and Getz Wold rallied for), on many of the same ideals as the Bretton Woods system. Both attempted to tear down economic and political dividing lines to increase mutual dependencies and weaken the potential for war. The snake came, in its establishment and function, to resemble a light version of the Bretton Woods system.[10] The government followed Norges Bank's advice and joined the snake. The referendum against Norway's membership in the European Economic Community in the autumn of 1972 did not change the outcome.[11]

With the final collapse of the multilateral fixed exchange rate system in the winter of 1973, the intimate relationship that Norges Bank claimed existed between exchange rate cooperation and exchange rate stability had been severely weakened. The key currencies now began, on a long-lasting basis for the first time, to float in relation to each other. In practice, this made it impossible to reach a completely stable exchange rate in relation to several key currencies simultaneously. During the 1970s, the West German authorities fought inflation more consistently and successfully than the United States, Great Britain, and other countries with floating exchange rates, which meant that the Deutschemark appreciated against other key currencies. Since the Deutschemark was the key currency in the snake cooperation, the currencies of other snake countries also appreciated. For many of them, this weakened their

---

[9] Straumann , *Fixed Ideas of Money: Small States and Exchange Rate Regimes in Twentieth-century Europe*, argues that this 'fear of floating' reflects the view that floating exchange rates would create unacceptable exchange rate instability and that such instability would be particularly harmful for small open economies like Norway's.

[10] Barry Eichengreen, *The European Economy since 1945: Coordinated Capitalism and Beyond* (Princeton University Press, 2006), 247–8.

[11] Norway participated in the snake cooperation from 1972. A break in this cooperation occurred in the autumn 1972, of which details remain unclear. See Kleivset, 'Inflasjon og akkomodasjon norsk valutakurspoli-tikk fra 1971 til 1986', 28.

competitiveness and foreign economic relations more than they were willing to accept. The tensions inside the snake throughout the 1970s led to frequent adjustments of the mutual exchange rates within the snake and a continuous flow of countries joining and leaving the cooperation, something that further undermined exchange rate stability.

In light of this development, it may seem surprising that Norges Bank so enthusiastically embraced the exchange rate cooperation with West Germany in 1972, and continued to do so through the bulk of the 1970s. As long as the krone was fixed relative to the Deutschemark, the authorities were required to keep inflation at the same low level as in West Germany. One might conceive that this would put severe restrictions on the Norwegian demand policy, which would have consequences on growth and unemployment in the short term.[12] The reason was in part that, given that the exchange rate was to remain fixed, there were few if any alternatives. Also, since in the beginning of the 1970s there still seemed to be considerable optimism that Norwegian authorities, with the help of income policy and other instruments, would be able to control inflation. It was also possible that insisting on the need for exchange rate cooperation, particularly with countries that carried out different economic policies, had set Getz Wold and others in Norges Bank in motion towards a position where exchange rate stability, when pushed to the extreme, would be more heavily weighed than the short-term goal of full employment.

Foreign Exchange Regulation under Pressure

At the technical level, throughout the entire postwar era (1946–86), Norges Bank, together with the responsible ministries (mainly the Ministry of Trade in the years 1948–80), came to play a leading role in the stable development of the krone exchange rate, first and foremost through foreign exchange regulation. Control of capital flows in and out of Norway gave the authorities the opportunity to isolate the Norwegian money market quite effectively, and this made it a relatively simple task to maintain a stable krone exchange. However, also in this area, the defence of a fixed exchange rate came under pressure during the 1970s.

The basis for the foreign exchange regulation, as previously mentioned, was already present during the war as a provisional law. This later became the Foreign Currency Act of 1950 and it remained pretty much unchanged until 1990. However, there was a clear shift in the basis for the regulations, from the rationing of the sparse foreign exchange reserves to the targeted isolation of the Norwegian money market.[13] In simple terms, regulation of capital flows meant that the Norwegian authorities could carry out an independent interest rate policy without interfering with the goal of a

---

[12] Erik Brofoss touched upon this in a memo 'Krisen i det internasjonale betalingssystem', NB, STAT 0017, box E, NAN.
[13] St. meld. 27 1977–8, Storting's proceedings.

fixed exchange rate, and on the other hand, were able to carry out a fixed exchange rate policy without consequences for the interest rate level. It was similar considerations for fixed exchange rates which were used as arguments during the Bretton Woods negotiations for allowing the member countries to regulate capital flows in and out of the countries.[14]

The processing of licence applications in Norges Bank and in the ministries allowed the Norwegian authorities to control the extent of direct foreign investments by Norwegians, like the purchase of securities, vacation homes, etc., as well as foreign investments in Norway. This foreign exchange control hindered large flows of money in search of higher returns or lower risks, flows that would quickly have put pressure on the interest rate level and the krone exchange rate.

Yet, not completely. Payments for goods and services that, for the most part were exempt, could be made, if the timing was right, taking return or exchange rate risk into account, and in turn contribute to destabilizing the exchange rates.[15] The international short-term money market, based on the so-called Eurodollar market, grew at the end of the 1950s into a considerable unregulated, transnational market for placing money in different currencies in the 1960s, eventually also for Norwegian kroner. This international market could abruptly turn towards the national money markets and put exchange rates and interest rates under pressure.[16] The increased capital mobility during the 1960s created problems for the exchange rate policy in many countries and became one of the mechanisms behind the collapse of the international fixed exchange rate system. For Norwegian authorities, destabilizing money flows were hardly a problem before into the 1970s.

Regulating capital flows in and out of Norway was always subject to a certain external pressure. Already when the Organisation for European Economic Co-operation was transformed into the OECD in 1961, the Norwegian authorities had (despite Erik Brofoss's writing off the whole thing as 'primarily of symbolic nature') committed themselves to liberalize the capital flows.[17] Throughout the 1970s and 1980s, there was also a steady, if not a very heavy, pressure on the Norwegian authorities from the OECD's side to deliver on these commitments.[18] In addition, an internal pressure had built up and the regulations were increasingly circumvented. Of course, money could always be moved across borders in a suitcase. More importantly, however, foreign

[14] Harold James, *International Monetary Cooperation since Bretton Woods* (International Monetary Fund, 1996).

[15] Jeffrey R Shafer, 'Experience with Controls on International Capital Movements in OECD Countries: Solution or Problem for Monetary Policy?', in *Capital Controls, Exchange Rates, and Monetary Policy in the World Economy*, ed. Sebastian Edwards (Cambridge University Press, 1995).

[16] For a description of the eurodollar market, see e.g. James, *International Monetary Cooperation since Bretton Woods*, 179–81. The eurokrone market which developed from the late 1970s is described in Geir Bergvoll, 'The Eurokrone Market and the Norwegian Economy', *Economic Bulletin* 52, no. 3 (1981): 198–204.

[17] Erik Brofoss, *Valutapolitikk: forelesninger ved Oslo universitet høstsemesteret 1966: 2*, 3.utg. ed., vol. 2 (Oslo, 1966), 261; Shafer, 'Experience with Controls on International Capital Movements in OECD Countries: Solution or Problem for Monetary Policy?'

[18] Thomas Nordbø Berg, Harald Bøhn, and Christoffer Kleivset, 'Fra regulering til marked: Et dokumentsjonsnotat om Norges Bank og utviklingen av penge-, kreditt og valutapolitikken 1965–1990' (Norges Bank, 2012), 65–6.

currency banks, shipping tycoons, and others with relative freedom to operate in foreign currencies could take out a loan or put money in locations or in forms that were difficult to monitor for both the foreign exchange and tax authorities.[19] As mentioned in Chapter 10, during the 1960s, a ceiling was placed on the foreign lending activities of the banks. Throughout the 1970s, Norges Bank's foreign exchange department became involved in solving and prosecuting more and more serious cases where violations of the Foreign Currency Act had, or could be assumed to have, taken place.[20]

After the collapse of the international fixed exchange rate system in 1973, the foreign currency market changed. Instability in the floating exchange rates led to an increasing need for exporters and importers to protect themselves against exchange rate risk. During the 1970s, in parallel with the original spot market, a significant market grew for the so-called forward contracts and foreign currency futures.[21] The major oil companies that were about to establish themselves on the Norwegian continental shelf earned income in dollars, but were required to pay taxes and salaries in Norwegian kroner, and had a great need for a secure exchange rate. These companies became the most important driving force behind the growth in the Norwegian forward currency market in the 1970s.

The need of the oil companies and other actors for a secure exchange rate increased the need of foreign currency banks for flexibility in currency trading. Norges Bank responded to this need and, at the recommendation of the foreign exchange department, proposed to replace the old regulation with a ceiling on foreign currency loans with the so-called zero total position regulation in 1978.[22] In short, the goal of this regulation, without going deep into technical details, was to make it possible for the foreign currency banks to adapt to the need of the industry of instruments that reduced their foreign exchange risk, and simultaneously make sure that this increased freedom did not manifest itself as exchange rate speculation. In sum, however, the zero total position regulation contributed to a substantial increase in the short-term funding of private banks' lending via the foreign exchange market. Throughout the 1980s, it became increasingly clear that this freedom contributed to the undermining of both the foreign exchange and the credit regulation systems.[23]

Changing conditions had an effect on how Norges Bank operated in the foreign currency market. Already in 1963, Norges Bank had stopped operating with fixed bid and offer rates for currency and instead made market interventions at given

---

[19] Shafer, 'Experience with Controls on International Capital Movements in OECD Countries: Solution or Problem for Monetary Policy?'

[20] The most prevalent of these cases is probably the Reksten case, although a string of lesser cases frequently surfaced in Norwegian newspapers. See e.g. 'Skipsrederi granskes for valutasmugling', VG, 27 December 1975 and 'Valutasmuglere skal avsløres', VG, 24 November 1976.

[21] Bjørn Rogstad and Odd Nordhus, 'Norges Banks swap og termin forretninger', Penger og Kreditt 7, no. 4 (1978).

[22] Steinar Juel, 'Endringer i reguleringen av bankenes valutaposisjoner', Penger og kreditt 7, no. 4 (1978).

[23] In short, this arrangement was that each bank's total foreign exchange position, i.e. the net worth of all spot and forward positions in foreign assets and liabilities, should be zero at the end of each trading day.

fluctuation margins around the fixed dollar exchange rate.[24] After 1971 these margins were expanded and later abolished against the dollar and instead made narrower against the Deutschemark and the other snake currencies. Due to the increasing instability between the exchange rates during the 1970s, Norges Bank frequently needed to operate in the market and defend these fluctuation margins with large interventions. Prior to its exit from the snake in December 1978, Norges Bank sold, for example, over the course of one month, foreign currency for around 5 billion kroner.[25]

Throughout the 1980s, the volume of international capital flows continuously increased. The large countries allowed their exchange rates to swing, and did not need regulations to keep the exchange rate fixed. In Norway, parts of the foreign exchange regulations were also relaxed. Business opportunities for both Norwegian capital abroad and international capital in Norway could more easily be exploited, increased the instability in the foreign exchange market, and put more pressure on the krone exchange rate. In 1983, at Norges Bank's initiative, the government established a committee to prepare for a revision of the foreign exchange regulations.[26] The committee's conclusion was clear. Regulating the capital flows was still important in reducing capital flows across country borders and decreasing pressure on the krone exchange rate.[27]

The Ministry of Finance Takes Control

Despite the agreement about Norges Bank's proposal to link the krone to the currency snake, Norges Bank's role and viewpoints were quickly challenged when the multilateral fixed exchange rate system collapsed in the winter of 1973. This was in part due to external events, when, over the course of 1973–4, the Ministry of Finance, on its own initiative, overtook case responsibility from the Ministry of Trade for exchange rate policy.[28] The Ministry of Trade, having had case responsibility since 1948, had usually supported Norges Bank's view about the exchange rate, most likely because it was more strongly influenced by international cooperation norms than the Ministry of Finance. In a wider context of exchange rate policy, it should be mentioned that the collapse of the old fixed exchange rate system and search for new solutions happened around the same time as the EEC's second round of enlargement, where the Norwegian government was in favour of Norwegian membership. In the intense debate that led up to the 1972 referendum on the question, civil servant ideals of neutrality in political questions were shattered on both sides. Civil servants from the

---

[24] Brofoss, *Valutapolitikk: forelesninger ved Oslo universitet høstsemesteret 1966: 2*, 2, 241.
[25] Harald Roseng and Geir Bergvoll, 'Likviditetsregulering og valutaintervensjonspolitikk', *Penger og kreditt 8*, no. 3 (1980).
[26] NOU 1983: 54, *Om revisjon av valutareguleringen* (Norges Offentlige Utredninger, 1983).
[27] NOU 1983: 54, *Om revisjon av valutareguleringen*, 8.
[28] Kleivset, 'Inflasjon og akkomodasjon: norsk valutakurspolitikk fra 1971 til 1986', 30, 35.

Ministry of Trade (and the Ministry of Foreign Affairs) engaged themselves passionately in the public debate in support of the government. Economists at the Ministry of Finance, with a few exceptions, were in strong opposition, as their teacher, Professor Ragnar Frisch, had been in the early 1960s. A main argument from their side was that the European common market would restrict the sum of available instruments for economic policy, and this would limit the possibility to conduct what they perceived as an optimal economic policy.[29]

The transfer of the responsibility for the exchange rate policy seems to have contributed to a change in the government's view on the relatively complex, specialized, and technical questions that were involved. Already in November 1973, and against advice by both the Ministry of Trade, the Foreign Exchange Council, and Norges Bank, the Bratteli government unilaterally revalued the krone by 5 per cent relative to the snake currencies.[30] Even though it was a revaluation, and as such did not resemble the competing devaluations from the interwar era that central bank Governor Getz Wold had warned about, and even though it was an isolated incident, it gave an early indication regarding the coming foreign exchange policy. The government revalued in a situation with a deficit in the balance of payments. This signalled a different attitude to the exchange rate question than that thought to rule the day in most other western European countries.[31]

Norges Bank's position on exchange rate policy was also challenged from within. Hermod Skånland, deputy governor since 1971, voted both in the board and in the Foreign Exchange Council in favour of the exchange rate change when it came up for discussion in the autumn of 1973.[32] Skånland came from the position as director general in the Ministry of Finance's economic policy department. Getz Wold had preferred the internal candidate, director of the monetary policy department, Einar Magnussen. The government selected Skånland after nominations from the board of representatives.[33] Skånland was not afraid to show that he held a different view on the krone exchange rate from that of his superior. The pressure on Norwegian authorities to conduct a particular policy when the large countries' currencies floated in different directions was minimal, Skånland argued in a talk on exchange rate policy in the autumn of 1974. 'It is a different question what we ourselves see fit in such a situation.'[34]

---

[29] Einar Lie, 'Masters and Servants: Economists and Bureaucrats in the Dispute Over Norwegian EEC Membership in 1972', *Contemporary European History* 24, no. 2 (2015).

[30] After Kleivset, 'Inflasjon og akkomodasjon: norsk valutakurspolitikk fra 1971 til 1986', 36–7; Qvigstad and Skjæveland, 'Valutakursregimer'.

[31] See e.g. the comparison between the Norwegian and Dutch revaluation in 1973 in Straumann, *Fixed Ideas of Money: Small States and Exchange Rate Regimes in Twentieth-century Europe*, 257. Straumann's discussion of exchange rate adjustments during the 1970s and 1980s shows that exchange rates were broadly revalued with current account surpluses and devalued with deficits, hence exchange rate adjustments were primarily used to improve current account balances. Straumann also provides examples indicating that other countries' authorities to a stronger degree restrained themselves from making exchange rate adjustments, compared with what Norwegian authorities did.

[32] Kleivset, 'Inflasjon og akkomodasjon: norsk valutakurspolitikk fra 1971 til 1986', 36–7.

[33] Eivind Erichsen, 'Glimt fra karrieren', in *Stabilitet og langsiktighet, Festskrift til Hermod Skånland*, ed. Jan F. Qvigstad og Sigbjørn A. Berg Kjell Storvik (Aschehoug, 1999), 47.

[34] Hermod Skånland, 'Kursfastsettelsen i det internasjonale valutasystem', *Penger og kreditt* 2, unpaged supplement (1974).

For Skånland and the Ministry of Finance, the collapse in 1973 of the multilateral fixed exchange rate system provided a seemingly attractive opportunity to use the exchange rate as a policy instrument.[35] Through the entire postwar era, Norwegian economists belonging to the Frisch school had been interested in the relationship between the exchange rate and price level.[36] In particular, they were interested in finding ways to counteract the effect of a constantly rising international price level on Norwegian prices.[37] Skånland came to reflect a view, also shared by the Ministry of Finance, that the exchange rate should be used in a pragmatic way, as one among many policy instruments, to ensure the best possible balance in the internal and external economy.

Skånland and the Ministry of Finance held understandably different views on the snake cooperation than those held by the Ministry of Trade and a majority of Norges Bank's Executive Board and in the administration. With its high ambitions for fixed exchange rates, the snake cooperation imposed potentially severe restrictions on this kind of use of the krone exchange rate as an instrument. The strong ambitions of integration that characterized the EEC, of which the snake cooperation was a key part, were also a potential threat to the autonomy of the Norwegian authorities in economic policy matters. This threat had formed a basis for the resistance from the Ministry of Finance. With the so-called Werner-plan from 1969, the exchange rate cooperation was the first step towards a monetary union between the EEC, later EU, countries. The monetary union implied a common currency as the unit of account, a common exchange rate, and a common interest rate.

The revaluation in the autumn of 1973 was one of many attempts by the Norwegian authorities to put a stop to the price growth in the beginning of the 1970s. As shown earlier, in the early 1960s, the Getz Wold committee had more or less accepted inflation as a necessary evil, an unavoidable consequence of full employment. This was a widespread position and continued to be so throughout the entire 1970s and a large part of the 1980s among Norwegian politicians and civil servants. The development of the early 1970s, with more than 10 per cent inflation in 1970 and prices continuously climbing in 1971–4, pushed the inflation problem right to the forefront of the economic policy discussion for a time.[38]

The incomes policy became the key instrument in the fight against inflation. The argument was that demand management and fiscal and credit policies could not be strongly tightened without threatening the goal of full employment. Instead, the Ministry of Finance attempted to influence price growth more directly, through wage determination and thereby the cost growth in the business sector. Incomes policy had been tested in a variety of different versions throughout the entire postwar era, with

---

[35] A similar picture is painted in Espen Søilen, 'Drømmen om inntektspolitisk samarbeid: Finansdepartementets kamp mot særinteresser' ([E. Søilen], 1993).

[36] Søilen, 'Drømmen om inntektspolitisk samarbeid: Finansdepartementets kamp mot særinteresser'.

[37] See Odd Aukrust and Tore Jørgen Hanisch, *Økonomisk forskning og debatt: utvalgte artikler 1942–1989*, vol. 75 (Statistisk sentralbyrå, 1990). See in particular the article on 'Konkurranseutsatte og skjermede næringer: historien om en idé' (1973), 230, 233.

[38] NOU 1973: 36, *Om prisproblemene*, 52–4.

mixed results. In 1973, the Ministry of Finance launched the first so-called *combined income settlements*.[39] The plan with the combined settlements was that employees would agree to lower nominal wage growth whereas the government would let the unions that negotiated on behalf of the employees have influence over economic policy. This applied first and foremost to the policies on taxes and duties, but also, as had been suggested by the committee that had launched the idea about the combined settlements, to revaluation of the krone exchange rate.[40] The committee was headed by Skånland.

The fact that the Ministry of Finance did not find it problematic to revalue in 1973, as opposed to later, and weaken Norwegian competitiveness, was, at least in part, oil related. In 1969, oilfields on the Norwegian continental shelf had been discovered. The unexpected high growth in the price of oil from 1973 onwards indicated that oil would entail significant future wealth. A stronger krone and weakened surplus in the old export industries was favourable because it would contribute to moving investments and the workforce from traditional industry over to the growing oil activities.

The revaluation in 1973 came in hindsight to stand out as a single incident. The results were disappointing. Both in 1973 and 1974, wages and prices continued to climb significantly. Competitiveness declined and the current account deficit increased. 'We have few if any examples of a similar unsuccessful measure in economic policy', Governor Getz Wold stated in retrospect.[41]

Disagreements on the Exchange Rate Policy

The Norwegian decision to leave the snake cooperation and establish a so-called basket system in December 1978, at the same time when the snake cooperation was about to become the EMS, implied that the Ministry of Finance took more direct control over the exchange rate policy. It also meant that the exchange rate policy was moving in the direction of more flexibility and less international commitment.[42] Skånland was the strategist behind this shift and the man behind what many saw as an internal rebellion against Norges Bank's governor, Getz Wold.[43] In numerous meetings, in the Foreign Exchange Council and in the bank's board, in the press and in memos to former colleagues in the Ministry of Finance—even in internal meetings of Skånland's own party, the governing Labour Party—Skånland had argued insistently through 1976, 1977, and 1978 for a reform of the exchange rate policy.[44] During 1977, Skånland

---

[39] After Espen Søilen, *Fra frischianisme til keynesianisme: en studie av norsk økonomisk politikk i lys av økonomisk teori 1945–1980* (NHH, 1998), 90; Kleivset, 'Inflasjon og akkomodasjon: norsk valutakurspolitikk fra 1971 til 1986', 36.

[40] NOU 1973: 36, *Om prisproblemene*, 52–4.   [41] KGWM, chapter 19, 19.

[42] James, *Making the European Monetary Union*, 146–8.

[43] Peter Ludlow, *The Making of the European Monetary System: A case Study Of the Politics of the European Community* (Butterworth Scientific, 1982), 276.

[44] Kleivset, 'Inflasjon og akkomodasjon: norsk valutakurspolitikk fra 1971 til 1986', 43, 47, 43, 47. Minutes from economic-political committee, 5 January 1978, Labour Party's archive, file '051–12 Økonomisk-politisk utvalg 1978–81', box 140, The Norwegian Labor Movements Archive and Library.

achieved a breakthrough in the Ministry of Finance. A memo from Skånland, titled 'Norwegian participation in the snake cooperation, pros and cons', was, in 1977, used by the ministry's civil servant network when face to face with the political leadership to facilitate the change in regime.

It was the impression during 1976–8 that Norwegian foreign economic relations faced major challenges in combining the goals of stable foreign economic relations and full employment, which brought the regime question to the forefront for Skånland. The decline in global demand in 1975, the deepest international recession of the entire postwar era, had triggered the challenge. Admittedly, the Bratteli government had met the recession with an expansive countercyclical policy in anticipation that demand would pick up again. This didn't happen, however, the expansive policy had contributed to a dramatic weakening of the current account and a high level of foreign debt. Oil production and oil prices were not high enough to compensate for this. Skånland maintained, most likely already in 1976, but clearly and unequivocally from 1977, that competitiveness of the mainland industry should now be a main objective for the Norwegian authorities in economic policy. In order to preserve or improve competitiveness without raising unemployment, the authorities needed to use all possible instruments. Snake membership, which Skånland expected would continue to push the krone exchange rate up and thus weaken competitiveness, would not provide an appropriate framework for such a policy.[45]

A Norwegian foreign exchange basket, of a similar kind that Finland had been experimenting with since the beginning of the 1970s, seemed to fit better with Skånland's proposed competitiveness policy because it, to a larger degree than the snake, would give a krone exchange rate that was better aligned with the countries to which Norway in fact exported. The snake cooperation was hit by a crisis in 1976 7, and more and more countries dropped out. A stable krone exchange rate relative to the remaining snake countries would guarantee increasingly less stability vis-à-vis what we today denote as the effective krone exchange rate, which reflects the importance of different currencies for Norwegian foreign trade.[46] A Norwegian foreign exchange basket could be constructed in such a way that a stable krone relative to the basket would provide for the highest possible degree of stability in the effective exchange rate and thus contribute directly to the largest possible amount of stability in competitiveness.[47]

Such a basket would also provide more autonomy in controlling the exchange rate, thus making eventual corrections easier. Since the snake exchange rates were multilaterally agreed, changes in the exchange rate needed to be negotiated with all partners. This often implied that exchange rate changes would occur at a time that was not necessarily optimal for Norwegian authorities. The other countries could also deny

---

[45] Hermod Skånland', Konjunkturperspektiver og norsk næringsliv', *Sosialøkonomen* 19, no. 10 (1977).
[46] The Foreign Exchange Council, 26 August 1977, NB, NAN.
[47] Skånland's claim that a currency basket implied a more stable system than the European exchange rate cooperation, rested on the assumption that *average* stability against all trading partners would yield better overall stability than an entirely stable exchange rate against a group of trading partners.

changes, which happened when Sweden wanted to devalue in the summer of 1977. After the transition from the snake to the EMS as from 1979, even more such limitations were to be expected. The basket, on the other hand, would give Norwegian authorities complete freedom, not only to change the exchange rate, but also to change fluctuation margins, exactly at a point of time of their discretion.[48]

Battling it Out in Public

Deputy Governor Skånland's campaign against the snake and in favour of the basket in 1976–8 triggered a deep conflict inside Norges Bank regarding the Norwegian exchange rate regime. For Governor Getz Wold and the foreign exchange department, the idea of a currency basket was perceived as a frontal attack on the core values of Norwegian exchange rate as well as foreign policy. For Skånland and his followers, defending the European exchange rate cooperation was perceived as being potentially harmful for the Norwegian economy. In 1978, Skånland and Getz Wold 'fought in public', according to the newspaper *Verdens Gang*, about the position Norges Bank should take on the question of snake versus basket.[49] Throughout the 1980s, even though Skånland's view won, the collaboration gradually deteriorated.

The core of the conflict was fundamental. For Knut Getz Wold, the basket system, and the increased autonomy that this system implied, was a dangerous road. On several occasions, like during the Foreign Exchange Council's meeting before Sweden's exit from the snake in 1977, Getz Wold spoke of 'the risk for competitive devaluations and protectionism' if international exchange rate cooperation became further undermined.[50] Weakening exchange rate cooperation was also bad for other reasons. Commitments to international exchange rate cooperation had a significant value in its own right, Getz Wold claimed in a personal memo in autumn 1977, 'not least in relation to advocacy groups that steadily will be able to require exchange rate adjustments in a less restrictive system'.[51] Also, Erik Brofoss, now out of the monetary policy area after three years as alternate director of the IMF (1970–3), became involved in the question. What would happen if everyone went around with 'their own little basket', he asked rhetorically, and with more than a little bit of sarcasm.[52]

The fundamental disagreement reflected and accentuated the differences between the 'internal' and 'external' areas of the bank's activities, and between the departments that worked with them. Whereas the leadership in Norges Bank's foreign currency

---

[48] Majority statement, in letter from the Executive Board to the Ministry of Finance, 6 December 1978, Da 0461, FD/ØKA file '490 Valutasamarbeidet EF og EMF [sic.] 1977–83', NAN.

[49] 'Men tøv å gjøre dette til EF-sak', *VG*, 7 December 1978.

[50] The Foreign Exchange Council, 26 August 1977, NB, NAN.

[51] GW/SAn 26.8.77, Norges stilling til slangesamarbeidet, box 20, EE.

[52] Eivind Thomassen's conversation with Jarle Bergo. Brofoss also used a somewhat derogatory term for a basket (in Norwegian 'kørj') in his writing: Letter from Brofoss to trade-political advisor Tore Tønne, 17 January 1979, enclosed Letter from Tore Tønne, Norwegian Export Council, to the Foreign Ministry 13 February 1979, file 44 37/16 '1' (untitled), UDA.

department shared Getz Wold's principal views on the exchange rate policy, with little sympathy for Skånland's opinions, Skånland had first and foremost support from the credit policy department.[53] Whereas the foreign currency department worked in close cooperation with central banks in the EEC to stabilize volatile foreign currency markets, the economists in the credit policy department struggled with the problems this created for domestic credit policy. In their view, there were tensions created by the foreign currency department and its large-sum interventions to defend the narrow intervention margins of the snake, which interfered with credit policy objectives. The interventions channelled liquidity to private banks and expanded their basis for increased lending.

The foreign currency department, and in a sense also Governor Getz Wold, were largely influenced by international organizations and foreign central banks, and they had close contact with the Ministry of Trade. The credit policy department and Skånland dealt, for the most part, with the Ministry of Finance. Even though the personal relations across the departments had never been as bad as they were between Getz Wold and Skånland, there was not much contact and mutual understanding between the departments in the day-to-day activities.

Skånland's and Getz Wold's personalities deviated from each other, despite certain similarities, on points that were bound to increase tensions and provide a personal dimension to the conflict. Whereas Getz Wold associated himself with the rigid civil servant ideal, with strict requirements on correct structures and the loyalty to formal hierarchies, Skånland was to a larger degree an individualist, almost an activist. For Getz Wold, Skånland's intense fight for the currency basket demonstrated his disloyalty to Norges Bank and to himself.[54] However, the relationship between the governor and deputy governor in the board was also affected by Getz Wold's health. During the 1980s, it became apparent that Getz Wold's health condition was weakening. A certain doubt regarding his capability to perform individual duties existed.[55] Skånland's high public profile, victories over Getz Wold (not only on foreign currency policy but also in votes in the board), and the chairman's illness during the 1980s, contributed to creating the impression, both inside and outside the bank, that Skånland was Norges Bank's true leader.[56]

---

[53] Bjarne Hansen in conversation with Kleivset, 11 March 2010.

[54] Conversations with Getz Wold's son, Bjørn Getz Wold, as well as Trygve Spildrejorde, who for many years worked closely with Arne Lie, head of the bank's foreign exchange department, and Getz Wold's closest confident in the bank, confirm this.

[55] Getz Wold contracted Amyotrophical Lateral Sclerosis (ALS), a rare disease of the nervous system. To what extent this disease, which in its first phase often manifests itself motorically, also led to a cognitive weakening during Getz Wold's term as governor—and eventually, when—is for obvious reasons hard to say. Lie and Venneslan, *Over evne: Finansdepartmentets historie 1965–91*, 351, write that the disease manifested itself from the late 1970s onwards. Furthermore, the disease, as it was perceived contemporarily, had an effect on Getz Wold's intellectual capacity (352). Trygve Spildrejorde and Bjørn Getz Wold, however, have indicated in conversations that clear signs of weakening first became manifest in the 1980s, but that Getz Wold's intellectual capacity remained strong. The prime minister at the time, Kåre Willoch, became aware of Getz Wold's disease in 1982, but found it hard to evaluate his condition (Kleivset, 'Inflasjon og akkomodasjon', 67).

[56] See Lie and Venneslan Venneslan, *Over evne: Finansdepartementet 1965–1992* (Pax forlag, 2010), 351–2; Kleivset, 'Inflasjon og akkomodasjon: norsk valutakurspolitikk fra 1971 til 1986', 351–2; Per Bang and Jon Petter Holter, *Norges Bank 175 år: mennesker og begivenheter* (Norges Bank, 1991).

Ignored and Devalued

From 1978 to 1986, the government largely ignored Norges Bank in its capacity as advisor on the foreign exchange rate question.[57] The old advisory Foreign Exchange Council, led by the central bank governor, was dissolved. The board still had a sort of formal decision-making role, but increasingly the government placed personal pressure on the Board members to ensure a majority vote for their own policy. This development was intimately connected with the fact that the government, during the same period, performed a series of devaluations or exchange rate adjustments, two in August and September 1982, and two in July and September 1984. The changes were met with sharp criticism inside Norges Bank.

The background for the exchange rate changes was partially the basket system's properties. No one had envisioned and even less desired that the basket system should form the basis for an 'active exchange rate policy' when it was introduced in 1978, and this was partly due to the fact that it did not deliver the increased stability Skånland had promised. On the contrary, since the US dollar played a key role in the Norwegian currency basket, the krone started to appreciate relative to the EMS currencies in the early 1980s due to strong dollar appreciation. This was contrary to what the strategist behind the currency basket, Skånland, had anticipated. He had expected that the dollar would continue to weaken in relation to the Deutschemark and that a large dollar weight of 25 per cent in the basket would have stabilized the krone against further EMS appreciation.[58] As from the beginning of the 1980s, however, the relationship (of relative strength) between the Deutschemark and the dollar flipped. Two to three of the devaluations in 1982 and 1984 (the number depends on the definition) came to take the form of so-called 'technical adjustments', which were justified as corrections within the basket concept, even though they always led to a weaker krone.[59]

However, the initiative came from the government. After a temporary wage and price freeze in 1978–9, wages and prices continued to climb and the competitiveness of the mainland industry continued to weaken. A new international recession in 1981–2 caused the demand for exports from mainland industry to drop. The year 1984 saw the rate of registered unemployment rise to 3.2 per cent, a hitherto unprecedented level in Norway in the postwar era. The government also made serious efforts to restrict wage growth in the Norwegian economy. The instruments used by the Labour Party governments in the 1970s had been a three-part cooperation between employees, employers, and the state, where the state had contributed with tax breaks to reduce the nominal extras. There was a split in opinion about the policy's principles and results. After a landslide election in favour of the civil parties, especially the Conservative Party, there was a change in government in 1981. The new prime minister

---

[57] Kleivset', Inflasjon og akkomodasjon: norsk valutakurspolitikk fra 1971 til 1986', 66–7.
[58] Skånland 'Norsk valutakurspolitikk', *Penger og kreditt* 1 (1983).
[59] Kleivset, 'Inflasjon og akkomodasjon: norsk valutakurspolitikk fra 1971 til 1986', 66.

was the Conservative party's Kåre Willoch, first from a minority government of his own party, and from 1983 as leader of a coalition together with the Centre Party (formerly the Farmers' Party) and the Christian Democratic Party.

For the prime minister from 1981 to 1986, Willoch, who was educated as an economist at the University of Oslo, experiments with the incomes policy of the kind used in the 1970s were not an optionrealistic. For him, exchange rate adjustments appeared to be a better strategy. By decreasing the international value of the krone, the government could compensate the effect of high wage growth on competitiveness and increase employment, or at least restrict the drop in employment in the short term.[60] The employment situation was, more or less explicitly, part of the background for all the exchange rate adjustments in 1982 and 1984.

Getz Wold and Norges Bank's foreign exchange department raised a series of protests against the government's foreign exchange rate policy. In the foreign exchange department, the technical adjustments were perceived as improper. In addition, the board raised the question of whether the devaluations really gave the results the government desired. And even worse, the 1982 Norwegian devaluations, which happened in the midst of a series of devaluations among the small western European countries, appeared to be of a similar kind of competing devaluations that Norges Bank had always warned against during the entire postwar era. The two Norwegian devaluations in 1982 followed two Danish devaluations earlier that year and were followed by a Swedish 'big bang' devaluation of 16 per cent in October. Both prior to and after Sweden, the Finnish markka was also devaluated. The exchange rate basket systems in Norway, Sweden, and Finland—which all attempted to align the effects stemming from the other countries' unilateral exchange rate adjustments with new adjustments which again affected all other exchange rates—created a very confusing and complicated exchange rate landscape during these months.[61] With the devaluations in 1982, not only did the Norwegian authorities participate in a non-solidary fight about market shares, but they did so as the only country with a current account *surplus*. This had to be perceived, as it was also admitted internally in the Ministry of Finance, as a breach of the rules of the game.[62]

Despite resistance, the government's devaluations were signed off by Norges Bank. In the midst of the summer holiday season, Deputy Governor Skånland called an extraordinary meeting of the board to decide an exchange rate change that the government had already proposed, although the proposition had not been submitted to Norges Bank or the Foreign Exchange Council in advance. Skånland had prepared a technical plan for the exchange rate adjustment with assistance from staff in the bank's department of information and research without involving neither the

[60] Erichsen, 'Glimt fra karrieren', 112.
[61] See 'Competing devaluations and exchange rate cooperation with third countries' [Konkurrerende devalueringer og nærmere valutapolitisk samarbeid med tredjeland], memo, 21 June 1983 from the Norwegian Embassy in Brussels, file 44 37/16 '2' (untiled), UDA.
[62] Exchange rate political issues, 26 April 1984, file 'Valuta 1971–87', box 24, EE.

governor, Getz Wold, nor the foreign exchange department. Getz Wold's protests at this meeting appear to have been the reason why the discussions were postponed for a week.[63] When the next meeting took place, Skånland and the government had succeeded, through personal persuasion, to position the other board members against the central bank governor.[64]

In March 1983, the economic policy department of the Ministry of Finance started to investigate what the government could do if Norges Bank would not approve the government's foreign exchange rate changes. One possibility, claimed the department in a memo a year later, was to use a royal decree and make a reference to the fact that the committee, which at that time was working on a revision of the Norges Bank Act, would give the king the authority to instruct Norges Bank. Another possibility was that the board could make the formal decision regarding the exchange rate change, but make it clear that 'this was done because the government wanted to, even though the Board advised something else'.[65] As long as possible, however, the government preferred nonetheless to use persuasion.

For Getz Wold the battle must have appeared lost already in 1982. In September 1982, he voted, as mentioned, for the devaluation. In September 1984, he also voted, despite raising some opposition, to weaken the krone, as it was stated in the board protocol, 'after expressed desire from the government'. [66] In the meantime, Getz Wold had on several occasions signalled that he wished to step down. For a number of reasons, he was asked twice to wait. The government did not want to name Skånland as Getz Wold's successor in the midst of the turbulent public debate about the high costs of Norges Bank's new bank building (see page 238).[67] When Getz Wold finally did step down in the spring of 1985 and Skånland was named as his successor, Skånland had already taken full control of the organization. In 1984, Skånland had initiated a comprehensive organizational reform, and with the relocation of the head office into a new bank building in the centre of Oslo in 1986, the old model with two separate departments for 'external' and 'internal' monetary policy was abandoned.[68] With the internal restructuring of the bank, the strongest critics of Skånland's position on exchange rate policy were relocated as well. With the former state secretary in the Ministry of Finance, Kjell Storvik, as the new deputy governor in Norges Bank, the relationship became more harmonious between the highest and next highest in command.

---

[63] Eivind Thomassen's conversation with Bjørn Getz Wold; Kleivset, 'Inflasjon og akkomodasjon: norsk val-utakurspolitikk fra 1971 til 1986', 66.

[64] Kleivset, 'Inflasjon og akkomodasjon: norsk valutakurspolitikk fra 1971 til 1986', 66–7.

[65] Quoted in Kleivset, 'Inflasjon og akkomodasjon: norsk valutakurspolitikk fra 1971 til 1986', 70.

[66] Ibid.

[67] Lie and Venneslan, Over evne: Finansdepartementet 1965–1992, 352–3. KGWM, chapter 31, 7.

[68] Egil Borlaug and Turid Wammer, 'Noregs Bank: Grunntrekk i administrasjon, oppgåver og historie' (2009): 54–5.

New Directions for Exchange Rate Policy

Over the course of 1986, the exchange rate policy was reformulated. The devaluation in May 1986, which we will discuss in more detail later, brought a shift in foreign exchange rate and monetary policies. From allowing prices and salaries to increase and solving the competitiveness problem with periodic devaluations, the authorities now attempted to maintain the fixed exchange rate by tightening demand, not least with the help of the interest rate policy. The major policy challenges facing the authorities in 1986 are partly to blame for this turnaround. During the first half of 1986, the oil prices dropped by more than half, turning the current account negative (Figure 11.1). From January to the beginning of May, Norges Bank sold foreign currency for close to 33 billion kroner to maintain the basket index level.[69] The foreign exchange regulations were tightened. Even the IMF recommended that Norway should devalue.[70] The devaluation, and the promise to maintain the new exchange rate, was the same strategy that Sweden, Denmark, and a series of other countries had chosen, successfully, to bring themselves out of foreign economic difficulties in 1982.

The shift could also take legitimacy from a growing discontent with the devaluation policy. Already in April 1984, before the round with the wage adjustments, the secretary general of the Ministry of Finance warned the finance minister in an internal

Current account (percentage of GDP, left axis)
Oil prices (US dollar per barrel, left axis)
Effective exchange rate index (right axis)

Figure 11.1   Current account, oil prices, and nominal effective exchange rate, 1973–90

[69] Annual report 1986, 16.
[70] Hermod Skånland, *Doktriner og økonomisk styring: et tilbakeblikk*, vol. 36 (Norges Bank, 2004), 99.

memo against undertaking more exchange rate adjustments. 'The experiences from other countries that have been labelled "devaluation countries" are frightening.'[71] The reactions to the Norwegian adjustments, especially from the EEC, were negative, and in December 1984, the Ministry of Foreign Affairs stressed internally that the authorities should no longer adjust the basket system 'in such a way that internationally we can be accused of carrying out hidden devaluations.'[72] The press also started to pay more critical attention towards the Norwegian exchange rate policy.[73] 'Some think they see the banana republic banner wave over the horizon', summarized economics professor Preben Munthe in retrospect.[74] When the krone was devalued in May 1986, there was widespread agreement that this must be the last time.

Also, Skånland, who during the course of 1986 was given the key role of defending the new krone exchange rate, had changed his view on exchange rate adjustments. This apparently happened abruptly. As late as the autumn of 1984, Skånland had defended the exchange rate adjustments that year by saying that they made krone placements riskier and therefore weakened demand and the pressure on the exchange rate. After the devaluation in 1986, and maybe especially around the end of 1986 and the beginning of 1987, he shifted to defending a stable krone exchange rate with all his authority and weight. Even though Skånland had always seen exchange rate adjustments as an 'emergency solution', it was not until at this point in time that devaluations were unequivocally rejected. Also, Skånland's own judgement regarding the exchange rate policy that had been carried out gradually became more apparent. 'Here at home, this line weakened the will for moderation in income settlements and internationally it weakened the trust in the Norwegian krone', he claimed, for example, in a review from 2004.[75]

Although Skånland's fixed exchange rate position from 1986 was pragmatic, as opposed to motivated by cooperation ideals, it also implied an attitude regarding the exchange rate which was undoubtedly closer to the position that Getz Wold and the foreign exchange department had maintained. It represented a break with the more unorthodox approach that Skånland himself, more than any other single actor, had advocated from 1976 to 1978, which, to such a large degree, had turned out to be so detrimental for the cooperation climate internally in Norges Bank.

Exchange Rate Selection and Deviation

Even though the Norwegian authorities did not give up on the goal for a stable exchange rate, this was undoubtedly given less priority during the 1970s and 1980s.

---

[71] Exchange rate political issues, 26 April 1984, box 24, file 'Valuta 1971–87', EE.
[72] Memo to the minister of foreign affairs, 6 December 1984 (TJ/hms), box 21, file 'Valutakurs 1982, 83 og 84', EE.
[73] See e.g. 'Frequent changes reduces credibility' [Hyppige endringer svekker troverdighet], Aftenposten 22 September 1984.
[74] Preben Munthe, 'Streiftog i Norges Banks historie', in Tre foredrag om Norges Bank 175 år: sentralbankens plass og oppgaver., ed. Hermod Skånland, Preben Munthe, and Karl Otto Pöhl (Norges Banks skriftserie 19, 1991).
[75] Skånland, Doktriner og økonomisk styring: et tilbakeblikk, 99.

Norwegian governments left the European exchange rate cooperation, established their own basket system, and carried out a series of exchange rate adjustments to strengthen Norwegian competitiveness, all the while in a situation with a surplus in the current account. Differences in opinion on the exchange rate regime created an internal conflict that further weakened Norges Bank as a contributor to the exchange rate policy up until it suddenly turned around in 1986.

The fact that opposing views on exchange rate policy turned out to be a root cause of such strong polarization internally tells us something about the institution of Norges Bank and its development during the postwar era. Whereas the bank's activities before the Second World War had been relatively closely integrated and focused on the setting of interest rates, they were in the postwar era split up into an internally oriented credit policy unit and an externally oriented foreign exchange policy unit, thanks to the regulations and the low interest rate policy. For more than a generation, from 1940 to the beginning of the 1970s, it had only been necessary for short periods to make joint considerations regarding these policy areas. This was reflected in how Norges Bank was organized into a foreign exchange department and a credit policy department; two departments, each reinforced by their physical separation in different buildings, which operated almost independently of each other and which developed diverging views influenced by different specialized environments.

The diverging views in these two departments was a reflection of the tense conflict that existed between Deputy Governor Skånland and his superior, Governor Getz Wold. Getz Wold, a civil servant since the war, had been actively involved in the building of both the 'internal' and 'external' parts of the Norwegian postwar economic policy regime. Starting in the 1950s, he came to be especially prominent in external relations, as the authority from the European cooperation gave him unchallenged weight in the Norwegian landscape. Skånland, on his side, had been involved with building up the domestic policy regime as one of the Ministry of Finance's largest capacities. Whereas the principles which represented Getz Wold's position in the exchange rate debate were firmly rooted in the international cooperation, Skånland's principles were the same as those of the Ministry of Finance.

The exchange rate policy during the last four years prior to 1986 represented an extreme point in Norges Bank's development in becoming the government's bank, which had characterized the bank during the postwar era. The multilateral fixed exchange rate system (1945–73) was a remnant of the metal standard system in which Norges Bank had been born and functioned in the nineteenth century, and in which Norges Bank, in the periods the system had worked, had played a key role. The role of Norges Bank in ensuring foreign exchange rate stability was fundamentally changed with the onset of the Second World War and foreign exchange regulations. Up and until 1986, Norges Bank did not have the opportunity to influence the foreign currency reserves or balance of payments via the traditional monetary policy instruments. However, both Norges Bank's role in the foreign exchange market, as well as in foreign exchange regulation and in international foreign exchange cooperation, gave the bank a certain weight as an advisor on exchange rate discussions. Through Norges Bank's use of this weight to emphasize the requirements underlying the fixed exchange rate, Norges Bank maintained a role of a sort of independent memento, a role that, as long as the exchange rate stability was respected by politicians, also implied a sort of last source of independent influence over economic-political decisions. If this influence was limited prior to 1973, the degrading of the fixed krone exchange rate target contributed, in the years that followed, to its complete removal.

12

Downfall of the Regulatory System
and Triumph of the Market

The system of low, politically determined interest rates and regulated credit lasted a long time in Norway. It was introduced by the Labour Party, with support in leading trade union circles. The period of non-socialist government from 1965 to 1971 brought no change in the main lines of that policy, but showed that the low interest rate policy and regulation of credit had gained credence across the political spectrum.

The dominant expert community of university-trained economists had been important in providing the low interest rate policy with a scientific rationale and legitimacy. From the early 1970s onwards, more and more economists in the leading premise-setting circles broke away. They were mostly to be found in Norges Bank, and had ample contact with international peers. The subsidiary effects of the regulatory system were pushed to the fore. Besides, it was more than doubtful whether extensive interventions actually served the objectives of distribution and facilitating growth, which had originally motivated the policy. In the 1970s and 1980s, Norges Bank also began to develop instruments with a view to steering economic policy under freer market conditions. But governments of changing political hues were unwilling to let go of the low interest rate.

The oil price fall in 1986 brought an abrupt change in interest rate and credit policy. The government's tightening actions included the introduction of a more binding fixed exchange rate policy. The frequent recourse to corrective devaluations—which were likely employed in a governance system unable on its own to maintain balance in the domestic and external economy—was to be a thing of the past. Hence there was justification for using the interest rate as an ongoing instrument to stabilize the exchange rate. This task fell to Norges Bank, as had been the case up to the Second World War.

The transition to an independent, active interest rate policy on the part of the central bank was abrupt and came as a surprise. Barely a year before the collapse of the oil price, the Storting had passed a law that made Norges Bank—at any rate as seen in academic quarters—one of the least autonomous central banks in all of western Europe.[1] Ill-advised decisions, disagreements within the Executive Board, and the

---

[1] Probably the most influential measurement of central bank independence in various countries is Alex Cukierman, *Central Bank Strategy, Credibility, and Independence: Theory and Evidence* (MIT press, 1992). In a comparison of legal status, based on law provisions in the countries concerned at the end of the 1980s,

Norges Bank 1816–2016. Einar Lie, Oxford University Press (2020). © Norges Bank.
DOI: 10.1093/oso/9780198860013.001.0001

central bank's general low standing had impaired the bank's ability to follow through. Norges Bank's advice to the government in the years immediately prior to devaluation in 1986 had also contributed to the crisis-like situation in which the Norwegian economy now found itself. Hence it was the external situation, and in no sense an increase in government's and the public's recognition of the bank and its institutional legitimacy, that restored greater operative autonomy to Norges Bank.

An Ineffective Regulatory System

As the 1970s progressed, the monetary and credit policy regulatory regime came in for strong disapproval at Norges Bank. The system was criticized by the chairman of the Executive Board, Knut Getz Wold, in his annual addresses to the Supervisory Council. The deputy chair, Hermod Skånland, argued in favour of a softer approach whenever the opportunity arose. However, the weightiest arguments were to evolve in the ongoing work on credit regulation, in what from 1977 onwards was known as the bank's credit policy department. Among the leading economists in this department, doubts about regulation developed along with a belief in the market that was stronger here than elsewhere in the administration.[2]

These economists were also products of the University of Oslo, which in the early postwar period had provided important intellectual rationales for the view that a lasting low interest rate would have a favourable effect on the economy. Many of the department's economists had spent multi-year periods of secondment to international organizations where freer market conditions in money and capital markets were considered advantageous, and virtually taken for granted. In general we find less acceptance of the principle of a low, nominal interest rate among economists who received their training in the postwar period, and especially among those with broad-based international contacts.

The Credit Act assigned responsibility for regulation to the Ministry of Finance. However, Norges Bank became increasingly responsible for selecting and applying the regulatory measures taken to meet the targets set out in the credit budgets. It was in large measure Norges Bank that proposed how the bond investment obligation and liquidity and supplementary reserve requirements should be applied in concrete terms, and that closely monitored credit institutions' compliance with those measures.

Cukierman ranked Norges Bank as the least independent central bank in the developed countries (p. 382), and as the third least independent in the world, after the central banks of Yugoslavia and Poland (381). See also Tobias Straumann, *Fixed Ideas of Money: Small States and Exchange Rate Regimes in Twentieth-century Europe* (Cambridge University Press, 2010), 180–1.

[2] Gunhild J. Ecklund, *Kredittpolitikken som redskap i den samfunnsøkonomiske styringen fra 1965 til 1980* (Universitetet i Oslo, 1995); Thomas Nordbø Berg, *Mellom politikk og marked? En studie av Pengepolitisk avdeling i Norges Bank, IMF og spørsmålet om den norske penge-og kredittpolitikken ca. 1965–1980* (Universitetet i Bergen, 2011).

The low interest rate, and the high credit demand that accompanied it, made it chronically difficult to curb and to steer the supply of credit. So long as borrowers wanted loans, many commercial and savings banks chose to accommodate them, even though high reserve requirements were liable to render the loans unprofitable. The lending quotas set out in the government's annual credit budgets were under constant pressure. In order to keep lending within the limits set, the authorities were on many occasions compelled to apply the most powerful policy instruments—the supplementary reserve requirement and the bond investment obligation. These measures were unpopular among the banks and politicians alike. Indeed, Norges Bank considered that the supplementary reserve requirement froze the competitive situation among the banks, thereby impairing the credit system's ability to function efficiently.

On a more fundamental level, it became clear that the low interest rate regime had consequences diametrically opposed to those on which the rationale for the objective of a low interest rate had been based. One such consequence was a shift in private credit institutions' lending *away* from the purposes which the politicians wished to prioritize through a low interest rate. Naturally enough, interest rates on such unregulated lending also rose. Moreover, a survey carried out in 1977 confirmed a suspicion that the low borrowing rates primarily benefited high-income groups of the population.[3] This was partly because high-income individuals had ample access to loans, but in particular because the Norwegian tax system allowed interest expenses to be deducted from gross income for income determination purposes. Thus, given the markedly progressive tax system, the highest earners qualified for substantial interest expense deductions, while lower earners qualified for relatively lower tax-related reliefs on their loans. This tore the ground away from much of the low interest rate argumentation seen in the immediate postwar period. In distribution terms credit was viewed as something allotted through various mechanisms *by* those who had built up substantial savings—loosely associated with wealthy capitalists—*to* persons who themselves had few assets, and needed to borrow. The low interest rate would thus appear propitious from a distributional viewpoint, in addition to financing sound long-term objectives.

In addition, the emergence of a 'grey', unregulated loan market became an increasingly conspicuous feature of the credit system. The low, regulated lending rates (which produced a negative real interest rate given the strong price growth in the early 1970s) incentivized the banks to grant loans of a type that were not subject to regulation. A plethora of new forms of lending and credit intermediaries had emerged.[4] Two committees concluded that the more the government authorities attempted to force on the credit market conditions other than those that the market itself would accept, the larger the unregulated market would become.

---

[3] Leif Eide and Einar Forsbak, *Norsk rentepolitikk*, Norges Banks skriftserie (Norges Bank, 1977).

[4] NOU 1974: 1, Finansieringsselskaper og låneformidling (Oslo 1974). Thomas Nordbø Berg, Harald Bøhn, and Christoffer Kleivset, 'Fra regulering til marked. Et dokumentasjonsnotat om Norges Bank og utviklingen av penge-, kreditt og valutapolitikken 1965–1990' (Norges Bank, 2012), 39.

A final reason for Norges Bank's displeasure with the regulatory system was doubt as to whether the low interest rates and the associated regulatory measures had contributed to higher economic growth. This doubt was also widely expressed among Ministry of Finance officials. The exceptionally high level of investment for which the credit policy of the 1950s and 1960s had laid the basis had failed to raise Norway above the average rate of growth in the OECD. The regulatory system removed the resource-allocating effect that market-determined interest rates would otherwise have had.[5] In addition, artificially low interest rates, along with tax rules that strongly favoured households and individual borrowers at the expense of business and industry, appeared to have resulted in overinvestment in housing.[6]

Money Makes its Reappearance

Norges Bank believed it would be better if the politicians allowed the market to play a bigger role in the pricing and allocation of credit than was the case in the 1970s. Intermediate solutions, involving a measure of regulation and a measure of market forces, were advised against.[7] But if the politicians removed both the low interest rate objective and the goal of political control of credit through the credit budget, what operational objectives should monetary policy in that case be aligned with? Based on historical experience, one might believe the answer to be the krone exchange rate. But that was not to be, in the first instance. In the first half of the 1980s, Norges Bank sought rather to realize a given, politically determined target figure for what the bank termed the 'domestic liquidity supply to the non-financial private sector'.[8] This would divert attention away from the postwar object of regulation in the financial system—the end product being credit to households and firms—and focus to a larger degree on a more controllable aggregate: the overall supply of credit.

The proposed new target should be viewed as a Norwegian variant of money supply management. 'Domestic liquidity supply' was derived from a money supply concept defined in much the same way as M2 in US monetary statistics.[9] The idea of exercising control by way of the growth in the money supply arose out of a long-term project at Norges Bank where the money supply was employed as a statistical variable and indicator of the effects of economic policy. With a basis in the bank's own accounts, statistics were compiled on overall liquidity among banks and other sectors as early as

---

[5] Einar Magnussen, 'Norsk penge- og kredittpolitik—sterke og svake sider', Norges Bank, Penger og Kreditt 1, no. 3 (1973).

[6] A description of the tax system and its significance for resource allocation and monetary and credit policy is given in Hermod Skånland, Doktriner og økonomisk styring: et tilbakeblikk, vol. 36 (Norges Bank, 2004), 50–69, 76–7.

[7] The rationale is provided by Eide and Forsbak, Norsk rentepolitikk, 16.

[8] 'Domestic liquidity supply to the non-financial private sector' was first proposed in Norges Bank's letter of 6 November 1981 to the Ministry of Finance concerning fiscal and credit policy in 1982, reprinted in Penger og Kreditt, no. 4, 1981, 318–22.

[9] Institutional factors have always made it difficult to define a money supply concept that is identical across all countries; see for example Terje Prøsch, 'Om budsjettering og regulering av pengetilgangen i Norge', Penger og kreditt 3, no. 1 (1975).

the mid-1950s onwards.[10] From 1971, Norges Bank published monthly overviews of various monetary statistics of which the money supply was the most aggregated. Figures for the 1970s showed that movements in this aggregate explained the trend in inflation and the external economy better than the estimates set out in the national budgets.[11] The money supply concept was introduced at an early stage in the work on Norges Bank's model for computing developments in the credit market.[12]

In tandem with its development of statistical overviews and relationships, Norges Bank took steps in developing tools with which to operate. From the end of the 1970s those tools gradually took on a more market-oriented character at the bank, a process geared to the ambition of liquidity management should the low interest rate policy be dispensed with. To this end, Norges Bank started out from the arrangements it had developed through the 1960s to enable commercial and savings banks to take out short-term liquidity loans with the bank in a more convenient and automatic manner than by discounting bills as in the old days. The first short-term borrowing arrangement that did not require the physical deposit of securities in Norges Bank was introduced in connection with the Credit Act in 1965. Because the private banks by various means learned to misuse the arrangements in order to increase their own lending by a greater margin than assumed in the credit budget, Norges Bank had to revise the arrangement time and again. From the start of the 1970s, automatic loans (A loans) were based on lending quotas set by Norges Bank—'tranches' corresponding to a given percentage of the lending bank's total assets. The interest rates rose for each tranche employed.

In parallel with this, Norges Bank developed an interbank market in Norwegian kroner which enabled banks with a liquidity surplus to lend to other banks with Norges Bank as a kind of clearing house. However, the dimensions of this purely krone-denominated market remained small. As early as the end of the 1970s—thanks to changes in foreign exchange regulation and increased oil tax receipts in 1978-9—an increasingly large portion of the redistribution of krone liquidity between the banks was effected by means of 'currency swaps' whereby kroner were exchanged for dollars for periods of varying duration.

The collapse of the fixed exchange rate system in 1973 and the transition to floating rates between several of the major currencies soon brought wider, more rapid movements in foreign exchange markets. When Norges Bank moved to defend the exchange rate by buying or selling kroner, it had substantial impacts on bank liquidity. This liquidity laid the basis for lending growth and had to be offset by credit policy measures that were faster working than the provisions of the Credit Act. Norges Bank started to intervene in the forward and swap markets. The bank introduced in addition market papers with a varying coupon. This instrument could be sold to

---

[10] Svein Gjedrem, 'Lividitetsstatistikk og -prognoser', *Penger og kreditt* 2, no. 4 (1976).

[11] Magnussen, 'Norsk penge- og kredittpolitik—sterke og svake sider'; Einar Forsbak, 'Pengemengde og pengemengdeanalyser', *Penger og kreditt* 3 (1976). Memo LTE/Fag (to the policy instrument group) 30 August 1982, file 420.4 'Policy Instrument Use 1981-83 A', Norges Bank Archive.

[12] Prøsch, 'Om budsjettering og regulering av pengetilgangen i Norge'.

commercial and savings banks in order to rapidly mop up liquidity, and served to strengthen and institutionalize the interbank market. Viewed collectively, market paper along with forward and swap transactions meant that by the start of the 1980s Norges Bank's abiding dream of engaging in open market operations appeared by and large to be fulfilled.

The in-house work on money supply analysis at Norges Bank from the end of the 1960s was undoubtedly encouraged and influenced by the growing international interest in monetary aggregates. Indeed, at the IMF headquarters in Washington, DC, where several of Norges Bank's subsequent leading economists were deployed in the 1960s, money supply concepts were at centre stage in the analysis of various countries' economic policies.[13] Extensive academic theorizing, empirical research, and debate about the significance of the money supply were also a feature of the US in the 1960s. The monetarists singled out growth in the money supply as the main explanation for the higher inflations rates. The best known among them, Milton Friedman, was awarded the Nobel Memorial Prize in Economic Sciences in 1976. In the 1970s and early 1980s several countries, in the first instance West Germany and the US, opted for growth in the money supply as the operational target with a view to bringing inflation under control, and in 1979 money supply management was recommended by the OECD.[14]

Hence when Norges Bank proposed to influence the money supply by way of the 'domestic liquidity supply to the non-financial private sector', it prompted some observers—as Skånland pointed out in one of his leaders in *Economic Bulletin*—to ask whether Norges Bank was advocating a Norwegian variant of monetarism.[15] 'Monetarism' was a controversial term at the end of the 1970s and start of the 1980s, and was regarded somewhat dubious in Norway. It was above all associated with Milton Friedman's heavy emphasis on steady money supply growth as virtually the *only* factor that government authorities should focus on in economic policy. Friedman's market liberal conviction, and what was seen as a breakthrough for his ideas in the US and UK in the early 1980s, aroused little enthusiasm in Norway. There is no doubt that Norges Bank, in its growing interest in the money supply and its various components, was—in common with most other central banks and with professional economists as a whole—*influenced* by the new orientation of monetary policy thinking which Friedman had headed up as far back as the 1950s.[16] However, the target for the domestic credit supply was by no means a rule for money supply growth of the type Friedman recommended. Nor did the economists at Norges Bank see themselves as 'monetarists', either in an economic theory or possibly a more

---

[13] Jacques J Polak, 'The IMF Monetary Model: A Hardy Perennial', *Finance and Development* 34, no. 4 (1997).

[14] Niels Thygesen, 'Penge- og kreditpolitiske udviklingstendenser i andre land', *Sosialøkonomen* 10 (1980).

[15] Espen Søilen, *Fra frischianisme til keynesianisme: en studie av norsk økonomisk politikk i lys av økonomisk teori 1945–1980* (NHH, 1998), discusses whether Skånland might be called a monetarist at the start of the 1980s. He, like others, finds no basis for doing so, and ends up placing Skånland close to Paul Samuelson, known as a Keynesian economist in the US, and his view of monetary policy.

[16] See in particular Forsbak, 'Pengemengde og pengemengdeanalyser'.

political-ideological sense, but as decidedly sober-minded practitioners.[17] 'We believe money is important', Skånland emphasized, 'but talking about money doesn't make one a monetarist'.[18]

The salient point in this context is that proposing a monetary variable such as the 'domestic liquidity supply to the non-financial private sector' as an operational target implied—possibly even more so than a target for money supply growth in, for example, the US—a marked upward adjustment of monetary policy's potential significance relative to fiscal policy and in relation to the role monetary policy had played thus far in postwar Norway. Setting a target for the 'domestic liquidity supply to the non-financial private sector' implied a changeable interest rate, one of whose missions was to counter—if necessary by raising the interest rate level—the effect of an overly expansionary fiscal policy.[19]

But the stumbling block was interest rate policy. For a period at the start of the 1980s, Norges Bank attempted to put its policy instruments on a more market-oriented footing. Through forward and swap transactions, use of market paper, and adjustments to the borrowing facilities, money market rates were forced upwards in order to curb lending by the private banks.[20] However, the interest rate declarations from the government prevented the high interest rate level from affecting lending rates and curbing demand for that portion of bank lending that was not subject to regulation. Foreign currency loans to business and industry, mediated by Norwegian commercial banks, also increased markedly in this period. Further influence in this direction was stopped by the government's interest rate cuts in 1983 and 1984. Open market operations nonetheless enabled the banks and Norges Bank to establish arrangements and gain experience of a market-based monetary policy, which supported the idea that overall liquidity could be established as a target for monetary policy.

Half-hearted Attempt at Reform

In the political and institutional environment in which Norges Bank operated there was, as far back as the start of the 1970s, a degree of acceptance that Norway's interest rate policy was ripe for reform. In summer 1978 the government appointed an *interest rate commission* presided over by Central Bureau of Statistics' director and former

---

[17] This also emerges clearly in the memo for Norges Bank's programme for 1982, in the target for domestic credit supply. LTE/Fag, to the policy instrument group, 30 August 1982, file 240.4, 'Policy Instrument Use 1981–83 A', NB.

[18] Hermod Skånland, 'Styring og likviditeten', *Penger og kreditt* 4 (1981).

[19] In retrospect Norges Bank could be thought to have overstated the leeway available to monetary policy. The government retained its official objective of a fixed exchange rate, which could be thought to constrain the use of interest rate policy in liquidity management. However, as we saw in Chapter 11, capital outflows and inflows were still subject to some control. It was not as clear then as it is now that this control rapidly deteriorated from the end of the 1970s. The transition to a currency basket system in exchange rate policy in 1978 featuring 'secret' intervention limits, possibly also periodic exchange rate adjustments, and may also have given a greater sense of scope for action. Cf. Thygesen, 'Penge- og kreditpolitiske udviklingstendenser i andre land'.

[20] Skånland, *Doktriner og økonomisk styring: et tilbakeblikk*, vol. 36, 42–3.

Labour Party finance minister, Petter Jakob Bjerve, with Skånland as Norges Bank's representative, which was to review Norwegian postwar interest rate policy and assess it in light of the objectives the government authorities had set for it. The commission was also to recommend 'fundamental guidelines for the interest rate policy in the years immediately ahead'. A sizeable, thoroughgoing recommendation was to hand in January 1980. In its recommendation the commission asserted, despite certain reservations related to the tax rules, 'that an interest rate determined in a sufficiently competitive market will on the whole have favourable effects on monetary and credit policy management and on resource utilisation'.[21]

The response in political quarters was lukewarm. True, the government attempted to some degree to act on the commission's recommendations, declaring in 1980 that the bond market was to be liberalized. However, the government soon proved unable to accept in full the consequences of such a policy. Interest rates on the central government's own loans were not revised upwards. Private credit institutions (which were still subject to a bond investment obligation) accordingly flocked to new, private bonds carrying higher interest. This development threatened both state bank funding and the credit budget's target figures. Instead of accepting the prevailing market conditions, the Ministry of Finance responded with more regulation. Supplementary reserve requirements and bond investment obligations were stepped up.

Ministry of Finance officials fully shared Norges Bank's concern regarding the fiscal policy trend since 1975 and the need for 'genuine demand-regulating measures'. Many of them agreed that monetary policy strictures and raised interest rates might be a way to achieve a better balance in the economy. But the Ministry of Finance did *not* want to weaken its overarching responsibility for coordinating fiscal and monetary policy based on an overall plan. Managing monetary policy was the prerogative of the Ministry of Finance, and isolated interim objectives could not be delegated to Norges Bank. Norges Bank's increased emphasis on money supply targets was at times supplemented by reference to the central bank's greater resilience to political pressure. However, such notions as to the advantages of an 'independent central bank' were rejected by Svein Gjedrem, new head of the monetary policy section in the Ministry of Finance as from 1979 (and central bank governor from 1999 onwards). 'The underlying argument from Norges Bank that political re-election is an important motive in the political decision process should not be accepted', he asserted.[22] Although Gjedrem had back in the day been brought in from Norges Bank's credit policy department, he clearly had little sympathy for Norges Bank's new aspirations.

---

[21] NOU 1980: 4, *Rentepolitikk*, 14; see also Skånland, *Doktriner og økonomisk styring: et tilbakeblikk*, 54 et seq.
[22] Quoted from Einar Lie and Christian Venneslan, *Over evne: Finansdepartementet 1965–1992* (Pax forlag, 2010), 348.

An Institution with Impaired Standing and Authority

Norges Bank was still left with little independent scope for action in monetary and credit policy. However, there is much to suggest that other factors at the start of the 1980s also played a part in the bank being taken less seriously as the government's adviser than it would have liked. Einar Magnussen, director of the monetary policy department since 1970, had left the bank in 1973 in favour of the Ministry of Trade, where he acted as a government minister for a time for the Labour Party. In the mid-1980s he returned to preside over an organization project. It was clear, Magnussen asserted in an early memo on the position of the organization, 'that our influence as adviser and instigator in policy areas is declining'.[23]

Norges Bank's gravest problem lay in the Executive Board. As we touched on in Chapter 11, relations between the chairman, Knut Getz Wold, and the deputy chair, Hermod Skånland, steadily worsened over the course of the 1970s and 1980s. The problems were in part personal, but were intensified and sustained by the shift in exchange rate policy from the end of the 1970s. Getz Wold's illness also played a part. The personal relationship between the chair and deputy chair led to awkward confrontations regarding the most trivial issues and weakened motivation both within and outside Norges Bank to draw the Executive Board into more processes than strictly necessary.

However, internal decisions with substantial and untoward consequences were also made in the period. The greatest and most untoward were undoubtedly related to the construction of the new headquarters in Oslo. A lack of office space had been a problem since the war, which Norges Bank had resolved by purchasing new premises elsewhere in the city. In 1971 the process of planning a building in tune with the times that could house the entire central bank eventually began. The foundation work at Bankplassen in Oslo, only a stone's throw from the old headquarters, started in 1979, and in August 1982 the foundation stone was laid. However, what should have been an institutional boost and vitamin injection proved to be virtually the opposite.

Norges Bank succeeded in constructing a modern, majestic, signal edifice with ample space for its entire staff.[24] However, the success cost an enormous amount of money. In 1975 the bank had put the construction costs at NOK 460 million (converted to 1984 kroner). When a government-appointed investigative commission took stock in 1990, the final price was set at NOK 2.5 billion (in 1984 kroner).[25] Even though allowance was made for expansions of the building area through the period, the commission concluded that the cost plan had been overrun to the tune of 188 per cent.[26] The causes of the cost overrun were manifold, and we shall not examine them in detail here. A number of complications involving choice of site and construction

---

[23] Changes in Norges Bank's organization, ORG/Mag/LTF, 4 January 1985, file 'Organisation Project 1984–85', box 003.4 Organisation Project, NB.

[24] *Byggekunst* (architecture magazine) 5 June 1987.

[25] NOU 1990: 25, *Norges Banks nye hovedsete* (Norges offentlige utredninger 1990).   [26] Ibid., 117.

process arose that had been difficult to foresee from Norges Bank's vantage point. However, much of the responsibility must be laid at the door of the construction management. In the planning, organization, and ongoing follow-up, many channels of influence were opened for actors with cost-driving requirements and recommendations. Little was done to ensure that clear-cut cost limits were formulated and abided by.[27]

The 'building scandal' was to some extent the upshot of general problems related to cost management at Norges Bank. When a German economist, Roland Vaubel, in 1997, compared the number of staff at all central banks across the world, he found that Norges Bank, based on certain criteria, was among the most overpopulated central banks in the Western world. Considering the substantial growth in employee numbers in the 1970s and 1980s, a period in which investments were made in new, efficiency-promoting technology for processing data, banknote production, and much else, and in which the tasks of the regional branches were growing fewer and fewer, this finding is not remarkable. Vaubel also found a clear statistical correlation between the number of staff and central banks' freedom to appoint their own personnel.[28] True, Norges Bank had introduced an operating budget in 1975. But the operating budgets were set up as the bank's administration itself saw fit, and the expenses were met out of the bank's profit without external involvement. The fact that the bank's self-management only produced such extreme effects in the 1970s and 1980s is probably in part due to an ineffectual Executive Board, and in part to the practice, initiated by Brofoss, of assigning administrative decisions to lower levels in the system.

The 'building scandal' proved to be what today would be termed a reputation problem for Norges Bank and in particular for Hermod Skånland, chairman of the building committee from 1981 onwards. As early as the autumn of 1983 the press began to show an interest in the building, with a particular focus on expensive details and choice of materials.[29] The erection of 'Uncle Hermod's money bin' came in for intense ridicule. In the public arena Skånland preached caution and moderation in a period of strong growth in investment and consumption in the Norwegian economy, and several cartoonists, then and for many years thereafter, found effective ways to contrast his apparent profligacy on his own institution's behalf with his public calls for savings to be made.

The 'building scandal' evidently aroused wider public interest in how Norges Bank had utilized its traditional autonomy in its in-house management.[30] Investigative journalists let loose. For example, a number of newspapers revealed in summer 1984 that mortgages granted to the bank's own staff were on terms more favourable than ordinary bank mortgages.[31] Moreover, Norges Bank's foreign exchange holdings were

---

[27] NOU (Norwegian Official Report) 1990, 25.
[28] Roland Vaubel, 'The Bureaucratic and Partisan Behaviour of Independent Central Banks: German and International Evidence', *European Journal of Political Economy* 13 (1997).
[29] 'Frontage at a cost of NOK 100 million', *VG*, 19 October 1983; 'Norges Bank sceptical of buying Norwegian materials', *Aftenposten* 23 November 1983.
[30] 'Deficient information on the bank's in-house management', article by E. Holte in *Aftenposten* 30 July 1984.
[31] 'Cheap mortgages at Norges Bank', *VG*, 22 June 1984; see also the *Vårt Land* newspaper of the same date.

growing strongly and earning good returns. When the campaign 'Yes to work' assembled 2,000 demonstrators in front of the Storting (parliament building) in December 1983, it was demanded that NOK 3 billion of Norges Bank's foreign exchange reserves should be spent on measures to counter unemployment.[32]

Although the Ministry of Finance had been closely involved in the decision to set in train the construction of a new head office, the ministry had little say in the actual building process. Responsibility for the use of the central bank's policy instruments had been definitively assigned to the Ministry of Finance after the war, but the bank's independent role in managing its own finances was retained. Hence the habitually vigilant and savings-minded Ministry of Finance had no say in the institution's budgets. In line with customary practice and legislation, this oversight was left to the bank's Supervisory Council, whose composition and remit were virtually unchanged since 1816. The Storting had been informed and indirectly involved in the decision via the Supervisory Council's resolution to build the new headquarters, but had in its capacity as legislative (and budgetary) authority passed no resolution on the matter. Once the spending became a public theme in the course of 1983, many observers were probably surprised by the large sums spent by a public institution without the Storting having appropriated a single krone. Who was ultimately responsible? It was—declared the Storting in 1991—the entire institution, but above all the rather secluded and uninfluential supervisory board that was to blame.[33] The Supervisory Council chair, Kristian Asdahl, stepped down.[34]

Now an old skeleton, the Hambro Scheme (see page 204), also fell out of the cupboard. The Bergen shipowner Hilmar Reksten had in 1976 been reported to the police (by Norges Bank among others) for breach of the foreign exchange regulations and the tax rules; he was charged and subsequently acquitted on his deathbed. In spring 1984 the report on the Reksten affair was up for consideration by the Storting. The leftist newspaper *Klassekampen* decided to investigate the government authorities' relationship to Reksten and quickly learned of the arrangement under which Norwegian foreign exchange holdings were used to subsidize Norwegian shipowners, including Reksten. Norges Bank's 'secret shipowner loans' were splashed over the newspaper's front page, followed by a number of critical commentaries over the course of the spring. In due course the affair was covered by further newspapers, leading to finance minister Presthus having to field questions in the Storting about decisions taken by Norges Bank almost twenty years previously.[35]

---

[32] '2000 march on the Storting', *Aftenposten*, 10 December 1983.

[33] Standing Committee on Finance and Economic Affairs' Report no. 2 to the Storting, 1991–1992: Consideration by the Storting of the recommendation of the Standing Committee on Finance and Economic Affairs' concerning the report of the investigative committee, 21 October 1991, *Proceedings in the Storting*, 1991–2: 276.

[34] Consideration by the Storting of the recommendation of the Standing Committee on Finance and Economic Affairs' concerning the report of the investigative committee, 21 October 1991, *Proceedings in the Storting*, 1991–2, 276.

[35] *Klassekampen* 10 April 1984. The blame for the initiative was laid largely at the door of the now deceased Erik Brofoss.

Central Bank Legislation Behind the Times?

The Willoch government's interest in the central bank's formal position was evidently limited.[36] However, the many controversies involving the bank in the 1980s meant that Norges Bank was a political problem for the government, compelling it to expedite the process of adopting new legislation. It was primarily the devaluations in 1982 that, directly and indirectly, moved the issue up the agenda. Knut Getz Wold's conduct in connection with the Executive Board's consideration of this matter (see page 224) prompted the government to begin to look into the formalities of Norges Bank's position. To what extent could the bank frustrate the government based on the act currently in force? The growth in Norges Bank's foreign exchange holdings, and the increase in its surplus that resulted from the devaluation of the krone and the concomitant increase of the krone value of the holding, were equally important. 'Unfortunately Ryssdal now has to get his commission moving', the finance minister noted in a personal comment in spring 1983. 'This is little short of a scandal, in particular now that the surpluses are so enormous.'[37]

Rolv Ryssdal, the chief justice of the Supreme Court, chaired the slow working commission that prepared a new law proposal for Norges Bank. The commission was appointed in the 1960s and the law proposal surfaced in September 1983. In large measure, it appeared to build on a draft prepared as early as in 1972, envisaged as tying Norges Bank more closely to the government and setting the stage for a more politically controlled monetary policy than the law dating from 1892 had done. This was in keeping with what broadly speaking had been the prevailing view among politicians and civil servants, and in Norges Bank, as early as the 1950s, 1960s, and 1970s. Aspects of Norges Bank's singular institutional status would, it is true, be carried forward. An objects clause confirmed the bank's role as executor of and adviser on monetary, credit, and foreign exchange policy. The freedom it enjoyed in terms of managing its own affairs was preserved. However, it was also made perfectly clear that the bank was obliged to comply with the politically determined guidelines for monetary and credit policy and to submit important decisions to the Ministry of Finance prior to adoption. Furthermore, the government was assigned the right of instruction, i.e. the opportunity to adopt decisions regarding the bank's activity and thus, if necessary, to overrule the bank's management team. All in all these provisions brought Norges Bank more tightly into the ambit of central government control than had the 1892 law, and in a firmer and more clear-cut manner than was customary in comparable countries.[38] True, the commission wished, through the strict requirements as to the form that such instruction could take, to *strengthen* Norges Bank's independent

---

[36] Lie and Venneslan, *Over evne: Finansdepartementet 1965–1992*, 338–9.

[37] Handwritten note by Rolf Presthus dated 24 April 1983, in folder '401.1 Act on Norges Bank: General, Ryssdal Commission 1984', box Da-0164, FD.

[38] Norges Bank's submission regarding NOU (Norwegian Official Report) 1983: 39 'Act Relating to Norges Bank and the Monetary System', submission of 27 April 1984, printed as Norges Bank's Occasional Paper 14, 17; see also Hermod Skånland, *The Central Bank and Political Authorities in Some Industrial Countries*, vol. 13, Norges Bank's Occasional Paper (Norges Bank, 1984).

position in relation to the ministry.[39] The government had to announce and justify any overruling—not, as previously, expect the bank to respond to current signals.[40] The Executive Board was replaced by a seven-strong Executive Board, all of whom were to be appointed by the government.

Although the law commission's recommendation was close to a Norwegian postwar consensus on how a central bank statute should look, Norges Bank in 1984 was dissatisfied. This was due to the new ideas that had evolved in the bank over the previous decade with regard to what objectives monetary policy, ideally speaking, should pursue and to the central bank's role in that regime. The Executive Board' formal statement rested on these objectives, and pointed out that new international trends imposed requirements on the central bank institution that differed from those imposed by the postwar credit and foreign exchange regulations.[41] In a copious review of central bank legislation in other countries, Skånland concluded that the law commission's proposal pointed in all essentials in precisely the opposite direction to that of the international tendency, namely to allow the central bank greater independent scope for action.[42] However, such objections were given little weight. When the bill reached the Storting for consideration in April 1985, the Ryssdal Commission's draft, including a few minor amendments by the Ministry of Finance, was adopted unanimously.

The Dam is Removed

By the time the new Central Bank Act was adopted, the government's liberalization policy had begun to undermine the assumptions regarding the political control of monetary policy for which the Central Bank Act sought to pave the way. The supplementary reserve requirement, which was designed to make it prohibitively expensive to breach the government's limits on lending, was dispensed with from 1 January 1984, and the bond investment obligation was scaled back. At the same time the low interest rate policy stood firm and was in fact reinforced by a rate reduction shortly afterwards. That decision triggered hefty lending growth, which simply accelerated into 1985 and 1986, completely undermining both the credit budget and the wider economic policy programme set out in the national budgets.

The policy relaxation has been discussed by a number of economists, historians, and governmental committees as a first mover leading to the major banking crisis in

---

[39] NOU (Norwegian Official Report) 1983: 39, 226: see also Carsten Smith, 'Norges Banks rettslige selvstendighet', in *Stabilitet og langsiktighet: festskrift til Hermod Skånland* (Aschehoug, 1994), 96–7.

[40] Skånland, *Doktriner og økonomisk styring: et tilbakeblikk*, vol. 36, 89; Hermod Skånland, 'Tilbakeblikk på 20 år med ny sentralbanklov', *Penger og kreditt* 3 (2005).

[41] Hermod Skånland, 'Ryssdalutvalget er for sterkt bundet til tradisjonen', *Sosialøkonomen* 6 (1984).

[42] True, the right of instruction could, in light of post-war practice, also be viewed as *strengthening* Norges Bank's position vis-à-vis the Ministry of Finance inasmuch as that right would be pursuant to the act ensuring that the bank's point of view was made known; Skånland, *Doktriner og økonomisk styring: et tilbakeblikk*, 84–5.

the early 1990s.[43] The rationale behind a deregulation marking the complete removal of quantitative controls on lending while the price of credit was kept artificially low (and the tax system continued to favour high borrowing) is complex and intricate. A brief overview follows, with the central bank's thinking and actions to the fore.

The non-socialist election victory and the formation of a Conservative government under Kåre Willoch in autumn 1981 had sparked hope of policy realignment at Norges Bank. True, the Conservative Party was dependent on cooperation with two centrist parties, the Christian Democratic Party and the Centre Party, which had joined the government in 1983. Moreover, the Conservatives had not explicitly committed themselves to deregulating the credit market or to realigning economic policy. Even so, several items on their programme—such as less emphasis on incomes policy and greater emphasis on combating inflation and the desirability of less state control of credit—could be expected to be reflected in a new policy at some point.[44]

Less than one month after the election, Norges Bank ventured, at the initiative of Skånland and the credit policy department, to gain support for a rapid realignment. By letter to the Ministry of Finance in November 1981, the central bank declared its intention to use open market operations to maintain overall growth in the 'domestic liquidity supply to the non-financial private sector' of between NOK 35 and 39 billion in 1982. A larger liquidity supply, particularly in connection with an overly expansionary fiscal policy, would of necessity prompt Norges Bank to tighten liquidity, resulting in a higher interest rate level. To achieve this, Norges Bank could no longer maintain a low, politically determined interest rate.[45] The target figure, NOK 35–9 billion, was taken from the national budget for 1982 and entailed a tightening in percentage terms over the previous year.[46] The target proposed by the bank was in that sense determined by the politicians themselves. Had the advice been followed it would nonetheless have meant a clear break with practical policy.

The move was summarily rejected. The responsibility for interest rate setting and credit management rested with the government.[47] The political assumptions appeared rather to move the government in the *opposite* direction. With a new interest rate declaration in summer 1983, Norges Bank was instructed, contrary to its recommendations and contrary to the intention of aligning the interest rate with market conditions, to *lower* the interest rate in the money market by one percentage point. The rate reduction was demanded by the supporting parties as condition for joining the government.[48]

---

[43] NOU 1992: 30 Bankkrisen (Norwegian Official Reports, 1992); Bankkrisekommisjonen, *Dokument nr 17 (1997–98) Rapport til Stortinget fra kommisjonen som ble nedsatt av Stortinget for å gjennomgå ulike årsaksforhold knyttet til bankkrisen*, Stortinget (Oslo, 1998); Thorvald G Moe, Jon A Solheim, and Bent Vale, *The Norwegian Banking Crisis* (Norges Bank, 2004).

[44] Conservative Party programme 1981–5, cf. Hallvard Notaker, *Høyres historie 1975–2005: Opprør og moderasjon* (Cappelen Damm, 2012); the apparent impact of these expectations on Norges Bank is also indicated by Hermod Skånland, 'Likviditetspolitikk—rentepolitikk', *Penger og kreditt* 2 (1982).

[45] Letter to the Ministry of Finance, 6 November 1981, Documentation file.

[46] Annual report and accounts 1981, 27.   [47] See Skånland, 'Likviditetspolitikk—rentepolitikk'.

[48] Skånland, *Doktriner og økonomisk styring: et tilbakeblikk*, 45.

For its part the Ministry of Finance was working on a separate strategy regarding how the credit policy management system should be relaxed. Whereas Norges Bank wished to start by freeing up the interest rate, the Ministry of Finance wished to start by tightening fiscal policy. Only if the 'liquidity supply to the non-financial private sector' from the government authorities was brought down sufficiently could private credit be allowed to increase by the same margin at the prevailing interest rate level. If credit was freed up while government-supplied liquidity remained as high as it was, the result would be far stronger liquidity growth than was warrantable in the present situation. However, this approach won little support in practice. Legislative treatment of the government budgets for the years 1982–5 pulled, instead, in the opposite direction.[49]

The decision regarding the period of deregulation came about specifically upon the recommendation of the Norwegian Bankers' Association and Norges Bank. The government was no doubt in favour of deregulating the credit market, but not for the time being in favour of raising the interest rate. For that reason Norges Bank, but also Skånland personally in several memos sent directly to the finance minister, recommended that Norges Bank should hold down interest rates through its open market operations.[50] As was pointed out by Ministry of Finance officials, this was a risky policy.[51] It could have led to a larger liquidity supply than envisaged in the national budget. Without supplementary reserve requirements and the bond investment obligation, the Ministry of Finance's hands would have been virtually tied in such a situation. The only way to halt an utterly unwarrantable growth in liquidity, warned the Ministry of Finance's economics department, would be to raise interest rates. Skånland acknowledged this, but with a different sign. For him, liberalization entailed a secure path towards an interest rate that was also flexible in an *upward* direction. In a more deregulated system an interest rate increase had to come at some point, either because developments were more benign than the authorities had expected, or more difficult than they had feared.[52]

However, in relation to the Ministry of Finance, Norges Bank emphasized that conditions were such that it would *not* be necessary to raise interest rates for a long while.[53] True, the credit budgets would be overrun, but in the first instance by loans in the grey market being moved to the banks' balance sheets. The operating target was of necessity the 'domestic liquidity supply to the non-financial private sector', and Norges Bank did not envisage this increasing in the short term. The government evidently accepted the bank's line of thinking and started the process of deregulation.[54]

[49] Lie and Venneslan, *Over evne: Finansdepartementet 1965–1992*, 319–24.
[50] Norges Bank's letter of 12 December 1983 to the Ministry of Finance concerning the use of credit policy instruments in 1984: our credit policy strategy, memo to the finance minister from Governor Skånland, 4 April 1984, box 26 EE; see also Lie and Venneslan, *Over evne: Finansdepartementet 1965–1992*.
[51] Memo, comments on Norges Bank's programme for controlling bank lending, to the minister from the economics department, 27 February 1984 (SG/GK) box 26, EE.
[52] Hermod Skånland, 'Hva slags ekspansjon?', *Penger og kreditt* 2 (1984): 4.
[53] Norges Bank's letter of 12 December 1983 to the Ministry of Finance concerning the use of credit policy instruments in 1984. Printed in *Penger og Kreditt* (4) 1984.
[54] Lie and Venneslan, *Over evne: Finansdepartementet 1965–1992*.

Norges Bank's advice was politically attractive, above all because it paved the way for both liberalization and continued low interest rates in the short term without the government needing to tighten the budget. But the consequences of the policy proved problematic. For the commercial and savings banks, the removal of the loan-regulating supplementary reserve requirement was contemporaneous with a move to make it easier for banks to establish new branches—the starting signal for a struggle to win market shares and to position themselves for a new liberal order.[55] More than at any time previously, expansion was in itself of such strategic importance for the banks that they were willing to accept losses in order to grow. Business enlargements, start-ups, and aggressive marketing of new loans contributed to pushing up lending figures.[56]

As such, removing the supplementary reserve requirement and the bond investment obligation constrained the Ministry of Finance's opportunities to curb lending effectively with the help of the Credit Act. However, in contrast to what Skånland's plan had premised, this constraint was not compensated for by freeing up the interest rate weapon. Norges Bank was still obliged to maintain the interest rate level desired by the government. In the summer of 1984 lending rates and the interbank rate were moreover *revised down*, absolutely counter to everything which—at all events in retrospect—appeared to make good economic sense.[57] The consequence was that lending overran all conceivable limits (Figure 12.1). For the rest of the year the Ministry of Finance fought a desperate battle using what little scope for control it had

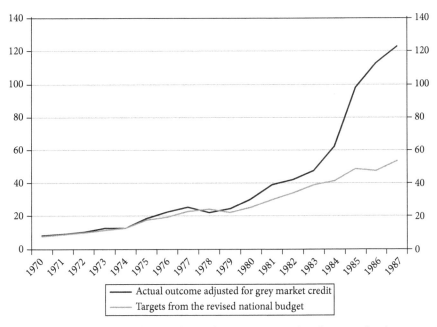

Figure 12.1 Credit target and actual loans from commercial and savings banks, 1970–87, billion kroner

[55] Einar Lie, *Den norske creditbank 1982–1990: en storbank i vekst og krise* (Universitetsforlaget, 1998), 35.
[56] Hermod Skånland, 'Om aggressiv markedsføring', *Penger og kreditt* 4 (1985).
[57] Statistisk sentralbyrå, 'Økonomisk utsyn 1984', 19.

left. In March the ministry raised the primary reserve requirement from 5 to 7 per cent and in September from 7 to 10 per cent. Over the course of 1985 the primary reserve requirement was pushed all the way up to 20 per cent, with no visible effect.

True, the interest rate declarations were dispensed with in September 1985. However, by instructing Norges Bank to maintain a given effective interest rate on government bonds and short-term market paper, the government would continue to be able to control the interest rate level. A general election was in the offing, and an interest rate hike of any significance was not on the cards this time round either.

In autumn 1985 capital began to leave the country. Inflation was high, lending figures high, and fiscal policy expansionary and interest rates low. Had it been allowed to proceed unchecked, the capital outflow from the autumn of 1985 would have brought a natural tightening of liquidity and a rise in the money market rate. However, at the meetings between Norges Bank and the Ministry of Finance, Skånland—the central bank governor from May 1985—interpreted the government's will to mean that the interest rate level was to remain fixed. The liquidity tightening was accordingly counteracted by means of a new lending facility, overnight lending, to the private banks.[58] Overnight loans enabled the banks to continue to increase their lending through 1986 and 1987.

A key point of the subsequent debate was for some time whether Norges Bank should have spoken out more clearly, or requested new instructions or a change in the guidelines from the government in accordance with the new law. The arrangement whereby formal instructions could be demanded would undoubtedly have served its purpose in this situation. However, Prime Minister Willoch has subsequently supported Skånland's statement that the government's will in this matter was absolutely clear. As we have touched on several times, Norges Bank had in the mid-1980s not built up sufficient standing, either with the government or the people, to have any hope of getting the government to change its mind. In addition, now that the government's right to overrule the bank was enshrined in the new law, demands for a new guideline or instructions would have come across as an ineffectual demonstration. It would hardly have strengthened the bank's standing at the time.

Still, for posterity, it would undoubtedly have looked better had Norges Bank used the act to make clear where the formal responsibility lay for the large supply of liquidity from the central bank.

The Final Devaluation and a Binding Fixed Exchange Rate Policy

In January the oil price started to plummet. Over the course of the first half of 1986 the price of crude oil fell from about USD 25 per barrel to below USD 10 per barrel at its lowest point. Much of the tax revenues from the oil sector thus fell away, central government finances weakened, and the current account balance moved from

---

[58] Karsten Gerdrup, 'Norges Banks rolle ved likviditetskriser i finansiell sektor', *Penger og kreditt* 4 (2004).

buoyant positive figures into markedly negative territory. In addition, inflation was now far higher than among Norway's trade partners. The wage settlement of spring 1986—featuring the first lockout since 1931—ended with the highest real wage growth in nine years.[59] The Willoch government had fought the election on an expansionary budget, lost its majority, and stepped down in May having failed to win the Storting's support for a package of austerity measures. Expectations of a devaluation prompted Norges Bank to purchase kroner worth a total of USD 4.6 billion from January to May.[60]

The situation faced by the new government, drawn from the Labour Party and headed by Gro Harlem Brundtland, involved a major and obvious need for a clean-up. The first step, as the market had both foreseen and contributed to fulfilling, was to devalue the krone. On 11 May the krone was devalued by about 10 per cent against the currency basket index. However, the fact that devaluation was not a long-term solution had been demonstrated on numerous occasions in the preceding ten years. In order to signal a clear change of tack the Brundtland government accordingly put the new krone exchange rate in pole position as an economic policy objective.

Hence it was the krone exchange rate that became Norges Bank's operational objective, not the 'domestic liquidity supply to the non-financial private sector', as the bank itself had proposed earlier in the 1980s. In practice the new operational object-ive made it impossible to maintain a low, stable interest rate as a target. Early on, the politicians were probably not entirely aware of the consequence, and certainly not aware that within a short space of time it would give Norges Bank practical control over this policy instrument. Immediately after the change of government the incom-ing government signalled in various ways its support for old principles: through the winter of 1985–6 Norges Bank had, as mentioned, continued to supply the banks with cheap liquidity.[61] The strong currency outflow in spring 1986, and possibly the real-ization that the Willoch government was in any case about to fall, prompted the finance minister to verbally grant Norges Bank temporary power to take management of the interest rate into its own hands.[62] Prior to the krone devaluation of 11 May Norges Bank had granted loans at interest rates as high as 50 per cent.

However, the temporary powers were withdrawn after the devaluation. There was a clear ambition on the part of the Brundtland government that the interest rate level, which was still seen as part of the politicians' remit, should decline in the longer term.[63] Had confidence in Norway's economic policy returned in the summer of 1986, efforts to uphold the principle of a low interest rate would likely have continued. But this was not to be. New assaults on the krone from the autumn of 1986 required a higher interest rate. The government demonstrated its willingness to keep its promise of a fixed exchange rate, despite the costs. Once again Norges Bank was given the

---

[59] Trond Bergh, *Kollektiv fornuft: 1969–2009*, vol. B. 3 (Pax, 2009), 271–3.   [60] Annual report 1986: 16.
[61] Skånland, *Doktriner og økonomisk styring: et tilbakeblikk*, 79–80.   [62] Ibid., 48.
[63] Lie and Venneslan, *Over evne: Finansdepartementet 1965–1992*, 386 et seq.

go-ahead to take control over the money market. On 2 December 1986 the overnight lending rate was raised from 14 to 16 per cent.[64]

Given this turn of events it was evident that the interest rate had to be aligned with the exchange rate.[65] True, the precise division of responsibility between the Ministry of Finance and Norges Bank had not been entirely clarified. The politicians continued to give the impression that they could intervene in the interest rate setting process if they so wished. Moreover, a wide-ranging discussion between the Ministry of Finance and Norges Bank was under way on whether interest rate changes had to follow political signals, or in the event be cleared with the ministry in advance.[66] Central bank Governor Skånland argued that the politicians, if they again sought to set the interest rate, would have to lay down new guidelines for the bank or impose instructions by way of a government decision with full disclosure. They could not do this without sowing doubts and impairing confidence in the fixed exchange rate regime among market actors. Under the pressure of the situation, the central bank governor's interpretation won the day, and through practice gradually became the established precept.

While victory for Norges Bank's autonomy in setting the interest rate was important, it should also be viewed in light of the almost unanimous consensus on what was an appropriate interest rate level. Looking at the two years preceding 1987 as a whole, Norges Bank had no objection to delivering large volumes of liquidity at low interest during the credit boom in autumn 1985 and winter 1986. The bank did not request instructions at this juncture, as it knew that that is what it would get. Two years later the institution advocated managing interest rate changes on its own, arguing that the government had to issue formal instructions if it desired a different interest rate. It was able do so because the political and economic costs of overruling the bank would be high—and because the Ministry of Finance was not in genuine disagreement with the decisions made. The introduction of a new, autonomous role for the bank in interest rate policy was in this sense more a reflection of the art of the possible than of high-level theorizing about how institutional autonomy could contribute to economic stability.

1986 as a Turning Point: A Summary

The fixed exchange rate regime introduced in 1986 was to form the backdrop to a more comprehensive phase-out of the objectives and mechanisms of the old management system. There was a remarkably strong consensus on the phase-out among politicians and senior government officials. The credit budgets were dispensed with in 1988. In 1990 what in a sense had been a prerequisite for the old monetary policy regime, i.e. the regulation of capital movements, was removed almost without debate.

---

[64] Skånland, *Doktriner og økonomisk styring: et tilbakeblikk*, 48–50.   [65] Ibid.
[66] Lie and Venneslan, *Over evne: Finansdepartementet 1965–1992*.

The market, providers, and demanders in the private sector needed to be given greater opportunity to decide the composition and paths of credit. They were, in the new line of thinking, far better in that respect than the political authorities had been, at any rate so long as the object was economic growth. The tax rules, which had favoured households at the expense of business and industry, were also variously revised as from 1987, in particular with the major tax reform of 1992.[67] The interest rate policy was put on a more effective footing by the same token. During the 1990s state bank lending was scaled back in earnest.[68] With the dismantling of policy instruments, economic policy objectives also had to be adjusted. The objectives of an interest rate that was not designed to clear the market, and of minimal unemployment in the very short term—core considerations for Norwegian politicians since 1945—were dispensed with.

At the policy's turning point in 1986, it was clear that the regulatory system was no longer able to curb and liberalize credit. The attempts to deregulate had exacerbated the situation dramatically. The repeated devaluations strengthened inflationary impulses and kindled expectations of new exchange rate cuts. The realignment may thus be characterized as a 'triumph of the market', a term used in a number of portrayals of other countries' central banks.[69] The title given to this chapter, 'Downfall of the Regulatory System and Triumph of the Market', alludes to the fact that the regulatory and deregulatory measures of the years up to 1986 plainly undermined the management system of the time.

Taking a more general view of the principles of economic policy, the objective was now to raise productivity throughout the economy in order to improve the growth figures. Other policy aspects, which are outside the scope of this book, marked an equally strong shift away from old principles. A number of wholly owned state enterprises had been established in the postwar period; these were almost without exception closed down, restructured, or sold. The power market, which had previously been tightly regulated, was liberalized, as was the telecoms market and a number of others. The underlying objectives were likely to some extent to be the same as previously— high growth, aiming to deliver high prosperity. But theoretical-economic reflections with an emphasis on efficient markets gradually won through as basic premises of economic policy. The underlying thinking had gradually evolved in the Ministry of Finance from the end of the 1970s, and the new ideas gained much prominence from 1986 onwards. All in all the main features of the entire economic management system were dismantled in the course of the first five years following 1986, with the oil price fall as the crucial game changer.

The central bank's new-found autonomy was accordingly a function of the new economic situation that was created, not of the new Central Bank Act, which was far and away a legacy of the postwar period's management ethos. Also in the realm of

---

[67] Skånland, *Doktriner og økonomisk styring: et tilbakeblikk*, 63–8.
[68] See NOU 1995: 11, 'Statsbankene under endrede rammevilkår'.
[69] Forrest Capie, *The Bank of England: 1950s to 1979* (Cambridge University Press, 2010); Charles Goodhart, 'The Evolution of Central Banks', *MIT Press Books* 1 (1988).

realities *contra* formalities is the fact that Norges Bank's subordination to the government took place under the old Central Bank Act, under which Nicolai Rygg also had functioned. A new act, with a clearer indication of areas in which the bank was subordinated to the government, came about at the same time that the central bank acquired greater operational autonomy. There is an element of irony here, in addition, naturally, to a small cautionary warning not to judge a central bank's de facto position by the formal legislation under which it operates.

13

In Search of an Anchor

The international trend towards greater central bank independence in the 1990s is usually explained by the virtually universal change of direction in the mid-1980s towards low and stable inflation as a primary objective of economic policy, and a focus on inflation as monetary policy's particular responsibility.[1] Economic policy in Norway was an integral part of this trend, though Norway developed its own version. The strict fixed exchange rate regime in operation between 1986 and 1992, with the krone pegged to currencies in countries with lower inflation, was an important tool in the efforts to bring down inflation. When a large-scale banking crisis occurred in Norway and global financial instability increased through the 1990s, followed by high oil price volatility, the suitability of the fixed exchange rate target in providing the basis for price stability was increasingly called into question. In 1993, Norges Bank argued in favour of supplementing the fixed exchange rate target, and in 1997 in favour of replacing it with an inflation target, with a view to maintaining inflation at a low and stable level.

However, the proposal to introduce an inflation target encountered stronger opposition in Norway than in many other countries. Neighbouring countries such as Sweden, Finland, and the UK had already adopted inflation targeting in 1992–3, while it was not introduced in Norway until 2001.[2] In Norway, the notion of an inflation target came into conflict with the desire to increase the involvement of the wage settlement partners in the work to stabilize price and cost inflation. Under the cooperative model that had been developed, the government, employers, and employees worked together to reduce unemployment and strengthen Norway's competitiveness. The responsibility assigned to this trinity could not also be given to the central bank. In addition, Norges Bank's authority in the political sphere was limited. Only when it became clear that the combination of income policy and fiscal policy was struggling to deliver the desired stability, did it become possible to present price stability as the central bank's policy guideline.

The introduction of an inflation target provided Norges Bank with greater scope for the exercise of independent judgement. Controversial increases in the policy rate in 2000 and 2002 demonstrated that Norges Bank was willing to use its increased

---

[1] Kathleen R. McNamara, *The Currency of Ideas: Monetary Politics in the European Union* (Cornell University Press, 1998).

[2] Denmark retained a fixed exchange rate policy against the ECU/euro and thus operated a regime that could be compared to Norway's. However, in contrast to Norway, Denmark had been a member of the EU since 1972 and participated in foreign exchange interventions in close cooperation with other European central banks.

Norges Bank 1816–2016. Einar Lie, Oxford University Press (2020). © Norges Bank.
DOI: 10.1093/oso/9780198860013.001.0001

independence. Amendments to the Norges Bank Act in 2003 weakened the scope of action available to the government and parliament to influence the bank's decisions, and the Executive Board largely became a council of economic experts. In addition, Norway's slightly inefficient central bank organization underwent major changes, with extensive outsourcing of non-core tasks, as defined by the new guidelines.

Combating Inflation

The fixed exchange rate target to which the government had committed in 1986 was the key instrument in bringing down inflation.[3] The stable exchange rate was what Norges Bank later referred to as a 'nominal anchor'.[4] Norges Bank set the policy rate necessary to maintain stability in the exchange rate, which was pegged to the currencies of Norway's main trading partners. Inflation was generally lower in these countries, and for some of them low inflation was a more explicit policy objective. High wage and price inflation would tend to weaken the krone exchange rate and had to be counteracted by raising the policy rate. In theory, the policy rate affected the exchange rate directly, by making the krone more attractive to investors, and more indirectly via overall demand in the economy. Despite lower growth, higher unemployment, and a major banking crisis in the early 1990s, Norwegian governments did not deviate from the political course they had chosen in 1986.

Monetary policy did not bear sole responsibility for achieving this policy objective. Fiscal policy was tightened after 1986 to contribute to internal and external balance in the economy. The conservative governments from 1981 to 1986 had also sought to end the government's participation in the formalized tripartisan cooperation on wage settlements. This tendency has subsequently become evident in a number of other European countries where wage setting is coordinated.[5] While most sectors after 1986 focused on finding market-conforming solutions to boost productivity, the Labour government moved in the opposite direction in the coordination of the labour market. Active use was made of the historically good relationship between the Labour Party and Norwegian unions to lay the basis for a coordinated effort to reduce inflation. This was particularly evident in the 1988 wage settlement. The favourable outcome of the wage negotiations was part of a larger understanding involving political decisions to introduce a new, advantageous early retirement scheme.[6]

Initially, the fixed exchange rate regime was not part of a policy to combat inflation, but was largely intended to curb devaluation expectations. However, as an increasing number of Norway's trading partners declared low, stable inflation to be a primary

---

[3] See e.g. the Long-Term Programme 1990–3, St. meld 4 (1989–90), 75, Storting's proceedings.

[4] This term appears to have been used for the first time in 'Det økonomiske opplegget for 1994' [Economic policy measures for 1994], Norges Bank's submission to the Ministry of Finance of 28 October 1993.

[5] Thorsten Schulten, 'A European Solidaristic Wage Policy?', *European Journal of Industrial Relations* 8, no. 2 (2002); Lars Calmfors, 'Wages and Wage-bargaining Institutions in the EMU: A Survey of the Issues', *Empirica* 28, no. 4 (2001).

[6] Einar Lie, *Norsk økonomisk politikk etter 1905* (Universitetsforl., 2012), 169.

objective of monetary policy, the expectations of this relationship became more prominent. Only when the government made the decision to discontinue the currency basket system and peg the krone unilaterally to the EEC's own exchange rate index, the European Currency Unit (ECU), in autumn 1990, was it made clear that one of the goals of the operation was to keep inflation at the same low level as on the continent.[7]

Banking Crisis

Chapter 12 showed how an expansionary monetary policy, low interest rates, and deregulation led to a lending boom from about 1984 and into 1987. When monetary policy was eventually tightened on a long-term basis in December 1986, and a more general downturn gradually gained momentum, an increasing number of borrowers encountered difficulties and banks began to incur losses.

Briefly described, the banking crisis itself, loss developments, and how bank solvency problems were managed can be divided into two phases. In the first phase of the crisis, from about 1987 to 1990, a number of small and some larger district banks experienced difficulties and had to receive capital support from the savings and commercial banks' own guarantee fund. Persistent underlying problems erupted in the second phase, after the krone was pegged to the ECU in autumn 1990 amid rising interest rate levels in Europe. Higher interest rates led to even more distressed borrowers and banks. In this phase, the government injected capital via a newly established guarantee fund, the Government Bank Insurance Fund. By the time the government, via the insurance fund, had taken over the three largest banks in the country, the economy was beginning to recover, and by 1993 loan losses had fallen and the banking crisis was over. In the course of the crisis, capital injections or capital guarantees were provided by the various guarantee funds to twenty-five commercial and savings banks. An even larger number of financial institutions received other forms of support.[8] At the height of the crisis, in 1991, Norwegian banks' losses were equivalent to 2.8 per cent of GDP.[9]

Norges Bank's role in the crisis management process itself was complex and very different from the role the bank had played in the crises of the interwar years. There appears to have been an even clearer idea among the economists of Norges Bank prior to the 1990s crisis that the central bank's primary crisis management responsibility, in line with internationally recognized theory, was to maintain the supply of liquidity.[10] As the bankers' bank and 'lender of last resort', Norges Bank's responsibility was to

---

[7] Hermod Skånland, *Doktriner og økonomisk styring: et tilbakeblikk*, vol. 36 (Norges Bank, 2004), 104.

[8] Bankkrisekommisjonen, 'Dokument nr 17 (1997–98) Rapport til Stortinget fra kommisjonen som ble nedsatt av Stortinget for å gjennomgå ulike årsaksforhold knyttet til bankkrisen' (Stortinget, 1998), 153.

[9] Knut Sandal, 'The Nordic Banking Crises in the Early 1990s—Resolution Methods and Fiscal Costs', *The Norwegian Banking Crisis* 33 (2004): 84.

[10] Karsten R Gerdrup, 'Three Booms and Busts Involving Banking Crises in Norway Since the 1890s', *The Norwegian Banking Crisis* (2004).

ensure that a loss of confidence between banks or in Norway's financial system did not dry up the supply of liquidity and prevent solvent banks from meeting their payment obligations. Norges Bank's liquidity support was particularly in the form of emergency liquidity assistance. In November 1991, Norges Bank provided billions of NOK in emergency liquidity assistance to the two largest banks in the country, Kreditkassen and DnB, for example, to enable them to meet their commitments to foreign creditors.[11] At the peak of the crisis, in March 1992, banks had received NOK 25.2 billion in this kind of credit.[12] It must be assumed that this type of support was the main reason this crisis, in contrast to the crisis in the 1920s, did not develop into a liquidity crisis.[13] It is likely that the overall liquidity problems of this crisis were much smaller compared with those of the interwar crises, largely because of the obligatory guarantee funds established for both savings and commercial banks under the 1961 banking legislation.

The banking crisis was a solvency crisis, and thus a crisis Norges Bank, according to the principle of the central bank as liquidity provider, could not take responsibility for *resolving*. If bank losses rose to a very high level, this would ultimately be the responsibility of the political authorities.[14] However, Norges Bank was also to play a role in the refinancing of failing banks. Developments through 1986 had left Norges Bank, even before the crisis had started, with large unsecured loans to private banks.[15] When the regionally important bank Sparebanken Nord-Norge encountered difficulties in 1989, Norges Bank contributed to the refinancing of the bank by writing down its loans by NOK 500 million.[16] The Ministry of Finance and the Storting's Standing Committee on Finance and Economic Affairs both subsequently pointed to the questionable nature, as a matter of principle, of Norges Bank's actions in taking it upon itself to write down loans, reducing the future return accruing to the government.[17] Direct or indirect support for banks should be provided by the authorities empowered to spend government funds. When the solvency crisis continued, and the banks' own guarantee funds ran out of money in 1990; this principle guided the authorities' management of the crisis from then on. The government established the Government Bank Insurance Fund in 1991, which was to provide capital support for failing banks, using funds allocated by parliament, via the banks' guarantee fund. Norges Bank was also to play a role in the technical management of various instances of support in its

---

[11] Harald Haare, Arild J Lund, and Jon A Solheim, *Norges Banks rolle på finanssektorområdet i perioden 1945-2013, med særlig vekt på finansiell stabilitet* (Norges Bank, 2015), 184–5.

[12] Ibid., 186.

[13] Nonetheless, there were some instances of near bank runs, see Sverre Knutsen, *Staten og kapitalen i det 20. århundre: regulering, kriser og endring i det norske finanssystemet 1900-2005* (Scandinavian University Press, Humanistiske Fakultet, 2007), 492.

[14] NOU 1992: 30, *Bankkrisen* (Norges offentlige utredninger, 1992), 92.

[15] Gerdrup, 'Three Booms and Busts Involving Banking Crises in Norway Since the 1890s'; loans from Norges Bank accounted for 13.9 per cent of commercial banks' total assets and 12.9 per cent of saving banks' total assets in 1986, NOU 1992: 30 Bankkrisen, 102–3.

[16] Haare, Lund, and Solheim, *Norges Banks rolle på finanssektorområdet i perioden 1945-2013, med særlig vekt på finansiell stabilitet*, 148.

[17] St. meld. 24 1989–90, 'Kredittilsynets, Norges Banks og Finansdepartementets behandling av Sparebanken Nord-Norge i 1989', Storting's proceedings.

role as secretariat for the Government Bank Insurance Fund and as observer on the fund's board.[18]

The Norwegian banking crisis was deep and far-reaching, although in terms of bank losses as a share of GDP, it was far smaller than the dramatic crisis of the 1920s.[19] It was also resolved relatively quickly. There were no interruptions in banking services, and the tasks performed by the financial industry suffered only limited and short-term damage. Government capital was quickly supplied where existing equity capital had been lost, but only after a bank's share capital had been written down by a corresponding amount. Shares were written down voluntarily or by government decision based on law. If a bank's equity capital had been wiped out, its share capital was written down to zero, as was the case with the three largest banks, Kreditkassen, DnB, and Fokus Bank. Members of parliament from the Conservative Party and the right-wing Progress Party protested, arguing that the existing shareholders should be allowed to keep at least a symbolic amount. But the government and the Ministry of Finance were adamant: public funds were not intended to supplement, but to replace risk capital that was now lost. And no residual amounts should be left behind as a symbol of anything else. Although this approach was based on fundamental micro and macro-economic principles, it also required a pragmatic view of government ownership that does not exist in the UK, and especially not in the US, where the authorities have generally relied on other solutions.

As for the authorities' system for the prevention and management of financial instability, the banking crisis confirmed and reinforced, rather than overturned, established institutional patterns. At Norges Bank, the crisis undoubtedly motivated increased focus on financial market analysis to expose the build-up of potential financial imbalances.[20] From 1994 onwards, the bank prepared quarterly reports providing an assessment of the risk of financial instability. This work was part of an international central bank trend, inspired by a string of financial crises that erupted in other countries throughout the 1990s. The work was done by the already established financial market department at Norges Bank, later the financial stability department, although in closer cooperation with the Banking, Insurance and Securities Commission. Even

---

[18] The interpretation of Norges Bank's role during the banking crisis has been the subject of debate. T. Gram, 'Når staten tar kontroll: bankkrisen fra 1991-1993', Masters thesis (University of Oslo, 2011) gives considerable emphasis to the bank's passive role in the management of the crisis, particularly from 1990 onwards. The picture is similar to that presented in E. Lie and C. Venneslan, *Over evne: Finansdepartementet 1965–1992* (Pax, 2010), which emphasizes the Ministry of Finance's leadership role in designing the institutional framework for the resolution of the crisis from 1990 and the absence of input to this work from other institutions. J. Bergo and J. Solheim, 'Kommentarer til Trond Grams artikkel i Samfunnsøkonomen nr. 4–2012', *Samfunnsøkonomen* 126, no. 5 (2012) 34–7, refute the impression created by these authors by noting that the Report to the Storting 24 1989–90 was a clarification of principles that had been agreed on by all parties, including Norges Bank, that these principles were set aside before the report was presented to Parliament, owing to special circumstances, and that the principles, once they had been drawn up clearly and deliberated in parliament in the form of Report to the Storting 24, had clear implications for Norges Bank's position in the management of the ongoing crisis. There was simply no expectation, inside or outside the bank, that Norges Bank would take a leadership role in resolving banks' solvency problems. Bergo and Solheim 2012 also point out that Norges Bank consistently contributed with crisis management advice to the Ministry of Finance and continued to do so after 1990.

[19] Hermod Skånland, 'Bankkrise og livet etterpå', in *Penger og kreditt* (1990).

[20] Arild Lund and Jon A Solheim, 'Finansiell stabilitet—et viktig mål for sentralbanken', i *'Sentralbanken i forandringens tegn: Festskrift til Kjell Storvik', Norges Banks skriftserie*, no. 28 (1999).

though a board of enquiry appointed by parliament in 1998 recommended assigning more formal responsibility for the financial system to Norges Bank, this proposal was not followed up by the political authorities.[21]

Similarly, a proposal to integrate the Banking, Insurance and Securities Commission into Norges Bank in 1991 was not followed up in practice. The commission, established in 1986 when the former Banking Inspectorate was merged with other financial supervisory bodies, was responsible for supervising individual financial institutions, i.e. microprudential supervision.[22] The Norges Bank Act gave the central bank a more general responsibility, which came to be referred to as macroprudential supervision. The combination of supervisory and central bank authority was not unusual in other countries, and merging the commission with Norges Bank had been discussed on a number of occasions during the postwar years.[23] Norges Bank favoured transferring the supervision of the financial industry to a separate institution.[24] It was also a widely held view that the commission had not functioned satisfactorily in the run-up to the crisis, and in 1992 the Ministry of Finance submitted a proposition to parliament that the commission's functions should be transferred to the central bank. But the government failed to win a majority for its proposal. The opposition's arguments largely focused on warning against an excessive concentration of power at Norges Bank.[25]

The most long-lasting consequence of the banking crisis for Norges Bank's institutional development was that the crisis gave the bank an additional argument in favour of a monetary policy regime more geared towards promoting stability. The many positive interactions between monetary and financial stability were a recurring theme in the bank's publications through the 1990s.[26] Attention was increasingly given to the costs of an unbalanced economic policy and the consequences that would inevitably follow. History clearly showed, said Governor Skånland in a speech to the Norwegian Savings Banks Association in 1990, how monetary policy could contribute to the build-up of financial imbalances. And the best way to guard against such developments was, according to Skånland, to grant the central bank greater independence.[27]

A Floating Krone and Price Stability

When Norges Bank first introduced price stability, in the sense of low, stable inflation, as an explicit, long-term objective of monetary policy in autumn 1993 and spring

---

[21] Ibid.; Haare, Lund, and Solheim, *Norges Banks rolle på finanssektorområdet i perioden 1945–2013, med særlig vekt på finansiell stabilitet*.

[22] Sverre Knutsen and Gunhild J Ecklund, 'Vern mot kriser? Norsk finanstilsyn gjennom 100 år' (Fagbokforlaget, 2000), 310.

[23] NOU 1983: 39, *Lov om Norges Bank og pengevesenet* (Norges offentlig utredninger, 1983).

[24] Hermod Skånland, 'Sentralbankens oppgaver i dag og i fremtiden' [The tasks of the central bank today and in the future], *Occasional Papers*, no. 19 (1991).

[25] Knutsen and Ecklund, 'Vern mot kriser? Norsk finanstilsyn gjennom 100 år', 310–12.

[26] A. Lund and J. Solheim, 'Finansiell stabilitet: et viktig mål for sentralbanken', in 'Sentralbanken i forandringens tegn: festskrift til Kjell Storvik", *Occasional Papers* 28 (1999), 62, Norges Bank.

[27] Skånland, 'Bankkrise og livet etterpå', 207.

1994, it was because the fixed exchange rate regime could no longer provide the clear framework around a stabilizing monetary policy that it had provided since 1986.[28] When the krone had to be allowed to float after intense speculative attacks in autumn 1992, Norges Bank spent much of 1993 assessing the alternatives available to the Norwegian authorities. A detailed report on monetary policy regime alternatives and the outline of a monetary policy plan were submitted to the Ministry of Finance in April 1994.[29] Norges Bank did not conclude by proposing the introduction of an inflation target: the bank was still in favour of the krone exchange rate as the operational target. Stable inflation as the explicit *long-term* target was, however, inspired by inflation targeting in other countries and laid the foundation, if the exchange rate was subjected to persistent pressure, for central bank-led developments in the same direction.

The speculative attacks on the krone in November and December 1992 were more intense than ever before. Major attacks in September had forced Finland and the UK to abandon the peg to the ECU they, like Norway, had established only two years before. Sweden followed suit on 19 November. These developments showed that there was little Nordic central banks outside the EU's joint currency intervention mechanism could do once currency speculation reached a certain level. In only the first hour after the devaluation of the Swedish krona, Norges Bank's Market Operations department sold NOK 14 billion in foreign exchange. In the course of one and a half trading days, Norges Bank's foreign exchange reserves had been depleted by more than half.[30] Norges Bank defended the krone and the pressure gradually receded, only to resume at the beginning of December. On the morning of 10 December, the government, on the advice of Norges Bank, suspended the obligation to maintain the krone's fluctuation margins against the ECU.[31]

Even though the krone stabilized after a 5 per cent fall in value, the exchange rate was from now on determined by supply and demand. The krone was technically floating. The extent of the attack, and further difficulties for the European exchange rate system in 1993, raised the question of whether, in a world of free capital movements, it would ever be possible to peg the krone to one or several currencies again.[32]

Even though the krone stabilized, there was concern at Norges Bank that with the suspension of the exchange rate target, the 'nominal anchor' had been lost: that the monetary policy discipline created by the clarity of the exchange rate would now come under political pressure, and that the bank, without the clear framework provided by the exchange rate regime, would not be able to stand firm. In the more or less interim exchange rate regulations issued between December 1992 and January 1993,

---

[28] The proposal was first presented in 'Det økonomiske opplegget for 1994' [Economic policy measures for 1994], Norges Bank's submission to the Ministry of Finance of 28 October 1993, cf. Einar Lie et al., *Norges Bank 1916–2016* (Fagbokforlaget, 2016), 427–9.

[29] 'Pengepolitikk under flytende valutakurser' [Monetary policy under floating exchange rates], Norges Bank's submission of 19 April 1994, cf. Ibid.

[30] Norges Bank's annual report 1992, 41.   [31] Norges Bank's annual report 1992, 26.

[32] Christoffer Kleivset, 'Fra fast valutakurs til inflasjonsmål, Et dokumentasjonsnotat om Norges Bank og pengepolitikken 1992–2001' (2012).

the Ministry of Finance also aimed for a cautious depreciation of the krone.[33] This is probably the background for Skånland's detailed review, in his last annual address in February 1993, of the importance of price stability and the need to make it a long-term objective of monetary policy.[34] That monetary policy should have a long-term, primary objective, in the form of an objects clause in the Norges Bank Act or in some other way, was for that matter something Skånland had been considering since the first half of the 1980s.[35] The proposal was repeated in a letter to the Ministry of Finance that autumn and in Skånland's successor Torstein Moland's annual address in February 1994.

Price stability as a long-term goal was clearly inspired by the large number of other countries from 1990 onwards that had made price stability in the somewhat longer term the direct objective of monetary policy, and at the same time allowed their exchange rate to fluctuate from one day to the next. New Zealand had experimented with a floating exchange rate since 1985 and launched an inflation target as the operational target of monetary policy in 1990.[36] Chile, Canada, and Israel followed suit in 1991. More importantly from a Norwegian standpoint, the UK in 1992 and Sweden and Finland in 1993 adopted inflation targeting to replace their suspended link to the ECU. Immediately after the suspension, Norges Bank's economists began to focus on the central banks in these countries to find out what they were really up to.[37] Key findings from their investigations were included in the bank's recommendation.

One finding was that inflation targeting offered the solution to a latent problem. In the years after 1986, it was usually emphasized that the fixed exchange rate target and the desire for economic stability often pulled monetary policy in the same direction.[38] When the economy heated up and prices rose, there was often also a tendency for the krone to depreciate. Both conditions implied that the policy rate should be raised. But this was not always the case. If cyclical developments in the countries whose currencies Norges Bank had pegged the krone to were different from developments in Norway, the fixed exchange rate policy could have an opposite, *destabilizing* effect. This problem was particularly relevant in light of Norway's special position as an oil exporter: when oil prices were high and the economy was in an upturn, such as in the period 1983–6, pressures in the Norwegian economy had been high *at the same time* as the krone came under upward pressure. Under such conditions in inflation-targeting countries, the policy rate could be raised to counteract inflationary impulses, even if the exchange rate appreciated.[39]

[33] Ibid., 12.   [34] Hermod Skånland, 'Økonomiske perspektiver; Årstale 1993' (Norges Bank, 1993).
[35] Cf. the description of Norges Bank's statement on the Ryssdal Commission recommendation, NOU 1983: 39, chapter 16.
[36] John Singleton, *Central Banking in the Twentieth Century* (Cambridge University Press, 2010), 245–6.
[37] This process is described in detail in Kleivset, 'Fra fast valutakurs til inflasjonsmål: Et dokumentasjonsnotat om Norges Bank og pengepolitikken 1992–2001'.
[38] See e.g. NOU 1989: 1, *Penger og kreditt i en omstillingstid: norsk penge- og kredittpolitikk i årene som kommer*, 19–20.
[39] Memo 'Notat pengepolitikk under flytende valutakurser' (PP3/ASk), 11 March 1994, Norges Bank.

Another feature of inflation targeting in other countries noted by Norges Bank was that inflation targeting strengthened the importance of the central bank's independent judgement in its conduct of monetary policy. While the policy rate in a system where the exchange rate was pegged to the ECU had to shadow the interest rates on the continent, policy rate decisions under an inflation-targeting regime had to be based on projected price developments months and years ahead, and on assumptions as to the effect of policy rate changes on these developments. While the krone exchange rate could be monitored in the market from one hour to the next, future price developments had to be projected using advanced models. And while the effects of a policy rate change were immediately observable in the krone market, the impact on inflation could only be observed later. This is what was meant when the bank referred in its statements to a 'greater use of judgement' in the conduct of monetary policy. And Norges Bank's role in the conduct of a monetary policy involving a greater use of judgement would be 'more visible than under a fixed exchange rate regime'.[40]

However, none of the advice given by Norges Bank and its governors to the Ministry of Finance in 1993–4 contained any proposal to introduce an inflation target. Skånland and Moland were probably sceptical as to whether such a proposal would be taken into consideration in the political situation of the time. And they were probably still in real doubt as to whether an inflation target would result in a better economic policy. For several floating rate countries, inflation targeting was the only option, simply because a fixed exchange rate target no longer had the confidence of the market. The Norwegian krone was still stable. In addition, the type of inflation targeting operated in Sweden and the UK could not in itself guarantee price stability, as noted in internal memos. On the contrary, the removal of the ties inherent in the fixed exchange rate regime might weaken discipline in fiscal policy and wage settlements and thereby undermine price stability. It would be difficult to create confidence in stability under a floating rate regime, 'particularly in light of Norway's history with regard to devaluation', as another memo put it.[41] Establishing the credibility of price stability under a floating exchange rate regime required a central bank that was formally and in reality strong enough to withstand pressure to lower the policy rate and weaken the exchange rate. Whether Norges Bank was capable of this was, in the light of both legislation and historical practice, in some doubt.

Norges Bank argued therefore in favour of supplementing fixed exchange rate regime guidelines with an explicit long-term price stability objective. Low inflation over time was a precondition for a stable exchange rate over time. And if the fixed exchange rate regime had to be abandoned for a period, Norges Bank argued that the price stability objective would be a working principle, providing direction for monetary policy in that period. A long-term guideline would thus prepare for developments in the direction of inflation targeting by providing Norges Bank, when

---

[40] 'Pengepolitikk under flytende valutakurser', Norges Bank's submission of 19 April 1994.
[41] 'Enkelte retningslinjer for pengepolitikken under flytende valutakurser—et foreløpig notat' [Some guidelines for monetary policy under floating exchange rates—a provisional memo], Memo 9/1993, 10 February 1993 ASk/KaM/924, p. 6, Norges Bank.

required, with the legal authority, for short or longer periods, to deviate from the operational exchange rate target.[42]

Policy of Cooperation Takes Precedence

The proposals of 1993/4 to make price stability a primary, long-term objective of monetary policy were not followed up by the government.[43] Instead, the Ministry of Finance issued a new exchange rate regulation in May 1994, confirming that a stable exchange rate would be monetary policy's only objective. This regulation was to provide the formal framework for Norges Bank's conduct of monetary policy until 2001.

The government did not disagree with Norges Bank about the need for price stability. Its rejection of the proposals was not because of the price stability objective as much as its treatment as something separate. 'The economic policy debate could then easily become a question of choosing whether the objective should be low inflation *or* full employment', said Svein Gjedrem, then director general of the economic policy department at the Ministry of Finance, at a meeting with representatives of Norges Bank in winter 1993.[44] The implication was that if the debate were conducted on these terms, price stability could easily draw the shortest straw. This understanding of the situation was fairly similar to Norges Bank's assessment, though with slightly less faith in the capacity of politicians to accept the consequences of price stability as a long-term guideline.

The background for the assessment was the support in parliament and among the social partners for the objective of nominal stability through exchange rate policy. In the years leading up to 1989, economic policy had led to internal discord in the labour movement and had been a contributing factor when the Labour Party fell from power. In autumn 1991, barely a year after she took over as prime minister after the Conservative government led by Jan P. Syse, the Labour leader Gro Harlem Brundtland took the initiative to establish a broadly composed commission, dubbed the Kleppe Comission, with a mandate to draw up a strategy for higher employment in the 1990s. Under the strategy the commission came up with, the so-called solidarity alternative, competitiveness would be improved by 10 per cent over five years by limiting average wage growth in practice to 3 per cent a year.[45] The stable exchange rate would prevent the improvement in competitiveness achieved through moderation in the wage settlements from being cancelled out by a krone appreciation, or nominal pay increases being weakened through devaluations and imported price inflation, as had been the case under the conservative government of the first half of the 1980s. The government

---

[42] 'Pengepolitikk under flytende valutakurser' [Monetary policy under floating exchange rates], Norges Bank's submission of 19 April 1994: 124.

[43] The signals were clearly conveyed in the contact between the governor of Norges Bank and the Ministry of Finance in late autumn 1993 (see Kleivset, 'Fra fast valutakurs til inflasjonsmål: Et dokumentasjonsnotat om Norges Bank og pengepolitikken 1992–2001', 14.).

[44] According to ibid., 10.   [45] Trond Bergh, *Kollektiv fornuft: 1969–2009*, vol. B. 3 (Pax, 2009), 369.

thus constructed a firm framework for the cooperative system, and the gains achieved had a more predictable and thereby more binding impact. Fiscal policy's responsibility in the system was to contribute to sufficient demand to reduce unemployment. And monetary policy would necessarily have to be linked to the objective of continued exchange rate stability.

The monetary policy regulation introduced in May 1994 required Norges Bank to keep the krone exchange rate stable against 'European currencies', the ECU index, at its initial range since 10 December 1992. The krone's initial range was unofficially set at between 103 and 108 on the ECU index.[46] In important aspects, Norges Bank's remark that it would no longer be possible to maintain the same fixed exchange rate as before 1992, and that the exchange rate objective would have to be given a more flexible design, was taken into account. Norges Bank was not required to keep the exchange rate within the range at any cost. On the contrary, it was emphasized that the instruments used to keep the krone within its initial range should not be as strong as if the system had been a traditional fixed exchange rate system. If the krone was forced outside its initial range, the use of instruments would, over time, be oriented towards bringing the krone back.[47] These provisions provided the legal authority in the second half of the 1990s for Norges Bank to 'suspend the use of instruments' and in practice allow the krone to float freely for a period. Apart from these tendencies towards a more flexible approach, however, the exchange rate regulation of 1994 essentially required Norges Bank to continue to set the policy rate as if it operated within the regime up to 1992.

Inflation-Targeting Campaign

The arguments both for and against an inflation target in Norway and a more flexible exchange rate became more pronounced from the mid-1990s. In 1996, Norges Bank's governor and his staff launched a campaign to convince politicians and government officials of the advantage of the inflation target compared with the exchange rate target and, over time, persuade them to adjust the exchange rate regulation in the direction of an operational inflation target.

From autumn 1995, this campaign was headed not by Torstein Moland, but the previous deputy governor Kjell Storvik. Moland had withdrawn owing to an incident involving penalty tax.[48] Other factors amplified the negative focus on Moland. The appointment of Moland as governor of Norges Bank in autumn 1993 and Moland's close links to key figures in the government of the time were subject to a critical review by parliament in 1994 that resulted in criticism of the Labour Party and a vote

---

[46] Kleivset, 'Fra fast valutakurs til inflasjonsmål: Et dokumentasjonsnotat om Norges Bank og pengepolitik-ken 1992–2001', 12.

[47] St.meld. 2 1993–4, (Revised National Budget 1994): 43, Storting's proceedings.

[48] For a summary, see 'Moland-sak i ny fase' [The Moland case reaches a new phase] NTB 19 November 1995.

of no confidence in the finance minister.[49] The government only narrowly secured a majority against the proposal. The tax penalty case, the political reaction, and massive pressure from the media eventually made it impossible for Moland to continue as governor of Norges Bank.

In his very first annual address in February 1996, Kjell Storvik asserted that the strict focus on the exchange rate Norges Bank was required to keep 'presents problems for an active use of monetary policy for short-term stabilisation purposes'.[50] Similar statements followed in Storvik's subsequent annual addresses. Dinners and meetings were held at the bank through 1997 and 1998 where academics and politicians discussed alternatives. Books and articles were written.[51] The reason given was to collect information and foster discussion on an important topic.[52] There is nonetheless little doubt that the governor and the executive management of Norges Bank hoped that spreading this information might speed up a regime shift they felt was better for Norway.[53] And in autumn 1997, the governor was able to gain the support of the Executive Board for a recommendation from the Ministry of Finance to change the regulation to introduce inflation targeting.[54]

The latent tension between the fixed exchange rate regime and the objective of price stability gradually became more pronounced. Through 1996, the upward pressure on the krone against the ECU increased to such an extent that Norges Bank had to suspend the use of the policy instrument in January 1997 and allow the exchange rate to adjust, as provided for in the regulation (see Figure 13.1). The policy rate had to be kept low throughout to curb the pressure on the exchange rate and, as from January 1997, bring the krone back to its initial range. A low policy rate had an expansionary effect in the context of a booming economy.

Norges Bank argued against such a change in the face of opposition from a fairly solid majority of experts. With the exception of some academics at the Norwegian School of Economics in Bergen, a symposium convened by Norges Bank in spring 1997 showed that a number of prominent Norwegian economists were positive regarding a fixed exchange rate target.[55] At the political level, the changes in government reduced the scope for changes in interest rate policy. Gro Harlem Brundtland, a widely respected prime minister with many years of experience, withdrew from office in 1996 and was succeeded by Labour Party colleague Thorbjørn Jagland. The following year, a centre-party coalition came to power. Jagland, whose power base lay with the left wing of the Labour Party, did not want to challenge the so-called solidarity

---

[49] Innst. S. 136 1993–4 Innstilling fra kontroll- og konstitusjonskomiteen om utnevnelse av ny sentralbank-sjef, Storting's proceedings, 24 May 1994: 3579–679.

[50] Kjell Storvik, 'Økonomiske perspektiver; Årstale 1996' (1996).

[51] As described in Kleivset, 'Fra fast valutakurs til inflasjonsmål: Et dokumentasjonsnotat om Norges Bank og pengepolitikken 1992–2001'.

[52] See e.g. the foreword in Anne Berit Christiansen and Jan Fredrik Qvigstad, *Choosing a Monetary Policy Target* (Scandinavian University Press, 1997).

[53] Conversations with Kjell Storvik, Jarle Bergo, and Jan Fredrik Qvigstad: looking back, it was, in their eyes, at least as late as in 1997–8, only a matter of time before Norway would have to switch to inflation targeting.

[54] 'Det økonomiske opplegget for 1998, Norges Banks brev 3.11.1997 til Finansdepartementet', printed in 'Penger og kreditt', April 1997.

[55] Christiansen and Qvigstad, *Choosing a Monetary Policy Target*.

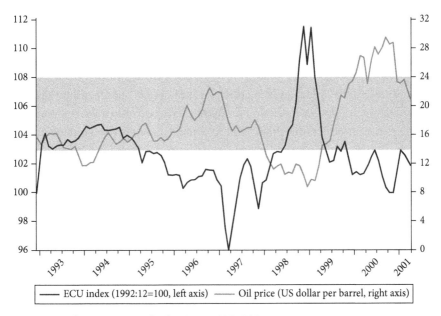

Figure 13.1 Exchange rates and oil prices, 1992–2001

alternative in an election year. The coalition government of 1997 took office on a very thin parliamentary basis and chose its battles very carefully. Norges Bank's pressure for a regime change was perceived as ill-placed by Ministry of Finance officials when the figures for growth, employment, and inflation were showing a positive trend and there was widespread consensus on economic policy.[56]

An important part of the picture in a political terrain focused on cooperation was that the Norwegian Confederation of Trade Unions (LO), and to a lesser extent the Confederation of Norwegian Enterprise (NHO), clearly favoured a continuation of the fixed exchange rate regime. The LO president used the media to convince politicians and voters that changes in the division of economic policy responsibilities would generate political discord. He declared Norges Bank to be the solidarity alternative's main enemy and ideological opposite. 'Norges Bank is the Norwegian economy's tool', the LO president declared in autumn 1998, 'not the opposite'. The daily newspaper *Dagbladet*—which voted the LO president most powerful man of the year in 1997—also referred to him as 'Norway's real central bank governor'. This is probably why the Ministry of Finance, in a meeting with Deputy Governor Jarle Bergo in autumn 1998, claimed that any official recommendation from Norges Bank to change the exchange rate regulation would put the government 'in a very difficult position'.[57]

Moreover, developments in competitiveness and unemployment had been clearly positive since 1992. These developments could be interpreted in two ways. For supporters of the solidarity alternative—many of whom were in the top echelons of the

---

[56] Eivind Thomassens conversation with Svein Gjedrem.
[57] After Kleivset, 'Fra fast valutakurs til inflasjonsmål: Et dokumentasjonsnotat om Norges Bank og pengepolitikken 1992–2001', 34.

LO and the Labour Party and among the economists who argued for it—the good reciprocal relationship between employer and employee organizations and the government had safeguarded an expansionary policy that stimulated the economy, while nominal wage increases every year up to 1996 ensured an improvement in competitiveness. Conservative calculations made by a number of economists indicated that the consensus of the Kleppe Commission might not have been the most important factor. Past experience indicates that high unemployment dampens wage demands during wage negotiations and particularly wage drift in companies. Calculations using historical data indicate that setting wages without an explicit 'solidarity approach' could have resulted in the same wage developments.[58] In that respect, there were several ways of achieving approximately the same goal, and Norges Bank argued that inflation targeting was in terms of the economy more reliable and more efficient. However, a transition from the 'solidarity approach' to inflation targeting would have entailed a direct and concrete transfer of responsibility and influence from political, cooperative arenas to Norges Bank. At the time, few other than Norges Bank voiced support for this solution.

In principle, Norges Bank could, under the Norges Bank Act, formally 'inform the ministry' when, in the opinion of the bank, there was a need for measures to be taken by institutions other than the bank. The Ryssdal Commission, which had prepared the act, had envisaged that governments would not be able to take this lightly. But in order to make such a formal submission to the ministry, the governor would have to have the support of the Executive Board.[59] Under the act, the number of external board members had been increased from three to five and had thus, compared with the previous system of directors, weakened the possibilities available to the two chairmen, employed full time, to garner a majority. It had also become practice for the government, at the request of parliament (although contrary to the Ryssdal Commission's intention), to select the candidates proposed by the various parliamentary party groups.[60] Politics thus moved directly into the central bank. The members of Norges Bank's Executive Board always included representatives of central government parties and the LO.[61] In autumn 1997, Storvik and Bergo were able to gather the support of the Executive Board, although with dissenting votes, behind a proposal to invoke this provision in a letter to the government and request an adjustment of the exchange rate regulations.[62] However, the message had been watered down during the board's processing of the bank's letter.[63] There is little evidence that the request was followed up in any way by the centre-party coalition government.[64]

---

[58] An overview of the debate is given in Roger Bjørnstad, 'Debatten omkring Solidaritetsalternativet: lønnsdannelsen i industrien-uendret også i perioden 1995-1997', Sosialøkonomen 52, no. 4 (1998).

[59] Memo to Norges Bank's management from B. Nyhagen, 12 October 1995, Norges Bank documentation file, NB.

[60] Hermod Skånland, 'Tilbakeblikk på 20 år med ny sentralbanklov' (2005).

[61] According to Kleivset, 'Fra fast valutakurs til inflasjonsmål: Et dokumentasjonsnotat om Norges Bank og pengepolitikken 1992–2001', 33.

[62] Norges Bank's submission to the Ministry of Finance of 22 November 1997 on economic measures for 1998.

[63] Kleivset, 'Fra fast valutakurs til inflasjonsmål: Et dokumentasjonsnotat om Norges Bank og pengepolitikken 1992–2001', 25.

[64] Ibid.

Real Inflation Targeting under a Formal
Fixed Exchange Rate Regime

The governor's attempt to put in place an inflation target by persuading the government to change the exchange rate regulation reached its peak—or anticlimax—with the sharp fall in the krone exchange rate in late autumn 1998.

The krone's fall in value was the result of the financial crisis in East Asia in summer 1997 and the subsequent fall in oil prices. From keeping the policy rate low to prevent a rise in the krone exchange rate, Norges Bank had to raise the policy rate through 1998 to prevent the krone from becoming so weak that it fell below its initial range. Authorized by the Executive Board, Governor Storvik raised the policy rate seven times in the course of spring and summer. The policy rate increases reduced pressures in the Norwegian economy, but not as gently as the bank had hoped. Nor did the rate increases prevent the krone from continuing to fall.

Even though the governor and the economists at Norges Bank made their recommendation to the government clear, the leeway for independent advice was limited. In his contact with the Ministry of Finance in autumn 1998, Storvik claimed that changing the guideline to inflation targeting, a system market participants were more familiar with, would have a calming effect.[65] According to the executive management of the bank, the situation again called for measures to be taken by institutions other than the bank under Section 3 of the act. However, this time the governor was not able to garner the support of a majority of the board.[66] 'All confidence in the krone could be lost', warned Storvik in a meeting in December, although this did not seem to make an impression on the board's members.[67] The majority, two of whom represented the LO and one the Labour Party, voted instead to postpone the discussion several times.

When the krone exchange rate plunged in August 1998, Norges Bank did not raise the policy rate further. This amounted to a temporary 'suspension' of the use of the instrument, in line with previous practice. The idea was that an even higher policy rate would not serve the objective of long-term stability. This was a few months before a new governor took office, which was to mark a clear transition to emphasis on the same long-term stability, but where the consideration of long-term inflation was in practice given precedence over exchange rate fluctuations. However, it should be stressed that August 1998 was obviously not perceived by contemporary market participants and observers as a change in monetary policy practice. The use of the policy instrument had been suspended on previous occasions and the fixed-rate regime resumed thereafter. According to Storvik, 'controlling the exchange rate, *and that alone*, is the basis for the use of instruments [author's emphasis]'.[68]

---

[65] Ibid., 31.   [66] Protocol 2 from Norges Banks Executive Board, 16 December 1998, NB.
[67] 'Talepunkter for KS i hovedstyret', 9 December 1998, Norges Bank Documentation file, NB.
[68] Speech at Forex Norway on 28 August 1998, Norges Bank Documentation file, NBA. It was precisely this excessively strict focus on the exchange rate that in Storvik's opinion followed from the regulation that was the argument for the persistent attempts to change it.

There was a basis for a more fundamental shift when the new governor, Svein Gjedrem, took office at the beginning of 1999. Gjedrem has been mentioned earlier in his capacity as head of monetary and credit policy at the Ministry of Finance, and later director general at the ministry's economics department. He became secretary general at the ministry in 1995 and held this office when he applied for the position of governor of Norges Bank. It is doubtful whether the position of governor carried more influence than the secretary general position at the Ministry of Finance when Gjedrem applied for it. But it carried considerably more influence after Gjedrem had been in office for a while.

As early as 4 January, Gjedrem maintained in a meeting with the press that the exchange rate regulation of 1994 allowed for the exercise of discretionary judgement by Norges Bank, and that the bank in its future exercise of judgement would give more weight to the consideration of stable inflation. As Gjedrem pointed out, the objective of a stable exchange rate over time was in any case dependent on the authorities being able to keep inflation at approximately the same level as the countries whose currencies the krone was pegged to. In an interview with Reuters, he confirmed that this interpretation could mean that the policy rate would be lowered even if the krone were well below its initial range. When the Reuters press release was issued at just past 11.00 am, the money market rate immediately fell. Even though Gjedrem emphasized that the exercise of discretionary judgement was in line with the regulation, the market, and in time some of the press, interpreted Gjedrem's statement to mean that monetary policy practice would be changed.[69]

This interpretation would prove to be correct. Only a few weeks later, the Executive Board followed up Gjedrem's statement by lowering the policy rate in response to expectations of lower price and cost inflation, even though the exchange rate, as mentioned, was considerably below its initial range. The further conduct of monetary policy through 1999 and 2000 consolidated this impression.[70] In a letter to the Ministry of Finance in October 1999, the Executive Board explained that Norges Bank no longer had credible instruments at its disposal to fine-tune the krone exchange rate, but should orient monetary policy towards the *fundamental* preconditions for exchange rate stability. In order to meet these fundamental preconditions, the bank asserted, 'monetary policy instruments must be oriented towards bringing cost and price inflation down to the level aimed for by the European Central Bank (ECB)'.[71] At this time, the ECB aimed to maintain the inflation rate at up to 2 per cent.

In the context of the picture created by some newspapers through 1997 and 1998 of Storvik's lonely struggle to introduce inflation targeting, and even more in light of what we know today about the tug-of-war in the Executive Board in autumn 1998, the signals and policy rate decisions through 1999 were remarkable. Less than a month

---

[69] According to Kleivset, 'Fra fast valutakurs til inflasjonsmål: Et dokumentasjonsnotat om Norges Bank og pengepolitikken 1992–2001'.

[70] Norges Bank's annual report 2000: 16.

[71] Den økonomiske politikken i 2000 [Economic policy in 2000], letter of 21 October 1999, Norges Bank documentation file, NB.

before the reduction in the policy rate in January 1999, the Executive Board did not want to adopt a recommendation to the Ministry of Finance to change the regulation in order to provide a better basis, in the eyes of the governor, for the policy now being pursued. The Executive Board's reinterpretation of the regulation also seemed to be in conflict with statements and documents by the current and previous government, which all placed the responsibility for price and cost inflation on the social partners, and emphasized exchange rate stability as the primary objective of monetary policy, without mentioning fundamentals at all.[72] In response to questions from puzzled parliamentary representatives, Finance Minister Gudmund Restad nonetheless confirmed that Norges Bank's practice was in line with the current regulation. The Stoltenberg government did the same when it took office in 2000.[73] However, neither Gjedrem nor government ministers would admit that Norges Bank was in reality operating an inflation-targeting regime.[74]

Support for a reinterpretation of the regulation, by the Executive Board and the government, partly depended on the immediate economic situation. Pressures in the economy had subsided. The krone's fall came to halt in December 1998. Oil prices showed signs of rebounding. There were favourable prospects for a rise in the krone, and a reduction in the policy rate was no longer such a clear breach of the regulation as it would have appeared in autumn 1998. The exchange rate also returned to its initial range. At political level, the policy rate reduction was received with relief after successive rate hikes through 1998. It was also important to the members of the Executive Board that the reinterpretation restored their involvement in the rate decisions.[75] It had undoubtedly been a source of reciprocal irritation between Storvik and the Executive Board that Storvik, owing to rapid developments in the foreign exchange market, had taken virtually all the rate decisions himself under a so-called general authorization.[76]

Svein Gjedrem, however, also played a substantial personal role in making the breach possible. A change in interpretation and practice was not formally agreed with the Executive Board in advance. Nor was there any completely consistent information about any informal contact Gjedrem might have had with individual board members prior to the press release on 4 January. The Ministry of Finance was informed the same day. Gjedrem claimed he had expected the reactions that came, and had probably also expected those that did *not* come, at a political level, at Norges Bank and in the market. Gjedrem came straight from a position as secretary general at the Ministry of Finance and knew the people and the sentiment among the bureaucracy, the government, and at Norges Bank very well.[77] In addition, it would have been difficult for the government to disavow a governor it had just appointed, and his reinterpretation also

[72] See e.g. the 1999 National Budget: 95–99, St.meld. no 1 1999, Storting's proceedings.
[73] Stortingstidende, 18 October 2000, 185, Storting's proceedings.
[74] Siv Jensen in Stortingstidende, 24 March 1999, 2476, Storting's proceedings.
[75] This paragraph is based on conversations buy Eivind Thomassen with Kjell Storvik, Svein Gjedrem, and the various Executive Board members.
[76] Kleivset, 'Fra fast valutakurs til inflasjonsmål: Et dokumentasjonsnotat om Norges Bank og pengepolitikken 1992–2001'.
[77] Eivind Thomassen in conversation with Svein Gjedrem.

entailed (as previously mentioned) a lower policy rate, which was favoured by the social partners. In that sense, the change in January 1999 was about the right person acting in response to the right situation.

A Regime Falls into Place

Some of the support was a result of the assessment of the solidarity alternative in light of the latest developments up to the change in practice. After the first five years of the solidarity alternative, the success of income policy had been failing. Attempts to maintain the solidarity alternative in a so-called 'reinforced' version in 1998 resulted in the highest rate of wage growth in the 1990s up to that point; for some groups, wage growth was as high as 10 per cent. On the initiative of Kjell Magne Bondevik's government, a more moderate wage settlement was achieved the next year and a plan was also made for moderation the year after. The plan did not hold: with strong pressures in the economy and the labour market, moderation was difficult to achieve. The main wage settlement in 2000, however, ended in strikes and new large wage increases.[78] The latter part of the developments, combined with the successful reinterpretation in 1991, prepared the ground for the new monetary policy guideline that was introduced in 2001.

The political process around the new economic policy guidelines showed broad support for the formal introduction of an inflation target. All parties were largely positive. Even the LO welcomed the inflation target.[79] In the Labour Party, the party that introduced the solidarity alternative and that was now at the forefront of support for inflation targeting, the two previous central bank governors, Moland and Skånland, had clearly been successful in their efforts to make inflation targeting Labour Party policy.[80] In parliament, only the Socialist Left Party opposed inflation targeting, on the grounds that it would give more weight to inflation than to unemployment in economic policy.[81]

The event that prompted the change in the monetary policy guideline, and that probably contributed to building political support, was the shift in fiscal policy and the establishment of a long-term rule for oil revenue spending over the central government budget. High oil revenues, central government budget surpluses, and financial wealth invested abroad through the Government Petroleum Fund since 1996 posed unprecedented challenges to fiscal policy. A substantial rise in oil prices, from approximately USD 10 per barrel at the beginning of 1999 to USD 30 in autumn 2000 contributed to the fund's strong growth and to political pressure to use the revenues. Oil-financed expansion, however, brought back bad memories. As stated in a Ministry of Finance press release, with a clear reference to the 1980s, 'Both our own and other

---

[78] Bergh, *Kollektiv fornuft: 1969–2009*, 379.   [79] Ibid., 468.
[80] 'Vurderer inflasjonsmål', *Dagens Næringsliv* 25 September 1999.
[81] Ø. Djupedals in the Standing Committee for Finance and Economic Affaires, Innst. St. 229 2000–2001, Storting's proceedings.

countries' experience has shown that excessive oil revenue spending can lead to high restructuring costs and unemployment.'[82]

Primarily in an attempt to stem the political pressure on fiscal policy and establish permanent framework conditions for oil revenue spending over the government budget, the Stoltenberg government launched new economic policy guidelines in spring 2001. According to the fiscal rule for oil revenue spending, the fund itself would be saved for the future, but the annual return on the fund (based on an estimate of expected real return, in order to cancel out fluctuations in actual return) could be spent over the government budget. The arguments in favour of the rule, i.e. the need for stable economic developments, and that the domestic economy had to be sheltered from an excessive supply of oil money, were supplemented by a regard for future generations, who were also entitled to their share of Norway's oil wealth.[83]

The fiscal rule was followed by new monetary policy guidelines partly because the rule would further strengthen the role of fiscal policy as a stabilization tool. But the effects of increased oil revenue spending would also be influenced by Norges Bank's monetary policy. One consequence of phasing in oil revenues in larger amounts, as described in the Ministry of Finance's preparatory work, was a larger transfer of resources from the exposed to the sheltered sector through weakened competitiveness.[84] An inflation target of 0–2 per cent, as in the euro area—the rate of inflation Norges Bank had in practice been targeting since January 1999—would lead to a weakening of competitiveness when the shift was made towards a more cautiously expansionary fiscal policy, through higher interest rates and a stronger nominal krone exchange rate.[85] It would be more acceptable if, instead, competitiveness declined because Norges Bank allowed wage and price inflation to be higher. Against this background, the inflation target was set at 2.5 per cent.

There are several reasons to view 2003 as a kind of endpoint for the shift in the monetary policy regime to inflation targeting. In summer 2002, Norges Bank raised the policy rate (with dissenting votes on the Executive Board), explicitly referring to public sector wage growth as a deciding factor. Many felt this was an overreaction.[86] The interest rate increase contributed to a sharp krone appreciation and a rapid deterioration in conditions for the exposed traded sector. Unemployment rose. At the beginning of 2003, trade union leaders from the largest manufacturing firms in Norway demonstrated in the streets of Oslo against Norges Bank's monetary policy.[87] At Governor Gjedrem's first open hearing before the parliamentary Standing Committee on Finance and Economic Affairs in December 2003, however, the committee members were on the whole positive. Gjedrem and Deputy Governor Bergo

---

[82] St.meld. 29 2001, 5, Storting's proceedings.
[83] Steinar Holden, 'Avoiding the Resource Curse: The Case Norway', *Energy Policy* 63 (2013).
[84] Utformingen av den økonomiske politikken i lys av de høye oljeinntektene, 9 January 2001, File 01/181, 430.0, Ministry of Finance's archive.
[85] Ibid.   [86] See e.g. Bergh, *Kollektiv fornuft: 1969–2009*, 469.   [87] Ibid.

later regarded the policy rate increase in 2002 as essential in establishing the right expectations as to Norges Bank's response pattern.[88]

The introduction of an official inflation target also laid the basis, as mentioned earlier, for an amendment to the Norges Bank Act in 2003. All the provisions referring to Norges Bank's relationship with the authorities pointed towards greater independence for the central bank compared with the original text of the act.[89] The rules allowing for the election of politicians to the Executive Board were tightened, and the board became more of a purely expert body. The legal authority to extend direct loans to the government was removed. And it is not uninteresting from a historical perspective that the Credit Act of 1965 and the Exchange Control Act were repealed at the same time.

In Chapter 10, 'The Government's Bank', we pointed out that the central bank's direction was mainly in line with new monetary policy principles, but also with broader trends in the organization of the government administration. The same can be said about the move towards greater independence around 2003. Two developments are relevant here: there were several reorganizations that would move important decisions away from government ministries. The police and the hospitals, for example, used to be under the direct government of the relevant ministry. Now a new police directorate was established with, in principle, wide policing powers. The hospitals were organized as regional enterprises with their own boards. Complex questions of setting priorities and decisions concerning mergers and closures would now be taken by presumably highly qualified managers and boards. Concrete individual decisions would thus be moved away from a vulnerable political level charged with negative connotations to governing bodies where professional competence played a decisive role.[90]

In addition, principles for the government's ownership stakes in commercial enterprise were more clearly established. In the years after 1986, the previously wholly state-owned manufacturing industry was largely reorganized, sold, or closed down. But the government gradually resumed its position as a large shareholder by holding controlling shares in large companies perceived as important for 'national' reasons, such as the industrial conglomerate Norsk Hydro, in which the government had held a large share (44 to 51 per cent) since the First World War. Following the financial crisis, the Norwegian state became a shareholder in the country's largest bank, DnB, and chose to retain a substantial ownership stake. The defence systems supplier the Kongsberg Group broke its back financially speaking in the late 1980s and was reorganized with the government as a major shareholder. Around the turn of the millennium, the state-owned oil company Statoil and the state-owned telecom giant Telenor, which was expanding internationally, were partially privatized and listed on Norwegian and international stock exchanges, as were other state-owned companies. About a third of

[88] Eivind Thomassen's conversation with Svein Gjedrem; Arne Jon Isachsen, 'Jarle Bergo: En profesjonell pengepolitiker går fra borde' (2008).
[89] Eivind Thomassen, 'Translating Central Bank Independence into Norwegian: Central Bankers and the Diffusion of Central Bank Independence to Norway in the 1990s', Review of International Political Economy 24, no. 5 (2017).
[90] Tore Grønlie and Yngve Flo, Sentraladministrasjonens historie etter 1945 (Fagbokforlaget, 2009).

the market capitalization of the Oslo Stock Exchange is now state owned, varying with oil prices and other factors.[91]

In each case, the norm was that boards were filled by persons with a corporate background who were well qualified in commercial terms. The administration of government ownership was professionalized and formalized to avoid companies being influenced by political decisions and 'signals' from government ministries. The main principles were that elected politicians should not be responsible for company decisions on expansions, closures, etc, and that minority shareholders' interests should be fully safeguarded. The latter group would, to put it simply, be protected against decisions that could be politically advantageous, but detrimental to company earnings.[92]

The changes in the administrative organization and government ownership of listed companies were justified as isolated and pragmatic changes, as they were for the central bank's mandate. But it is difficult not to see it as part of a more fundamental position, where the solutions chosen were influenced by similar perceptions of how the boundaries between political and professional decisions should be drawn up.

Concentration on New Tasks

The introduction of inflation targeting prompted a succession of changes in Norges Bank's organization and working methods. Inflation targeting and a floating exchange rate changed the basis for interest rate setting from developments in the foreign exchange market to analyses of future price developments. This shifted the organization's centre of gravity from the operators in the Market Operations department to the bank's analysis departments, which was eventually named the monetary policy area. With a more long-term orientation of interest rate setting, analyses of financial stability could also be included in the decision-making basis, at least tentatively. The Executive Board could also be assigned a larger and more systematic role in interest rate setting. As early as 1999, the Executive Board began to hold regular and pre-announced interest rate meetings to assess and decide on changes in the policy rate.

Even though these were not the only reasons for the strong concentration of Norges Bank's organization around inflation targeting and financial stability, these tasks became a particularly prominent feature of the bank's development after the turn of the millennium. Anything that could not be categorized under these two labels, referred to as the bank's core tasks, or that was not an essential support function, was discontinued in one way or another. The Royal Mint was spun off as a separate company in 2001 and sold in 2003. Operation of the settlement function was outsourced in 2003, and a number of banking services for public institutions were discontinued in 2004. The bank's work on statistics was transferred to Statistics Norway in 2005.

---

[91] Einar Lie, 'Context and Contingency: Explaining State Ownership in Norway', *Enterprise & Society* 17, no. 4 (2016).

[92] Einar Lie, Egil Myklebust, and Harald Norvik, *Staten som kapitalist: Rikdom og eierskap for det 21. århundret* (Pax forlag, 2014).

It caused a stir, of course, when the printing of notes, the part of the bank's operations that perhaps most clearly demonstrated continuity back to the founding of the bank in 1816, was outsourced in 2007.[93] However, the most important event, as part of a long history and as an organizational process, was the closure of the bank's regional branch network. All the remaining regional branches were closed or transferred to other duties for the partially Norges Bank-owned NOKAS Cash Handling in 2001. As a result of these processes, the number of bank employees fell from well over 1,000 in the mid-1990s to about 300 in 2007.

The desire for continuous change in the direction of a leaner, more focused, special-ized, and cost-efficient organization was not unique to Norges Bank. In the period to the turn of the millennium, other central banks sought to implement organizational changes of the same kind.[94] However, the motivation for such a departure was par-ticularly strong at Norges Bank. As we have seen, internal discord had weakened the bank's influence in the 1980s. The cost overrun during the construction of the new Norges Bank premises raised more general questions about governance and resource use that unavoidably made internal reform particularly important. Moreover, the legacy from the 1970s and 1980s may perhaps partly explain why Norges Bank eventually managed to slim down the organization, particularly a widespread regional branch network, to the extent that it did compared to some other European central banks. There was quite simply plenty of 'fat' to cut.

The issue of the regional branches had been raised at regular intervals in the postwar period, and after an extensive internal process, eight branches were finally closed down or converted into cash offices in the course of 1988–9. There was little change after this period. The Executive Board certainly still held the opinion that the bank's departmen-tal structure, as the board put it in a letter to the Ministry of Finance, was 'historically conditioned on the situation in the business sector and communication prevailing in the previous century'.[95] However, the Supervisory Council had proved to be opposed to closures in 1988. When the Standing Committee on Finance and Economic Affairs complained about how difficult it was for politicians to close down regional branches, decision-making authority was assigned to the council. The Supervisory Council, for-mally the bank's highest body, was formally parliament's supervisory body, established in 1816, with the same composition and approximately the same tasks almost 200 years later. For an institution that printed its own money and was not subject to the govern-ment's general budget procedures, the council might have been expected to take on a more critical and investigative role with regard to the bank's organization and use of resources. This was not how the Supervisory Council functioned: a place on the coun-cil was a comfortable position for deserving citizens. The episode mentioned earlier, when the chairperson had to resign after the building budget scandal in the 1980s, was an abrupt, though transient, reminder of parliament's formal responsibility.

---

[93]   Harald Bøhn, 'Norges Banks distriktsavdelinger 1983–2001', in *Staff Memo* (Norges Bank, 2012), 3.
[94]   Singleton, *Central Banking in the Twentieth Century*, 205–6.
[95]   In a letter to the Ministry of Finance, according to Bøhn, 'Norges Banks distriktsavdelinger 1983–2001', 7.

Svein Gjedrem's governorship from 1999 was also a turning point for internal developments in the bank. Gjedrem was a driving force in the work to phase out or outsource operations that were not categorized as the bank's core tasks and to privatize the regional offices. The Ministry of Finance's ideal of thrift came to Norges Bank with Gjedrem. Gjedrem put considerable energy and willpower into removing anything that involved a waste of time or money. He was also to break with the collegiate forms of governance that had developed through Norges Bank's organization in the postwar years in favour of a streamlined system of clear, distinct lines of responsibility.[96]

All in all, Norges Bank's organization and working methods were almost completely changed, at the same time as the bank's independence in its conduct of monetary policy increased. The task of managing the rapidly growing oil fund, described in Chapter 14, strengthens the impression of a break with a shadier past and growth into a new governance regime for the Norwegian economy.

Price Stability Between the Past and the Future

By the beginning of the new millennium, Norges Bank was leaner, stronger, and more self-assured than it had been for a long time. Norges Bank's independence in interest rate setting had certainly already been considerably expanded when the exchange rate target was introduced in 1986. Compared with the preceding period, when the interest rate was largely decided by politicians, this was a major transition, at least as significant as the transition to inflation targeting. Inflation targeting, nonetheless, was a significant step towards independence. Inflation targeting and a floating exchange rate placed greater responsibility for inflation on the central bank and thereby a greater joint responsibility for general stability than exchange rate targeting. Not least, the introduction of an inflation target entailed support for a monetary policy Norges Bank had long argued in favour of and that was in line with best practice in central banking internationally.

Norges Bank won approval for its arguments because the other solutions to the stability challenges in the 1990s preferred by the authorities—income and fiscal policy—demonstrated in a number of ways that they could not fill this role. On a deeper level, inflation targeting gained support because of basic agreement on the objective of price stability, the objective that in practice had been chosen in 1986 and that every government since then had committed to. The discussion about inflation targeting was a conflict about *how* the authorities could best ensure low and stable inflation for the future. The cooperative ideals related to monetary policy had long had precedence. When the confidence in fiscal and income policy failed, monetary policy was left as the only tried and tested and internationally recognized alternative.

---

[96] Egil Borlaug and Turid Wammer, 'Noregs Bank: Grunntrekk i administrasjon, oppgåver og historie' (2009): 78; Haare, Lund, and Solheim, *Norges Banks rolle på finanssektorområdet i perioden 1945–2013, med særlig vekt på finansiell stabilitet*, 340.

The monetary policy regime change in 2001 was thus not a direct reaction to high inflation. On the contrary, inflation had been low, while economic growth had been high and the employment rate had risen sharply throughout the 1990s. Oil price volatility, the rise in wage growth, and the calls for an increase in oil revenue spending at the end of the 1990s nonetheless raised the question as to whether the existing regime could also adequately safeguard stability in the future. Memories of the 1980s played a decisive role for the conclusion reached by the authorities. Virtually all of the arguments in favour of a regime change referred more or less explicitly to the uncontrolled expansion of the 1980s and the high cost of restoring control in the late 1980s and early 1990s. The Ministry of Finance referred to the experience of the 1980s when explaining its cautious approach to oil revenue spending. And this experience was probably the most important intellectual foundation among politicians and government officials for the new economic policy guidelines introduced in 2001.

As had been the case for the fixed exchange rate regime since 1986, inflation targeting was largely a policy to meet future challenges based on past experience. This will often be the case, and there is no particularly deep insight to be found here. All policy aims to be forward looking, but the experience underlying the decisions and the mistakes to be avoided must necessarily be in the past.

14

The Investment Manager

The management of the nation's long-term savings in what is now the Government Pension Fund Global brought Norges Bank a brand new responsibility from the mid-1990s, and an unusual one for a central bank.[1] While many central banks have historically played an important part in contributing to government financing and investing government debt in liquid securities, this has never been one of Norges Bank's main roles—indeed one of the key aims of the acts of 1816 and 1892 was to prevent the government from funding itself through the central bank.[2] From the mid-1990s, however, Norges Bank was in a way given the opposite task: a separate mandate to manage the country's financial wealth on behalf of the government by investing it abroad in long-term bonds, shares, and eventually real estate.

Within twenty years, thanks to high oil prices and substantial inflows from the government, the fund's market value soared from nothing to around NOK 7 trillion, or almost three times mainland GDP.[3] In 2012, the fund overtook the Abu Dhabi Investment Authority to become the world's largest sovereign wealth fund.[4] In recent years, the fund's rapid expansion and financial importance have brought Norges Bank—and Norway—at least as much international attention as the bank's more traditional roles in monetary policy and financial stability.

The Government Petroleum Fund that was formed in 1991 was originally more of a budgetary vehicle than a response to how and where the nation's financial wealth should be invested. With its institutional autonomy and freedom to manoeuvre, and its historically contingent mix of both proximity to and distance from the political authorities, the bank found itself in a seemingly ideal position to house such a fund. Even after rising oil prices from the mid-1990s transformed the outlook for the fund, both the Ministry of Finance and the bank itself remained in favour of the bank managing the fund. The mandate gave the bank an important role in a brand new area and helped strengthen both its own self-image and the external perception of the central

---

[1] Of the international funds that Norges Bank in 1997 considered comparable with the Government Petroleum Fund, as it was then known, only Singapore's reserve fund had a connection to the central bank, in that the bank's governor acted as its CEO. See the report of the working group on the cost, aims, and organization of investment management, 2 May 1997, Norges Bank Administration. (Documentation file.)

[2] While this principle was set aside during the First World War and to some extent in the years after that, the financing of government never became one of Norges Bank's principal activities.

[3] Statistics Norway's latest estimate of the market value of GDP in 2014 is NOK 2,527,409 million.

[4] According to the Sovereign Wealth Fund Institute, the GPFG was the single largest sovereign wealth fund in 2015, although some countries do have funds that together have a greater value. The fund is nevertheless smaller than the two largest private funds. As reported in newspapers, with titles such as 'Oil Fund is the World's Largest' (author's translation), see 'Oljefondet er størst i verden', *Aftenposten*, 5 November 2012.

Norges Bank 1816–2016. Einar Lie, Oxford University Press (2020). © Norges Bank.
DOI: 10.1093/oso/9780198860013.001.0001

bank as an institution with a very special responsibility for the long-term stability of the Norwegian economy.

But the management of an ever-growing fund would also expose the bank to considerable institutional risk. The focus on risk taking and returns made very different demands on central banking in terms of expertise and organization. The creation of a new internal unit specializing in investment management—Norges Bank Investment Management (NBIM)—and this unit's expansion and evolution in line with the fund and expectations for the fund—presented considerable governance challenges and created institutional tensions. The fund's growth and substantial investments meant that its management attracted political attention on a completely different level than the rest of the central bank's activities. Much of this institutional risk was to crystallize during the financial crisis of 2008–9, which brought heavy losses and widespread criticism.

A Buffer Fund

The awareness that oil revenues might one day produce surpluses for the government that would need to be invested somewhere arose around the time of the oil crisis of 1973 and the introduction of a new restrictive tax regime on the Norwegian continental shelf in 1975. As the Ministry of Finance noted in its 1974 white paper on the position of the oil industry in Norway, future surpluses would need to be invested in assets abroad in the interests of both the economy and coming generations.[5] But these surpluses were a long time coming. When the Government Petroleum Fund was created as an account at Norges Bank in 1991, there was still no immediate prospect of any wealth to invest.

This was partly because more oil revenue than expected was being spent. That the country's oil wealth should benefit the whole of society had been a premise ever since the 1974 white paper launched the political slogan of the decade—'building a better Norway'. At the same time, it was explicitly stated that injecting oil revenue into the economy too quickly could cause problems—it needed to be phased in over a long period. The original solution to this problem had been to attempt to limit oil production, but this proved difficult in practice. In key parts of the 1970s and 1980s, Norway also showed a talent for spending money before it arrived.

The fund set up in 1991 was not intended in the first instance to solve the problem of how surpluses from oil production should be invested. The aim was to uncouple the production side, which generated the revenue, from the spending of that revenue, so ensuring that the latter was steadier and more predictable than the revenue itself. The idea of a 'buffer fund' was mooted as early as 1983 by the Tempo Committee as an alternative to regulating production. The committee's chairman, Hermod Skånland, then deputy governor at Norges Bank, was the brains behind the proposal.

---

[5] 'St. meld. 25 (1973–1974), 'Petroleumsvirksomhetens plass i det norsk samfunn', Storting's proceedings.

The committee argued that revenue from oil production should be transferred to the fund and no longer be recognized as revenue in the government budget. This would encourage the government to budget its expenditure on the basis of other, more long-term criteria. The Storting would still be able to withdraw as much money from the fund as was needed to cover any deficits, however, so the fund was not in itself an impediment to unsustainable fiscal policy. The main argument for the buffer fund was that parliamentary approval of transfers to and from the fund would nevertheless make it more obvious and politically risky for governments to spend more oil money than permitted by the long-term guidelines.[6]

The Tempo Committee's proposals were welcomed by the Willoch government. Key opposition politicians also embraced the fund concept. In 1983, oil revenue was still high, and many probably saw the fund primarily as a vehicle for investing future wealth. Contrary to the committee's proposals, however, many advocates of the fund concept argued that it should be used to finance domestic infrastructure investments. Civil servants at the Ministry of Finance feared that an independent fund might serve as a channel for bypassing the ordinary government budget.[7] They would proceed to stall the process, helped along by external developments.[8] When oil prices slumped in early 1986, any prospect of an accumulation of wealth in the fund became a distant dream. When the short-lived right-wing coalition government took up the matter again in 1989, the fund was more of a symbolic notion.

The Tempo Committee did not look in depth at how the fund should be managed. It indicated, however, that the simplest option would be to deposit inflows of oil revenue in a krone account at Norges Bank, which would then invest the money in foreign securities in the same way as its foreign exchange reserves.[9] Should these inflows hit a certain level, parts could then be managed with a view to higher returns. The returns generated could then be credited to the krone account under an agreement between the Ministry of Finance and Norges Bank. In practice, this was the solution that the Ministry of Finance plumped for in 1990 and has stuck with ever since. At the time, investing the money abroad was a key point. Heavy domestic investment funded with oil money could lead to excessive demand in the Norwegian economy in the longer term. Norway's own experience from the 1970s and developments in the Netherlands before that—the dreaded 'Dutch disease'—were a major source of concern. There were also persistent fears among the civil servants developing the fund structure that the fund would end up as a source of 'cheap' financing for populist initiatives outside the normal thorough budget process, as previous funds had tended to be. Once it was established that the money would be invested abroad, however, it was easier to focus on performance objectives and avoid fighting over the most desirable recipient of government investment.

---

[6] NOU 1983:27, *Petroleumsvirksomhetens fremtid* (Norges offentlige utredninger, 1983).
[7] Einar Lie, 'Learning by Failing: The Origins of the Norwegian Oil Fund', *Scandinavian Journal of History* 43, no. 2 (2018).
[8] Einar Lie and Christian Venneslan, *Over Evne: Finansdepartementet 1965–1992* (Pax forlag, 2010), 343–7.
[9] NOU 1983: 27, 101–2.

A Brand New Role

Not until new forecasts for oil prices and oil production came along in the mid-1990s did it become clear that the petroleum fund would indeed grow to a significant size. In the revised national budget for 1995, the government announced the prospect of net transfers to the petroleum fund account for the very first time. In the very next paragraph, the government noted the long-term challenges facing the welfare state in the form of an ageing population and peak oil.[10] Over the next two years, forecasts for oil production and prices were revised substantially, and the fund was projected to hit NOK 400 billion by the year 2000. The prospect of the fund growing to such a size made the issue of principles and rules for the management of the fund suddenly more acute.

One of the Tempo Committee's arguments for assigning the management of the petroleum fund to Norges Bank was the latter's long experience with investing its own foreign exchange reserves. These were mainly invested in liquid government securities and bank deposits, at the time chiefly in European currencies. Back in 1996, when the first billions were transferred to the petroleum fund, there was still a strong case for managing the fund in a similar fashion. Estimates during this first phase suggested that transfers to the fund would decline again after 1996, and that there would soon be a need to make withdrawals.[11] However, rapid upward forecast revisions would subsequently indicate that the fund needed to adopt a more long-term investment horizon and look for broader, more diversified investments. A fast-growing fund would need to consider investing in more long-term and less liquid assets, in various types of equity instruments, and eventually maybe also in real estate and commodities. The bank was particularly keen on investing in shares in foreign companies. This position was reached on the basis of historical data from the US and the UK showing that a mixed portfolio of equities and bonds was less risky than a portfolio consisting entirely of one or the other, and that the equity allocation bringing the lowest risk to the portfolio increased with the investment horizon.[12] 'Professional managers would not have any strong objections to an equity portion of at least 30 per cent', the bank concluded in spring 1997.[13]

The management of hundreds of billions of kroner in multiple asset classes with a long-term return objective was an unfamiliar task for a central bank and presented Norges Bank with challenges both large and small. Most obviously, it required expertise that the bank did not possess. The bank was also a bureaucratic institution unsuited to generating returns, critics claimed. It was furthermore in possession of market-sensitive information about other countries' central banks and their decisions. Expectations that the fund would be invested in other assets sparked debate, as early

[10] St. meld. 2 (1994–1995) 'Revidert nasjonalbudsjett for 1995', Storting's proceedings.

[11] Harald Bøhn and Birger Vikøren, 'Petroleumsfondet-en ny stor oppgave for Norges Bank', *Norges Banks Skriftserie H* 28 (1999): 133.

[12] St. meld. 2 (1996–1997) 'Revidert nasjonalbudsjett for 1997', 78, Storting's proceedings.

[13] 'Future management of the Government Petroleum Fund', letter from Norges Bank to the Ministry of Finance of 10 April 1997, documentation file, NB.

as 1995, on whether the bank should be given operational responsibility for the fund if it were to be managed in this way. Representatives of the financial sector argued that the fund should instead be used to build up a private investment management industry in Norway that could live on after the oilfields ran dry.[14]

Many critics may have had their own interests in mind when questioning the choice of Norges Bank as manager, but counterarguments also coloured the bank's own stance in 1996–7. An internal committee set up in December 1996 to examine various aspects of the extended role as investment manager found that managing the petroleum fund might complicate the bank's core central banking duties. For example, the committee noted that one sure-fire way for the bank to generate an excess return for the fund would be to take currency positions against those of other central banks having to intervene heavily to defend their currencies.[15] To be associated with operations of this kind would be unprecedented for a central bank. Another issue was that the fund might grow to such a size that it would steal management's attention away from core central banking duties. Poor investment results and the ensuing negative press coverage might also damage Norges Bank's reputation.[16] Underlying these arguments was an implicit fear that managing the fund could undermine the bank's independence.[17] When the committee's report was submitted to the Executive Board in May 1997, the conclusion was that, if the bank was to continue to manage the fund, it should loosen the ties between central banking and investment management as far as possible by setting up a separate subsidiary with its own board and offices outside the bank.

While the challenges associated with investment management at Norges Bank were clear, neither the civil servants at the Ministry of Finance nor the bank's own management seem to have been in any doubt that the fund should be managed by the bank. The government never wavered in its position that the bank would continue to manage the fund.[18] The bank's governor, Torstein Moland, also rounded on the critics in autumn 1995, offering to compete with private players for the management of the fund. He pointed out that there had already been moves towards higher required rates of return in the bank's existing management of the foreign exchange reserves.[19]

The solution of assigning the fund to Norges Bank would eventually fall neatly into place. Other than some internal concerns at the bank about the changes involved, and constant pressure from players in the financial sector, the balance of opinion was in favour of the central bank. It is interesting how little traction was gained by arguments in favour of using this capital to strengthen the Norwegian financial sector. In fact, there were fears that a large, independent entity with close ties to the financial sector might acquire a degree of informal influence that would undermine democratic control and the general credibility of the fund. This was definitely not wanted.

---

[14] Christoffer Kleivset and Tine Petersen, 'Etableringen og utviklingen av NBIM' (Norges Bank, 2013).
[15] Ibid., 52.   [16] Ibid., 6.
[17] Sigbjørn Atle Berg, who chaired the committee, in conversation with Christoffer Kleivset on 2 May 2012.
[18] St. meld. 2 (1994–1995) 'Revidert nasjonalbudsjett for 1995', 70, Storting's proceedings.
[19] Kleivset and Petersen, 'Etableringen og utviklingen av NBIM'.

It is understandable that this would be the outcome in a Norwegian political context. Historians have noted that business interests have generally had limited legitimacy in Norway. To a greater extent than in many other countries, it is believed that power and influence in important areas of society should be linked directly to democratic institutions. This is where legitimacy lies.[20] Historically, this may be a legacy of the nineteenth-century 'civil servant state', which was built on explicitly expressed democratic and egalitarian norms—it was civil servants working for the common good, rather than businessmen, who were the powerful and normatively dominant elite, as discussed in this book's early chapters. The dominance of the Labour Party after the Second World War helped cement some of these attitudes. The party welcomed growth and production, but tended to be wary of the men and interests of the business world.

The financial sector, especially the big institutions, has generally been viewed with some scepticism. The low interest rate policy was motivated by the good results that low interest rates would bring. But underlying this was scepticism about those who could be thought to benefit from high interest rates: the wealthy and those who managed their wealth. In the government sector, the Ministry of Finance acted as both policy-maker and regulator for the financial sector. From its perspective, there was little doubt that the financial sector was something to be regulated, and relations between the ministry and the industry were not especially warm. Until the 1990s, for example, there was an active policy to limit the growth of the big three banks (despite their comparatively small size by global and even Nordic standards) in order to make space for small and regional banks. One internationally oriented executive at the largest bank of the 1980s, DnC, commented at the time that he wished the Norwegian authorities shared the attitude of their counterparts in the UK, where banking was seen as a valuable sector that generated money and created value. In Norway, the general perception was that of a service industry in need of restraint and of lower intrinsic value than the more 'productive' side of the business sector.[21] By the late 1990s, policies and practices had begun to move forward, but calls for private management of the country's oil wealth in order to increase the expertise and earnings of Norwegian financial institutions fell on unusually stony ground.

The need to oversee the fund's management, and fears that decentralized management would mean weaker returns, also spoke in favour of a solution in the government sector, with Norges Bank undoubtedly the preferred option. The Storting already had an established control mechanism in the form of Norges Bank's Supervisory Council and established reporting procedures. Svein Gjedrem, then chief mandarin at the Ministry of Finance, wrote several memos to the minister pointing out that the bank had great technical expertise and must also have the capacity to handle such a task.[22]

It became clear in talks with the bank's management early in 1997 that the ministry also wanted the management of the fund to take place *within* the bank's existing

---

[20] Einar Lie, 'Context and Contingency: Explaining State Ownership in Norway', *Enterprise & Society* 17, no. 4 (2016).

[21] Einar Lie, *Den norske Creditbank 1982–1990: En storbank i vekst og krise* (Universitetsforlaget, 1998), 24.

[22] Svein Gjedrem in conversation with Einar Lie, 18 August 2015.

organization. Above all, the ministry seems to have been concerned that a subsidiary, as proposed internally at the bank, might, like a fully external solution, develop an excessive degree of independence. With the management of the fund within the central bank, the ministry would also avoid moving into uncharted territory in terms of international tax rules, which would probably have been necessary with both a private sector solution and the subsidiary model.[23] With the Executive Board directly responsible for the fund, it would come under a well-established governance and reporting system.

Creating a New Unit

Although the management of the fund was kept within Norges Bank's existing organization structure, this side of its operations would have considerable autonomy. One important driving force in the creation of the investment management unit was Knut Kjær, previously a senior executive at the insurance company Storebrand, who from May 1997 led the internal project group tasked with preparing and implementing the phasing in of an equity portfolio and systems to safeguard the fund. As the subsequent head of the fund from 1998 to 2007, he would be a key practitioner of the independence that he himself had fought for as chair of the project group.

Kjær quickly realized that investment management requires a keener focus on results than ordinary central banking operations, and that this could best be cultivated in a separate organization.[24] This focus on results also meant that responsibility needed to be assigned undiluted to the management unit, and that this responsibility had to be backed with considerable freedom to take the decisions that the unit itself deemed necessary. Similarly, the various components of its role were to be delegated right down through the unit to the individual employee. This principle was an argument for transferring ever more functions to the unit's own management and cutting ties with the rest of the central bank's operations.

Not only should the investment management unit have independent responsibility and greater freedom, but it also needed a more relaxed regulatory framework than the rest of the bank. Investment management demanded a different approach to personnel and remuneration policy. Whether it was to manage the portfolios itself or 'manage the managers' by overseeing external suppliers, the unit would need to recruit people with investment management expertise. To do so, it would need to offer competitive pay packages. Although part of the strategy was that the fund should not be a pay leader, the need for competitiveness meant higher pay levels than were generally seen elsewhere at the bank. Although this need for special pay terms was broadly accepted at management level, it did not necessarily sit well with all staff.[25]

---

[23] Kleivset and Petersen, 'Etableringen og utviklingen av NBIM', 6.
[24] See, for example, Knut Kjær, 'Rammer for organiseringen av KAP' [Framework for the organization of investment management], 31 October 1997, Norges Bank Administration. Documentation file, NB.
[25] Kleivset and Petersen, 'Etableringen og utviklingen av NBIM'.

The tensions between the new, more freestyle unit and the rest of the bank were apparent from an early point in its relationship with Market Operations, the department responsible for managing the foreign exchange reserves. For practical reasons, a number of tasks—mainly related to oversight and strategic advice for the bank's executive management—were initially assigned to Market Operations. Based on the line management principle and dissatisfaction with how some of these tasks were handled, Kjær argued in 1998 that most of them should be transferred to Investment Management. Market Operations supported retaining the previous arrangement. The question was ultimately settled in Kjær's favour.

An Active and Growing Investor

The year 1997 brought the broad lines of a management strategy that, with few significant changes, has provided the framework for the fund's operations ever since. This work covered a wide variety of technical issues, such as allocations to different currencies and geographies, and how risk should be measured and managed. There was also the important split between fixed income and equity—government bonds and shares—which Norges Bank and then the Ministry of Finance set at 60/40 (with a degree of flexibility).[26]

Most important of all for the manager's role, however, was the proposal that the fund should largely be managed passively as an index fund, but with a small element of active management. This meant that the fund was to be invested on the basis of a broad benchmark index that reflected developments in the various markets. By investing in line with this index, the fund's investments would be well diversified and generate a return identical to the market. With passive management, both transaction and management costs would be low, and it would be easier to monitor and assess performance. The guidelines for investment management that the government approved in autumn 1997 on the basis of Norges Bank's own recommendations also focused on returns following a broad benchmark index constructed by the Ministry of Finance after consulting the bank.

From the outset, however, it was clear that the fund was also to aim for an excess return over the benchmark through a degree of active management of parts of the portfolio. This could be achieved in various ways. The most obvious was 'active index management', or systematically using information about when a stock will enter or exit a known index and trading in anticipation of these events. Without some element of this, transaction costs would probably pull returns below the market average. Another option was to try to beat the index by picking stocks expected to outperform.

[26] A fact based presentation of the investment strategy is presented on NBIMs homepages, https://www.nbim.no/en/publications/features/2011-and-older/2009/from-40-to-60-per-cent-equities/ (accessed 19 June 2019).

The project group under Kjær embraced and defended this ambition to generate an excess return through active management from an early point.[27] As early as May 1997, he presented a vision of Norges Bank building up a management unit 'among the international elite'.[28] Almost as much as the excess return per se, the main argument seems to have been that aiming for an excess return would help develop the unit and give it something to reach for—a motive for continuous improvement. This applied not only to the relative return but also to the requirement for low management costs. Organizational factors have also, implicitly or explicitly, played a key role subsequently when Norges Bank has defended the ambitiousness of its goals for the management of the fund. In a letter to the ministry in 2009, Norges Bank wrote: 'A passive, uninformed approach to operational decisions is an alternative without a sound theoretical or practical justification.'[29]

The balance between passive and active management was set out formally in the Ministry of Finance's rules on relative volatility. Under the regulations laid down in 1997, the amount of risk that the manager was permitted to take was determined by a limit for tracking error—how far the fund could deviate from the benchmark index.[30] On the bank's recommendation, this limit was eventually set at 1.5 per cent. Since this was a limit for the whole fund's deviation from the benchmark index, and most of the fund was to be managed passively with relatively little risk, the permitted tracking error could be concentrated in such a way that individual portfolio managers within specific mandates could operate with much higher levels of expected relative volatility and hence much higher potential returns on their investments. In keeping with the line management principle, Kjær split this risk between different portfolios, and the senior portfolio managers delegated the risk further, right down to the individual investment manager.[31]

With a growing fund due to substantial transfers from the government, an independent internal management unit, and a degree of active management, the scene was set for substantial organizational expansion. As explained in the fund's annual report for 2003, different forms of active management required considerable expertise across a wide variety of fields. As a result, 'the Bank wishes to build a very diverse investment management structure'.[32]

One concrete mechanism in this process was the potential for cutting costs. Kjær noted at an early stage that the experience of external index managers was disappointing, and that there was clear scope to realize economies of scale by bringing this management in-house. Even in the far more specialized field of active management, where

---

[27] See also Knut Kjær, 'Strategi for kostnadseffektiv meravkastning i aksjeporteføljer', *Sentralbanken i forandringens tegn: Festskrift til Kjell Storvik* (Norges Bank, 1999).
[28] Kleivset and Petersen, 'Etableringen og utviklingen av NBIM', 19.
[29] 'Active management of the Government Pension Fund Global', letter from Norges Bank to the Ministry of Finance, 23 December 2009. (Documentation file.)
[30] 'Proposal for guidelines for the Government Petroleum Fund', letter from Norges Bank to the Ministry of Finance, 22 August 1997. Documentation file, NB.
[31] See feature article 2 in the Norwegian version of NBIM's annual report for 2003, *Forvaltning av Statens Petroleumsfond–Årsrapport 2003* (Norges Bank, 2003).
[32] Ibid., 44.

costs for external managers were very high, there would be clear advantages to the bank building up its own expertise internally. In the ensuing years, both index management and active management would increasingly be insourced. In 1999, NBIM took over an entire floor of Norges Bank's extensive headquarters in Oslo. A few years later, it had taken over another floor and opened offices in London and New York. By 2005, there were thirty-four staff at these overseas offices, mostly working on active management.[33] An office in Shanghai followed in 2007, and, with great fanfare, another in Singapore in 2010.[34] In terms of staff numbers, NBIM overtook the rest of the bank in 2012 and is now considerably larger.

Capital and Ethics

Historically, there has been scepticism in Norway about the influence that comes with large concentrations of capital and the financial sector. Norwegian authorities have also long been concerned about their reputation and role in an international context, in peacekeeping and the development of international law and standards. In this light, it is unsurprising that the matter of ethical and political guidelines for what the fund should and should not invest in arose early. More surprising, perhaps, is that it took so long for explicit ethical guidelines to fall into place.

The fund's manager—Norges Bank—was by no means keen on guidelines of this kind. In its letter on principles for the management of the fund in spring 1997, the bank argued that any criteria beyond pure financial returns would make it difficult for politicians and the public to assess its performance.[35] Similar arguments were aired by the Ministry of Finance's experts and political leadership. The ethical principles for the fund came about mainly due to pressure from opposition parties and a series of press exposés. In many cases, these were the fruits of long-term work by non-governmental organizations with a clear agenda for change.

An early attempt to accommodate the calls for ethical guidelines was nonetheless made in 1999. The government proposed setting up a separate environmental fund amounting to 0.5 per cent of the oil fund's capital. It also proposed that the fund should not be permitted to invest in the tobacco industry, but this was not backed by the Storting. Nor were any mechanisms developed to enable the fund to avoid specific companies.[36]

More extensive and politically demanding criticism of the fund's concrete investments would emerge a couple of years later, from 2001 until the creation of a government committee to examine the matter in 2003. Investments in cluster munitions, child

---

[33]   *Statens Pensjonsfond Utland—Årsrapport 2005* (Norges Bank, 2005), 33.

[34]   'Oljefondet slo ut håret i Singapore', *Dagens Næringsliv*, 30 December 2010.

[35]   'Future management of the Government Petroleum Fund', letter from Norges Bank to the Ministry of Finance, 10 April 1997.

[36]   Maren Diesen Kristensen, 'From Avoidance to Activism: The Responsible Investment Frameworks of the Norwegian Government Pension Fund Global, the New Zealand Superannuation Fund and California Public Employees' Retirement System 2000–2016' (University of Oslo, 2016).

labour, the military dictatorship in Myanmar, and landmines—this last example only shortly after campaigners against these weapons had received the Nobel Peace Prize—were among the revelations of who and what was helping grow the nation's savings.[37]

NBIM and the bank's management argued explicitly against ethical guidelines during this period. The fund's management considered it most appropriate to 'invest in the world as it is', as CEO Yngve Slyngstad later put it.[38] Governor Svein Gjedrem explained to the press in 2001 that in an international economy it was impossible to 'differentiate between white knights and black knights'. Large, complex conglomerates could have operations in countless industries. Gjedrem also pointed out that Norway's armed forces already did business with arms manufacturers that also produced landmines. The underlying principle here was that the government should not apply different standards in different areas. At the same time, the governor noted that the most pressing matter was to reach a political consensus on where the line was to be drawn, and then stick to that line in the longer term.[39]

Not that the fund was completely without ethical guidelines in the early years of the new millennium. It was not permitted to invest in production that was unlawful or discouraged by international conventions. But most of the fund's influence as an owner was expressed through its voting at general meetings and on corporate actions. As it still does today, the fund voted against proposals that contravened the principle of equitable treatment of all shareholders, the re-election of chairmen who were also CEOs (a model common in the US), and various types of remuneration, including options that were based on past performance or resulted in substantial transfers from shareholders to management. While these principles were not ethically neutral, they were not primarily ethical in purpose—all were founded on the fund's overall goal of the greatest possible long-term return on its investments.[40]

New guidelines were introduced in light of the findings of the 2003 government committee mentioned above. In addition to active ownership through voting at general meetings, two new principles were introduced. One was negative screening, which meant that producers in certain areas were not to be part of the fund's investment universe. These included parts of the arms industry, and subsequently also the tobacco industry. The other was individual exclusions. After individual consideration on the basis of general guidelines, specific companies could be excluded from the same universe. Based on the committee's proposals, a new Council on Ethics was formed to advise the Ministry of Finance on exclusions.[41] A variety of companies have been excluded over the years. The most renowned, especially outside Norway, is probably US retailer Walmart, which was excluded in 2006 for reasons that included its anti-union stance.[42]

[37] Kaare Mikael Bilden, "'Vi kan ikke leve med disse skandaleavsløringene": Hvordan aktualiseres den globaliserte økonomiens problemstillinger i norske nyhetsmedier i debatten om etiske retningslinjer for oljefondet' (University of Oslo, 2005).

[38] Conversation with Yngve Slyngstad, 19 June 2015.   [39] *Bergens Tidende*, 10 March 2001.

[40] 'Forvaltning av Statens Petroleumsfond'. Annual report 2003.

[41] NOU 2003: 22, *Forvaltning for fremtiden* (Norges offentlige utredninger, 2003).

[42] Bilden, "'Vi kan ikke leve med disse skandaleavsløringene": Hvordan aktualiseres den globaliserte økonomiens problemstillinger i norske nyhetsmedier i debatten om etiske retningslinjer for Oljefondet'.

The reaction in the US was strong: Walmart had contravened neither national nor international rules, and perhaps not even norms for how employers in its home country should behave. The whole point of the ethical framework, however, was that the fund's principles should reflect not universal rules but important *Norwegian* norms. The reasoning here was that shareholders' participation in a company is not purely financial, and so they cannot wash their hands of its conduct. The ongoing debate about the ethical rules has often focused on the consequences—whether they contribute to a better world. The background documents behind the new rules did not, however, say much about what the effects of exclusion or screening might be. The emphasis was on the importance of being able to say no to investments in companies from which the fund wished to distance itself on the basis of an independent ethical assessment. This had a particular appeal when it came to the nation's savings, as the population should not be made 'complicit' in activities that contravened the values that Norway otherwise sought to uphold.

Given the political risk associated with the fund, the system introduced in 2004 provided important clarification. Decisions on screening and exclusion now rested with the political authorities. The fund would remain an active owner, but this would be about individual decisions less controversial than those now assigned to the Ministry of Finance and the government. However, subsequent reports from external consultants criticized the fund and the Council on Ethics for poor coordination and collaboration.[43] In 2014, the Solberg government proposed resolving this by discontinuing the Council on Ethics and transferring the responsibility for exclusions to Norges Bank, but a majority of the Storting opted instead for a hybrid solution. The Council on Ethics would remain in place, but its advice would now be submitted to Norges Bank which, from 2015 onwards, would take the final decision. The idea was to create greater coherence and consistency between ongoing ownership activities and exclusions, but it has also increased the institutional risk from alleged or actual misjudgements in this politically charged area.

There is also a need for sensitivity to ensure that Norges Bank's position is aligned with that of the Storting. The principles for negative screening are still a parliamentary matter. In spring 2015, the Storting resolved to exclude coal producers from the investment universe. The same parliament decided that the government should issue financial support for continued coal production on Svalbard, to a company in which the fund would not have been able to invest had it been a foreign company. The political consistency that Gjedrem took for granted back in 2001, when considering the issue of excluding arms manufacturers that were customers of the Norwegian armed forces, does not therefore seem to have prevailed. Such inconsistent treatment of domestic and international companies serves to make the normative foundation in important Norwegian values less robust.

---

[43] The Albright Group LLC and Simon Chesterman, 'Assessment of Implementation of Article 3 and 4 of the Ethical Guidelines for the Government Pension Fund—Global', ed. Ministry of Finance (Regjeringen, 2008).

Capital and Politics

With the oil fund's growing size, the 'political' dimension has also become prominent in areas other than ethical equity investments. Investing in government bonds and other securities used for the long-term financing of governments and economic activity can never be politically neutral. The key role played by the big investment banks in financing both their own and other governments up until the interbellum period is an old story. At times, these investments would bring considerable unofficial influence. NBIM's ascendancy has been more restrained, and its portfolio more diverse, than those of the Rothschilds, Barings Bank, and J.P. Morgan in their heydays, but a number of episodes show how capital and high politics can also be closely intertwined when it comes to the oil fund.

One early episode was extensively covered in the Norwegian and international press before and during the financial crisis. The fund had substantial investments in the Icelandic economy until around 2005. These were then sold for purely financial reasons. At times, the fund also had short positions in Icelandic fixed-income instruments—a technique used to bet on a decrease in the value of an asset. This clear lack of confidence in the Icelandic economy prompted vocal protests from Iceland itself, which is after all part of the relatively close Nordic community in many areas. But pan-Nordic cooperation and solidarity were not part of NBIM's agenda, and in hindsight the handling of its exposure to Iceland turned out to be right for the fund's return.

The most persistent challenge in European politics in the wake of the financial crisis has been Greece's enormous government debt, which would grow to slightly more than—and more recently slightly less than—the value of the oil fund. When the EU proposed a deal to refinance this debt in 2011, NBIM voted against it. For the EU, this was a political issue, but not in Norway. The Ministry of Finance—and hence the government—was not consulted before NBIM voted. The position at NBIM and Norges Bank was that the refinancing package clearly contravened the principles the fund was to follow.[44] NBIM found that the package failed in numerous ways to take account of existing contracts between lender and borrower, and that creditors were not being treated equitably, and was very sceptical about Greece's ability to service its old debt. Repeated refinancing inevitably also brings a lack of control over how the burden is distributed between creditors.

The most recent example worth mentioning arose during the Crimean crisis in 2014. A relative strengthening of the economies of eastern Europe, and especially Russia, meant that they had come to make up a larger share of the benchmark for NBIM's investments. Based on the principle of staying one step ahead of the benchmark, NBIM started buying up Russian government securities. Soon after, Russia occupied the Crimean peninsula, leading to extensive discussion at NBIM and among Norges Bank's senior management of whether increased financing for Russia was

---

[44] Conversation with Svein Gjedrem and Yngve Slyngstad.

desirable. Both political and financial arguments played a role in this discussion. Following this internal process, the bank contacted the Ministry of Finance with a proposal to amend the benchmark index so that the bank was not obliged to increase its investments in Russian securities. The solution was to find a technical justification for assigning Russian government bonds a much lower weight in the benchmark portfolio than before.[45]

The Fund and the Financial Crisis

In terms of the return on the oil fund, the financial crisis was primarily a matter of the collapse in the prices of shares and fixed-income instruments in autumn 2008. But the crisis would also have more prolonged effects for both the fund and financial markets. Globally, the first signs of trouble came in the form of liquidity problems and losses at a number of major banks, most notably BNP Paribas in France and Northern Rock in the UK in autumn 2007. Leading stock indices were not affected by these signals and hit new highs that same autumn. There was then a gradual decline, with a full-scale collapse after the Lehman Brothers bankruptcy in September 2008, but it was not until spring 2009 that equity prices hit their lowest levels. The clean-up process in the financial sector was to last much longer still.

NBIM analysed the situation in depth in August 2007. Three main scenarios were considered, the bleakest 'apocalypse scenario' being far worse than actual events over the next eighteen months.[46] Autumn 2007 was a busy and complicated period, especially for fixed-income management. Results were relatively weak, but without this sparking any major debate in the outside world. When Knut Kjær finished as CEO of NBIM early in 2008 and was succeeded by Yngve Slyngstad, previously chief investment officer for equities, a series of organizational changes were made to improve risk management in general and the oversight of fixed-income management in particular. Substantial changes were made to the external side of fixed-income management, with a sharp reduction in the number of external managers. Internally too, major changes were made. Of the three senior portfolio managers, one was transferred, one left, and one stayed on. This extensive change process was undoubtedly important for NBIM's internal culture and organization, which we will not go into in detail here. The two investment areas—equity and fixed income—were largely separate within the office and used different IT systems. Staff on the fixed-income side came to work in the open-necked shirts and sweaters that were the standard dress code of the central bank, and had Norwegian as their working language. Slyngstad's equity managers favoured ties and dark suits, and had English as their working language. From spring 2008, however, the fixed-income side was gradually subsumed into the equity side's style and expression.

---

[45]   Conversations with Svein Gjedrem, Yngve Slyngstad, and Trond Grande.
[46]   Conversations with Svein Gjedrem, Yngve Slyngstad, and Trond Grande, 19 June 2015.

Although NBIM was prepared for a substantial downturn, it was not impossible in practice to avoid heavy losses. 'There was nowhere to hide' is how the governor put it at a press conference early in 2009 when the results from the autumn were unveiled. NBIM operated under a mandate with fairly clear limits on how assets could be invested, and there were considerable declines in every asset class, with both equities and fixed income falling sharply in value. One problem for NBIM, however, was that the losses from its active management were greater than would have been the case with purely passive index management. The Storting had also amended Norges Bank's mandate in 2007, most notably by increasing the allocation to equities from 40 per cent to 60 per cent. This had been a controversial move both politically and in the public debate. While the change had not been implemented by the time the markets crashed, the events of autumn 2008 provided ammunition for those arguing that the stock market presented excessive risks for a sovereign manager, and prompted generally fierce criticism of attempts to beat the market through active management.

Active management had generated an excess return for the fund every year until 2007, and the equity portfolio had significantly outperformed the fixed-income portfolio. The fund was also growing in size. The white paper on the fund published by the Ministry of Finance in spring 2008 therefore proposed a number of changes to the investment strategy. By far the most important was the increase in the equity share from 40 per cent to 60 per cent. It also proposed increasing the number of companies the fund could invest in by including small-cap companies in the benchmark portfolio and increasing the weight of emerging markets. The ministry further proposed that real estate and infrastructure should become a new investment area for the fund, and that NBIM should be permitted to invest in unlisted shares.[47]

NBIM and Norges Bank had themselves proposed an increase in the allocation to equities, but had not put any number on it. The Ministry of Finance came up with this big leap independently. It was, however, backed by all parties in the Storting other than the Progress Party, which consistently dissented on a number of aspects of the fund's management during this period.[48]

The annual white paper in 2009 reported that the decline in the markets in which NBIM operated had been bigger than any previously recorded.[49] The fund's equity investments had therefore fallen sharply, contributing to a reduction in the value of the fund as a whole of more than 24 per cent in international currency. The press and the public debate focused on this drop in value, generally as part of a debate about NBIM's general investment approach and vulnerability to the vagaries of the stock market. Internally at NBIM and Norges Bank—and soon also the Ministry of Finance—the focus was rather different. Over the previous five years, the previous three years,

---

[47] 'Report to the Storting No. 24 (2006–2007) on the Management of the Government Pension Fund in 2006, Section 3.1', ed. Ministry of Finance (Regjeringen, 2007).
[48] 'Recommendation to the Storting No. 283 (2007–2008)' (Storting).
[49] 'Report to the Storting No. 20 (2008–2009)' (Stortinget). It should be noted here that the actual 'crash' in autumn 2008 saw a smaller drop in share prices in most countries than in 1929. This is because 1929 followed a boom–bust pattern, whereas 2008 was a year of almost constant decline even before the bottom fell out of the markets in the autumn, hence the record-breaking decline over the year as a whole.

and 2008 itself, the equity portfolio had performed reasonably well relative to the benchmark in terms of both returns and relevant risk metrics, and had performed well in comparison to large funds with a similar risk profile.

The problem was with fixed income. While 2007 was a poor year both in absolute terms and relative to the benchmark, 2008 was a really bad year. The year as a whole brought relatively strong returns in fixed-income markets, due partly to large risk premiums, but fixed-income prices were highly volatile, and NBIM was not ideally positioned in the situation that arose. The 'negative excess return'—the difference between the return on the benchmark and the return on the fund's actual holdings— was no less than 6.6 per cent (−0.52 per cent vs +6.08 per cent), which was remarkably large in an area that is generally much more stable than equity investments. The fund had a low weight of government bonds, but relatively large holdings of asset-backed securities (ABSs), which generally fell sharply in the wake of the subprime mortgage crisis in the US. ABSs accounted for almost half of the losses recorded on fixed-income investments at the end of the year. The fund also had relatively large holdings of bank bonds, which formed part of the bank's reserves. Here too, there were losses. Other types of fixed-income instruments contributed to the negative excess return as well, but it was these two classes that saw the greatest downturn and performed worst against the risk metrics presented earlier.[50]

One conclusion of internal and external reviews was that the crisis had brought a systematic confluence of credit risk and liquidity risk, which had together resulted in a greater downside risk to these securities than previously anticipated. The liquidity risk in particular hit many of these investments. Bonds fell in value because there were few buyers with any money in the market. In late 2008 and early 2009, the coolest heads realized that much of this value would return once markets normalized. But the losses were 'real' in the sense that existing holdings could at this time be acquired in the markets at lower values.

When the final results for the year were announced, NBIM came in for strong public criticism. The press drew on a steady stream of academics in economics and finance who finally had proof that active management cannot pay in the long term. Those who had knocked the fund's move into the stock markets now had substance to their arguments. The press carried features on what these huge losses 'mean for you'.[51] We could read about how many tens of thousands of hospital beds these losses equated to, what they meant in terms of the government's access to oil revenue. The Ministry of Finance and the government were also very critical of NBIM in early 2009, both publicly and privately. Internally, it was not the heavy losses due to the general decline in the markets that were the problem, but the active management of fixed-income investments. As mentioned above, a substantial underweight of high-quality government bonds and overweight of other types of instrument from private issuers had

---

[50] See NBIM's annual report for 2008 and Report to the Storting No. 20 (2008–9), which is based largely on reports from international firms hired to verify NBIM's reporting.

[51] For example, *Nettavisen*, 11 March 2009.

contributed to the weak relative performance in 2008 and, to some extent, 2007. The ministry viewed this as part of systematic and relatively 'simple' risk taking, which also had positive effects on fees to NBIM's managers in good years in the form of performance bonuses.

The ministry probably shared the view that most of the recorded losses would be reversed once the market recovered. Several of the ministry's experts also argued that, with a fund as large as the recently renamed Government Pension Fund Global, it would be entirely rational to accept considerable amounts of liquidity risk, because the fund did not have the same need as other funds and investors for instant access to cash during a crisis. But if this was to be a conscious strategy, it should have been communicated and approved, and it had not. The losses therefore fuelled doubts as to whether Norges Bank was adequately equipped to handle the fund's management, and one important aspect of this question was whether the Executive Board was in a position to conduct adequate oversight.[52]

Svein Gjedrem has commented in hindsight that, had the fund not been part of Norges Bank but had 'a board of City types in sharp suits', it would not have been able to retain its management structure through the turmoil of 2009.[53] This view seems plausible, as the head of asset management at the Ministry of Finance at the time has also since stated that, had the oil fund's domestic parallel—the Government Pension Fund Norway—reported similar losses, the question of consequences for the board would have arisen.[54] But the government never discussed holding Norges Bank's board and management to account for the losses. The bank generally enjoyed a strong reputation. It would also have been wholly inappropriate to undermine the central bank's power and authority in the midst of the crisis that still raged in 2009.[55] This episode from autumn 2008 thus illustrates not only that the management of the fund brings institutional risk for Norges Bank, but also that the central bank brings stability to the management of the fund—which was indeed one of the reasons the bank was given management of the fund in the first place.

Presumably, NBIM and Norges Bank benefited from there being a majority government at the time, and one leaning to the left. The two smaller parties in the ruling coalition had previously been critical of the management of the fund, and their public reaction would probably have been strong had they sat in opposition. When the white paper on the fund came before the Storting, the vast majority endorsed the government's criticisms and self-criticisms, and the proposals to limit the scope for risk taking to some extent, but the basic principles for the management of the fund were largely retained.

The following year, the fund bounced back strongly, with an overall return of no less than 25.5 per cent, 4.1 percentage points more than the benchmark.[56] This excess

[52] Conversation with Martin Skancke, 10 August 2015.
[53] Conversation with Svein Gjedrem, 10 June 2015.
[54] Conversation with Martin Skancke, 10 August 2015.
[55] Conversation with Kristin Halvorsen, 21 August 2015.
[56] Government Pension Fund Global Annual Report 2009 (Norges Bank Investment Management, 2009), https://www.nbim.no/globalassets/reports/2009/nbim_annualreport09.pdf.

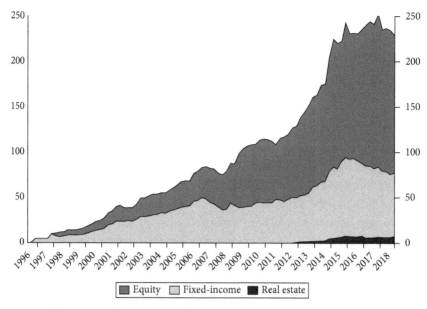

Figure 14.1   Norwegian Sovereign Wealth Fund, percentage shares of GDP

return was partly a reflection of many of the previously recognized liquidity losses reversing as the markets stabilized somewhat, but the equity portfolio also produced strong results. The implementation of the increase in the equity share to 60 per cent also took place at the height of the financial crisis, and these huge purchases of cheap shares turned out very well for the fund (see Figure 14.1). NBIM has delivered strong results in recent years too. The debate about risk, costs, and results continues, especially when it comes to active management. And so it should, as part of a constructive debate about such a large part of the nation's wealth. But viewed over the long term, from 1998 until today, via the greatest crisis in the global economy since the depression following the crash of 1929, NBIM has delivered strong results relative to relevant benchmarks.

The Getting to Norway: The Oil Fund as a Historical Phenomenon

Norges Bank has been profoundly influenced by the state's large savings of oil revenues from the continental shelf. The savings are mainly the result of an efficient system for securing a high government take from the oil extraction, combined with restraint in spending the revenues. The so-called 'fiscal rule', introduced in 2001, is at present relatively uncontroversial. Various governments, comprising parties of the centre-right and centre-left, have embraced the rule and prepared their national budgets according to it.

In the resource curse literature, Norway has at times been seen as an outlier, as a nuisance to general understandings of how large windfall gains affect the overall economic and partly political system. A part of the overall assessment of the Norwegian oil experiment is that Norway, unlike all OECD countries and most small oil producers, has been able to create positive linkages between petroleum extraction and other parts of the economy, mainly a vital, globally oriented supply and service industry at an advanced technological level

In a small textbox in their survey, *The Resource Curse Revisited*, Paul Stevens et al. explain the Norwegian case by pointing out that Norway, when it first struck oil, was a long-established, fully functioning democracy with a history of very low levels of corruption in the public sector. Its small population was extremely well educated, and only a very small percentage was considered to be living in poverty. As a seafaring nation, it was used to offshore activities and international business. 'Norway, arguably, is a special case—the only way its experience can be replicated is to start with 4.5 million Norwegians.'[57]

These are all good insights; let us still add a few elements. First, the fiscal rule is also relatively firmly established in the corporative system surrounding government and political parties. In Norway's internationally exposed economy, a rapid expansion of domestic demand would lead to a deterioration of competitiveness. This has been well understood and has also been made a fundamental part of institutional practices in the corporative surroundings of party politics. In the exposed, internationally competing sectors of the economy Norway has a high rate of unionization, and these unions have had a strong position within the Norwegian Confederation of Trade Unions and considerable influence within the Labour Party throughout the twentieth century.[58] The result is that a labour movement, which otherwise could have become a strong advocate of high wages and expensive social welfare benefits, has thought and acted within a context where their own interests would suffer if Norway did not set aside a portion of oil revenues.

Moreover, Norway has long traditions for high government investments and strong state finances, as mentioned in Chapter 10. From the 1800s until the present, the state's legitimacy as a vehicle for growth and protector of common interests has been high. Large infrastructure projects during the nineteenth century (roads, harbours, and above all railways) were usually financed by large state loans. To avoid running deficits in the national budgets, future taxes and custom fees necessary for servicing the debt were calculated in detail. The postwar period is broadly similar, with exceptionally high levels of public and private investments, facilitated by low interest rates, favourable corporate taxation, high taxation of households, and a disciplined budgetary policy. In both periods, government prioritized high savings (in real capital), at the expense of suppressed private or public consumption, especially in the postwar decades. The 'rule' applied was to avoid running deficits in national budgets. Exceptions are found during the two world wars, and in the 1970s, 1980s, and 1990s. In these decades, oil revenues appeared in government budgets and were spent without any

---

[57] Paul Stevens, Glada Lahn, and Jaakko Kooroshy, *The Resource Curse Revisited* (Chatham House, 2015), 12.

[58] Eivind Thomassen and Lars Fredrik Øksendal, *Modellbyggere: Det tekniske beregningsutvalget for inntekts-oppgjørene 1967–2017* (Pax forlag, 2017).

explicit rule—until the fiscal rule was introduced in 2001 to establish a broad consensus around the principles of government spending and savings.

We find a similar consensus around state ownership of domestic commercial enterprises (outside the oil fund). Government is a major owner in five out of the seven largest companies on the Oslo Stock Exchange (oil, fertilizers, aluminium, telecoms, finance). Their management and boards are recruited on the same professional basis as in other parts of the business sector, and there is a broad consensus that they should be operated on ordinary commercial terms.[59] The role of the state's shares is mainly to preserve a long-term national ownership. Although different from the structure and scope of the oil fund, we find the same kind of pragmatic consensus in trusting state institutions with huge values on which future welfare depend. Moreover, the high legitimacy of the state is, as Stevens et al. point out, partly rooted in a long-standing perception of the state apparatus as competent and honest, with negligible levels of briberies and serious malpractice. The non-biased prescriptions of the heavy 'silver tax', when the forced payments were distributed by parliament and local politicians following the founding of Norges Bank in 1816 (Chapter 1), is an early and striking example of how integrity and trust were expressed and developed.

If we move from the factual to a more interpretive or even speculative terrain, the linguistic figures used in explaining and defending the principles behind the fiscal rule are closely tied to some old virtues, which might have a larger bearing in Norway than in many other countries. Except from the crowding-out type of arguments for saving, the main imperative behind the oil fund is that it is the responsible thing to do: oil has been here since prehistoric times, its revenues thus belong not only to the few cohorts of Norwegians living in the age of drilling, but also to future generations. A preferred metaphor of former Prime Minister Jens Stoltenberg (2000–1 and 2005–13) and Finance Minister Sigbjørn Johnsen (1990–6 and 2009–13) was that of responsible forest stewardship: prudent foresters knew that they on average should chop down only the natural annual increase and leave the forest stock volume intact. This echoes the norms and values found in the traditional farming sector of society. Land and values were passed on through generations; and they should be handed to the following generation in the same, of preferably better, state than they were when received.[60]

The ethos of work, discipline, and savings is to some extent a shared feature of many traditional societies. Still, it might have a stronger position in this north-western corner of Europe than in most societies. Thomas Robert Malthus made some interesting contrasting observations during his travels in Norway in late 1799. The main thesis of his then recently published treatise on population was that the mass of the population would stabilize at the subsistence level. As population growth naturally tends to outstrip increases in the food supply, growth beyond subsistence would be kept in check by starvation and death. In Norway, however, he witnessed what the pioneer social

---

[59] Einar Lie, Egil Myklebust, and Harald Norvik, *Staten som kapitalist: Rikdom og eierskap for det 21. århundret* (Pax forlag, 2014); Lie, 'Context and Contingency: Explaining State Ownership in Norway'.

[60] This argument is developed further and in more detail in 'Wealth in Norwegian', in *On Managing Wealth*, ed. Jan Fredrik Qvigstad, Occasional Papers (Norges Bank, 2012).

scientist Eilert Sundt would later describe in detail, namely that marrying and starting families were deferred until young adults could take over a farm or sustain their families in relative comfort. This, in a fundamental sense, was a philosophy of moral and economic restraint, of sacrificing immediate rewards for a better future for one self and ones descendants, an observation that inspired the somewhat brighter spots in Malthus' revised editions of his *Essay on the Principle of Population*.[61]

Leaving the metaphors and connections to the pre-petroleum age aside, the fiscal rules, which ensures a continued large fund that needs to be managed, is now solidly established. An expression of the broad support came in early 2019, when representatives of the government announced that they considered financing two particular projects outside the fiscal rule. The projects were the reconstruction of government buildings, partly destroyed in the devastating terror attack of 22 July 2011 (which include the killings of sixty-nine youth at summer camp the same day), and the later casualty of a frigate of the Norwegian navy. As the state is self-insured, the idea was that these events were extraordinary, and the resulting cost could be treated extraordinarily in the budget. However, a number of protests soon appeared from economists, media, organizations, and other politicians, and the government soon concluded that the fiscal rule needed to apply to all public expenditure, however extraordinary they were.

[61] See Agnar Sandmo, *Samfunnsøkonomi: En Idéhistorie* (Universitetsforl., 2006), 64ff.

Conclusion

Norges Bank and the State, Past and Present

A central theme in this book has been the shifting relations between the state and Norges Bank. To some extent—but only to some extent—the bank's independence from political institutions has been at the centre of the narrative. The concept of independence is useful when studying the means available to the bank in contributing, for example, to financial stability and efficiency in the payment system. For understanding its long-term institutional development, the bank's fundamental *dependency* of political institutions should be the starting point. Norges Bank has undoubtedly enjoyed various forms of autonomy in its activities throughout its history. But the bank was established by parliament, its legal foundations debated, revised, and altered at numerous occasions. Government took control over the main instruments of monetary policy in the postwar era, as a result of a general, public support of a new line of economic policy thinking and a general distrust of the pre-war central bank institution. The last decades have brought back a stronger operational independence in monetary policy and Norges Bank has been trusted with a new task, managing the huge and growing Norwegian oil fund. The stronger independence in monetary policy-making has been line with the international development of the central bank, which is, for obvious reasons, a result of new riches and willingness to put large parts of them aside for the future. Anyhow, both changes have resulted from new debates and new formal decisions in the parliament and government.

Concluding, we will make a broad overview of the changing character of the bank's dependence by looking at Norges Bank's role in handling financial crises. The relations between a central bank and political institutions are normally brought to the forefront during a crisis, as financial breakdowns have widespread effects outside the financial system itself. These relations are at times being put to the test, but are always clarified, implicitly or explicitly. We will start with the most recent shock, the financial crisis of 2008/9, before outlining a number of differences and similarities with its role in previous episodes of financial instability.

Managing Crises

As mentioned in Chapter 14, the first effects of the financial crisis were felt in 2007, but Norwegian financial institutions were not particularly affected. Spring 2008 saw

Norges Bank 1816–2016. Einar Lie, Oxford University Press (2020). © Norges Bank.
DOI: 10.1093/oso/9780198860013.001.0001

an upturn in the Norwegian economy with rising inflation, and the bank's key policy rate was raised to 5.75 per cent, its highest level since 2003. The following autumn, however, brought a severe liquidity shock to global money markets, and that part of the crisis did have a significant impact in Norway. Interbank lending markets ceased to function, liquidity dried up, and interest rates soared. From late autumn 2008 and on into 2009, Norges Bank and the Ministry of Finance both feared that the crisis would deliver a hard blow to economic activity in Norway, with attendant consequences for banks' financial strength.

In autumn 2008, Norges Bank took a series of steps, both conventional and more unorthodox, to boost liquidity. Banks were given access to more loans and loans with longer maturities, and the collateral requirements were relaxed. There was also a precarious shortage of foreign exchange as a result of the drought in global money markets. Norges Bank therefore used its foreign exchange reserves to lend to banks and shored up the reserves with a direct loan from the Federal Reserve of USD 15 billion against collateral in NOK. In this way, Norges Bank allied itself directly with the source of USD for redistribution to Norwegian financial institutions.

The most innovative solution by historical standards was the swap arrangement whereby banks were able to exchange covered bonds for liquid government securities. Covered bonds carry limited credit risk but nevertheless proved difficult to trade in autumn 2008. The arrangement had similarities with a contemporaneous scheme in the UK, and it was the governor himself who worked out the proposals both internally and with the Ministry of Finance.[1] The Storting approved the swap arrangement in late October, and the bank was given the job of administering it. Norges Bank attached importance to this being a type of measure that needed political support. Although the objective was liquidity assistance, there was an undeniable risk of loss should a financial institution file for bankruptcy or be placed under public administration.[2] This made the arrangement rather more than a standard liquidity management mechanism.

On top of these acute measures to create liquidity, interest rate policy played an important role. The key policy rate was lowered by half a point on both 15 and 29 October, a larger cut of 1.75 points was made in mid-December, and further reductions followed in 2009. In all cases, the division of duties between Norges Bank and the Ministry of Finance worked well. The Executive Board reached its decisions on the basis of preparatory work at the bank, and the Ministry of Finance was informed about the decisions before they were announced. There were exceptions: one was the 1.75 point cut, which was formally put before the ministry because the bank considered this a sufficiently big decision to trigger the obligation in the Norges Bank Act to submit decisions of special importance to the ministry.[3]

---

[1] Interview with Jan F. Qvigstad.
[2] The arrangement is described in detail in Proposition No. 5 to the Storting (2008–9) and on p. 99 of Norges Bank's annual report for 2008.
[3] Interviews with Svein Gjedrem and Kristin Halvorsen.

In January 2009, the government unveiled a wide-ranging package of fiscal policy measures. Two major funds were started up during the spring to supply financial institutions with new core capital and give them improved access to long-term funding: the Government Finance Fund and the Government Bond Fund. Norges Bank had little to do with the creation and operation of these funds. Although they served an important function, less use was ultimately made of them than many had anticipated—or feared—when they were set up. The downturn in the real economy was limited, due partly to these various measures and partly to activity holding up well in parts of the oil-related industries. The year 2009 saw a moderate drop in GDP, but the upturn in 2010 more than made up for this lost ground. There were therefore no waves of bankruptcies among Norwegian bank customers, and banks' loan losses were very moderate.

The main effect of the financial crisis in Norway was thus a liquidity crisis and a sharp decline in the country's net lending. Norges Bank came to play a key role in both areas. The contrast to the banking crisis of the early 1990s is striking. That was predominantly a solvency crisis, not part of a global financial crisis with marked liquidity effects. There were funding issues back then as well—the recovery phase in 1991–2 saw particular concern that the supply of funding could dry up due to a loss of confidence in the Norwegian financial system. But this did not happen. Once the Norwegian banks had been recapitalized, they were readmitted to global financial markets.

The banking crisis of the early 1990s stands out historically in that, all things considered, the central bank played only a minor role. Not only did Norges Bank have limited duties in light of the nature of the crisis, but it was absent when the principles and guidelines for handling looming problems were drawn up in 1989 and 1990. This should probably be seen mainly in the light of the central bank's relatively modest role in the economic policy system in the preceding decades and limited institutional awareness of the importance of establishing clear authorities and responsibilities. The division of duties was likely also determined de facto by the Ministry of Finance taking clear and far-reaching action before the crisis became established. The head of the economic policy department, Svein Gjedrem, was the key player in this respect.

It is an interesting coincidence that Gjedrem was first a key player in the institution with the lead role in resolving a major solvency crisis in the early 1990s, and then headed the institution responsible for liquidity management and financial stability in what now seems primarily to have been a dramatic evaporation of liquidity and funding from conventional sources. A full documentary and interview analysis of the handling of the financial crisis in Norway will no doubt emerge in time, but there is little doubt that Norges Bank's management of the crisis benefited from, and was coloured by, Gjedrem's experience and unique authority in political-administrative circles. He kept a low profile externally, with little enthusiasm for media appearances. Internally, however, his position was very strong among those who remained at Norges Bank after his extensive purges and concentration of its operations.

Previous crises too had been managed effectively, and based on largely the same principles for Norges Bank's intervention. The last crisis before the solvency crisis of the 1990s was the double banking crisis of the mid-1920s and early 1930s. At Norges Bank there was no doubt that the role of the central bank was as lender of last resort, while it was up to private capital—and possibly other public institutions—to provide new equity if a bank's existing equity was lost. This principle came to the fore back in the previous century during the resolution of the Kristiania crash of 1899, but it was not easy politically to set this out explicitly.

For one thing, in the age of the metal standards, there were limits to how far Norges Bank could go without compromising its role as defender of the value of money. Today, this role is formulated as maintaining low and stable inflation. During a severe crisis, inflationary pressures will often ease or evaporate, providing scope for a major injection of liquidity. However, the monetary protection provided by the silver and gold standards entailed the free exchange of banknotes for metal and so clear legal limits on how many notes could be put into circulation. Unless the central bank had built up substantial reserves, this presented clear limitations for liquidity management. Moreover, it was never good to know in advance what was liquidity support and what was solvency support in the form of 'permanent' equity. It could be difficult to value collateral in an ailing economy. When conditions are steadily worsening, liquidity assistance in the form of injections or loans can be lost in practice if the bank's losses are large enough. Third, a clearly defined function for the central bank during a crisis requires a well-functioning division of responsibility between political institutions.

The limitations of the metal standard were clearly exposed during the crises of 1848 and 1857. In both cases, Norges Bank was more of a bank than a bankers' bank. As the bank of issue, it had an overarching role and possibly also a responsibility extending beyond itself. But this responsibility meant that the institution could not do much to supply liquidity to banks and customers in need. In 1848, the bank found itself in violation of its note-issuing rights, and the head office in Trondheim decided to temporarily suspend the redemption of notes for silver at two of the bank's branches. This move was heavily criticized and was not repeated in 1857. By then, Norges Bank had somewhat larger reserves with which to provide assistance to customers and banks. But the most important form of support for a troubled economy was delivered by the government in the form of a large emergency loan that was transformed into short-term loans to banks and businesses. Norges Bank thus contributed a form of liquidity assistance for finance houses and bankers in Hamburg and Altona, as their customers would not accept Norges Bank's bills of exchange to cover their claims. The branch in Kristiania—today's Oslo—sent large quantities of silver by steamer to provide the safest and most liquid means of payment. This probably acted as a form of liquidity support, but the main aim was to preserve confidence in the central bank and its silver coins.

The Kristiania crash of 1899 came after the new Norges Bank Act had been drawn up, a true head office had been established and transferred to the capital, and thoughts about the bank's role as a bankers' bank had become reasonably well rooted. The explicit guideline for crisis management was that Norges Bank should and could issue liquidity loans to banks as long as the recipient was solvent and could provide collateral. This was also the central bank's policy when the first banks ran into difficulties. The rescue operations were conducted in consultation with the Ministry of Finance, partly in tandem with the government. But private banks too were involved in the rescue operations to save crisis-stricken banks. Norges Bank also organized funding solutions involving municipal authorities, first in Kristiania and then in southern Kristiansand when the city's largest bank ran into trouble. In this sense, money was sourced from wherever it could be found, and not least where there were institutions and authorities with a strong obligation or self-interest in preventing the destructive effects of a major bank failure.

There was close collaboration with the Ministry of Finance during the Kristiania crash. But the political criticism of the rescue operations is interesting and illustrates the underlying norms and realities surrounding Norges Bank's role and unique position: some representatives complained that the government was assuming responsibility and spending money in yet another area of society when it helped to 'rescue' failed banks. That was supposed to be Norges Bank's job. This argument shows that the bank was not seen as part of the state, as we view a modern central bank, or as a fully integrated part of the executive. Norges Bank was, in a way, a bankers' bank rather than the state's instrument of monetary policy. It could, however, rescue banks and organize rescue operations together with other banks. This points back to an important reality: Norges Bank was a limited company with many private shareholders all requiring a return, and so not part of the state apparatus. Nor was the chairman a civil servant, although he could, under the special legislation that applied, be dismissed by the government.

During both the Kristiania crash and the 1920s crisis, Norges Bank's task as a provider of liquidity management was widened and extended, partly because the bank was *not* an integrated part of the state. The argument was that Norges Bank's main role was to give liquidity support to troubled banks. Still, in a situation where the state could go no further, the private bankers' bank could step in with its reserves if it was willing to rescue an insolvent bank.

During the major banking crisis of the 1920s and its successor in 1931–2, the principle that Norges Bank's primary role was to provide sufficient liquidity was retained. But the crisis was so severe, there was so much at stake, and the actions of the government and the Storting were so varied in strength and aim, that it soon became difficult to comply with such a principle. Even in the earliest operations, Norges Bank supplied core capital to the banks in the form of subordinated loan capital. The main reason was that previous liquidity loans had to be converted into core capital. In the subsequent major reconstructions, capital was obtained from the sources that were available. Several of the changing governments were reluctant to step in, as government finances were also under pressure. Storting president Otto B. Halvorsen challenged Norges Bank late in 1922 to provide what the government did not have and the private banks could not. Norges Bank duly participated in various ways, but Nicolai Rygg did not contribute such large sums that the central bank itself ran into financial difficulties.

He did not want to print money and expand the overall liquidity too much. Conversion to gold was suspended, but the aim was still a return to pre-war parity.

Norges Bank therefore contributed far more than liquidity assistance—and at the same time the government provided support ranging from core capital to liquidity assistance. The Handelsbanken rescue operation clearly illustrates the absence of a clear definition of duties: when that bank ran into trouble and needed help in 1923—with the future of the entire banking sector at stake in the eyes of both Norges Bank and the government—the government decided to make a substantial deposit in the bank to improve the situation. In principle, the bank was classed as solvent, but Rygg refused further liquidity support because Handelsbanken could not provide acceptable collateral as required by his terms of reference. Prime (and finance) minister Abraham Berge neglected to inform the Storting about the liquidity support he then decided to make on behalf of the government. Perhaps this was because he did not consider it necessary to disclose a deposit in a solvent bank—it is more budgetary allocations than deposits that concern the Storting. But this money was lost, as was so much else in the 1920s. The impeachment trial that followed was therefore also the story of a shifting and unclear division of duties between the government and Norges Bank. What was not unclear, however, was where the real authority lay. It was Rygg who led and organized the resolution of by far the most severe financial crisis in Norwegian history.

His de facto leadership was particularly accentuated when the country's two largest banks ran into difficulties after the crisis year of 1931. The politicians' unwillingness to use government funds meant that, in practice, Norges Bank took charge. Most of the right-wing parties believed that the banks had to be rescued, but without the Storting allocating any funds. The Labour Party did not want Norges Bank to put its money into saving the banks either. Rygg received most of the authorizations he asked for, which were to give an unlimited guarantee for the two banks' future operation. In the debate where the Storting laid down the gauntlet to Norges Bank, a systematic distinction was drawn between the roles of 'government authorities' and Norges Bank. It was the limited company Norges Bank, with its reserves and its governance structure, that stepped in. But part of the reason why the bankers' bank was now able to rescue the remains of the two big banks was undoubtedly that the krone was no longer tied to gold. Norges Bank now had greater freedom if really large sums were needed to supply liquidity and new core capital to the banks.

The interbellum governor was keen to have support from political decisions, preferably from the Storting and ideally in the form of legislation. However, this did not necessarily mean that the central bank operated within fixed legal bounds. A number of ad hoc laws were passed along the way, legislation was amended, and the governor worked tirelessly to secure support for the vision that he himself and the board believed to be correct in the face of major issues. For the most part, Rygg got what he wanted in terms of both bank support policy and monetary policy. These victories came at the cost of the institution's legitimacy in the political and professional circles that established the premises for economic policy after the Second World War. The central bank's authority would not have been the same anyway as it was under the gold standard and in the years when the relationship between the ministry and the central bank was regulated in the spirit of the act of 1892. The cost associated with the parity policy—declining production and high unemployment—were acceptable to the two leading political parties founded in the 1800s (the Conservative and Liberal parties). But they were unacceptable for the coming Labour Party, which never displayed any affinity for 'the rules of the game' or the result it provided, and turned explicitly against the institution that symbolized them.

Preventing Crises

One key role of a good central bank is, without doubt, helping resolve financial crises. But an even more important one is to make sure that they do not happen in the first place. In this area, too, Norges Bank's contributions have been mixed.

The bank was set up in the wake of the most chaotic situation Norway's finances have ever been in. In the period with a functioning metal standard, Norges Bank contributed with discounting that resulted in the supply of capital in difficult periods and temporary tightening during upturns. But the bank's decentralized structure and limited reserves hampered its ability to play an important role until the act of 1892 converted Norges Bank from what was essentially a loose network of semi-autonomous banks subject to the Storting's guidelines and control, into something more akin to a modern central bank. The bank's stabilizing role was first put to the test in the run-up to the Kristiania crash. Observers of the time rightly criticized Norges Bank for having done little to prevent the speculative bubble that had built up. The problems inherent in reining in a local boom using the discount rate—there were no licensing or bank supervision arrangements to turn to—were obvious, however, and Norges Bank came in for little criticism in the years that followed. The First World War was worse. Here Norges Bank clearly failed in its duties. The main reason for this backsliding has to be found in other areas: in government policy and stock market speculation. But Norges Bank did not stick to its principles, which could have helped to restrain and caution. The government's accounts were overdrawn, the volume of notes in circulation increased sharply, and large foreign loans helped push up domestic liquidity. When the new governor of Norges Bank took over in 1920, a clean-up process began with clear elements of self-searching.

The next major crisis—the banking crisis of the early 1990s—also followed major imbalances. Bank lending increased sharply in the mid-1980s, interest rates were too low, and the real interest rate after tax was even lower for many borrowers until the move towards gross taxation was made in the late 1980s. Banks' financial strength was poor, and it was all too easy to obtain funding without adequate collateral. Here too, Norges Bank made a contribution in the middle of the decade, with extensive central bank funding for the banking sector which was used, in turn, for further lending. The regulatory failure was clear, not least in what was previously and has subsequently been the central bank's area of responsibility. At the same time, Norges Bank was relatively explicitly brought under the control of the political authorities, and there was, as mentioned earlier, little interest in drawing up clear rules on what should be the central bank's contribution to general stability. It was presupposed that this responsibility rested with the political authorities. The general lack of interest in formal definitions of responsibilities was most obviously reflected in the legislation governing the central bank. After the Second World War, everyone agreed that the act of 1892 was outdated. But it was not until 1985 that a replacement was finally passed.

The run-up to the financial crisis in 2008 was different. There was scarcely any liability to be apportioned domestically. The financial situation was relatively stable in Norway despite substantial oil revenues. The crisis came from outside. And it never had any major direct consequences for the Norwegian real economy, although the difficult situation in the global and especially the European economy has in subsequent years helped shape the context for Norwegian economic policy.

A Central Bank in a Parvenu State

Norges Bank is today in the historically welcome position of having played a major role in successfully resolving a crisis that it did not itself help create. In addition, the central bank probably has greater influence and authority than ever before, other than in the interbellum period. But this authority has not been won through unpopular measures in tough times, but through an advanced position in easier years. The principle of the state's responsibility for growth and employment has long been established in government policy, which now implicitly includes Norges Bank's actions. The bank's position in the arsenal of policy instruments is also relatively prominent. The most important guideline for the central bank's monetary policy is the inflation target, but other factors, such as growth and employment, are increasingly being incorporated into the guidelines for Norges Bank's interest rates settings.

The government's present guidelines underline that Norges Bank, in its interest rate setting, should include considerations about 'real economic stability', meaning that the central bank should take the effects on future employment and economic growth into consideration.[4] This is in broad line with international models, as monetary policy has become an increasingly powerful tool in economic policy-making. In a historical perspective, this is an interesting widening of Norges Bank's target spectrum. During the times of the metal standard, convertibility, loosely associated with financial stability, was the main aim of Norges Bank's monetary policy measures. After the First World War, discretionary policies aimed at promoting growth and employment were at the heart of all economic planning and policy-making, though controlled and conducted by the government and Ministry of Finance. The integration of tools within

---

[4] 'New Regulations on Monetary Policy', press release, 2 March 2018, http://www.regjeringen.no/en/aktuelt/new-regulation-on-monetary-policy/id2592551/.

government was a key aspect of 'democratic control' over economic life, an ideal incompatible with an autonomous central bank.

After 1986, various versions of 'nominal anchoring' have been applied, with a de facto operational autonomy for Norges Bank. Still, inflation targeting arrived late in Norway, partly because of the framework for wage negotiations, partly because of Norges Bank's relatively weak standing in political and public life. Throughout the 1990s, there was also a widespread scepticism against giving 'inflation' priority over unemployment. The central bank viewpoint was these were not competing aims in the long run; that predicable, low inflation was the only feasible route to growth and high employment. Around the turn of the century, Norges Bank's political superiors accepted that it was useful for overall economic policy-making that the central bank would secure a relatively stable inflation rate, as this was a precondition for stability in output and employment.

The widening of the monetary policy's target area implies that inflation normally will be kept close to the target set. But short-term deviations will be accepted if they are judged to secure stability in employment and stabilization in the long run. By broadening the scope and extending the horizon, the 'real economy considerations' are thus given a higher priority in Norges Bank's policies and, above all, are integrated with the aims related to monetary values. This is strangely similar to the thinking underlying the integration of all-powerful policy means in the Ministry of Finance after the Second World War. Government (and modern-minded economists) found that interest rates were important for employment and growth, and consequently should be taken from the central bank and placed at the centre for economic policy and decision making. After a relatively short period with a more confined inflation target, real economy considerations are reunited with the interest setting, but this time in Norges Bank, which is becoming increasingly independent from its political peers in its interest rates policy. We have thus moved closer to the integration of aims and means of the 1940s and 1950s, yet a long step further away from the ideal that important policy means should be placed under the control of government, or 'democratic institutions' as they were labelled by mid-twentieth-century Labour politicians and ideologists.

One reason for these changes coming about without controversy is probably that Norwegian government has huge financial reserves. Temporary fiscal policies seems relatively confined to following the budgetary rules in public spending. Still, the government is, contrary to the majority of European countries, able to use fiscal policy measures to stimulate aggregate demand. Regardless of this, the increased autonomy and widening of economic policy targets is undoubtedly an expression of an increased trust in the central bank institution. Norges Bank has, at present, wider responsibilities than ever before in its more than 200 years history—the management of the huge oil fund included. Norges Bank's controversial interwar years are no longer quoted and the bank has definitely moved out of the troubled shadows of the 1970s and 1980s.

Still, 2020 is not the end of history, no more than the interwar years or the 1980s were. For many years now, there has been no need to raise interest rates to unpopular levels to curb inflation, as was the case in the first years after inflation targeting was introduced. Cheap imports from Asia and then stable or falling prices among our trading partners in an economic crisis have resulted in low external inflationary pressures. For much of the time since 2008, Norway has also seen a historically very unusual combination of crisis or sluggish growth in surrounding countries and extremely high prices for its most important export products, most notably oil and gas. The former has made inflation targeting less prone to political and popular criticism, while the latter has allowed the build-up of substantial reserves, particularly in the Government Pension Fund Global, managed by Norges Bank.

Norway will remain a wealthy country for many years to come. But it is possible, and maybe even probable, that it will become more difficult to manage the wealth and the appurtenant regulatory framework in years to come. The historical norm where stability sometimes requires a tightening of policy, partly through unpopular high interest rates, will undoubtedly return. The bank's investment management has won considerable recognition, but probably more outside Norway than within its borders. This is also an area with ever present financial, operational, and political risk, which can be expected to increase in the future. The fund's policy present is to keep holdings in selected companies up to as much as 10 per cent. Should any of the companies in which the fund has large holdings behave in ways that are viewed by Norwegian politicians and the public as completely unacceptable, a latent institutional risk will be triggered—whether the fund and the central bank choose to be active or passive. There is also an obvious political risk on the fixed-income side, as the examples of Iceland, Greece, and Russia in Chapter 14 indicate.

There is neither pessimism nor concern in these observations on risks and drop height in the present state of central bank business in Norway. From a historical perspective, this is exactly how it should be. A central bank should, at its best, contribute to stability and income growth. But when turbulence and difficulties arise, it will find itself right in the thick of things unless it has made itself an irrelevance. And Norges Bank, as a mixed central bank and fund manager in a small, nouveau riche economy, is at present far from irrelevant.

Bibliography

Archival Sources

A number of abbreviations are used in the footnotes that refer to archival sources. They cover the following archives:

AEP   Alf Eriksen's archive, Norges Bank
EB   Erik Brofoss' archive, the Norwegian Labor Movement's Archive and Library
EE   Eivind Erichsen's archive, Ministry of Finance
FD   Archives from the Ministry of Finance, NAN
FINL   Archives from the Ministry of Finance in London (1940–5), NAN
GJ   Gunnar Jahn's diary, National Library of Norway
KGW Knut Getz Wold's archive, NAN
KGWD Knut Getz Wold's diary, KGW
KGWM Knut Getz Wold's manuscript, KGW
NAN   National Archives of Norway
NB   Norges Banks's archives
NBL   Archives from Norges Bank in London, NAN
STAT Archives from the Statistical Department, NB
STGR Archives from the Storting's investigation of the Reksten case, Stortinget S-1013
UDA   Archives from the Ministry of Foreign Affaires (Utenriksdepartementet)

Literary Sources

Aall, J., 'Om Bank- og Pengevæsenet, og sammes Indflydelse paa de viktigste Næringsveie i Norge' (J. Aall, 1832).

Aly, G., *Hitler's Beneficiaries: Plunder, Racial War, and the Nazi Welfare State* (Macmillan, 2007).

Andvig, J.C., *Ragnar Frisch and the Great Depression: A Study in the Interwar History of Macroeconomic Theory and Policy* (Norsk utenrikspolitisk institutt, 1986).

Asdahl, K., 'Kjære Knut Getz Wold', *Penger og kreditt* 15, Supplementary Issue (1985).

Aukrust, O. and P.J. Bjerve, *Hva krigen kostet Norge* (Dreyer, 1945).

Aukrust, O., and T.J. Hanisch, *Økonomisk forskning og debatt: utvalgte artikler 1942–1989*. Vol. 75 (Statistisk sentralbyrå, 1990).Austnes, M., *Kampen om banken: Et historisk perspektiv på utformingen av det nye Norges bank- og pengevesen Ca. 1814–1816* (Norges Bank, 2016).

Bagehot, W., *A Practical Plan for Assimilating the English and American Money: As a Step Towards a Universal Money* (Longmans, Green, 1889 [1869]).Bang, P. and J.P. Holter, *Norges Bank 175 år: mennesker og begivenheter* (Norges Bank, 1991).

Banke, N., 'Om Adam Smiths forbindelse med Norge og Danmark', *Nationaløkonomisk Tidsskrift*, no. 93 (1955).

Bankkrisekommisjonen, *Dokument nr. 17 (1997–98) Rapport til stortinget fra kommisjonen som ble nedsatt av Stortinget for å gjennomgå ulike årsaksforhold knyttet til bankkrisen* (Stortinget, 1998).

Bartel, R.J., 'International Monetary Unions: The XIX-Century Experience', *The Journal of European Economic History*, 3 (1974) 689–704.

Berg, R., *Norge på egen hånd 1905–1920*. Vol. 2. (Universitetsforlaget, 1995).

Berg, T.N., *Mellom politikk og marked? En studie av pengepolitisk avdeling i Norges Bank, og spørsmålet om den norske penge- og kredittpolitikken ca. 1965–1980* (University of Bergen, 2011).

Berg, T.N., H. Bøhn, and C. Kleivset, 'Fra regulering til marked. Et dokumentasjonsnotat om Norges Bank og utviklingen av penge-, kreditt og valutapolitikken 1965–1990'. Staff memo no. 27 (Norges Bank, 2012).

Bergh, T., 'Norway: The Powerful Servants', *History of Political Economy* 13, no. 3 (1981) 471–512.

Bergh, T., *Storhetstid 1945–1965* (Tiden, 1987).

Bergh, T., *Norge fra u-land til i-land: vekst og utviklingslinjer 1830–1980* (Gyldendal, 1983).

Bergh, T., *Jernbanen i Norge: 1854–2004. Nye spor og nye muligheter: 1854–1940* (Vigmostad & Bjørke, 2004).

Bergh, T., *Kollektiv fornuft: 1969–2009* (Pax, 2009).

Bergo, J. and J. Solheim, 'Kommentarer til Trond Grams artikkel i Samfunnsøkonomen nr. 4–2012', *Samfunnsøkonomen* 126, no. 5 (2012) 34–7.

Bergvoll, G., 'The Eurokrone Market and the Norwegian Economy', *Economic Bulletin* 52, no. 3 (1981) 198–204.

Bilden, K.M., ' "Vi kan ikke leve med disse skandaleavsløringene": Hvordan aktualiseres den globaliserte økonomiens problemstillinger i norske nyhetsmedier i debatten om etiske retningslinjer for oljefondet', (University of Oslo, 2005).

Bistrop, E., *Oslotelefonen 1880–1985* (Oslo Teledistrikt, 1990).

Bjerve, P.J., *Økonomi og politikk* (Aschehoug, 1971).

Bjerve, P.J., *Økonomisk planlegging og politikk* (Samlaget, 1989).

Bjørnstad, R., *Jorden og mannen. Jon Sundby* (Bøndenes forlag, 1968).

Bjørnstad, R. 'Debatten omkring solidaritetsalternativet: lønnsdannelsen i industrien-uendret også i perioden 1995–1997', *Sosialøkonomen* 52, no. 4 (1998) 22–9.

Bomhoff, K.G. 'Erindringer [unpublished memoirs]', available in Norges Bank library (1923).

Bøhn, H., and B. Vikøren, 'Petroleumsfondet – en ny stor oppgave for Norges Bank', *Norges Banks Skriftserie*, no. 28 (1999).

Bøhn, H. 'Norges Banks distriktsavdelinger 1983–2001', Staff Memo, no. 24 (Norges Bank, 2012).

Bordo, M.D., 'Long Term Perspectives on Central Banking', Paper prepared for The Norges Bank Symposium 'What is a Useful Central Bank?' Oslo, Norway (2010). Available from https://www.norges-bank.no/contentassets/d0a6369493ae406f9f71df31018f54e0/bordo_paper.pdf.

Bordo, M.D, and E.N. White, 'A Tale of Two Currencies: British and French Finance During the Napoleonic Wars', *The Journal of Economic History* 51, no. 2 (1991) 303–16.

Bordo, M.D, and H. Rockoff, 'The Gold Standard as a "Good Housekeeping Seal of Approval" ', *The Journal of Economic History* 56, no. 2 (1996) 389–428.

Bordo, M.D., and L. Jonung, 'The History of Monetary Regimes: Some Lessons for Sweden and the EMU', *Swedish Economic Policy Review* 4 (1997) 285–358.

Bordo, M.D., Ø. Eitrheim, M. Flandreau, and J.F. Qvigstad, 'Introduction', in *Central Banks at a Crossroads: What Can We Learn from History*, ed. by M.D. Bordo, Ø. Eitrheim, M. Flandreau, and J. F. Qvigstad (Cambridge University Press, 2016).

Borlaug, E. and Wammer, T. 'Noregs Bank: Grunntrekk i administrasjon, oppgåver og historie'. Staff memo, no. 9 (Norges Bank, 2009).

Børresen, E., 'Norges Banks gullpolitikk etter 1945', *Norges Bank skriftserie*, no. 12 (Norges Bank, 1983).

Broadberry, S., and K. O'Rourke, *The Cambridge Economic History of Modern Europe*. Vol. 2 (Cambridge University Press, 2010).

Broch, O.J., 'Beretning angaaende den i Paris afholdte Internationale Myntkonferents' (Stortinget, 1869).

Broch, O.J., 'Om Myntforandring i de tre Skandinaviske Riger', in *Tids-Tavler*, ed. by L.K. Daa (Cammermeyer, 1872) 87–194.

Broch, O.J., *Statistisk Årbog for Kongeriget Norge 1867–71* (C.C. Werner, 1871).

Brofoss, E., *Vekst- og strukturproblemer i norsk økonomi: Forelesninger ved Universitetet i Oslo høstsemestret 1963: 4: Fjerde del* (University of Oslo, 1964).

Brofoss, E., *Valutapolitikk: forelesninger ved Oslo universitet høstsemesteret 1966: 2. 3.utg.* (University of Oslo, 1966).

Buchan, J., *Frozen Desire: The Meaning of Money* (Farrar Straus Giroux, 1997).

Calmfors, L. 'Wages and Wage-bargaining Institutions in the EMU: A Survey of the Issues', *Empirica* 28, no. 4 (2001) 325–51.

Capie, F. H., C. Goodhart, and N. Schnadt, *The Development of Central Banking* (Bank of England, 1994).

Capie, F., *The Bank of England: 1950s to 1979*. (Cambridge University Press, 2010).

Capie, F., G. Wood, and J. Castañeda, 'Central Bank Independence in Small Open Economies', in *Central Banks at a Crossroad: What Can We Learn from History?* ed. by M.D. Bordo, Ø. Eitrheim, M. Flandreau, and J.F. Qvigstad (Cambridge University Press, 2016).

Christiansen, A.B. and Qvigstad, J.F., *Choosing a Monetary Policy Target* (Scandinavian University Press, 1997).

Collett, J.P. and B. Frydenlund, *Christianias handelspatrisiat: en elite i 1700-tallets Norge* (Andresen & Butenschøn, 2008).

Cox, E.F., 'The Metric System: A Quarter-Century of Acceptance (1851–1876)', *Osiris* 13 (1958) 358–79.

Cukierman, A., *Central Bank Strategy, Credibility, and Independence: Theory and Evidence* (MIT press, 1992).

Daae, L., *Politiske dagbøker og minner*. Vol. 2 (Den norske historiske forening, 1938).

De Cecco, M., 'European Monetary and Financial Cooperation before the First World War', *Rivista di storia economica* 9, nos. 1–2 (1992) 55–76.

De Kock, M.H., *Central Banking* (Staples Press, 1956).

Degen, H., 'Om den Danske Oversættelse af Adam Smith og Samtidens bedømmelse af den', *Nationaløkonomisk Tidsskrift* 3, no. 44 (1936).

Denzel, M.A., *Handbook of World Exchange Rates, 1590–1914* (Ashgate Publishing, 2010).

Ecklund, G.J., *Kredittpolitikken som redskap i den samfunnsøkonomiske styringen fra 1965 til 1980* (University of Oslo, 1995).

Ecklund, G.J., *Creating a New Role for an Old Central Bank: The Bank of Norway 1945–1954* (Handelshøyskolen BI, 2008).

Ecklund, G.J. and S. Knutsen, *Vern mot kriser? Norsk finanstilsyn gjennom 100 år* (Fagbokforlaget, 2000).

Egge, Å., 'Statens diskonteringskommisjoner: Finansdepartementet som statsbank i det 19. århundre', Doctoral-thesis (University of Oslo, 1988).

Eichengreen, B., *Gold Fetters: The Gold Standard and the Great Depression 1919–1939* (Oxford University Press, 1995).

Eichengreen, B., *The Gold Standard in Theory and History* (Psychology Press, 1997).

Eichengreen, B., *The European Economy since 1945: Coordinated Capitalism and Beyond* (Princeton University Press, 2008).

Eichengreen, B. and M. Flandreau, *The Gold Standard in Theory and History* (Routledge, 1997).

Eide, L., and E. Forsbak, 'Norsk rentepolitikk', *Norges Banks Skriftserie*, no. 5 (Norges Bank, 1977).

Eitrheim, Ø. and J.T Klovland, ed. by J.F Qvigstad, 'Historical Monetary Statistics for Norway 1819–2003', *Norges Bank's Occasional Papers*, no. 35 (Norges Bank, 2004) 293.

Eitrheim, Ø. and E. Lie, *Noen riktig lange linjer: Statens inntekter, utgifter og gjeld* (Finansdepartementet, 2014).

Eitrheim, Ø., J.T. Klovland, and L.F. Øksendal, *A Monetary History of Norway, 1816–2016* (Cambridge University Press, 2016).

Engebretsen, E., *Norsk Bankvesen: Et historisk riss med særlig vekt på forholdene etter verdenskrigen* (Tanum, 1939).

Engebretsen, E., *Christiania Bank og Kreditkasse 1848–1948* (Aschehoug, 1948).

Englund, P. and L. Werin, *Från räntereglering till inflationsnorm: det finansiella systemet och Riksbankens politik 1945–1990* (Stockholm, 1993)

Erichsen, E., *Økonomiske problemer idag, og i tiden framover: artikler skrevet i tiden 14. mai - 25. august i Dagbladet* (Halvorsen & Larsen, 1945)

Espeli, H., '"Det gavner ingenting å gjøre store vanskeligheter i små saker. Dette er ikke store saker"—Norges Bank, administrasjonsrådet og etableringen av okkupasjonskontoen i 1940', *Historisk tidsskrift* 90, no. 4 (2011) 559–84.

Espeli, H., 'Central Banks Under German Rule During World War II: The Case of Norway', *Norges Bank Working Papers* (Norges Bank, 2012).

Espeli, H., and Y. Nilsen, *Riksrevisjonens historie 1816-2016* (Fagbokforlaget, 2016).

Feinstein, C.H., P. Temin, and G. Toniolo, *The European Economy between the Wars* (Oxford University Press, 1997).

Fforde, J., *The Bank of England and Public Policy, 1941-1958* (Cambridge University Press, 1992).

Flandreau, M., 'Central Bank Cooperation in Historical Perspectives: A Sceptical View', *Economic History Review* 50, no. 4 (1997) 735-63.

Flandreau, M., 'The Economics and Politics of Monetary Unions: A Reassessment of the Latin Monetary Union, 1865-71', *Financial History Review* 7, no. 1 (2000) 25-44.

Flandreau, M., 'The French Crime of 1873: An Essay on the Emergence of the International Gold Standard, 1870-1880', *The Journal of Economic History* 56, no. 4 (1996) 862-97.

Foreman-Peck, J., *A History of the World Economy* (Pearson Education, 1995).

Forsbak, E., 'Pengemengde og pengemengdeanalyser', *Penger og kreditt* 3 (1976).

Fuglum, P., *Én skute-én skipper: Gunnar Knudsen som statsminister 1908-10 og 1913-20* (Tapir, 1989).

Gallarotti, G.M., *The Anatomy of an International Monetary Regime: The Classical Gold Standard, 1880-1914* (Oxford University Press, 1995).

Gerdrup, K.R., 'Norges Banks rolle ved likviditetskriser i finansiell sektor', *Penger og kreditt* 4 (2004) 190-8.

Gerdrup, K.R., 'Three Booms and Busts Involving Banking Crises in Norway Since the 1890s', in *The Norwegian banking crisis* ed. by T.G. Moe, J.A. Solheim, and B. Vale (Norges Bank, 2004) 145-72.

Gilbert, E., '"Ornamenting the Facade of Hell": Iconographies of 19th-Century Canadian Paper Money', *Environment and Planning D: Society and Space* 16, no. 1 (1998) 57-80.

Gilbert, E. and E. Helleiner, 'Nation-States and Money', *The Past, Present and Future of National Currencies* (Routledge, 1999).

Gjedrem, S., 'Lividitetsstatistikk og -prognoser', *Penger og kreditt* 2, no. 4 (1976) 101-7.

Goodhart, C., *The Evolution of Central Banks* (MIT Press, 1988).

Gram, T., 'Når staten tar kontroll: bankkrisen fra 1991-1993', Masters thesis (University of Oslo, 2011)

Grønlie, T., *Ekspansjonsbyråkratiets tid 1945-1980* (Fagbokforlaget, 2009).

Grønlie, T., 'Norges Bank—og andre "uavhengige" statsinstitusjoner', *Historisk Tidsskrift* 96, no. 03 (2017) 336-47.

Grønlie, T. and Flo, Y., *Sentraladministrasjonens historie etter 1945* (Fagbokforlaget, 2009).

Haare, H., Lund, A.J., and Solheim, J.A., *Norges Banks rolle på finanssektorområdet i perioden 1945-2013, med særlig vekt på finansiell stabilitet* (Norges Bank, 2015).

Hagen, M.G. 'Samarbeidsnemnda, en studie i samarbeidet mellom staten og de private kredittinstitusjoner 1951-1965', Masters thesis, (University of Oslo, 1977).

Hagen, I., *Blåfargen fra Modum: en verdenshistorie. Blaafarveværket 1776-1821* (Scandinavian Academic Press, 2014).

Hanisch, T.J., 'Kryssløpet mellom vitenskap og politikk: Odd Aukrust og forskningen i Statistisk sentralbyrå', in *Økonomisk forskning og debatt: utvalgte artikler av Odd Aukrust 1942-1989. SØS 75* (Statistisk Sentralbyrå, 1990).

Hanisch, T.J., E. Søilen, and G.J. Ecklund, *Norsk økonomisk politikk i det 20: århundre: verdivalg i en åpen økonomi* (Høyskoleforlaget, 1999).

Hansen, B., 'Synspunkter på valutapolitikken', *Sosialøkonomen* 31, no. 6 (1977) 26-30.

Hansen, P.H., 'Cooperate or Free Ride? The Scandinavian Central Banks, Bank for International Settlements and the Austrian Financial Crisis of 1931', *Scandinavian Journal of History* 37, no. 1 (2012) 87-107.Harket, H., *Paragrafen: Eidsvoll 1814* (Dreyers forlag, 2014).

Hartmann, P., *Bak fronten: fra Oslo og London 1939-1945* (Aschehoug, 1955).

Heftye, T.J., *Om Norges Myntcirkulation* (Cappelen, 1873).

Helleiner, E., 'National Currencies and National Identities', *American Behavioral Scientist* 41, no. 10 (1998) 1409-36.

Henriksen, I. and N. Kærgård, 'The Scandinavian Currency Union 1875-1914', in *International Monetary Systems in Historical Perspective*, ed. by J. Reis (Palgrave Macmillan, 1995).

Henriksen, I., N. Kærgård, and C. Sørensen, 'Den Skandinaviske Møntunion', *Den jyske historiker*, nos. 69–70 (1994) 88–97.

Hertzberg, E., *Om Kredittens Begreb og Væsen* (Malling, 1877).

Hertzberg, E. and N. Rygg, *Den norske Creditbank, 1857–1907* (Den norske Creditbank, 1907).

Hjort, J., *Utenrikspolitiske oplevelser under verdenskrigen* (Gyldendal, 1927).

Hodne, F., *Norsk økonomisk historie 1815–1970* (Cappelen, 1981).Hodne, F. and O.H. Grytten, *Norsk økonomi i det tyvende århundre* (Fagbokforlaget, 2002).

Holden, S. 'Avoiding the Resource Curse: The Case Norway', *Energy Policy* 63 (2013) 870–76.

Hood, C., 'The "New Public Management" in the 1980s: Variations on a Theme', *Accounting, Organizations and Society* 20, nos. 2–3 (1995) 93–109.

Horsefield, J.K., 'The Origins of the Bank Charter Act, 1844', *Economica* 11, no. 44 (1944) 180–9.

Humphrey, T.M., 'The Real Bills Doctrine', *FRB Richmond Economic Review* 68, no. 5 (1982) 3–13.

Isachsen, A.J., 'Jarle Bergo: En profesjonell pengepolitiker går fra borde' (2008).

Jacobsen, R., *Trygve Bratteli: en fortelling* (Cappelen, 1995).

Jæger, O., 'Udsigt over de forandringer som Norges Banks virksomhet har undergået ved den nye banklov', *Statsøkonomisk Tidsskrift* 8, no. 1 (1894) 63–81.

Jæger, O., 'Guldspørgsmaalet', *Statsøkonomisk Tidsskrift* 30, no. 2 (1916) 110–31.

Jahn, G., A. Eriksen, and P. Munthe, *Norges Bank gjennom 150 år.* (Norges Bank, 1966).

James, H., 'The Causes of the German Banking Crisis of 1931', *Economic History Review* 37, no. 1 (1984) 68–87.

James, H., *International Monetary Cooperation since Bretton Woods* (International Monetary Fund, 1996).

James, H., *Making the European Monetary Union* (Harvard University Press, 2012).

Johansen, H.C., 'Om at skrive bankhistorie', *Historisk tidsskrift (DK)* 15, 5 (1990) 384–404.

Johansson, S.S.F., '"Til Christiania for at Søge Forlindring i de Store Tyngsler": Bondetogene på Østlandet og bøndenes motstand mot skattepolitikken i 1818', Masters thesis (University of Oslo, 2009).

Jonung, L., 'Riksbankens politik 1945–1990', in *Från räntereglering till inflationsnorm: det finansiella systemet och Riksbankens politik 1945–1990*, ed. by P. Englund and L. Werin (SNS Förlag, 1993) 386–90.

Juel, S., 'Endringer i reguleringen av bankenes valutaposisjoner', *Penger og kreditt* 7, no. 4 (1978) 305–10.

Kaartvedt, A. and L.C. Hartsang, *Kongeriket Norges hypotekbank 1852–1952* (Hypotekbanken, 1952).

Keilhau, W., *Norge og verdenskrigen* (H. Aschehoug & Company, 1927).

Keilhau, W., 'Menn og tanker i statsøkonomisk forening', in *Den Statsøkonomiske Forening 1833–1933*, ed. by Statsøkonomisk forening (Aschehoug, 1933) 9–36.

Keilhau, W., *Det norske folks liv og historie i vår egen tid* (Aschehoug & Company , 1938).

Keilhau, W., *Den norske pengehistorie* (Aschehoug, 1952).

Kenwood, A.G. and A.L. Lougheed, *The Growth of the International Economy 1820–1980* (George Allen & Unwin, 1983).

Keynes, J.M., *A Tract of Monetary Reform* (Macmillan, 1923).

Kjær, K., 'Strategi for kostnadseffektiv meravkastning I aksjeporteføljer', in Sentralbanken i forandringens tegn: Festskrift til Kjell Storvik, Norges Bank Skriftserie, no. 28 (Norges Bank, 1999).

Kjeldstadli, K., *Et splittet samfunn 1905–35.* Aschehougs norgeshistorie (Aschehoug, 1994).

Kleivset, C., 'Inflasjon og akkomodasjon: norsk valutakurspolitikk fra 1971 til 1986', Masters thesis (University of Oslo, 2010).

Kleivset, C., 'Fra fast valutakurs til inflasjonsmål: Et dokumentasjonsnotat om Norges Bank og pengepolitikken 1992–2001', Staff memo no. 30 (Norges Bank, 2012).

Kleivset, C. and T. Petersen, 'Etableringen og utviklingen av NBIM', Unpublished memo (Norges Bank, 2013).

Klovland, J.T., 'Monetary Aggregates in Norway 1819–2003', in *Historical Monetary Statistics for Norway 1819–2003*, ed. by Ø. Eitrheim, Norges Bank Skriftserie (Norges Bank, 2004) 181–240.

Knutsen, K., 'Samarbeidet mellom distriktenes utbyggingsfond og Norges Bank', *Penger og kreditt* 9, no. 3 (1981) 212–16.

Knutsen, S., 'Kritisk historisk forskning om økonomisk politikk', *Sosialøkonomen*, no. 3 (2000) 10–15.

Knutsen, S., *Staten og kapitalen i det 20. århundre: regulering, kriser og endring i det norske finanssystemet 1900–2005* (Scandinavian University Press, 2007).

Knutsen, S. and G.J. Ecklund, *Vern mot kriser? Norsk finanstilsyn gjennom 100 år* (Fagbokforlaget, 2000).

Kobberrød, J.T., 'Christiania er, som Hovedstad betragtet, Rigets viktigste Stad', in *Riket og regionene: Grunnlovens regionale forutsetninger og konsekvenser*, ed. by I. Bull and J. Maliks (Akademika, 2014).

Koht, H., *Johan Sverdrup 1870–1880* (Aschehoug, 1922).

Kristensen, M.D., 'From Avoidance to Activism: The Responsible Investment Frameworks of the Norwegian Government Pension Fund Global, the New Zealand Superannuation Fund and California Public Employees' Retirement System 2000–2016', Masters thesis (University of Oslo, 2016).

Krogh, C., *Kampen for tilværelsen* (Gyldendal, 1952).

Kuusterä, A. and J. Tarkka, *Bank of Finland 200 Years—Parliament's Bank* (Bank of Finland and Otava Publishing Company, 2012).

Lie, E., 'Pengesanering og reguleringsøkonomi', *Historisk tidsskrift* 73, no. 1 (1994) 54–71.

Lie, E., *Ambisjon og tradisjon: Finansdepartementet 1945–65.* (Universitetsforlaget, 1995).

Lie, E., *Den norske Creditbank 1982–1990: En storbank i vekst og krise* (Universitetsforlaget, 1998).

Lie, E., 'Statistical Thinking in Norway in the Nineteenth Century', *Scandinavian Economic History Review* 49, no. 1 (2001) 5–22.

Lie, E., 'Norsk økonomisk politikk i det 20. århundret', *Historisk Tidsskrift* 85, no. 4 (2006) 645–64.

Lie, E., *Norsk økonomisk politikk etter 1905* (Universitetsforlaget, 2012).

Lie, E., 'Wealth in Norwegian', in *On Managing Wealth*, ed. by J.F. Qvigstad, Occasional Papers (Norges Bank, 2012) 23–32.

Lie, E. 'Masters and Servants: Economists and Bureaucrats in the Dispute Over Norwegian EEC Membership in 1972', *Contemporary European History* 24, no. 2 (2015).

Lie, E., 'Context and Contingency: Explaining State Ownership in Norway', *Enterprise & Society* 17, no. 4 (2016) 904–30.

Lie, E., 'Learning by Failing: The Origins of the Norwegian Oil Fund', *Scandinavian Journal of History* 43, no. 2 (2018) 284–99.

Lie, E., J.T. Kobberrød, E. Thomassen, and G.F. Rongved, *Norges Bank 1816–2016* (Fagbokforlaget, 2016).

Lie, E., E. Myklebust, and H. Norvik, *Staten som kapitalist: Rikdom og eierskap for det 21. århundret* (Pax, 2014).

Lie, E. and H. Roll-Hansen, *Faktisk talt: statistikkens historie i Norge* (Universitetsforlaget, 2001).

Lie, E. and C. Venneslan, *Over evne: Finansdepartementet 1965–1992* (Pax, 2010).

Lindboe, A., *Fra de urolige tredveårene: Dagboksnedtegnelser og kommentarer* (Tanum, 1965).

Ludlow, P., *The Making of the European Monetary System: A Case Study of the Politics of the European Community* (Butterworth Scientific, 1982).

Lund, A. and J.A. Solheim, 'Finansiell stabilitet–et viktig mål for sentralbanken', i 'Sentralbanken i forandringens tegn: Festskrift til Kjell Storvik', *Norges Banks skriftserie*, no. 28 (Norges Bank, 1999).

McNamara, K.R., *The Currency of Ideas: Monetary Politics in the European Union* (Cornell University Press, 1998).

Magnussen, E., 'Norsk penge- og kredittpolitikk—sterke og svake sider', *Norges Bank, Penger og Kreditt* 1, no. 3 (1973) 162–73.

Manthey, A.C., *Dagbøger for Aarene 1856–1874* (Den norske historiske forening, 1919).

McGouldrick, P., 'Operations of the German Central Bank and the Rules of the Game, 1879–1913', in *A Retrospective on the Classical Gold Standard, 1821–1931*, ed. by M. Bordo and A.J. Schwartz (University of Chicago Press, 1984) 311–60.

Meltzer, A.H., *A History of the Federal Reserve* (Chicago, 2003).

Meyer, H., *Den første arbeiderregjering* (Det norske Arbeiderpartis forlag, 1928). Milward, A.S., *The Fascist Economy in Norway* (Clarendon Press, 1972).

Moe, T.G., J.A. Solheim, and B. Vale, *The Norwegian Banking Crisis* (Norges Bank, 2004).

Monnet, E., *Controlling Credit: Central Banking and the Planned Economy in Postwar France, 1948 1973* (Cambridge University Press, 2018).

Mouré, K., *The Gold Standard Illusion* (Oxford University Press, 2009)

Munthe, P., 'Streiftog i Norges Banks historie', in 'Tre foredrag om Norges Bank 175 år: sentralbankens plass og oppgaver', ed. by H. Skånland, P. Munthe and K.O. Pöhl (ed), *Norges Banks Skriftserie*, no. 19 (Norges Bank, 1991).

Munthe, P., *Christen Smith: Botaniker og økonom* (Aschehoug, 2004).

Nielsen, A., *Den Skandinaviske møntunion* (Børsens forlag, 1917).

Nordvik, H.W., 'Bankkrise, bankstruktur og bankpolitikk i Norge i mellomkrigstiden', *Historisk tidsskrift* 71, 2 (1992) 170–91.

Norges Bank, *Norges Bank under okkupasjonen* (Norges Bank, 1945).

Norges Bank, *Beretning fra direksjonen for Norges Bank om virksomheten i det frie Norge og i London i tiden 22. april 1940 til 13. juli 1945* (Norges Bank, 1946).

Notaker, H., *Høyres historie 1975–2005: opprør og moderasjon* (Cappelen Damm, 2012).

NOU 1973: 36, *Om prisproblemene* (Norges offentlige utredninger, 1973).

NOU 1974: 1, *Finansieringsselskaper og låneformidling* (Norges offentlige utredninger, 1974).

NOU 1990: 25, *Norges Banks nye hovedsete* (Norges offentlige utredninger 1990).

NOU 1983: 27, *Petroleumsvirksomhetens framtid* (Norges offentlige utredninger, 1983)

NOU 1983: 39, *Lov om Norges Bank og pengevesenet* (Norges offentlige utredninger, 1983).

NOU 1983: 54, *Om revisjon av valutareguleringen* (Norges offentlige utredninger, 1983).

NOU 1992: 30, *Bankkrisen* (Norges offentlige utredninger, 1992).

NOU 2003: 22, *Forvaltning for fremtiden* (Norges offentlige utredninger, 2003).

Nysæter, E., 'Sosialistene og pengepolitikken 1920–1928', Masters thesis (University of Bergen, 1972).

Olsen, E., and E. Hoffmeyer, *Monetary History of Denmark 1914–1960*, (Danmarks Nationalbank, 1968).

Olstad, F., *Einar Gerhardsen: en politisk biografi* (Universitetsforlaget, 1999).

Olstad, F., *Med knyttet neve: 1899–1935* (Pax, 2009).

Pearson, R., *Redd gullet! Historien om den norske gulltransporten i 1940* (Dinamo, 2010).

Penrose, J., 'Designing the Nation: Banknotes, Banal Nationalism and Alternative Conceptions of the State', *Political Geography* 30, no. 8 (2011), 429–40.

Peters, B.G., *The Politics of Bureaucracy* (Routledge, 2014)

Petersen, E., *Norsk arbeidsgiverforening, 1900–1950* (Grøndahl, 1950).

Petersen, E., *Den norske Creditbank 1857–1957* (Fabritius, 1957).

Petersen, T., 'Da Norge forlot gullet: Norges Bank og kurspolitikken 1931–1933', Masters thesis, (University of Oslo, 2011).

Polak, J.J., 'The IMF Monetary Model: A Hardy Perennial', *Finance and Development* 34, no. 4 (1997) 16–19.

Polillo, S., and M.F. Guillén, 'Globalization Pressures and the State: The Worldwide Spread of Central Bank Independence', *American Journal of Sociology* 110, no. 6 (2005) 1764–1802.

Prøsch, T., 'Om budsjettering og regulering av pengetilgangen I Norge', *Penger og kreditt* 3, no. 1 (1975) 25–8.

Qvigstad, J.F., and A. Skjæveland, 'Valutakursregimer', in *Stabilitet og langsiktighet—festskrift til Hermod Skånland*, ed. by K. Storvik, J.F. Qvigstad, and S.A. Berg (Aschehoug Forlag, 1994).

Rasmussen, J.R., 'Love and Hate Among Nations: Britain in the Scandinavian Mirror, 1800–1920', *European Journal of English Studies* 8, no. 2 (2004) 219–32.

Riste, O., *The Neutral Ally: Norway's Relations with Belligerent Powers in the First World War* (Universitetsforlaget, 1965).

Rogstad, B. and O. Nordhus, 'Norges Banks swap og termin forretninger', *Penger og Kreditt* 7, no. 4 (1978).

Rongved, G.F., 'Money Talks', in *Scandinavia in the First World War*, ed. by C. Ahlund (Nordic Academic Press, 2012).

Rongved, G.F., 'The Slide from Stability: Monetary and Fiscal Policy in Norway 1914–1920', Doctoral dissertation (University of Oslo, 2014).

Rongved, G.F., 'Blurring the Borders: How the Central Banks of the European Neutrals During the First World War Became Part of the State Machinery: Examining the Case of Norway', *The International History Review* (2018) 1–22.

Rooth, G., *Ivar Rooth Riksbankschef 1929–1948, En autobiografi intalad för och utskriven av Gösta Rooth* (Gösta Rooth,1988).

Roseng, H. and G. Bergvoll, 'Likviditetsregulering og valutaintervensjonspolitikk', *Penger og kreditt* 8, no. 3 (1980) 227–332.

Roset, I.A., *Det norske Arbeiderparti og Hornsrud regjeringsdannelse i 1928* (Universitetsforlaget, 1962).

Rostoft, A., 'Valutauro og valutapolitikk', *Penger og kreditt* 1, no. 1 (1973) 21–8.

Rubow, A., *Nationalbankens Historie: 1878–1908* (Gyldendal, 1920).

Rygg, N., *Handelspolitisk samarbeide* (Norstedt, 1917).

Rygg, N., *Norges Banks historie, 1* (Norges Bank, 1918).

Rygg, N., *Norges Bank i mellomkrigstiden* (Gyldendal, 1950).

Rygg, N., *Norges Banks historie, 2* (Emil Moestue AS, 1954).

Sandal, K., 'The Nordic Banking Crises in the Early 1990s—Resolution Methods and Fiscal Costs', *The Norwegian Banking Crisis* 33 (2004) 77–111.

Sandmo, A., *Samfunnsøkonomi: en idéhistorie* (Universitetsforlaget, 2006).

Schulten, T., 'A European Solidaristic Wage Policy?', *European Journal of Industrial Relations* 8, no. 2 (2002) 173–96.

Schweigaard, A.M., 'Anmeldelse Av Jacob Aalls bok "Nutid og fortid" ', *Vidar* 1, nos. 21–2 (1832).

Schweigaard, A.M., *Ungdomsarbeider* (Aschehoug, 1904).

Seip, J.A., *Et regime foran undergangen* (Tanum, 1945).

Seip, J.A., *Ole Jacob Broch og hans samtid* (Gyldendal, 1971).

Seip, J.A., *Utsikt over Norges historie* (Gyldendal Norsk Forlag, 1974).

Sejersted, F., *Den vanskelige frihet 1814–1851* (Cappelens forlag, 1978).

Sejersted, F., *Historisk introduksjon til økonomien* (Cappelen, 1985).

Sejersted, F., 'Demokrati og rettstat. Et perspektiv på 1800-tallets politiske brytninger', in *Demokrati og rettstat*, ed. by F. Sejersted (Pax Forlag 2001), 153–99.

Sejersted, F., *Den vanskelige frihet: Norge 1814–1850* (Pax, 2001).

Sejersted, F., 'Ideal, teori og virkelighet: Nicolai Rygg og pengepolitikken i 1920-årene', in *Demokrati og rettsstat*, ed. by F. Sejersted (Pax forlag, 2001).

Sejersted, F., 'Den norske sonderweg', in F. Sejersted, *Demokratisk kapitalisme* (Pax, 2002) 311–51.

Shafer, J.R., 'Experience with Controls on International Capital Movements in OECD Countries: Solution or Problem for Monetary Policy?', in *Capital Controls, Exchange Rates, and Monetary Policy in the World Economy*, ed. by S. Edwards (Cambridge University Press, 1995) 119–56.

Singleton, J., *Central Banking in the Twentieth Century* (Cambridge University Press, 2010).

Skånland, H., *Det norske kredittmarked siden 1900* (Aschehoug, 1967).

Skånland, H., 'Kursfastsettelsen i det internasjonale valutasystem', Appendix to *Penger og kreditt* 2, (1) (1974).

Skånland, H., 'Konjunkturperspektiver og norsk næringsliv', *Sosialøkonomen* 19, no. 10 (1977), 9–13.

Skånland, H., 'Styring og likviditeten', Introduction to *Penger og kreditt* 9 (4) (1981).

Skånland, H., 'Likviditetspolitikk—Rentepolitikk', *Penger og kreditt* 10 (2) (1982) 99–101.

Skånland, H., 'Norsk valutakurspolitikk', *Penger og kreditt* 11 (1) (1983) 124–35.

Skånland, H., *The Central Bank and Political Authorities in Some Industrial Countries.* Occasional Papers no. 13 (Norges Bank, 1984).

Skånland, H., 'Hva slags ekspansjon?', *Penger og kreditt* 12 (2) (1984) 3–4.

Skånland, H., 'Ryssdalutvalget er for sterkt bundet til tradisjonen', *Sosialøkonomen* 6 (1984) 14–6.

Skånland, H., 'Om aggressiv markedsføring', *Penger og kreditt* 13 (4) (1985) 335–6.

Skånland, H., 'Bankkrise og livet etterpå', *Penger og kreditt* 18 (4) (1990) 199–208.

Skånland, H., 'Sentralbankens oppgaver i dag og i fremtiden', *Occasional Papers*, no. 19 (Norges Bank, 1991).

Skånland, H., 'Økonomiske perspektiver; Årstale 1993', in *Foredrag av sentralbanksjef Hermod Skånland på Norges Banks representantskapsmøte torsdag 18. februar 1993* (Norges Bank, 1993).

Skånland, H., 'En skjev historie', *Sosialøkonomen*, no. 8 (1999) 2–5.

Skånland, H., *Doktriner og økonomisk styring: et tilbakeblikk* (Norges Bank, 2004).

Skånland, H., 'Tilbakeblikk på 20 år med ny sentralbanklov', *Penger og kreditt* 3 (2005) 168–71.

Slagstad, R., *De nasjonale strateger* (Pax forlag, 1998).

Smith, C., *Bankrett og statsstyre* (Universitetsforlaget, 1980).

Smith, C., 'Norges Banks rettslige selvstendighet', in *Stabilitet og langsiktighet: festskrift til Hermod Skånland*, ed. by S.A. Berg, K. Storvik, and J.F. Qvigstad (Aschehoug, 1994).

Søilen, E., 'Drømmen om inntektspolitisk samarbeid: Finansdepartementets kamp mot særinteresser', Masters thesis (University of Oslo, 1993).

Søilen, E., 'Fra frischianisme til keynesianisme: en studie av norsk økonomisk politikk i lys av økonomisk teori 1945–1980', Doctoral thesis (Norges Handels Høyskole, 1998).

Solbakken, E.T., 'The Wealth of a Young Nation: On Voting Rights, Financing Plights, and Long-Run Wealth Inequality in Norway', Doctoral thesis (University of Oslo, 2018).

Sørensen, A.R., 'Monetary Organization and National Identity: A Review and Considerations', *Journal of Cultural Economy* 9, no. 2 (2016) 173–85.

Spang, R.L., *Stuff and Money in the Time of the French Revolution* (Harvard University Press, 2015).

Statistics Norway, *Historisk statistikk 1968* (Statistics Norway, 1978).

Statistisk Sentralbyrå, 'Statistisk-økonomisk oversikt over året 1931', (Statistisk sentralbyrå, 1932).

Statistisk Sentralbyrå, 'Historisk statistikk 1968' (Statistisk sentralbyrå, 1969).

Statistisk Sentralbyrå, 'Historisk statistikk 1978' (Statistisk sentralbyrå, 1978).

Steen, S., *På fallittens rand* (Cappelen, 1953).

Stevens, P., G. Lahn, and J. Kooroshy, *The Resource Curse Revisited* (Chatham House, 2015)

Storthings-Efterretninger 1814–1833 (Jacob Dybwads Forlag, 1878).

Storthings-Efterretninger 1836–1854, vol. 1 (Jacob Dybwads Forlag, 1888).

Storthings-Efterretninger 1836–1854, vol. 2 (Jacob Dybwads Forlag, 1893).

Storthings-Efterretninger 1836–1854, vol. 3 (Jacob Dybwad Forlag, 1904).

Storvik, K., 'Økonomiske perspektiver; Årstale 1996', in *Foredrag av sentralbanksjef Kjell Storvik på Norges Banks representantskapsmøte torsdag 15. februar 1996* (Norges Bank, 1996).

Straumann, T., *Fixed Ideas of Money: Small States and Exchange Rate Regimes in Twentieth-Century Europe* (Cambridge University Press, 2010).

Talia, K., 'The Scandinavian Currency Union 1873–1924: Studies in Monetary Integration and Disintegration', Doctoral dissertation, (Stockholm School of Economics, 2004).

Tarkka, J., 'Investment Doctrines for Banks, from Real Bills to Post-Crisis Reforms', in *Preparing for the Next Financial Crisis: Policies, Tools and Models*, ed. by E. Jokivuolle and R. Tunaru (Cambridge University Press, 2017), 63–88.

Tarkka, J., 'The North European Model of Early Central Banking', in *Designing Central Bank* (Routledge, 2009), 48–81.

The Albright Group LLC and S. Chesterman, 'Assessment of Implementation of Article 3 and 4 of the Ethical Guidelines for the Government Pension Fund—Global' (Ministry of Finance, 2008).

Thomassen, E., 'Knuten på perlekjedet: Securitas-aksjonen og Norges Bank 1925–1928', Masters thesis (University of Oslo, 2012).

Thomassen, E., 'Nytt blikk på Hornsrud-regjeringens fall: Sentralbanken, sosialistene og securitas', *Historisk tidsskrift* 92, no. 03 (2013) 425–47.

Thomassen, E., 'Translating Central Bank Independence into Norwegian: Central Bankers and the Diffusion of Central Bank Independence to Norway in the 1990s', *Review of International Political Economy* 24, no. 5 (2017) 839–58.

Thomassen, E. and L.F. Øksendal, *Modellbyggere: Det tekniske beregningsutvalget for inntektsoppgjørene 1967–2017* (Pax forlag, 2017).

Thomassen, Ø. 'Herlege tider: Norsk fysisk planlegging ca. 1930–1965' (Norges teknisk-naturvitenskapelige universitet, 1997).

Thygesen, N., 'Penge- og kreditpolitiske udviklingstendenser i andre land', *Sosialøkonomen* 10 (1980) 9–14.

Toniolo, G. and F.A. Olivetti, *Central Banks' Independence in Historical Perspective* (W. de Gruyter, 1988).

Toniolo, G., *Central Bank Cooperation at the Bank for International Settlements, 1930–1973* (Cambridge University Press, 2005).

Trøite, R., *Norges Banks uavhengighet i etterkrigstida: en analyse av sentralbankens uavhengighet fra 1945 til 1970 i et komparativt perspektiv* (Oslo, 2010).

Stefano, U., *The Evolution of Central Banking: Theory and History* (Palgrave Macmillan, 2017).

Ulvund, F., *Fridomens grenser 1814–1851* (Scandinavian Academic Press, 2014).

Værholm, M. and L.F. Øksendal, 'Letting the Anchor Go: Monetary Policy in Neutral Norway During World War I', *The International History Review 32*, no. 5 (2010) 661–86.

Van der Wee, H. and Verbreyt, M., *A Small Nation in the Turmoil of the Second World War: Money, Finance and Occupation. Belgium, its Enemies, its Friends, 1939–1945* (Leuven University Press, 2009).

Van Dormael, A., *Bretton Woods: Birth of a Monetary System* (Macmillan, 1978).

Vanthoor, W.F.V., *The King's Eldest Daughter: A History of the Nederlandsche Bank 1814–1998* (Boom, 2005).

Vaubel, R., 'The Bureaucratic and Partisan Behaviour of Independent Central Banks: German and International Evidence', *European Journal of Political Economy* 13 (1997) 201–24.

Wee, H.v.d., *Prosperity and Upheaval: The World Economy, 1945–1980* (Penguin, 1987).

Wenzlhuemer, R., 'The History of Standardisation in Europe', *European History Online* (2010). Retrieved from: https://d-nb.info/1020545348/34.

Wergeland, H., *Avhandlinger Oplysningsskrifter 1834–1837*. Samlede Skrifter: Trykt Og Utrykt (Steenske forlag, 1924).

Wetterberg, G., *Pengarna och makten: Riksbankens historia* (Atlantis, 2009).

Willoch, K., 'Hvor uavhengig bør sentralbanken være?', in *Stabilitet og langsiktighet, festskrift til Hermod Skånland*, ed. by S.A. Berg, K. Storvik, and J.F. Qvigstad (Aschehoug, 1994).

Wold, K.G., *Norges Banks samarbeid med statsmaktene, bankene og utlandet* (Norges Handelshøyskole, 1972).

Wold, K.G. and J.T. Kobberrød, 'I samarbeid', *Norges Banks Skriftserie*, no. 52 (Norges Bank, 2017).

Øksendal, A., *Gulltransporten* (Aschehoug, 1974).

Øksendal, L.F., 'En fast kurs: Norsk betalingspolitikk 1945–58', Masters thesis (NTNU, 2001).

Øksendal, L.F., 'Essays in Norwegian Monetary History, 1869–1914', Doctoral dissertation (Norges Handelshøyskole, 2007).

Øksendal, L.F., 'Trondhjem som hovedsete for Norges Bank—noen faktiske og kontrafaktiske betraktninger', Staff memo, no. 8. (Norges Bank, 2008).

Index